MILLENNIUM ODYSSEY

A Review of Belgrave Harriers' 21st Century Road & Country

W V L Cockerell

Millennium Odyssey

This book was first published in Great Britain in paperback during October 2022.

The moral right of W V L Cockerell is to be identified as the author of this work, in accordance with the Copyright, Designs and Patents Act of 1988.

Email: ads2life@btinternet.com

ISBN: 979-8354927692

CONTENTS

PREFACE

A man runs. He travels, quickly. His body is bronzed a chestnut hue, courtesy of some warm weather training and not merely a "holiday", as some have wondered aloud. He has a lead of 150 yards over a runner he on 'on par' with, and there are 3kms to go before his club is crowned National Champions, for the first time in 50 years at any road and country race. His physiology sings down the road as he easily keeps pace with the lead bike.

Sweet dreams are made of this.

Just then two fellows in green and white tracksuits amble into the road and start running alongside. One of them leans into him and bellows: "He's dying! *He's f***ing DYING!!*"

Who is the loudmouth referring to? And who is he shouting at? The situation becomes uneasy, and confusing.

The dream has turned into a nightmare.

ABOUT THE AUTHOR

Will Cockerell is a sports writer, athletics coach and distance runner. He worked for several years at the fledgling news digest *The Week* and in the early 2000s wrote for numerous Premiership football websites; was chief reporter for the televised *World Series of Backgammon*, and contributed commentaries for the online service *Guerilla Cricket*. His column "Will's World" began at *Athletics Weekly* in 2007, and his first book "The 50 Greatest Marathon Races of all Time" was described by *The Times*: "at last the marathon has found a book worthy of its long and epic journey."

At Belgrave he has turned in some 350 races in 24 years, and holds numerous club appearance records including most scoring runs at the Surrey League, Southern cross, National cross and Southern 12 Stage. He served as club captain for four years, club secretary for seven and a combined 13 years as Team manager for the men and women's Road & Country. He has coached numerous individuals, and both senior and junior running groups at the club.

His two children, Seb & Imogen are both keen Belgravians, and he lives in Wimbledon, just up the road from Belgrave Hall.

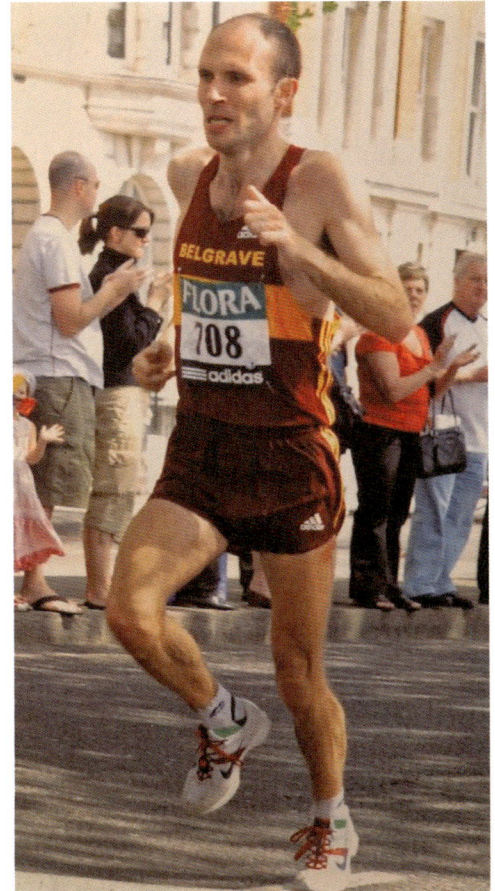

ARM

INTRODUCTION

The Mammoth is not yet extinct!

This is a very old Belgrave joke that would be trotted out when our legendary and beloved gazette would have one of its slumbers and go MIA. But then she'd return, after a year or three and this merry line would greet the readers.

This tome is basically rousing the mammoth again and in some ways is just an enormous *Belgravian*. But it is of a specialist variety: Only 21st Century, and only Road and Country. Whither Track and Field, I hear you ask?! Well, it has been pretty amazing, particularly in the period 1990-2010, but it's another tale, for another day, and the subject too large and not of this reporter's expertise – however many round trips I made to Wigan to do a dodgy 'chase.

Another query of this book might be whither Road and Country pre-2000? Well, the subject matter is enormous, and they are at least in print in *The Belgravian*, and between 1975-1997ish we were actually very quiet as a club so we'd be going way back, circa 1930-1972 for the really good stuff. That period will never be forgotten and is hugely responsible for making Belgrave the epic, household name that it is today. Its history does at least remain in print via those gazettes, although full copies may be down to around half a dozen. Reference will be made to those heroes throughout these pages.

Does such a strict time-frame really warrant an entire book though? Yes. A resounding yes.

How to define the magic of club athletics – did Capone put it best?

"Enthusiasms… What draws my admiration? What is that gives me joy?" asked Al Capone to a roomful of goons in *The Untouchables*.

"*Dames! Music! Booze!*" they chant back.

"Baseball!" he replies to raucous laughter. "A man stands alone at a plate, this is the time for what? For *individual* achievement. There he stands alone; but in the Field, what? Part. Of. A. Team."

"Looks, throws, catches, hustles. Part of one big team. Bats himself the livelong day… Babe Ruth, Ty Cobb *and so on…*"

"But if the team don't field. What is he? Follow me? No one!"

"Sunny day, the stands are full of fans. What does he have to say? I'm going out there for myself. But… I get *nowhere* unless the *team* wins…"

And that right there – in the Field - is the glorious, intangible magic of club athletics. The individual stakes are well and good and why we all took up the sport, but the team race is where the true thrills lie. Where we fight for each other, experience the adrenaline of team ambition and the entire club counting on us; why we run and train in packs, work out strategic relay orders and hunt in groups over the mud.

For all these great Belgrave teams down the years, and the 100-odd titles you won this Century, and some 200 podiums… this book is for you.

Key Raison d'Etres and Dating issues

Most sports books have the problem of 'dating' the moment they're published, but this shouldn't diminish their value. The book is what it is: a snapshot of a "moment in time". If the club does go on to have a great run in the coming years, that's wonderful – the perfect problem to have – I certainly can't lose in that respect by producing this. And as for all the players in here – and their perhaps soon to be dated statistics? They are the architects and forerunners for all that is to come. My comrade Kevin Kelly over at Herne Hill spent some 30 years compiling his epic annals for them, and they promptly went on a magical run of form for the next decade and beyond. But Kevin's 2001 *magnum opus* doesn't feel too dated. It feels like a great work that helped to trigger all of their subsequent success, which is now never lost. 20 years on and I still consult it often. Besides, what's to say an updated edition to these pages, some years from now?

Battling back against Cyber Losses

Another key reason for this tome is the fragility of cyberspace and website ownership. In 2014 the committee relieved Alan Mead of his astonishingly classy and detailed club website that he'd compiled since shortly after the birth of the internet. It was a magnificent work of art with well over a million views, and we were the first port of call for clubs all over the country on a Monday morning after the big road relays, because they knew we'd run a lavish report.

Our website remains strong, but its archiving and history sections are fragile. There are reports of the last 7 years, but only if you go to News and keep pressing the 'Older' tab, some 30 times to get back to the start. And before that, the incredible run of the Belles between 2011-2014 is nearly all lost and the epic era of 2000-2012, one of the greatest R & C eras in our history, is lost too. It alarmed me terribly at the time, and I knew that it'd be a shocker if that era's reportage disappeared to the sands of time forever; particularly as the club was so diligent as to never lose a report for nearly 100 years, before the axe fell on Alan's site.

Well, Alan has rebounded from his sadness at losing the site and is constructing a pretty epic History site for us at www.belgraveharriers.info, which is a work in progress, but now has scores of fascinating pages. So all is not lost. This book only covers around 5% of the vast scope of Alan's site – but in somewhat more detail. We do also still have 'emergency, hit-and-miss' access to Alan's work on the website *WayBackMachine* that has taken billions of imprints of webpages of popular websites in history, and fortunately we are one. To give a taste of our reporting values, and indeed our standard in competition, here we are in 2004 providing the women's National Cross champion, and us briefly having 6 in 36 for the men's race:

An historic day for Belgrave

Any doubts as to whether our men's team were serious about the race were blown away on the stiff Yorkshire breeze when the team manager turned up at Temple Newsam Park on the Friday afternoon to check out the course and found that half his team were there, having had similar ideas.

And that course was bit of a shock. The steep rise from the start at the lowest point in the park was tougher than anything Parliament Hill could offer: undulations, tussocks of grass and boggy patches added to the torture of that relentless 800 metre climb which would also have to be tackled at the finish. Then there was the farmland and the general rough nature of the ground throughout the rest of the loop. Although, of course, one has to say, "It's the same for everyone," there's no doubting that this time it was a real cross country runner's course.

Later in the evening, pre-race speculation among the supporters over a drink or two in the Toby Carvery centred on the fact that Birhan Dagne was reportedly looking for a medal to raise her profile in her quest to obtain selection for the Olympic Marathon and that the men's chances, although good, were by no means certain. Regular rivals Newham & Essex Beagles had been so dominant in the "Southern" while the holders, Leeds AC, were sure to be strong on their home ground. Everyone felt that we had five men who would normally be equal to any other team's five – but Paul Freary was suffering from a little niggle while 1500m/5000m man Stephen Sharp was not enamoured with the course. And who would that sixth man be? We reckoned he'd need to be home in 60th-70th but would it be Will Cockerell (always solid and looking for that something special), Hassan Raidi (sometimes brilliant), or Simon Marwood (a very promising 'chaser but an unknown quantity over the country). At least all were agreed that it was going to be exciting.

Race day dawned still and cold. The tent party had completed their task by 8am, and before heading back for breakfast they looked back down on the scene from the heights of Temple Newsam House. The claret, gold and blue Belgrave pavilion stood in splendid isolation on the brilliant green of the course below.

Four hours later and the park was a hive of activity. Shelters of every kind now surrounded our marquee. Most displayed the colours of hopeful teams and there, in the centre, below the Belgrave flag, our team began to assemble. Let the tournament begin!

Birhan Dagne wins our first senior individual gold

Reigning champion Hayley Yelling (WSE&H) had chosen to miss the race in favour of warm weather training in the USA but when the starting gun fired there were plenty of positive runners making a bid for a forward position, not least among them being our own Birhan Dagne. Louise Damen of Bournemouth, the winner of last year's Junior race and the favourite for this, was soon at the head of the field and as they descended to the farmland it was Birhan taking up second spot although already 30 metres behind.

At the end of the first lap the Mick Woods coached Bournemouth girl had extended her lead to 50 metres but Belgravians were delighted that Birhan appeared to be on course for a silver medal. She was well clear of third and running freely down that bumpy slope to the farmlands. The majority of spectators now made their way to the last half-mile of the course, lining the route to greet the leader. The tide of applause preceded the runners up the final climb and, amazingly, it was the compact figure of Birhan that finally hove into view first. Louise Damen had not been able to match Birhan's strength and experience over the second circuit and the Belgrave woman ran into the finishing straight a full 120 metres to the good. Belgrave's first senior "National" winner! Tremendous!

Team title returns to Belgrave after 56 years

Down at the foot of the hill the tension was rising. The three minute warning had sounded and still Belgrave runners had no intention of getting down to their racing strip. Finally, thirteen men in claret and gold stood line abreast intending to get the best start possible. The weeks of anticipation, persuasion and organisation were over and the best Belgrave cross-country team seen in almost a lifetime was in action.

A huge roar from the 1500 runners followed the starter's gun and as they burst up the slope there seemed barely time to scurry across to the next section of the course before the runners could be seen tearing at breakneck speed down to the bottom again. Coventry Godiva's Glyn Tromans, a winner at Stowe in 2000, was already clear. He was up for it and no mistake! But the pack behind was full of Belgrave runners and after the first full lap we had the glorious site of six of our men in the top 36 – Barden at 4, Graffin 7, Nash 11, Freary 25, Sharp 26 and Raidi 36. What a start.

These wonderful reports, so lovingly constructed, may now be rather lost – but at least this book revisits many of the halcyon days and summarises them as best as time and space allows.

ILLUSTRATION CREDITS AND KEY

I am enormously grateful to the photographers in this book. There are many of you and your contributions are superb and bring the pages alive. I have tried wherever possible to credit you, usually by initials, the key to which may be found here.

If an image is not credited it is either my own, or I have been unable to find the source, or am not certain of its origin. Feel free to let me know if an uncredited image was yours and I'll be sure to update for future versions.

Photographers, in alphabetical order, credited via initials

AR	Adrian Royle
ARM	Alan Mead
CDM	Chris de Mauny
GG	Gigi Gianella
JH	Jeremy Hemming
JHM photography	
KM	Keith Mayhew
KMcC	Keith McClure
LC	Leo Coy
LM	Leonard Martin
MS	Mark Shearman
NB	Nigel Bramley
RB	Rex Bale
RO'D	Ray O'Donohue
RX	Richard Xerri
SG	Steve Gardner
SH	Sophie Harris
SSP	Sussex sport photography
SW	Steve Wicks

GLOSSARY OF ABBREVIATIONS, NICKNAMES & INITIALS

Throughout these pages, names are given, but often not in full. This propels the narrative along and many autobiographical sports books go down this route. Nobody wants to read the same well known name in full up to 50-100 times, which sometimes may not trip off the tongue. What of course I don't wish for though is for readers to come across monikers and wonder who on earth I'm talking about. Well, there are five failsafes to this:

1) I have constructed a gargantuan Index where everyone's coverage is presented in full.
2) I will often have referred to the person earlier in the piece, so it should be fairly obvious to whom I refer.
3) A brief glance to the full results in each section give the identities of the athletes for that race.
4) The athletes to whom I attribute abbreviations, nicknames or initials will be well known protagonists at the club. I expect a small amount of "emotional investment" from my reader, and if you're not willing to work out who, say, "Wicksy" is, then this may not be the publication for you.
5) I present to you this Glossary! Run your eyes up and down it, and you'll see that what I've done is not rocket science. So, use these five failsafes freely and thank you for allowing me to run the narrative along more smoothly, and may I suggest more colourfully, than if I had to give every name in full, every time.

Glossary of Nicknames and abbreviations:

AJ	Andrius Jaksevicius
Alan	Alan Mead
Andy	Andrius Jaksevicius
Anne	Anne Hegvold
ARM	Alan Mead
Catherine	Catherine Eastham or Bryson [context]
CB	Catherine Bryson
CD	Charlie Dickinson
CE	Catherine Eastham
Charlie	Charlie Dickinson
Chas	Charlie Dickinson
Cockerpillar	Will Cockerell
DA	David Anderson
Danders	David Anderson
Fairbs	James Fairbourn
Fee	Fiona Maycock
Flic	Felicity Cole
Gnasher	Kevin Nash
HBR	Hester Barsham-Rolfe [Scotton]
Hursty	Lee Hurst
Jess	Jessica Saunders
Jim	James Kelly
JK	James Kelly
JJR	Jojo Rhodes
Jojo	Jojo Rhodes
Jon	Jonathan Blackledge
Jonesy	Simon Jones
Kerimac	Keri Mackenzie

Kev	Kevin Nash
Kezza	Keri Mackenzie
Knut	Knut Hegvold
Lee	Lee Hurst
LGS	Lizzie Goldie-Scot
The Lion	Paskar Owor
Liv	Olivia Papaioannou
Lizzie	Lizzie Goldie-Scot
Lou	Louise Blizzard [nee Cooper]
The Machine	Richard Ward
Mal	Malachi Byansi
Mark	Mark Miles
Mel	Mel Wilkins
Mhairi	Mhairi Hall
Mike	Mike Trees
Milesey	Mark Miles
MM	Mark Miles
MW/MJW	Mel Wilkins
Nagongera Lion	Paskar Owor
Neil	Neil Speaight
Nick	Nick Goolab or Buckle [context]
Northern Lightning	Knut Hegvold
Panthera Pardus	Paskar Owor
Paps/*Papsrunslaps*	Olivia Papaioannou
Paul	Paul Freary
Phil	Phil Wicks
The Pillar	Will Cockerell
PO	Paskar Owor
Polly	Mark Pollard
Rog	Roger Alsop
Roy	Royston Maddams
Rich	Richard Ward
Rose	Rose Grace [O'Brien]
Ruds/The Rudster	Craig Ruddy
SA	Samantha Amend
Sammy G/Sam	Sam Gebreselassie
Sammi/Sam	Samantha Amend
Sharpy	Stephen Sharp
SJ	Simon Jones
Smurph	Sarah Murphy
Sp8y	Neil Speaight
Sophie	Sophie Harris
Spen	Spencer Barden
SS	Stephen Sharp
Terry	Terry O'Neill
Tilly	Tilly Heaton
Tinos	Konstantinos Touse
Tish	Tish Jones
TO'N	Terry O'Neill
Trondheim Stallion	Knut Hegvold
Wardy	Richard Ward
Wicksy	Phil Wicks
The Vixster/Vicki	Vicki Goodwin
YJB	Young Jonny Blackledge
ZLD	Zoe Doyle
ZVS	Zoe Vail Smith

1999-2022 ROAD AND COUNTRY RESULTS - WOMEN

YEAR	Surrey rd relay	Southern 4 stage	National 4 stage	Southern XC relay	National XC relay	SOT team	SOT champs	Surrey XC champs	The Southern	Surrey League	The National	Southern 6 Stage	National 6 Stage	London Marathon
1999-2000	3	-	-	[race	-	n/a	n/a	3	-	4	-	-	-	3
2000-2001	-	-	-	founded	-	n/a	n/a	-	-	9 [R]	-	21	-	
2001-2002	6	-	7	2011]	-	-	n/a	2	-	1 [Div 2]	-	4	5	3
2002-2003	3	16	15		-	-	n/a	13	-	3	31	7	11	
2003-2004	3	5	20		-	-	n/a	1	-	1	-	7	-	1
2004-2005	4	11	28		-	3	-	-	18	2	12	2	21	
2005-2006	3	13*	12		-	-	-	-	13	2	15	8	17	3
2006-2007	5*	-	26		-	-	-	1	-	1	-	11	10	
2007-2008	-	-	18		-	-	-	-	-	12	-	-	-	
2008-2009	17*	-	20		-	-	-	-	-	2	21	-	-	3
2009-2010	-	-	49		-	-	-	-	-	6	-	11	-	
2010-2011	12*	30	42	3	-	-	-	-	-	15 [R]	-	4	24	2
2011-2012	4*	-	25	-	-	-	3	-	3	1 [Div 2]	16	12	11	1
2012-2013	5	3	17	1	-	6	3	-	6	3	6	4	13	1
2013-2014	1*	19	15	6	33*	1	1	3	2	1	4	2	9	
2014-2015	-	16	17	2	-	1	1	5	2	1	5	2	8	
2015-2016	-	33	17	2	-	2	3	8	16	9	30	10	8	
2016-2017	6	24	23	4	-	3	1	5	6	2	37	17	15	
2017-2018	7	10	10	2	-	-	2	6	3	5	18	n/a	-	
2018-2019	-	16	7	3	-	1	1	-	13	7	20	6	8	
2019-2020	-	27	25	8	-	2	-	3	5	3	11	Cov 19	Cov 19	
2020-2021	Cov 19	Cov 19	Cov 19	Cov 19	Cov 19	Cov 19	Cov 19	Cov 19	Cov 19	Cov 19	Cov 19	Cov 19	Cov 19	
2021-2022	2	Cancelled	9	3	-	-	1	3	4	1	5	2	-	

*non-scoring team due to county ineligibility; repeating a runner or late entry

Gold:	19
Silver:	19
Bronze:	25

1999-2022 ROAD AND COUNTRY RESULTS -MEN

YEAR	Surrey rd relay	Southern 6 stage	National 6 stage	Southern XC relay	Nat XC rel Lnd chmps	SOT team	SOT champs	Surrey XC champs	The Southern	Surrey League	The National	Southern 12 Stage	National 12 Stage	London Marathon
1999-2000	2	9	4	n/a	-	2	1	-	6	1	6	3	17	
2000-2001	2	4	6	n/a	-	4	-	5	9	3	8	3	2	
2001-2002	2	3	1	n/a	-	4	5	-	14	1	9	1	1	
2002-2003	2	1	1	n/a	-	4	-	-	10	3	28	1	1	
2003-2004	1	1	1	n/a	1	-	-	-	-	3	1	1	2	
2004-2005	1	1	1	n/a	2	4	1	-	8	2	6	1	1	3
2005-2006	2	1	1	n/a	8	14	2	7	-	3	7	1	3	
2006-2007	1	3	4	n/a	8	9	1	5	6	3	17	2	3	
2007-2008	1	1	1	n/a	1	-	2	4	4	3	19	1	3	
2008-2009	1	1	1	n/a	7	3	1	3	4	4	13	1	1	
2009-2010	6	2	2	n/a	8	-	1	3	-	3	7	2	8	
2010-2011	1	2	2	-	5	5	-	2	14	4	19	5	10	
2011-2012	3	5	14	1	8	3	5	2	-	3	25	9	6	
2012-2013	4	13	3	2	-	12	5	1	6	6	-	-	-	2
2013-2014	6	7	2	5	5	5	7	3	19	5	21	10	19	
2014-2015	-	23	10	1	-	2	5	2	2	6	15	6	10	
2015-2016	14	2	-	2	-	2	3	3	10	8 [R]	25	6	-	
2016-2017	2	24	-	3	-	1	3	3	8	1 [Div 2]	27	6	8	1
2017-2018	-	21	-	3	-	2	5	7	9	7	39	n/a	25	3
2018-2019	-	49	-	2	-	3	6	6	17	7	52	5	-	
2019-2020	-	17	-	-	-	5	8	-	11	6	36	Cov 19	Cov 19	
2020-2021	Cov 19	Cov 19	Cov 19	Cov 19	Cov 19	Cov 19	Cov 19	Cov 19	Cov 19	Cov 19	Cov 19	Cov 19	Cov 19	
2021-2022	3	Cancelled	30	-	-	-	-	2	5	2	19	13	26	

Gold: 44
Silver: 34
Bronze: 32

Total medals: Women: 63   Men: 110

10

CAST FOR "THE BIG 11" - WOMEN

109 female athletes have scored for Belgrave in the 11 Championship races since the '99-00 season, excluding the Surrey League & London Champs:

	Total	Surrey 4	SEAA 4	SEAA XC 3	ERRA 4	SOT team	SOT champs	Surrey xc	SEAA XC	ECCA XC	SEAA 6	ERRA 6
Tilly Heaton	45	3	1		9	2	2	8	8	4	4	4
Samantha Amend	43		2	6	4	1	7		5	5	6	7
Sarah Murphy	25	1			4			6	4	5	1	4
Jojo Rhodes	23		2	1	2	2		2	2	3	4	5
Juliette Clark	21	1	2		3			3	1		6	5
Mel Wilkins	20	1	2	1	3	1	3		3	2	2	2
Zoe Doyle	20		1	3	2	2	2		2	2	2	4
Louise Blizzard [Cooper]	20		2		4	1			2	1	3	7
Catherine Eastham	18	4	1			1		1	3	3	2	2
Tania Sturton	18	3	1			2		3	3	1	3	1
Fee Maycock	17		2	1	2	1	2		2	2	3	2
Saron Haileselase	16	2	2	3	2	1	1				2	3
Zoe Vail Smith	16	2		1	4	2	3	1			2	1
Catherine Bryson	15	1		2	4			1	2	1	2	2
Mhairi Hall	14	1			1	3	2	1	2	2	1	1
Tish Jones	14		1		2	1	1		2	2	2	3
Birhan Dagne	13				5			1		1	2	4
Felicity Cole	12			2		2	1	4	1		2	
Lizzie Goldie-Scot	12		2				3	1	1	2	1	2
Anne Hegvold	11	1	1	1	1			1		3	2	1
Vicki Goodwin	11				1	1	3	3			2	1
Georgie Fenn	10						1	1	2	3	1	2
Helen Smethurst	10		1		1					1	4	3
Helen Cole [Alsop]	10	4	1					1			2	2
Sophie Harris	10		1		2	1	2	1	2	1		
Megan Bailey	10	1	2				1	2		2	1	
Keri Mackenzie	10		2	1		2	2	1			1	1
Nelle Quispell	9	1			2		1		1		2	1
Angela Walker	9	2	2		1			1	1	1		1
Rosie Powell	8	1	1		1						3	1
Syreeta Stracey	8	4	1					1	1		1	
Rachel Brown	8				1		1		2	2	1	1
Olivia Papaioannou	8			1	1			1	2	2	1	
Rose Grace [O'Brien]	8	1	2	1							2	2
Christina Pennock	7						2	2	2	1		
Jen Beecroft	7	1			1				2	2	1	
Sarah Gailey	7	1			1	1			1		2	1
Hester Scotton [B'm-R'lfe]	7	2	1			1	2		1			
Sophie Carter	6				1				1		2	2
Maria Sharp	6				2						2	2
Fiona Maddocks	5	1	2		1					1		
Erica Fogg	5							3	1			1
Vicki Edwards	5	1			2				1			1
Rebecca O'Kill [Prince]	5	1			1		1	1			1	
Mimi Corden-Lloyd	5		1				2		1	1		
Rieko Trees	5	1	1				1				1	1
Iona Cousland	5	1				2		2				
Emma Howsham	5			1		2	1		1			
Alice Reed	5								2	1	1	1
Mary Grace Spalton	4						1			1	1	1
Jane Vongvorachoti	4		1		2						1	
Sally Underhill	4		1		1					1		1
Getenesh Tamirat	4		3		1							

	Total	Surrey 4	SEAA 4	SEAA XC 3	ERRA 4	SOT team	SOT champs	Surrey xc	SEAA XC	ECCA XC	SEAA 6	ERRA 6
Helen Auden [White]	4		2			1					1	
Steph Hewitt	4	1			1	1					1	
Jess Saunders	4			1			1	1			1	
Grace Richardson	4			1	1					1	1	
Sarah Astin	4				1				1	1	1	
Victoria Clarke [Knight]	3										1	1
Maureen Noel	3	1					1				1	
Amy Linford	3		1		1							1
Emily Barrett	3		1	1				1				
Justine Lynch	2						2					
Jess Reed	2									1		1
Lenka Vseteckova	2										1	1
Camilla Barden	2						1	1				
Jacqui Smiter	2	1									1	
Caroline Shanklyn	2	1									1	
Kate Dillane	2	1						1				
Jodie Favell	2	1			1							
Katie Ellen-French	2			2								
Rachel Weston	2	1		1								
Heidi Cayzer	2	1		1								
Anoushka Johnson	2	1		1								
Runa Bostad	2	1		1								
Catherine Lovegrove	2		1			1						
Natalie Beadle	2						1	1				
Laura Goodson	2	1							1			
Jan Whittington	2								1	1		
J Emery	1										1	
Debbie Hearn	1										1	
Jayne Lawrence	1										1	
Julie Mitchell	1										1	
Christin Bertram	1										1	
Chrissie Wellington	1						1					
Kerry Renshaw	1						1					
Samantha McClary	1						1					
Laura D'Albey	1						1					
Celine Durraffourd	1						1					
Ellen Van der Velden	1						1					
Angela Pike	1									1		
Liz Horrobin	1									1		
Petra Kasperova	1									1		
Orna McGinley	1				1							
Laurel Bray	1						1					
Nikki Haines	1								1			
Amy Pike	1								1			
Nina Mills	1								1			
Katherine Swanson	1								1			
Deborah Noel	1								1			
Nici Cahusac	1								1			
Kate Houston	1	1										
Claire Stokes	1	1										
Sophie Cowper	1	1										
Bethany Brown	1	1										
Laura Suggitt	1			1								
Vicky Jones	1					1						
Carly Weeks	1					1						
Naomi Lenane	1										1	

CAST FOR "THE BIG 12" - MEN

187 male athletes have scored for Belgrave in the 12 Championship races since the '99-00 season, excluding the Surrey League:

	Total	Surrey 6	SEAA 6	SEAA XC 4	ERRA 6	Nat xc 4	SOT team	SOT champs	Surrey xc	SEAA XC	ECCA XC	SEAA 12	ERRA 12
Will Cockerell	112	13	8	4	2		5	8	15	15	17	15	10
Paskar Owor	81	7	8	8	5	3	4	7	10	8	6	8	7
Phil Wicks	62	3	6		6	5	5	4	8	4	7	8	6
Stephen Sharp	53		10		10	8					1	12	12
James Kelly	40	2	5		4	1		3	5	4	5	4	7
Richard Ward	36	5	4	2	2		1		2			9	11
Paul Freary	34		6		6	3				2	4	6	7
Mike Trees	28	1	3	1			1	5	5	4	1	5	2
Knut Hegvold	27	8	1				1	4	4	3	2	4	
Roger Alsop	27	6	4				3			3	1	2	5	3
Nick Goolab	26		5	1	4	4						8	4
Andrius Jaksevicius	25			1			5	5	4	3	2	3	2
Malachi Byansi	24	3					2	3	3	3	5	3	2
David Anderson	23		3		4	2		1			2	5	6
Nick Buckle	23	1	3	3			1	2	2	5	2	4	
Alister Stewart	22	2	2		3	1		1	1		3	4	5
Simon Jones	21		3		5	2				2	1	3	5
Royston Maddams	21	2	2	2			2	2	4	2	2	2	1
Kevin Nash	20		2		1	1	1	1	2		2	7	4
Jon Blackledge	20		4		2	1	1					6	7
Mark Pollard	19		2		2	2				2	1	4	6
Arne Dumez	18				1		2	2	3	3	3	2	2
Neil Speaight	17		1		3	1		1				5	6
Mark Miles	16	2			5	2					1		6
Lee Hurst	15	2			3					3	3	2	2
Spencer Barden	15	2			7	1					1		4
Alex Miller	15			1			1	3		3	2	3	2
James Fairbourn	13	2		1				2	2	3	3		

	Total	Surrey 6	SEAA 6	SEAA XC 4	ERRA 6	Nat xc 4	SOT team	SOT champs	Surrey xc	SEAA XC	ECCA XC	SEAA 12	ERRA 12
Nick Bundle	13		1					2	1	3	2	2	4
Dan Mulhare	13	2		3		1					1	2	4
Charlie Herrington	12		1		1			1		1	2	4	2
Steve Davies	12		1		5							2	4
Gus Upton	12	2	1	1	1		1					3	3
Don Anderson	12						3		5	1	2		1
Warren Lynch	12	1					3	1	3	4			
Craig Ruddy	11		2		2					2		2	3
Hassan Raidi	10	1	1							1	2	4	1
Edward Auden	10		2	1			1	1				3	2
Lander Eguia	10						2	1	2	2	1	2	
Kris Gauson	9		1	1	2	1						2	2
Pete Willis	9						1	2		1	1	3	1
Kevin Quinn	9	3					1	1				3	1
Tim Watson	8		1					1		1		2	3
Matt Welsh	8		2	1				1	1			1	2
Phil Carstairs	7									4	1	1	1
Dave Mason	7	3						1	1	1	1		
Richard Stannard	7			1				2	2	1		1	
Nick Smallwood	7	1	1					1	1	1	1	1	
Mark Humphrey	7	4					1		2				
Rob Norville	7	3	1					1	1			1	
Conall McNally	7	1			1					1	2	1	1
Lloyd Catley	6	1							1	1	3		
Rob McHarg	6		1						1		2	1	1
Taras Telkovsky	6						1	1	1		1	1	1
Tim Weeks	6	1					1	1	1	1	1		
James Browne	6	3					1			1	1		
Ross Finlay	6		1				1	1	2	1			

	Total	Surrey 6	SEAA 6	SEAA XC 4	ERRA 6	Nat xc 4	SOT team	SOT champs	Surrey xc	SEAA XC	ECCA XC	SEAA 12	ERRA 12
Ben Hurley	6	1	1				2	1			1		
Marty Dent	6	1	1		1							1	2
Jason Lobo	5				2					2	1		
Allen Graffin	5				1						2		2
Russ Dessaix-Chin	5							1			1	1	2
Jim Estall	5	2	1									1	1
Alex Mills	5		2							1	1	1	
Tom Ellacott	5	1					1	2				1	
Stephen Kennefick	5	1	1				1	1				1	
Joachim Wolf	5						2			1	1	1	
Callum Stewart	5						1		1	2		1	
Sam Gebreselassie	5	1				1			1			1	1
Jonny Neville	5								1	1	1	1	1
Zek Abery	4							1		1	1	1	
Paul Evans	4				1							1	2
Mike Kazimierski	4							1	1	2			
Patrick McDougall	4								1	1	1		1
Lee Greatorex	4	4											
Andrew Connick	4		1							1		1	1
Brad Courtney-Pinn	4		1					1	1			1	
Junior Galley	4	3	1										
Padraic Buckley	4	1					1					1	1
Andrew Fyfe	4			1			1					1	1
Bruce Barton	4						2	1					1
Steve Gardner	4									1		1	2
Tom O'Beirne	3							2			1		
John Kimaiyo	3							1		1	1		
Tom Hadfield	3							1		2			
Paul Lowe	3							1		2			
Najibe Hliouat	3											2	
Steve Clarke	3											2	1
Kassa Tadesse	3					2							1
Stephen Trainer	3					1				1			1
Shugri Omar	3							1				1	1
Rick Hayman	3											1	2
Chris Moss	3											1	2
Steve Zealey	3							1	1		1		
Simon Marwood	3	1										1	1
Shaun Moralee	3		1									1	1
Yacin Yusuf	3	1	1		1								
Adam Leane	3	1	1										1
Matthew Graham	3		1	1	1								
Martin Holm	3						1				1		1
Will Johnson	3						1			1			1
Dan Wallis	3											1	2
Ewan Somerville	3					1						1	1
Eliot Lyne	2							2					
Oliver Young	2							2					
John Charles	2									1		1	
Matt Taylor	2							1		1			
Andrew Cumine	2							1		1			
Matt Edgar	2							1		1			
Soren Lindner	2									1	1		
Alex Bodin	2							1				1	
Doug Morton	2										1	1	
Dan Gauson	2										1		1
Fraser Logan	2											1	1

	Total	Surrey 6	SEAA 6	SEAA XC 4	ERRA 6	Nat xc 4	SOT team	SOT champs	Surrey xc	SEAA XC	ECCA XC	SEAA 12	ERRA 12
Michael Mulhare	2					1							1
James Williams	2								1		1		
Tom Fordyce	2								2				
Neil Wilson	2	1			1								
Kevin Gadd	2	1									1		
Paul Coughlan	2	1											1
Gregg Clark	2	2											
Konstantinos Touse	2			1								1	
Graham Adams	2	1	1										
Rob Harding	2						1	1					
Matt Whiting	2						1				1		
Alister Jones	2						1			1			
Reece Edwards	2								1	1			
Angus Lamb	2	1									1		
Jonny Scott	2								1		1		
Tommy Taylor	2				1								1
Henry Hart	2										1	1	
Alex Hutchinson	2		1									1	
Clive Gilbey	1											1	
Fabien Bernard-Gaudien	1											1	
James Beech	1											1	
Yitbarek Dinku	1							1					
Steve Nelson	1							1					
Will Ireson	1							1					
Eduard Egelie	1							1					
Alistair Lang	1							1					
Alex Luce	1							1					
Matt Young	1							1					
Garrett Lee	1							1					
Kyle Marks	1										1		
Luke Pikett	1										1		
Steve Jones	1										1		
James Morris	1										1		
Michael McCarthy	1										1		
David Walsh	1										1		
Tom Corbett	1									1			
John Clarke	1									1			
James Nutt	1									1			
Ben MacCronan	1											1	
Ted Oldman	1											1	
Andrew Swearman	1											1	
Stuart Kollmorgen	1											1	
Sam Shore	1											1	
Tom Chandy	1											1	
Scott Mills	1												1
Erwin McRae	1												1
Adam Zawadski	1												1
Andy Graffin	1												1
Justin Chaston	1												1
Erwin Lemenager	1								1				
Richard Merrick	1								1				
Dan Agustus	1								1				
Steve Fowler	1	1											
Paul Chapman	1	1											
Matt Morgan	1	1											
Trygve Reitan	1	1											
Graeme Hyett	1		1										
Will Stockley	1		1										
Jasper Taylor	1		1										
Geremew Wolde	1						1						
Jerome Curtat	1						1						
Frank Ward	1						1						
Lars Rehn	1						1						
Harry Corbett	1						1						
Chris Sweeney	1						1						
Patrick Bogues	1						1						
Clayton Scott	1						1						
Matt Foord	1						1						
Euan Campbell	1											1	
James Fox	1											1	
Rob Kelly	1												1
Ross Christie	1												1
Valentin Rigori	1												1

SURREY 4 STAGE ROAD RELAY - WOMEN

Four bronze and a reigning silver

Due to our smallish squad size over the years and the strict county qualification, we have not had vintage returns at this season curtain-raiser, but it is worth noting that five medals have been scored, including four between 1999-2005, so let's revisit those efforts now.

The 1999-2000 season was kicked off by a fine thriller when Helen Maskrey [Cole] came home in 2nd, and Tanya Sturton and Catherine Eastham held onto bronze. Enter Kate Houston for an almighty assault on the silver medals, which would have happened given another 150 yards or so of land. But by just 4 seconds, Ranelagh held on.

A blob followed by a 6th ensued before we were back on the podium in 2002 with Vicky Edwards, Angela Walker and Syreeta Stracey running superbly to set off Helen Alsop in the lead. Helen's halcyon days were a decade earlier, and she was up against major opposition in SLH's O'Connor and Liz Kipling of Ranelagh, and had to give best, whilst holding off Herne Hill for bronze.

In 2003 we again tasted the lead, this time on one through Angela's sparkling 16:44 and again on anchor, a much fitter Helen blasted us from 5th to 3rd! So net level par for her last two years then.

A hard fought 4th with Rachel Weston excelling, was followed by more bronze in a race of dodgy standard, but hey, tell it to the record books, and to Ranelagh who won in a good time. Kudos to the TM Catherine Eastham for stepping onto the dancefloor to ensure we medalled.

Bronze ambition. Kate Houston nearly had lift-off to silver in '99. RO'D

The less said about the decade that followed the better – a barren wasteland indeed! We interweaved between illegal teams and DNF's (or DNS's) and the only liftage from the gloom came in 2012 with a hard fought 5th. It was a quirky team of Genia Marek who'd been with us since she was around 11, kicking off in 10th, Alison Heydenrych moving up a notch, Rieko Trees another, and Catherine Bryson blasting round in 17:41. Would that be enough to sneak CB into the outstanding squad for the Southern 4 stage three weeks hence – which would medal?! It was a very tough choice and I went with Lou Blizzard in a call correct by just 2 ticks. One of those devilish ones…

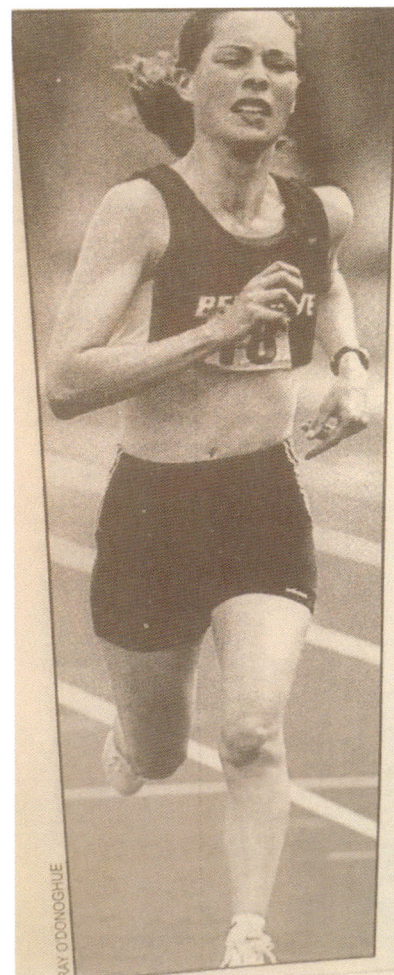

Back with a BANG!

There were flickers of life with 6th and 7th in 2016 & 17, before a riotous post-Covid return to form. Where had we been for 20 years?!

In a dramatic race, Steph Hewitt blasted off into 2nd behind a front-loading Thames who naively wasted by far the best runner of the day, Ruby Woolfe, on one; how they might rue that. Laura Goodson was soon accosted by the talented Carolyne Baxter of Guildford, and setting off with LG I observed the entire saga-laden run: The frantic Baxter-dragged start, the mid-race sag and then after a quiet word from me when I caught her with 650 to go, a riotous finish. The last thing she needed was me prattling in her ear, and it's very rare to be able to rescue a relay run like that, but she managed it thanks to drawing oh-so-deep. Guildford's team was amazing as Sophie Cowper's 16:45 was upended by a 16:40 from Suzie Monk.

We had a 57 second buffer on Thames in 3rd, but Bethany Brown on anchor was not feeling well, and as it went the entire B team [Corden-Lloyd, Bray, Goldie-Scott & Barrett] would take care of her. They would place an impressive 6th. But BB was there on the back of a good 1,500 in the summer and a lot of those B's were on the comeback trail, and not deemed prudent to risk. Also, Bethany gave the leg what it needed, a steady and pragmatic approach, and I was able to tell her with 1,200 to go that she was safe – so why blast it? 18 seconds was the final margin over a fine Thames team who needed to give their weaker runners much more help early doors. It is so alluring to give the best runner the chance to get a great time, but to what end?

A classic day's racing and cameraderie in 2021. Clockwise from top left: Mhairi Hall, Lizzie Goldie-Scot, Laurel Bray, Sophie Cowper, Bethany Brown, Steph Hewitt, Mimi Corden-Lloyd, Laura Goodson, Tommy Taylor, author, AJ Elsadig, Chris Warren, Neil Wilson, Dave Walsh, Phil Wicks, Sam Gebreselassie, Ben Hurley, Conall McNally, Angus Lamb, David Lewis & Nick Buckle

RESULTS

Year	Team	Name (team position)	Time								
1999	3	H Maskrey (2)	17:48	T Sturton (3)	19:44	C Eastham (3)	20:08	K Houston (3)	18:51
2001	6	T Sturton (4)	18:09	K Dillane (3)	19:56	J Smiter (7)	23:16	C Eastham (6)	20:24
2002	3	V Edwards (4)	17:55	A Walker (3)	18:51	S Stracey (1)	18:46	H Alsop (3)	18:52
2003	3	A Walker (1)	16:44	T Sturton (5)	21:18	S Stracey (5)	18:53	H Alsop (3)	18:14
2004	4	A Hegvold (8)	18:25	S Stracey (5)	18:47	H Alsop (5)	19:34	R Weston (4)	18:05
2005*	3	H Cayzer (6)	19:08	R Powell (4)	19:05	C Eastham (5)	21:51	J Clark (3)	18:32
2012	5	G Marek (10)	19:37	A Heydenrych (9)	19:37	R Trees (8)	20:23	C Bryson (5)	17:41
2016	6	F Maddocks (13)	19:41	M Bailey (13)	20:11	I Cousland (8)	19:08	R Prince (8)	18:17
2017	7	M Hall (14)	19:47	C Stokes (12)	21:21	S Haileselase (8)	17:27	R O'Brien (7)	19:32
2021	2	S Hewitt (2)	17:22	L Goodson (3)	17:57	S Cowper (2)	16:45	B Brown (2)	18:56

*long course

SURREY 6 STAGE ROAD RELAY - MEN

An absolute pearl in '99

My Belgrave career started with this one in 1998, where this remarkable 'headfry' of a course around Wimbledon Park made its debut turn. What a journey it is! A ferocious half-mile of climbing, a savage 500 metre descent and then that mile-long piece of fast, flat running in the park. The course may have a personality disorder and can be a little heartless, but what a true battle of wits and skill it is. Our Surrey team in '98 was comprised of lads from Kent, Middlesex, Morocco and New Zealand, and even then we failed to finish. Inauspicious stuff perhaps, but the touchpaper was lit in no uncertain terms in '99 with one of the best relays I ever saw. And it started a stunning sequence of ten top two-finishes in a row – what a roll!

The penny hadn't quite dropped for me in 1999 about how exciting relay-running was but goodness it did during this marvellous race – about half way round I was hooked on the drama of Belgrave and Herne Hill locked in a battle of wills. We kicked off with a swansong run from Steve Fowler. Along with Marcello Bizio, Steve one of our 90s big-hitters, who I caught the last embers of in their career before they vanished off the scene. I enjoyed two super sessions with Marcello at Battersea in '98, and then, just when I thought I had a training partner sent straight from the angels, he disappeared from my life. Steve and I shared a couple of runs out from the hall, and that was that. Very nice guy though. But running is such a fragile sport, that you never quite know the last time you'll see a comrade. Steve got a stodgy 12th here before Kev Quinn also struggled, only finding us a couple of spots. I had a horror run in the Bs and I remember Kev and I chatting after and being so disappointed in ourselves. Imagine then, us both being National 12 champions five years hence – albeit Kev for Aldershot. But there's a lesson there: horror runs do not make a man.

Jim Estall had a peach to haul us up to 4th – another man soon to regretfully disappear from the Belgrave scene – but what a career he had for us – and then Junior Galley started a streak of 'over-performing' at this one, and suddenly we were 2nd with two legs to go. We all knew by now the trouble that awaited Roger Alsop on 6: Dave Taylor no less, who the previous year had placed 4th in the Commonwealth Marathon. So it was down to "Coggie" [Paul Coughlan] to not only bridge the 13 second gap to Herne Hill, but then put some serious distance between us and them. The final damage was 31 seconds, or a slender 160 yards if you will. Could Rog possibly protect that precious allotment of real estate? No. It was gripping but Taylor caught him with a kilometre left to run, as Rog's excellent 14:23 was trumped by DT's absolutely stunning 13:33. What can you do?

**Author's note.* On a balmy summer's evening 23 years later I saw a greying ghost-like figure shuffling along the path at just where Taylor took out Rog. It was Taylor himself! He was limbering up for a return to competition after four years out, and a track 3k, where, pushing 60 he nailed a 9:48. Class – you never lose it.*

Irrepressibly good

Paul Coughlan has flogged himself and the team into a 31 second lead, but will it be enough? RO'D

An excellent team came to race in 2000, but SLH were not just "Irrepressible" [their moniker] but a sensation. Look at these times for nigh on 3 miles: 14:25, 14:21, 14:09, 14:50, 15:02, 14:14. You can only admire, raise your hands and say, "too good!" In the 1950s SLH were by some distance the greatest running club in the land, and their 60+ years of struggle since is a little curious. But occasionally they dazzle & shine, and remain to this day a sharp outfit, with the occasional pearl. We were no mugs ourselves with Rog, Kev, Yacin, Gerry, Jim and Al easily good enough to win most years, but here they had to give best by over 2 minutes.

Another crackerjack race

In 2001 my long love affair with the race began and I enjoyed a good run on the way back from injury. Back in June I'd laced on track spikes too tight, and had battled severe pain in the top of my foot ever since. But I squeaked into the team and we enjoyed a brilliant duel with SLH who had calmed down a tad whilst we had strengthened by half a minute. But they still hit us right between the eyes with Stuart Major and Gary Staines up front. Some one-two gut punch that, and we were 1:45 back. But that was some severe front-loading from them whilst we had saved Al Stewart for 3rd. Al nailed one of the finest runs of his career for a remarkable 14:02, and as he ripped by with 600 to go, I guffawed to Roger, "that's amazing". "No it's not," Rog barked. "He's mispaced it. No-one should be able to run that quick with less than 2 minutes to go…" Haha, no pleasing some people. Al of course had struck the bullseye and was top runner of the day, six seconds up on Belgrave life member Staines.

Lloyd Catley and Robbie James then ran lock-step, so I had a 45 second deficit on my hands on 5. Alan told me I could be going into the lead. "But what about him?" I said pointing to Kevin Tilley. "Oh, forget about him!" Alan said. It was impeccable management to make me *believe* SLH were there for the taking. Well, I took 37 seconds out of Kevin, so at least Roger had the redoubtable Jason Simpson "only" 35 yards up the way. But Simpson was no joke and it wasn't to be. Cracking race though and we hit them hard.

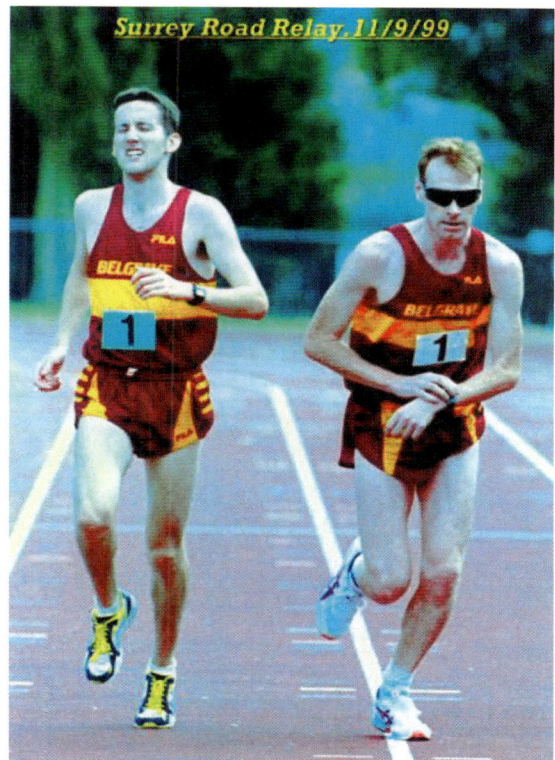

Getting annoying…

For the fourth year in a row we had to settle for 2nd in 2002. I led off with a bit of a stormer (14:17), but this time, in yet another thriller, it was back to Herne Hill to nick us, in a near action replay of the gem of '99. Lee Greatorex ran well to turn my 3rd into 1st, whilst James Browne and Roger cemented the lead. However, an unfit Steve Kennefick toiled a tad which opened the door for Herne Hill to take a minute out of us and it meant that our old warhorse Junior Galley had a world of trouble on his hands as Simon Stevens was a very able runner. His lead was just 10 seconds but the result wasn't decided until the last half a klik as SS ran 14:52 to JGs 15:15. It was the classic 'running on former glory" run from Junior, and shows how much competitive fire in the belly counts for.

"Apres moi, le deluge…"

One is reminded of Roger Bannister's words with our travails at this one. After all these chastening blows, the floodgates opened for us – in a very big way as we nailed six wins in the next eight years – incredible stuff. Warren Lynch and Junior started us off nice and steady in 2003 and we were nestled in 5th, but then it was the Marty Dent show and we ran away comfortable 2 minute winners over Thames; who in turn had a suave Aussie of their own in Phill Sly. A dreadful field couldn't get near us in 2004 – one of those days, they happen – whilst we were rock solid throughout; whilst in 2005 SLH bounced back well to defeat us in an interesting race, but they were on one of their benders. I had a surreal day in that I observed 90 minutes of the crucial 5th Ashes Test at the Oval, leapt on my bike, did the race, and got back half way through the afternoon session. Not a bad little workout that.

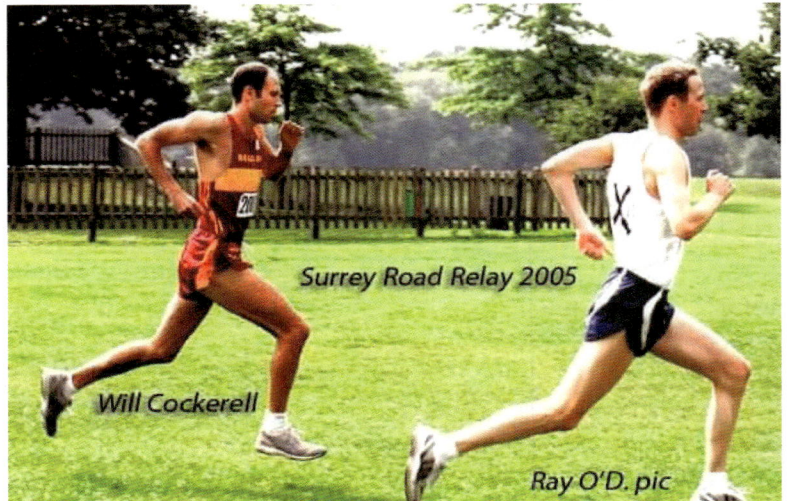

Tired of watching Hayden and Langer flog England all over Kennington, a different type of flogging was imbibed a few miles up the road, via SLH and Thames' Darren Talbot. RO'D

Another rather ghoulish field turned up in 2006, and we won by over half a mile, although we did witness John Mcfarlane return one of the best sessions I've ever seen. He ran a 14:07 on one, 14:19 on 4, and 14:24 on six. What a runner. He'd go on to place 17th at London the following spring.

The drama returns

Finally, another wonderful race in 2007. We were getting lonely at the top! I was managing the lads as Alan was stuck in the results tent. It was a fallible team built mainly of engine-roomers, and SLH had Simpson and Major. This was going to be close. Malachi was still in fine form after 'the year of his life', and a brilliant, straight out of left field, 32nd at London; whilst Wardy was a tad off colour but fair enough. Fairbs and Dave Mason kept us in 2nd, before we 'unleashed the beast!' New man James Kelly ran a stonking 14:12 and that was with going off course for some 100 yards. But it all meant for a thrilling denouement with our fabled Trondheim stallion Knut Hegvold up against our old friend and foe Stuart Major who had gone sub 14 around here. Surely 29 seconds was too little to give Knut? But actually he was right at the top of his [46 year old] game, whilst Stuart was on the comeback trail. It meant that these two fine runners ran basically lock step and Stu could only take 4 seconds out of KH. A terrific race.

2008 saw Belgrave at its imperious best with a very straightforward win, although it was a welcome sight to see as many as four teams within four minutes of us. Perhaps the depth of the race was on the rise.

RESULTS
long course

Year	Team	Name (team pos.)	Time										
1999	2	S Fowler (12)	15:51	K Quinn (10)	15:46	J Estall (4)	14:48	J Galley (2)	14:51	P Coughlan (1)	14:55	R Alsop (2)	14:23
2000	2	R Alsop (3)	14:44	K Quinn (3)	14:42	Y Yusuf (2)	14:47	G Adams (2)	15:10	J Estall (2)	14:58	A Stewart (2)	14:56
2001	2	J Browne (6)	15:13	K Quinn (5)	15:04	A Stewart (3)	14:02	L Catley (2)	14:49	W Cockerell (2)	14:57	R Alsop (2)	14:43
2002	2	W Cockerell (3)	14:17	L Greatorex (1)	15:13	J Browne (2)	14:40	R Alsop (1)	14:24	S Kennefick (1)	15:34	J Galley (2)	15:15
2003	1	W Lynch (6)	15:17	J Galley (5)	15:18	S Marwood (2)	14:49	M Dent (1)	13:53	R Alsop (1)	15:19	W Cockerell (1)	14:42
2004	1	M Humphrey (10)	15:29	A Leane (3)	15:08	L Greatorex (2)	15:15	R Alsop (2)	15:00	W Cockerell (1)	15:03	K Hegvold (1)	15:03
2005*	2	L Greatorex (4)	15:52	W Cockerell (2)	15:45	K Hegvold (2)	15:54	T Ellacott (2)	16:13	M Humphrey (3)	16:55	J Browne (2)	16:11
2006	1	P Buckley (4)	14:52	M Humphrey (3)	15:27	K Hegvold (3)	15:36	W Cockerell (4)	15:14	H Raidi (1)	14:30	R Ward (1)	14:40
2007	1	M Byansi (3)	14:52	R Ward (2)	15:08	J Fairbourn (1)	15:31	D Mason (2)	15:47	J Kelly (1)	14:12	K Hegvold (1)	14:59
2008	1	K Hegvold (2)	14:54	L Greatorex (1)	15:07	R Ward (1)	14:53	T Weeks (1)	15:48	W Cockerell (1)	15:00	J Kelly (1)	14:46
2009	6	M Humphrey (9)	15:48	B Hurley (5)	15:31	K Gadd (5)	15:34	D Mason (5)	16:40	P Chapman (6)	17:01	R Norville (6)	16:59
2010	1	K Hegvold (8)	15:44	M Byansi (5)	15:09	M Morgan (4)	15:17	W Cockerell (5)	15:04	R Ward (3)	14:50	P Owor (1)	13:58
2011	3	J Fairbourn (7)	15:30	R Ward (1)	14:33	D Mason (2)	16:11	W Cockerell (2)	15:56	M Byansi (4)	16:41	P Owor (3)	14:27
2015	14	G Clark (14)	15:53	W Cockerell (13)	16:08	P Owor (10)	16:10	P Wicks (6)	13:29	G Upton (4)	15:01	R Maddams (14)	28:41
2016	2	N Smallwood (10)	15:44	P Owor (1)	13:58	W Cockerell (4)	16:17	P Wicks (2)	13:48	G Upton (2)	14:46	G Clark (2)	16:07
2021	3	S Gebreselassie (1)	14:10	N Buckle (3)	15:16	C McNally (4)	15:18	P Wicks (3)	14:42	A Lamb (3)	15:29	N Wilson (3)	15:14

And another absolute classic

Lots transpired against us in 2009 [including my daughter's christening] to see us well out of the medals, but we were yet again on the gold standard in 2010 in a thrilling struggle. We knew we were fallible and insisted on back-loading to keep ourselves competitive right till the end. Knut, Malachi and Matt Morgan saw us into a solid 4th at the half, and then my run saw us leak a spot, but little damage was done as the field had massively bunched up. So! It was Belgrave in 5th, Thames 4th, HW 3rd, Herne Hill 2nd and a guesting Shaftesbury in 1st, who were about to combust. Hercules leapt into the lead, Thames kept their 4th, lining up Major (enjoying a sojourn with them), and Herne Hill kept silver, with Wardy's tasty run advancing us to 3rd. Pity poor Richard Xerri on anchor for HW. Rich is a talented runner but his star shone brightest some 15 years earlier. He ran ok, but was no match for Stu or Dave Mulvee, whilst Paskar was in just about the form of his life, and tore off a sub 14 run, for an ultimately comfortable win. But what a great race it had been.

HW had their revenge in 2011 as a woefully out of touch Mal dampened our allure, although I see I toiled as well. But it was another fine race, and we were still less than a minute off the gold, only a little behind a strong Saltire effort. We led at the half in 2012 but then ran out of men big time and had to close with a non-scorer, and had an even bigger dnf shocker in 2013, albeit still leading after 2. We had fun with it though as as we could savour the "battle of the brother-in-laws". The husband of Knut's wife's sister Runa [a Belgrave star in her own right, see SEAA 4 stage], Trygve Reitan, was in town, and I knew him to be a slugger, having vacationed with him in Trondheim a decade earlier. That cruel strength similarly dismantled Knut 16:06 to 16:22. A bronze then, if we could somehow shoehorn this Northern outpost of Norway into the Surrey boundaries. But we couldn't.

Farewell to The Machine

2014 was my first year at the TM helm, and we had a good team but it needed Wardy to apply the *coup de grâce*. It was deemed only a minor hitch when he reported a wedding in Tonbridge the night before. No problem. We agreed he'd perhaps reign it in slightly at the festivities, and he could hop back to town the next morning and we could put him on a late stage. Maybe the wedding would cost him 20-30 seconds. But as the race drew near, Rich admitted he found the prospect untenable [or perhaps unpalatable], and pulled the plug, which triggered a Bels DNS. I knew in my heart that it wasn't really the wedding that was the problem: Rich, christened "the Machine" in his early teens by *AW*, had retired from competitive athletics; he just didn't know it yet. We never saw him again in the claret, but what a terrific Bels career he enjoyed for some 14 years – one of the doyens for sure.

We looked very dangerous in 2015 but Roy Maddams' notorious difficulties with transport [and navigating] was very costly. PO had also had the summer off, while Wicksy's 13:29 was a shameful waste by us, but despite Roy starting about a quarter of an hour late on anchor, we still got 14th. Four months later, more Roy travel sagas hastened our exit from the Surrey league… a bit harsh to put it all on the lad, but when he wrote in to say: "body under a train," I had a grim feeling about our league chances, such was his reliability and strength (when we could get him to start).

Much better fare followed in 2016 as we fought tooth and nail with SLH just as in 16 years earlier. The soon to depart Nick Smallwood got 10th and we let the lion off the leash. The perfect example about why NOT to start with your ace. He creamed us into the lead, whilst an aging Cockerpiller leaked to 4th. Phil ran beautifully again, but he was up against a stunner from Kev Quinn (over 1:30 up on that '99 run). Gus Upton did what he could with Tom Higgs which left a rather injured Gregg Clark to have an isolated run in silver. But that SLH team was magnificent.

Disgraceful treatment from SCAA in '17

I've had some run-ins with officialdom in my time, but the Surrey County AA behaved awfully in 2017, disqualifying us for a late entry when I got us in on the correct day. Yes, you read that right. But they told me they wanted us by noon. It's pathetic, ham-fisted bureaucracy for a fairly low-key race, where the entries could easily be handled on the day, not days in advance; and all it served to do was ruin the race as a spectacle. I asked why the spurious noon deadline was in place and they said that it was to allow problems to be dealt with that afternoon. Well – here was a problem! No amount of pleading would get them to see sense. These officials – and certainly this applies to the SEAA and ECCA as well, so often forget that they're in place to *provide* competition, not *deny* it. We had a good team (with Wicksy on board); we [well, ARM] had dutifully done the results for the last decade; we had won the race six times since 2002; and all we basically got back was, "piss off". It is so not how to run grassroots sport.

I wrote to the other clubs to apologize for Belgrave's non-appearance and the replies were mystified. Naturally the spectacle at the sharp end was pretty dull but it did at least mean that Dorking popped up with an unlikely set of medals. Kudos to them. Before the race, Surrey County put out a begging letter for marshals… um, thanks but no thanks. It's an obvious organization for me to serve in future years, but the contempt they treated me with was quite chilling. It wasn't just the "no", but the anonymous, sarcastic, autocratic style of no which is so out of place for a community event like this, where we're all supposed to be trying to promote the sport.

**As a rider to this tawdry episode, in May of 2022 there was outcry at the abysmally low entries for the Track and field County champs. Once again a far out noon entry, which was then extended due to numbers at eye-wateringly low figures, like, say two for the women's 1,500 or five for the men's. If these officials put in even a quarter of the effort into marketing what used to be a sizzling affair, as they do into such rubbish as draconian, spurious "noon" deadlines, then they would undoubtedly get more patrons. What about social media interaction? Or letters to clubs and team managers? Campaigns to say: "save our Championships! Don't let parkrun have it all their own way! For goodness sake do the Surrey 5k and not parkrun on this day!" Something like that. I am forever amazed at how little the SEAA and SCAA interact with the grassroots. I don't think I've seen a compulsive social media advert or had a personal letter from them extolling their wares in my time in the sport.

Lots of blobs, but finally a podium refound

The team fell apart in 2018 for another DNS, and Arne and Steve let the race go in 2019 in their first year 'on the job' preferring to focus on the Southerns. The race does come at a fiddly time, with the track season still in swing. But finally we were back in play, post-Covid in 2021 and we hit the race hard. Too hard in fact, as the fearsome Sam Gebreselasie was let off on one. It's very damaging to burn your ace with still 83.3% of the race to go, as he gives the rest of leg 1 such a great tow, and your 2nd man is then savagely feasted on. 1st after one doesn't mean a thing if you can't hold it. Anyway, Nick Buckle battled manfully to come back in 3rd and Conall McNally leaked one more in a terrific field to land us in 4th. It was wonderful to see Wicksy back in the team, but both Guildford and Hercules were on electrifying form. Indeed GG ended with 14:08 man George Dallner. But Angus Lamb was solid on 5 and Neil Wilson had a pleasantly surprising 15:14 on achor, keeping well clear of the dangerous Ollie Garrod for SLH. Hercules won a superb race by just 14 seconds, and 1:47 up on the Bels. Goodness, Guildford must have fancied their chances at the gun. They were basically half a man short of the win, as one of their flock ran 15:53.

What a journey then it's been at this one, and we can be well happy with our return. A dream decade followed by the very splotchy one, but the roaring '20s have started well.

For an image of the men's squad, please consult the women's race

SOUTHERN 6 STAGE - MEN

An astonishingly good ride

There was a special feeling in the air for the 1999 race. I recall a bunch of us walking up to the start and 2.66 teams being allocated their men. I'd not been too respectful in that I'd run the Serpentine Last Friday of the month the day before, and the subtle slopes of the great Rushmoor Arena would prove very telling. I anchored the B team round in 25th, and felt every step of that 6k. In the As we had a rock steady team of strength and experience, who in turn were hard-pressed by several of the Bs, particularly new man Rob McHarg who was a 45 second flub to leave out. Now we knew…

After granite-like Jim Estall cruised round in 17th progress was generally solid with Kev, Lee, Junior [making one of his last major forays in an A team vest], Rog and Gerry to nail 9th.

More progress came in 2000 with a now terrific team that saw the likes of Gnasher and myself with noses pressed to the glass. In fact, with Kev Quinn, Najibe, Rick Hayman and Joachim Wolf also on board, our baby Bees had a bit of a stunner in 14th. The C-team of "International All-stars" found 32nc/88. Up front, we began with Chas Herrington, he of the most bulging calves of perhaps any Bel in the last 40 years. "These are my guns!" he used to proudly say. A rocking 18:25 had us on the tail of the leaders in 7th and after a slightly off-colour run from Rog, 10th crept all the way up to 4th by the denouement. A little way off the medals though. Up front Hounslow were incredible – they needed to be, what with dying their hair blue and white, painting their faces likewise and donning t-shirts with "the boys are back in town." The late Sam Haughian led from the front, and backed up by the likes of Ben Whitby, Mike Simpson and Mo Farah ["For the first time I got stitch, I had nothing to chase"], it began a decade long battle between us and Farah-led teams. What absorbing struggles they were.

Medals!

The acorn continue to grow in 2001 – with a team would go on to win the National 6 stage the following month (with the odd super-sub). I narrowly missed out on selection as I often did for this one, but the selectors got it just right with Steven Kennefick edging me out by 4 seconds. SK wasn't with us for long but he did some good, strong races. Hounslow had merged with Windsor and Mo Farah was quite simply sensational. "Did you see Mo?!" asked a wide-eyed Bill Laws after he'd flown down one of the slopes. Indeed I had, and I thought right there and then he could be one of the best runners in the world. Nobody runs like that! Mo was the day's fastest with an incredible 17:29 and with Haughian running 17:48, Windsor were far too hot to handle. How on earth could we beat them the following month, with a 2:05 gap to Newham and 2:40 to us? See that chapter to find out.

Meanwhile, after Lee's strong opener, Paul F. ripped us into 2nd, which Roger held and a debutant called Stephen Sharp leaked a spot albeit with our best of the day. Goodness weren't we in for a treat with that one! SK and Al Stewart brought home the medals. Mr Sharp would not miss another major relay for us until the year again ended in 1, and even that took divine intervention.

A Mo slugfest for the gold

Would 2002 be our year? We were very strong as even my sharp 14:17 at the Surreys for the day's 7th fastest didn't guarantee selection, but finally I was given the nod over Lee Hurst, who took it ok, but was placed on 1 for the B's and made clear his intention to "take me down, all the way down…" To add to the pressure I came down with a cold the night before, which I persuaded myself was one of those ones that you could barter with. This is possible with colds of course; you just feel absolutely rotten. Leg 1 was to be my lot as well, and a big crowd lined up in front of the runners, for 100 metres up the straight. This, I told myself, was 'it': leading off a white-hot team, for a hoped for win. The first lap was amazingly quick and I came through the 3k in 8:54, which was nigh on my pb for the distance, on a hilly course, with another lap to come – with a cold. I was asking for trouble - and I got it. A grisly 45 second decline was my penance, but others leaked too, and I got 6th as Spencer Barden had 25 seconds to make up on Ipswich in the lead and four other souls.

Like a sharpshooter, he took care of his quarry one by one and spent his second tour extending the gap by nearly half a minute. Paul Freary was very fit but twanged a hammie, still extending the lead to a minute. And now? Roger Alsop versus Mo Farah – who had destroyed us for the last couple of years. Wow - what a contest this was turning out to be, as Mo (slightly unfit) ripped 40 seconds out of Rog on lap one. The announcer was sure that Windsor would take the lead, but in one of his most obdurate runs, Rog held Mo off by just 2 ticks. Elsewhere, another superstar in the making Chris Thompson was running an incredible 17:29. Sharpy set off pursued by the hollering Maria and gradually extended us into unsurmountable territory, and we still had the outstanding new talent of David Anderson to come, who refused to cruise, and ran to our 2nd fastest. It had been a day of high drama, and Windsor sorely missed Sam Haughian, but even then I think we would have had them covered – just!

Thommo Meltdown

The team held firm for 2003, but never did we, or specifically 'T', envisage the nightmare that would envelop us – deep into the race. It was all going so well… SS began with an outstanding 3rd and YJB [young Jonny Blackledge – a play on 'Young Jonny Bairstow's' moniker] did superbly to step smoothly into a sick Wardy's shoes. Just a fortnight beyond his 19th birthday, Jon won a ferocious duel with the incoming Team GB'er Huw Lobb to advance to 2nd with a heavily front-loaded Thames (courtesy of Phill Sly) in the lead.

Thames had the legendary Lazza Mathews on 3, but his heyday was a decade-plus earlier and Freary was far too good. This all set up *Danders* to scorch to an attempted sub 18, which ended up being 18 flush. As I awaited my comrade and 'roomie', I was slightly surprised to see the *Shots'* Chris 'Thommo' Thompson stride to the start and then make something of a show of removing his tracksuit top. I almost wanted to tap him on the shoulder and warn him not to get cold – our lead was a quarter of a mile.

Mayhem!

I set off and flew down the slope at the end of the first K. A panicky John Jeffery was there to greet me: "EVERY. SINGLE. METER. COUNTS!" he bellowed. What was he on about? Surely no-one was catching the Cockerpillar today. But there was another problem too. Something felt off with my body. A weakness and lethargy I couldn't quite place. Racing with a huge lead can do that – it's a very lonely business and doubt, unexpected fatigue and just general malaise can set in. A bit like perhaps being 2 sets to nil up in a tennis match. Where do you go from there, and how do you dig really deep? Some other squawkers started up too and was that even shouts of "Go on Thommo!"? Naaaaahh. But as I came through lap 1, Alan greeted me with a mood I'd never before seen from the ice-cool one: "*Come on Will!* This is *SERIOUS!!*," he bellowed. I glanced at my watch, and for sure my time of around 9:20 was sub-optimum. But at least I was starting to snap out of my malaise, as I knew I had a real race on.

The AFD boys started cleverly ganging up on me, by stepping up close and roaring in my ear: "Go on Thommo!!" to give the impression Chris was just behind. It was fairly terrifying stuff as I still had 2K to go. Nothing for it but to patter on down the road.

Finally, as I re-entered the arena with 700 to go, the footsteps of doom were heard and this masterful young athlete cantered by. I tried to get into his slipstream and hang on for as long as I could. I couldn't help but admire the poetry in motion before me as his smooth stride reminded me of pistons on a steamtrain. The gap grew to 4 or 5 seconds, but finally Chris ran out of road. I felt pretty wretched that I'd let AFD back into the race, but my time [18:45] wasn't *toooo* bad, and we were probably still favourites. Marty Dent was approaching international standard while AFD's Elliot Robinson was "only" rock solid. Elliot would in turn come under fire from top South African Greg van Hest of Bedford, and our winning

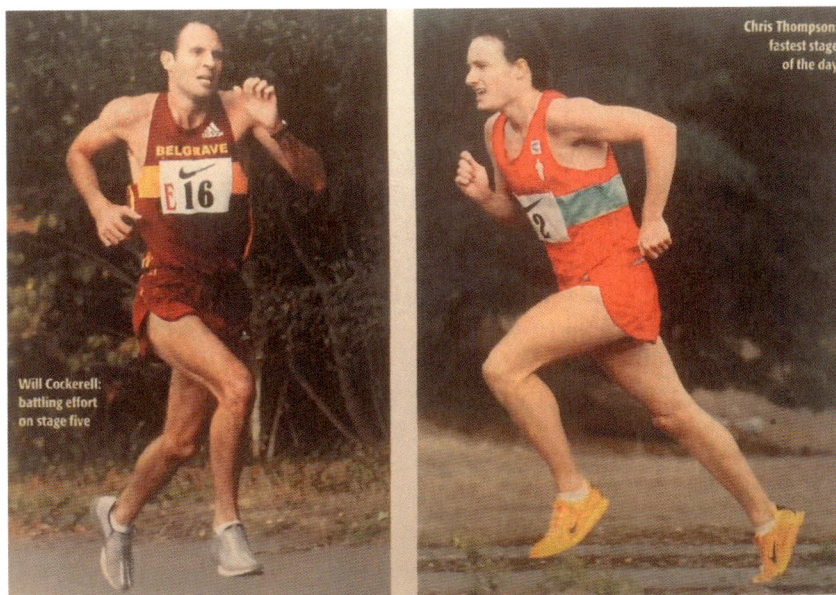

How AW saw the duel. MS

margin was 40 seconds over them and 41 over Aldershot, with Newham hovering too. It had been a wonderful race, and now for part two: straight back to town, and on a flight for a business trip to New York. Which I missed – by miles – not even close! It was one of those days when the clock always seemed to tick too fast.

More absorbing relay magic

To my minor regret I skipped '04 in favour of the Great North Run, where I got a tangy 68, but can't help but think that a Championship gold was more important. Little did I realise I wouldn't get back into the squad for another seven years. These spots are precious. Adam Leane was my like for like replacement, although he had a minor shocker on one: we were 24th.

A downpour had hit the course as Paul F took a deep breath and splashed his way up the slope. This was going to be interesting. Paul had an excellent run and by the time his work was done, 14 men were in the sack. Right, what chance of a further advance from Blackledge? Oh so high! A monumental 18:11 followed – one of our best ever on the course, and with legs buckling under a peaking sun, we had a precious place in the top 6, but the gold was over a minute away. This was some race.

Enter the Gnasher. He was solid as ever despite a hip injury over the summer. Kev steadily advanced us into third with the top two some 30 seconds adrift, but as Alan writes, we had: "a kick like a whole rake of mules."

This was *some* back-loading! I've written a lot in the book about the discipline and nerve back-loading takes, and not blowing your best runners early. Well we hadn't done that for sure with the small matter of SS and Mark Miles to offer the enemy. Stephen ripped off a fine first lap with coach Terry not daring to say how fast it was. That was the Beagles accounted for, now for Wells. Soon they were drifting back to our man who would have dearly loved that evasive sub 18. ARM writes:

"First words from Steve after the take-over were, 'What time was it?' The reply of 'seventeen ...' was drowned in a cry of delight."

The biggest concern left was relay great Keith Cullen limbering up for Highgate – what a prospect. But such is Milesey's self-belief he wouldn't have found going out on KC's shoulder particularly distasteful. Cullen turned in a pretty magical 17:24, but Mark's 17:37 was awesome too, and 67 seconds was the damage in the end – but what a journey to get there.

A rake of mules: YJB, SS, MM, Gnasher and Leaney. MIA Paul

"Bels Rampant at Rushmoor"

Thus spake ARM's headline in his 2005 report. The C team were 16th! To be sure it was a squad sent straight from the angels and it took the B's until lap 3 to catch the Cs who began in 6th through 19 year old Shugri Omar – with a run good enough for the As. Al Stewart was back in the squad and ran to a superb 2nd which Wicksy on debut around these slopes duly massaged into 1st. A decade later Phil would again be shooting for the lead at this one, more on that in 2015. Messrs Watson, Barden and YJB were always in control, even when Newham wheeled out a riotous Mo Farah, and steadily worked the lead up to 1:28 by the end of their tours. It didn't leave Sharpy much to do but he duly saw his medal count rise to 16 SEAA and AAA team golds, and he was only about half done!

Mic drop from Clarkey, and a Stumble

Anchoring for the B's, John Clarke uttered one of the most whamboozling sentences ever to come from the lips of a relay man: "take my phone will you? My wife's giving birth in 8 minutes."

It had been a practically perfect Olympic cycle of racing, but we returned in 2006 with a couple of kinks – or five. Only Sharpy returned from the previous year, but I failed to pounce on the chance of a spot, still recovering from the largesse of marriage. It was still a fine side and Wardy, making a rare sojourn to this one, found a very good 7th on 1. But then disaster as Hassan Raidi was fasting on the first day of Ramadan, but neglected to share this nugget of info with the TM. Maybe he thought his body would be ok, but I can't really think of a course which punishes those feeling weak more than this. Six spots were lost and the win was surely out the window. Stephen repaired the damage but 7th at the end of 3 is a world of difference to end of 1. Paul had one of his best runs at Rushmoor to take us into the medals, determined not to go out too fast he concentrated solely on a 3 minute first K… and still found 2:50. Such are the mysteries of racing – where does that extra power come from?

Milesy was rock solid on 5 but on this occasion the gaps were simply too large for an advance, as Moumin Geele ripped into Wells' lead which duly fell, to give Mo Farah a 1 metre lead on Ben Tickner. What a proposition for that developing runner. Mo always ran relays in a cagey fashion in the first half, due to his enormous self-belief. I saw it time and again over the years. "Is he ok?" "Is he feeling it today?" but when the touch paper was lit the result was always spectacular, and in this case Mo fell just 7 seconds short of Andy Bristow's course record from 1989. To sum up our day, Simon Jones had come down with a cold, but it probably only cost 20 seconds and the bronze was easily secured. On this day though, NEB were far too good.

Hunger to retain the gold

I was in good shape in 2007, but the only possible way into the squad was via a returning to fitness Danders. We had a 6k time trial in Batts and my derriere was handed to me on a plate. A sub 19 followed for me, opening for the B's whilst David found a super 18:14 for 3rd. With Polly leaking just one spot, Jonesy was at his best and the lead was ours at the half-way stage. Stephen then stretched the lead out and Phil ran a startling 8:41 for the first lap, not far off course record pace. He had majorly over-cooked it, but no matter and still went sub 18. Dave Mitchinson was a fine runner but there was no way he was going to be able to pull back 90 seconds on our 24-year-old Anglo-American James Kelly, who had a "mature run", to only give up 26 ticks to our Essex friends.

Polly's obdurate run leaves the lead in Jonesy's sights

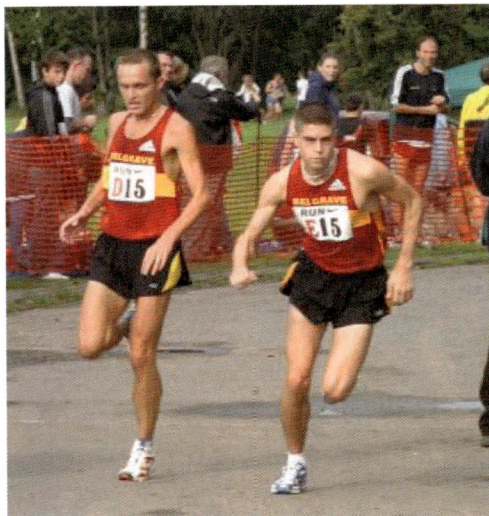

Graceful Bels, but Swan Lake this ain't. One can see how Phil is about to record a slightly barmy 8:41 opener, with a 9:18 coming home

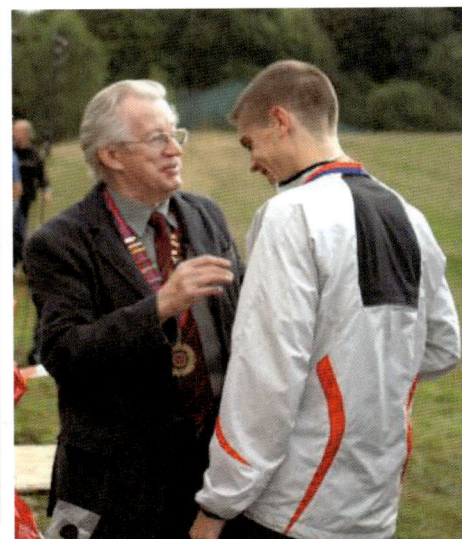

I could get used to this! The late Gordon Biscoe tells Phil Wicks that as SEAA President he's quite happy to keep meeting like this

Hypnotic AFD duel

If 2003's AFD battle was gripping, this in 2008 was even better. The hosts were getting *super hot* now with their squad, under the precocious Mike Boucher, becoming ever more dangerous, and this was a ripper from the start. We had a couple of chinks in our armour and I was so very close to making the cut, and this time would beat an A-teamer by 50 metres, and almost another. Next time! Some slightly profligate front-loading began with Nick Goolab setting us off in 3rd. Would we come to regret using up such a big gun so soon? We now had to find spots for Shaun Moralee and Graeme Hyett. Maybe having two such new and inexperienced men together 2 & 3 was too much of a clash. How about Hyett, Goolab, Moralee? Anwyay, Shaun found his position distinctly uncomfortable, and after an early lunge into 2nd, he dropped 47 seconds on the second lap and 7 spots with a time 10 seconds off the author in the B's.

After Jon Blackledge called in injured we turned to Graeme Hyett. More of a mudlark, Graeme dipped sub 19 with a solid run and claimed back two spots, but we were some considerable distance off the lead. "What followed was extraordinary and set the race up for a grandstand finish," ARM writes. With AFD's Andy Vernon tearing through the field in 6th, Dan Mulhare somehow found a way to jump on this International's back. Just behind he had the excellent Jermaine Mays snapping away. The five athletes up ahead all surrendered as Vernon smashed into the lead with Dan running to the point of oblivion, "lying on the tarmac gasping for air".

New skipper Sharpy felt a cold coming on, but teamed up with Beagler Dan Pettit who had crept up on him. Détente was called as the two athletes had one thing on their minds: to claw back Elliot Robinson's AFD lead. The 150 metre difference inched down to 60 as Ben Moreau set off. It had been a magnificent stage of racing, one of the best I ever saw, and we now had yet another duel to savour. Moreau did everything he could to keep Phil at bay, but still on the comeback trail from knee niggles, Phil was simply outstanding with a 17:41 to BM's 18:03 – still a tremendous time. We savoured what had been a thrilling race and looked forward to more at Sutton Park the next month.

A brace of deuces

An electric Aldershot got their revenge in 2009 and despite a sensational opener from Neil Speaight, who hugged Ben Whitby tight on one [2nd], while the amazing Jonny Hay lurked in 4th. We then had JK slip a little, assaulted by Ben Lindsay's 18:14, whilst Sharpy *only* allowed 3 more ticks to the deficit to become 22 overall at the half. Nick Goolab then gained 9 seconds on Matt Ashton in another slugfest of a duel, but the race was smashed wide open by Ben Moreau on 5, who was simply too good for Jonesy. 53 seconds is a lot to ask of anchor and an impossible task when that anchor is Andy Vernon. What a team it was from AFD and Phil's electric run for once was made to look ordinary – rare to say that about him!

RESULTS 1999-2009

Year	Team	Name (team pos.)	Time										
Rushmoor Arena:													
1999	9	J Estall (17)	19:06	K Nash (13)	19:11	L Hurst (7)	18:22	J Galley (10)	19:46	R Alsop (8)	19:01	G Adams (9)	19:52
2000	4	C Herrington (7)	18:25	R Alsop (10)	19:26	Y Yusuf (6)	18:49	R McHarg (6)	19:15	P Freary (5)	18:47	A Hutchinson (4)	19:01
2001	3	L Hurst (9)	18:38	P Freary (2)	18:25	R Alsop (2)	19:16	S Sharp (3)	18:21	S Kennefick (3)	19:20	A Stewart (3)	18:32
2002	1	W Cockerell (6)	18:33	S Barden (1)	17:54	P Freary (1)	18:29	R Alsop (1)	18:48	S Sharp (1)	18:10	David Anderson (1)	18:02
2003	1	S Sharp (3)	18:16	J Blackledge (2)	18:29	P Freary (1)	18:24	David Anderson (1)	18:00	W Cockerell (2)	18:45	M Dent (1)	17:53
2004	1	A Leane (24)	19:13	P Freary (10)	18:27	J Blackledge (6)	18:11	K Nash (3)	18:35	S Sharp (1)	17:57	M Miles (1)	17:37
2005	1	A Stewart (2)	18:09	P Wicks (1)	18:09	T Watson (1)	18:24	S Barden (1)	17:54	J Blackledge (1)	18:27	S Sharp (1)	18:15
2006	3	R Ward (7)	18:31	H Raidi (13)	19:36	S Sharp (7)	18:28	P Freary (3)	18:25	M Miles (3)	18:06	S Jones (3)	18:42
2007	1	David Anderson (3)	18:14	M Pollard (4)	18:34	S Jones (1)	18:12	S Sharp (1)	18:14	P Wicks (1)	17:59	J Kelly (1)	18:26
2008	1	N Goolab (3)	18:12	S Moralee (9)	19:17	G Hyett (7)	18:58	D Mulhare (2)	17:58	S Sharp (2)	18:18	P Wicks (1)	17:41
2009	2	N Speaight (2)	18:03	J Kelly (2)	18:51	S Sharp (2)	18:29	N Goolab (2)	18:35	S Jones (2)	18:47	P Wicks (2)	17:45

It was more of the same in 2010 as AFD were majesterial. Stephen experienced a minor back pang on one, but 10th set up Wardy to plunder 5, and another old fave in Jon took that to 4th. Enter Goolab! His 18:21 was punchy, but better was to come with Paskar's 18:13. The team had done well and nursed a silver, but what can you do about a team who were now 1:26 up, and had one of the most precocious GB juniors of all time waiting in the wings? Jonny Hay had stunned the community in the summer with a 14:02 aged 18 and that included a 56 last lap. Dan took a deep breath and relieved JH of 21 seconds of the lead, but could do nothing about the other 65. An unwell Wicksy would perhaps have meant just a few seconds in it either way on this day, but one can't look at it like that, as the six we had were bang on point and hugely able – sometimes you just have to say 'hats off'.

Three fun ones for ARM to finish

What a dozen year sequence for Alan, and the fun didn't stop there. Real drama awaited in 2011 as minor capitulation saw the author force his way back in, we *still* nursed medal hopes, but it was going to be close. We started with Polly who would be the first to admit that his athletics career was a little 'uneven'. But that's because the heights he hit were so electrifying – only the mediocre are always at their best. Well, this was one of the clunkers, and there were only a few for us, and the great days were far more in abundance. But we were in a bit of a pickle here for 28th. Steve Davies loved the challenge in front of him though and found an imperious 17 spots – one of our greatest rises in a 6

Stage surely. A very sparky Wardy was back in the fray too and we were 8th at the half. JK "only" gained one but the field up ahead concertinaed. I was given the task of holding the fort before we unleashed the beast. This I did, taking care of Tonbridge but having to bow to Highgate which meant PO had four to find on anchor. It's an awful lot, but if anyone could... Bedford and Highgate were swifty dispatched with Winchester and Kent visible up the way. Alas, the lion ran out of road with 34 seconds still to find. Entertaining race though!

2012 was a bewildering team for Alan to raise, as the "bar of soap syndrome" came to the fore. At noon I was still still in bed, eating a danish and reading the funnies, in my status as reserve, admiring the horizontal monsoon that lashed against the window, which was a huge departure from the previous day's glorious sunshine when the Belles has struck a superb bronze. But then the text: "you're in".

JK ran a superb opener for 4th, and thereafter we dovetailed between the solid and the stars. Mike Trees stepped into the breach, then over to Matt Graham, back to Wardy not at his best and then PO to canter along. I was set off in around 10th and had to settle for 13th as the likes of Dan Watts of SBH and WGEL 800 star Matt Shone were slightly above my paygrade. I was good friends with Shone and hit him with a ribald greeting as he came by. Fortunately he completely misheard it for something far more affectionate. Skippy Wardy kindly gave me 'man of the match' though for being our 4th best.

Commonwealth Games 800 man Matt Shone was an old buddy; and famous for running 10 miles home from Soho nightclubs at 4am in his brogues. He has misheard my greeting here for something benign, when it was anything but

Coast to Coast Like Buttered Toast

The team continued to take hits, and the front-loading chided in these pages was fully kosher in 2013. As ARM writes: "With a few guys missing we were not going to be able to turn out a medal winning team so with the team manager suspecting that Nick Goolab was in good form, he took the decision to front load the six and showcase our colours. Having lit the blue touch-paper he then retired to a safe distance to watch the fireworks; and weren't they spectacular!"

Indeed they were as we confirmed that Nick was one of the most dramatic and entertaining runners in the club's history. He simply battered the first lap and was inside Andy Bristow's course record pace at the bell – amazing. 37 seconds were then leaked, but the gift to James Kelly was a 28 second lead. Remarkably, instead of the field coming up to molest James, he drew further away, and although were were rather weak on this day, we were surely going to be leading at the half. Another thankless task followed, as the oh so brave "Rudster" [Craig Ruddy] extended further, to 36. Perhaps he would have run 20 seconds quicker with company. It was lovely to be enjoying the fun of the fair though, but now we had to take an arrow though the neck, with a gas bill attached.

Exactly 10 years earlier I'd sampled the heady isolation of the lead at Rushmoor being chased by Aldershot, and here I was in the same position – oh! – and being aggressively accosted by AFD yet again. Some things never change. I also had to let Bedford by, before a remarkable run from Mike Trees. The wrong side of 50, Mike dipped well under 20 to only leak one more spot. Roy Maddams was in the firing line for sure, but he refused to be freaked out by 4th in such a prestigious race. He got his head down and plugged away. The big guns of Kent, Highgate and Tonbridge came by, but that was it for Roy. Our rear-gunner opened his stride a little on the second lap and Alan called the result "marvellous". He wrote:

Knut Hegvold was a loyal servant for us from his late 30s to mid-50s, and was very good value for his 40 Surrey league scores. He now does great things over at Hercules' youths

"Sometimes a non-medalling performance can be as pleasing as one that gets us on the podium. This was such a run."

And you can't say fairer than that, it was an apt note for Alan to close on – his boys fighting tooth and nail for the gaffer. All those years on from 9th in 1999, and we were now 7th. But that hardly tells the tale.

Jekyll and Hyde from the new TM

Well, mainly Hyde! I had some rebuilding to do upon replacing our fearless leader, and could attract few to the party in 2014. However, the squad for the National looked much better, so all we had to do was qualify [top 25]. Goodness, it was a close run thing. Front-loading with PO was good fun and he blasted us through into the lead, before I threw hot new kid Gus Upton to the lions. Gus responded with a mildly bonkers 4:30 for the first 1500 and still the lead held. And then things started slipping for the next hour or so. And slipping. The top 25 encroached, until finally I set off on anchor after Knut's tour, left, in 24th, still drunk from the Club awards dinner the night before. "*NONE shall pass!*" was my Black Knight of the *Holy Grail* mantra, and fortunately that held: we were going to the National. A rabble of misfits perhaps, but tomorrow, is another day. We then led that National till the end of stage 4.

Resurrection!

We hadn't seriously tested the gold standard for five years, but in a hark back to the glory days, a fine squad came to race. We started off in 2015 with the mercurial Andy Connick who had run a quite brilliant Southern Cross two years earlier (15th). But there was bizarrely no gas in the tank on this day for a horror start of 28th. The lion loves a good chase and ripped us back into it by claiming 16 spots. This all had shades of four years earlier. Nick Goolab was originally a no, because "he didn't want to let me down." I had to gently explain that an off-colour Goolab still has 90 secs on his stand-in… Nick ran fine and we were into 8th at the half but still an awful lot of work to do. Next came an electric run from Craig to place us on the back on bronze, with silver 30 seconds away. Phil has enjoyed many superb runs around this course and here he was the day's fastest. Sadly for us though, Highgate were having a phenomenal run and that opening wound was proving fatal. After an incredible 8:40 opening lap Phil barked at the TM: "What is it?!" About 50 seconds, I lied. It was rather more. "*Fuuu**in' 'ell*", came the despairing reply. How do you chase a man you can't see? But Phil never gave up and Kris Gauson on anchor flayed himself for the first 1500 to see if he could get a glimpse. The time for that was 4:22, rather too quick to hold but with silver safe, he had to go "all in".

It had been a fine, dramatic race but the acquisition of Andy Maud to Highgate from the Chasers turned a strong squad into an unbeatable one. Congrats to them – a passionate club, full of fire and brimstone, quite literally sometimes as they like to stoke up a barbie on the course to give the runners a tempting waft of burger and onions as they run by. But it's all in good humour and fine rapport, and they have replaced Shaftesbury as North London's top club. For now… SBH tend to stoke themselves up just when they get forgotten.

Some rather sleepy years

In 2016 we shlepped up to the Bedford Aerodrome which I thought was rather a cool venue, albeit with a hellish wind. But the course was beautiful for running and the race remained competitive. Nothing really beats Rushmoor though – how blessed we were all those years, and what a shame things have fallen through for now. We were rather weak though and after PO's good start, it was left to Ed Auden and Matt Welsh to run strongly to have us in 13th at the half. The short-lived Nick Smallwood was ok too, whilst I had a minor shocker, and came under some attack from Rob Norville, who we were delighted to welcome into the squad, after so many years with us. Good things come to those… our times were an OCD dream in depreciation: 17, 18, 19, 20, 21 & 22. But you know what? 24th isn't the end of the world and we came, saw, fought and got stuck in.

2017 saw a strong 5 searching for a solid 6th man at another venue of Crystal Palace, a very pleasant park to run in, with some testing climbs. Would it be the author or new prospect Alex Mills? A run-off was avoided when AM pointed to a solo Wandsworth 5k time trial in 16:45, which was way too hot for me. He was in. After PO's expert opener in 14:47 [for a spot on equivalent to 5k given the climbs], messrs Buckle, Auden and Welsh grouped well between 15:41 to 15:56 to keep us in the top 10 and then Nick Bundle found a 16:21 and we were still in 12th. Now for Alex to find another 16:45. It wasn't there as the hills hurt him, and we concluded in 21st. Again, not so bad, just missing a star or two.

After many years at the Bels coalface it gave the TM a warm feeling in his belly to welcome Rob Norville into the 6 Stage team. More of a 4/8 track man, Rob has uncomplainingly served the XC teams because he knows it's good for him, and scored in nearly 20 Surrey Leagues. Here he adds another arrow to his quiver: Paskar's back man! The start gun is looming, and the only way to iron out those kinks is a spot of body surfing. All in a day's work for Rob

2018 brought a reality check as we had a real shocker: 49th! We thought those early 20s runs weren't *too bad*, now we could believe it. All due respect to the hardy souls who ran, but we had lost our way with the race, which may or may not have had anything to do with some grim committee battles I was having. Something had to give…

Uptick under new management

By the 2019-20 season we had welcomed Arne and Steve to breathe new life into the squad. Phil was welcomed back with open arms after four years off, while Paskar was now raging against the dying of the light. It was his fourth opener in a row and he could "only" find 27th. New Bel Will Stockley really looked the part though and claimed 8 souls. With Emily, wife of Phil, having had an excellent day earlier for AFD, Phil reduced the damage further, with a time only 5 seconds off PO. Another new recruit came and went in Jasper Taylor, and along with Brad Courtney-Pinn a top 20 position was maintained. It was then left to skipper Buckle to run an excellent time to not only edge out Will but turn 19th into 17th. It was a respectable and encouraging start to a new look Bels.

Appalling cancellation

Little could we dream that the race would then be cancelled for the next two years. First by Covid, then a disgraceful decision by the South in 2021 to deem the Palace unsafe. It was such a spurious,

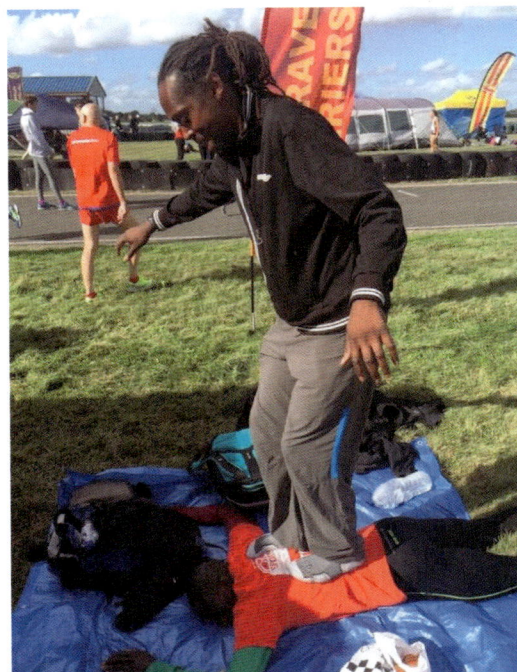

weak, insipid call. So, a stand had a crack in it? So what - don't use the stand. The community firmly felt we were in gravely uncommitted hands. The South sit on half a million in cash and many of their events are a licence to print money. The clubs are happy to print them that money, but we do expect a race or two in return. Not only was the cancellation made very late but they also *refused* to look for another venue, despite the likes of myself and Mike Boucher at AFD saying we'd find one, no problem. 3km stretches of macadam *do exist* over 62,000 square Km of Southern England. We found about four quickly, told the South, who rejected our request to keep it as a Championship, for reasons unknown. We opted for Milton Keynes, put on a fine race and had a really nice day out. But having no Championship to play for, sucked all the air out of the occasion [and our squad].

For years I've had multifold battles with the SEAA and it's just getting worse. There is genuine concern in the community as to what should be done, because one thing we all know – things can't go on like this. What on earth is that EA fee for if we're not getting a good service in return?!

What a race this exciting relay has been for us though, and all six wins are of course treasured by the club. When will we medal in it again? Who knows, but given the superb strength and depth of both squads, it may not be so long.

RESULTS 2010-2019

Year	Team	Name (team pos.)	Time	Name	Time	Name	Time	Name	Time	Name	Time	Name	Time
Rushmoor Arena:													
2010	2	S Sharp (10)	18:24	R Ward (5)	18:56	J Blackledge (4)	18:39	N Goolab (3)	18:21	P Owor (2)	18:13	D Mulhare (2)	17:53
2011	5	M Pollard (28)	19:36	S Davies (11)	18:18	R Ward (8)	18:35	J Kelly (7)	18:32	W Cockerell (7)	19:40	P Owor (5)	17:58
2012	13	J Kelly (4)	18:20	M Trees M45 (18)	20:32	M Graham (8)	18:37	R Ward (11)	20:11	P Owor (10)	18:30	W Cockerell (13)	20:08
2013	7	N Goolab (1)	17:37	J Kelly (1)	18:32	C Ruddy (1)	18:50	W Cockerell (3)	20:04	M Trees M50 (4)	19:49	R Maddams (7)	20:43
2014	23	P Owor (1)	18:04	G Upton (8)	19:29	M Trees M50 (14)	19:49	R Maddams (17)	20:06	K Hegvold M50 (23)	21:13	W Cockerell (23)	20:14
2015	2	A Connick (28)	19:42	P Owor (12)	18:05	N Goolab (8)	18:45	C Ruddy (4)	18:16	P Wicks (2)	17:45	K Gauson (2)	18:59
Bedford Aerodrome:													
2016	24	P Owor (3)	17:26	E Auden (9)	18:48	M Welsh (13)	19:04	N Smallwood (16)	20:07	W Cockerell (20)	21:14	R Norville (24)	22:00
Crystal Palace:													
2017	21	P Owor (4)	14:39	N Buckle (8)	15:46	E Auden (ca. 9)	15:41	M Welsh (10)	15:56	N Bundle (ca. 12)	16:21	A Mills (21)	18:11
2018	49	P Owor (15)	18:00	N Buckle (34)	19:42	R Finlay (48)	20:49	A Mills (46)	20:24	B Hurley (46)	20:48	W Cockerell (49)	21:28
2019	17	P Owor (27)	17:28	W Stockley (19)	17:47	P Wicks (16)	17:33	J Taylor (18)	18:17	B Courtney-Pinn (19)	18:28	N Buckle (17)	17:45

SOUTHERN 4 STAGE - WOMEN

Steady as she goes, with one dream day

For the first decade of the Century the Belles were circumspect at this one. Not sure what it was, but the race largely failed to capture their imagination or of their TM, or both. In my very first race at the helm of Belgrave road-running I put out my attendance request for Aldershot in September 2009. Of the 25-odd runners we had then, 20 replied. Not bad! The result? 19 No's and a maybe. This was gonna' be a tough little mission. But you know what? That little "maybe" consitutes 12.5% of a team. The feedback could've been worse.

Farewell to club life for an icon

The most notable moment in the early part of the Noughties was Anne Hegvold toeing the line in 2001, glancing across and finding her opponent was Paula Radcliffe – fresh off the mother of all "domestics" with husband Gary at Edmonton the previous month. It was to be Paula's last ever club race at the young age of 27. Surely she could have taken the odd nostalgic tour in the blue and white in the ensuing years, but try as Bedford might, this was it. She turned up to the National 4 stage in 2005 to great excitement from all, but a cold stopped her racing. I was sure Paula would don the club vest for her farewell marathon in 2015, but she opted for a red Nike vest instead. Could Bedford and Nike not have come up with a Bedford vest with a big swoosh? Hey ho, that's commerce for ya' – no mood for messin'.

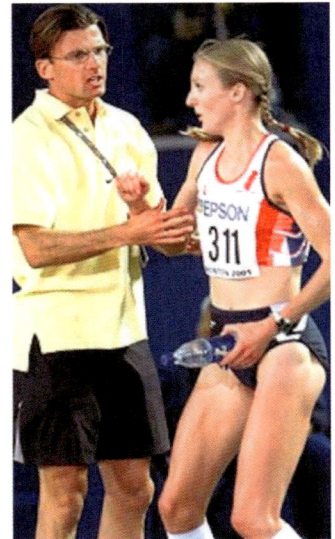

Paula Radcliffe bade farewell to the club world once and for all, a month after this public little spat

Alas, Belgrave were incomplete that day after a good start, before a gnarly 16th in 2002 followed by an absolute cracker: 5th. I have elsewhere grumbled about us front-loading strong teams too much, but on this occasion Catherine was saved from the flub when Getenesh pleaded to being very tired, so went off last, and blasted to the day's 6th fastest. It is no coincidence that this triggered such a fine return as it meant the ladies were always chasing rather than being devoured. There was a minor selectoral *snafu* with Tilly in the B's beating Helen in the As by 32 seconds and us missing the medals by 33, but that's a minor grumble on an otherwise superb day.

More solid fare came in 2004 with 11th highlighted by Juliette Clark, a W40 running to our 3rd fastest ever. A maddening dnf came in 2005, with a late withdrawal proving impossible to cover. Tilly vowed to run twice which she did for an unofficial 13th in the results, but we can't really count that! Thus it was five straight years of no result before stopping the rot after my blank in 2009, with a 30th in 2010. It may have been a bit of a tough watch at times as tenth at the half was tripled, but it was good to be back in this championship race.

I felt I was starting to crack it in 2011: six strong runners for the four spots on Thursday… which became 5, and four on Saturday morning, and then 3. *What the?!* I cancelled the remaining trio and took the kids off to the Science museum in a mild fury, only to get an email from the athlete who'd dropped to say 'maybe her cold wasn't so bad, so perhaps she could get round after all'. Too late! Incredibly this cost us another Championship appearance – indeed a gold – the following week, when Nelle Quispel went to Aldershot [this cancelled venue] instead of Biggleswade for the SEAA cross relay in a team that was nailed on for the win. You couldn't make it up.

One of the great days!

Fast forward a year and I was convinced that this was a race that could be cracked. Things began to happen… I was getting plenty of yesses, and Sammi met a diminutive but powerful athlete at a race called Tish Jones, and put us in touch. It was clear that 'sight unseen' this was someone I'd be chucking in at the deep end, and Tish and I made a 'hot Rusmoor date' for a month after our first chat; but in the meantime she had an outward bound mission with the army, where she'd be camping and living on wild berries, and incommunicado until the day before the race. Not ideal, but one just had to keep a steady nerve. Elsewhere, Runa Bostad, sister of Anne Hegvold, gave the nod, nine years after taking the Surrey road 5k title. Sammi was an easy 3rd pick, but who to round out this little nest of vipers?

It came down to a straight shoot-out between stalwart Lou Blizzard and Catherine Bryson, one of the finest Belles of all time, but on the comeback trail from injury. What a choice. Lou had scored a remarkable run at the National 6 stage in the spring, but she'd since cooled a little. CB was going better and better in training. I went with Lou, and put CB on two for the B's, who then ripped them from 26th to 14th. What could Lou do about that?! I got the call right by 2 seconds. Phew! Horrid to get the big ones wrong.

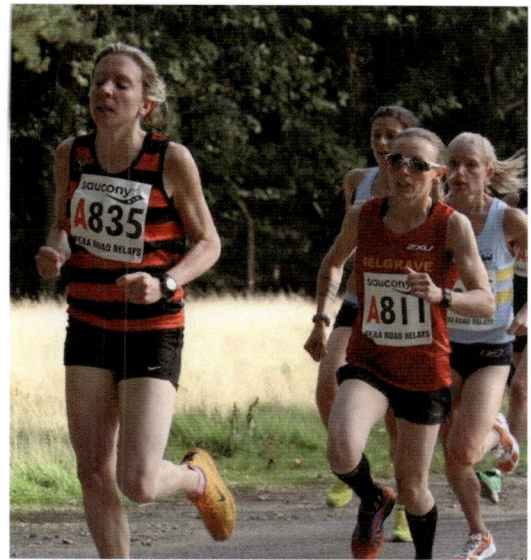

Introducing a legend! With one of Europe's most unforgiving workhorses in Ros Kieran for company, Tish Jones stamps an indelible mark on the Belgrave - and she wouldn't look back

To the race, and Tish commenced her fabled Belgrave story like a fox let loose in a chicken hutch. She fought ferociously, although this was a level of athletics hitherto unseen for her. It was a case of hammer it early and hang on as she was knifed at the half by a stitch. She simply refused to release her grip on the leaders though, who included teenage sensation Jess Judd. 4th was her result, to set up Sam a beaut. A very tough run followed but only one position lost and now Lou's steady, nerve-wrecking run, which saw the medallists sneak further afield, but crucially kept our dream alive, and didn't leak any spots.

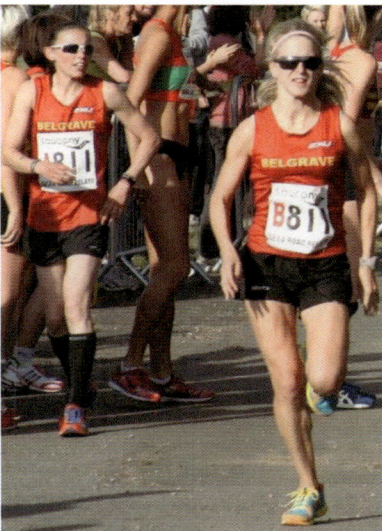

With a barnstorming run in the can, Tish hands off to SA in a lofty perch of 4th

I had grappled a lot with the running order and didn't like the thought of putting Runa last, lest she be wasted. But finally, on a scamper the evening before, it hit me between the eyes: of course Runa must go last – I was being a baby and she could handle the enormous gaps that she may have to bridge.

Well the gap to bronze was indeed a bit scary and Runa set off to only empty road, but she still ran like a woman possessed, with rock-steady self-belief. The gap to bronze was 44 seconds and the owner [Vicky Walker of Shaftesbury] had a 10:08 3k. It was a problem.

"The gap was 44 seconds… now it's 20!" I screamed at Runa at half way. She had let rip for sure, but maybe too much? Ex-Belle Nikki Neale was the first impediment though and she was dealt with into the final K. Into the last 350, and the margin was still 10 seconds… maybe 8? It was going to be desperately close, but it looked like heartache.

Runa wound up her finishing burst, having recently outkicked Makestad Bovim (who placed 6th at the 1,500 Daegu Worlds). 100 to go and the gap was 2 seconds, and Walker kicked herself in a valiant claim on the medal. But Runa was not to be denied and eased away in the final yards for a wonderful triumph for this brave team. Silver was just 13 seconds away, in the form of the Aldershot B's. So no other club aside from them beat us.

Only 14 clubs in the South of England had an answer to our B team of Maycock, Bryson, Rhodes and Vail Smith [placing 18th], whilst the Cs came 44/62. It was quite the day, and it was obvious this was now a squad 'going places'.

Given the moment... given the match... it's hard to name many better Belles' relay runs in history. Lou's work is done, and we still have a 10% chance of medals to which Runa might say: "hold my beer"

The tribe enjoys the warm afterglow of a thrilling race. L-R: WC, Runa, Genia Marek, Catherine Bryson, TJ, SA, Vicki Goodwin, LB, Fee Maycock and Laura d'Albey. Front row is the wistful Max, sad that the mad humamoids have ceased their galloping

To highlight the brilliance of that day and to show what a tricky race this is, we "only" found 18, 16, 33 & 24 in the four years that followed.

Not great, but not terrible. Charlie then awoke the sleepy giant with a fine 10th in 2017 in a team comprised of Lizzie GS, Saron, Sophie and Helen White. Sophie in particular had a humungous tour, chalking 4th= quickest of the day and only eight ticks from the top.

A good effort came in the wind tunnel that was the Bedford Aerodrome in 2016, as Fi Maddocks, Sally Underhill, Helen White and Megs Bailey took 24th

A terrific 10th in 2017 and medals not so far beyond the imagination. L-R: Simon & Saron, Sophie H, Lizzie GS, CD, Fi Maddocks, Megs Bailey & the two Mhairis, Hall and McDonald

One more master-blaster in there would have medalled. [West Suffolk it was for the bronze, 1:29 up]. It rightly sits as our third best performance of all time. A solid 16th followed with Thai Olympian Jane Vongvorachoti in cracking form, before a gutsy 27th to 'keep the kettle boiling.' Then Covid struck, before the South appallingly cancelled in 2021 for the most spurious of reasons, and a strong squad ready to rock. Next time...

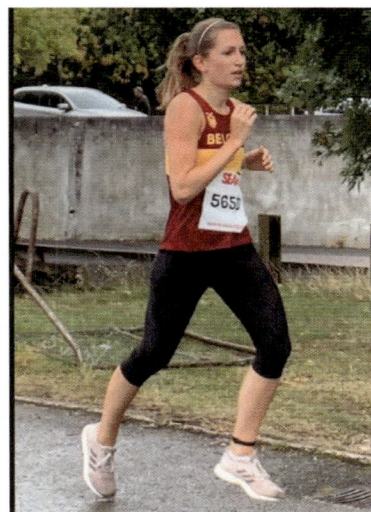

Emily Barrett calmly sees the class of '19 home. Little could we dream we'd not then set foot on the course for three years

RESULTS

Rushmoor Arena:

Year	Team	Name (team pos.)	Time	Name	Time	Name	Time	Name	Time
2001	-	G Tamirat (4)	13:28	A Hegvold (7)	14:41	C Eastham (13)	16:55		
2002	16	G Tamirat (3)	13:18	T Sturton (14)	15:12	S Stracey (14)	14:52	A Walker (16)	15:30
2003	5	A Walker (16)	14:04	R Powell U20 (9)	14:14	H Alsop (13)	14:47	G Tamirat (5)	12:58
2004	11	H Smethurst (23)	14:39	L Cooper (19)	15:13	J Clark W40 (15)	14:08	R Weston (11)	14:25
2005	-	M Heaton (19)	14:27	H Cayzer (15)	14:30	J Clark W40 (9)	14:16		
2010	30	S Amend (10)	13:46	A Linford (10)	14:45	R Trees (16)	16:20	A Johnson (30)	18:25
2012	3	T Jones (4)	13:14	S Amend (5)	13:42	L Blizzard (5)	14:06	R Bostad (3)	13:15
2013	18	M Wilkins (23)	14:28	R O'Brien (23)	14:57	Z Doyle (21)	14:30	F Maycock (18)	14:35
2014	16	M Wilkins (13)	13:46	K Mackenzie (14)	14:27	C Lovegrove (19)	15:24	F Maycock (16)	14:26
2015	33	J Rhodes (29)	14:32	M Bailey (35)	16:02	H Barsham-Rolfe (34)	16:03	R O'Brien (33)	15:49

Bedford Aerodrome:

Year	Team	Name (team pos.)	Time	Name	Time	Name	Time	Name	Time
2016	24	F Maddocks (38)	18:41	S Underhill (29)	17:57	M Bailey (30)	19:35	H White (24)	18:04

Crystal Palace:

Year	Team	Name (team pos.)	Time	Name	Time	Name	Time	Name	Time
2017	10	L Goldie-Scott (21)	13:39	S Haileselase (14)	12:54	S Harris (5)	12:05	H White (10)	14:31
2018	16	S Haileselase (4)	16:46	J Rhodes (20)	20:06	J Vongvorachoti (11)	17:28	L Goldie-Scott (16)	21:17
2019	27	F Maddocks (37)	18:16	K Mackenzie (25)	17:35	M Corden-Lloyd (29)	19:36	E Barrett (27)	18:26

SOUTHERN XC RELAY - WOMEN

What an entertaining caper this is, overlooked by the caperers of Wormwood Scrubs. I've always enjoyed this day that still suffers through dismal marketing from the SEAA which in the early years was all but non-existent, and one year saw more officials than teams. However, things are starting to pick up nicely now.

2011 and the Belles fightback from obscurity begins

The course at the Scrubs is firm and fair and an excellent test of sustained tempo running. We pitched up at the inaugural event in March 2011 with a team of old faves and an exciting new face, and were pleasantly surprised to come away with hardware; and look at that consistency from Catherine B, Zoe VS and Flic: 13:05, 13:03; 13:03.

One can pretty much trace the passage of the Belles' fortunes over the last decade-plus to this image, of two pioneering Belles frantically reaching for a higher plane, in this case Zoe Vail Smith with a premature lunge at Flic Cole

Brilliant stuff. We gave AFD a scare and were bearing down on Highgate by the end. It all went to show that we could easily switch on our aspirations again, as a club of note and worth, after the mortification of Surrey League relegation the previous month as the famous Eastham reign ran out of puff. We'd cement this day the following month with a 4th at Milton Keynes in the SEAA 6 stage.

An almighty cock-up and a fine coup

The race needed to be better placed in the calendar and hence it switched to October, seven months hence. I raised a wonderful side in Catherine again, Sam and Nelle Quispel. But then horror of horrors Nelle travelled to the previous week's venue [Aldershot, which we cancelled] and not Biggleswade in Suffolk. It was an awful and very embarrassing moment as the other two had made sacrifices to be there. The frustration was heightened by the athlete whose withdrawal pulled the plug on Aldershot, then came *back in* after we'd cancelled, and of course if Nelle had gone to Aldershot as scheduled, she would have read her emails more closely! Such is the fine line TMs walk between triumph and disaster. We still won in Biggleswade but with Dorchie [the wife] in the colours, who is with Thames.

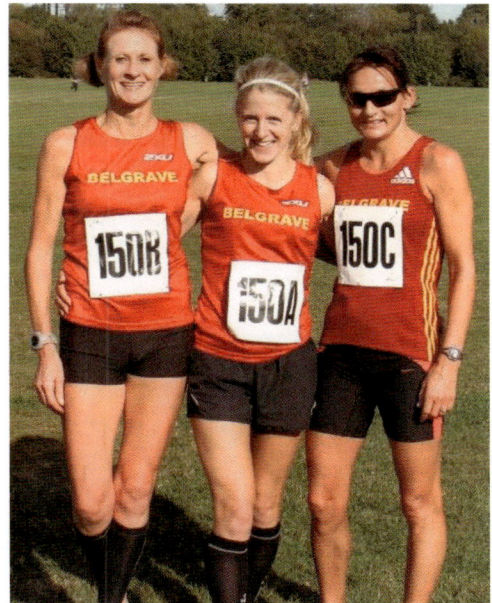

A team grabbed for the jaws of oblivion. Fee, Sam and Anne savour a job well done

2012 and another all but fatal loss to our aspirations, this time from dear old Tish on race day with a jumpy knee. We gave her maximum possible time to make the call, and basically had the '*Maycock Massive*' sitting in motorway lay-bys waiting on whether to drive down or give-up. Tish finally said nay, but I decided to hit my little black book one final time and the last athlete I tried was Anne Hegvold who had already done a big session for the day. But she also happened to be in West London and grimly gave the nod. We were back in play!

In what was a super performance, the ladies had a tremendous duel with Heathside. Sam came through in second, Fee had a brilliant sub 13 run to claim us a 5 second lead, and now it was over to an exhausted Anne to use all her experience to calmly steer us home by over 40 seconds. Two years, two very different life experiences!

We had two aces in Doyle and Amend to throw at the race in 2013, but were short that third piece of the puzzle yet again. It came down to a shoot-out between heptathlete superstar Jodie Albrow and engine-roomer Hester Barsham-Rolfe. On reflection, I should have probably stuck in the endurance junkie, but I was slightly dazzled by the bright lights of Jodie, who will be the first to admit the extra distance played havoc with her fast twitch muscles. But Zoe enjoyed whipping us from 17th to 9, and Sam got within a minute of the medals.

The TM couldn't resist seeing what our top-rated heptathlete could do at the Scrubs. It was a huge ask, and not an unqualified success, but one has to admire her courage - this was way out of her comfort zone!

Maureen Noel [solo for the B's], Zoe, Jodie & Sam. A remarkably eclectic 'fab four'. Maureen, a race-walking expert, often loyally plugged a road and country gap. All four athletes would win medals all over the world in the Masters categories at a quite bewildering array of events. Their range is 100 metres to 100 miles.

A remarkable sequence of races

There then followed a period of pretty amazing Belles performances in this race although a second win has always remained elusive, but what a superb streak, missing medals just once till 2019, and that was 4th.

2014 was a wonderful thriller as a squad led out by Kerimac in 6th, became 3rd thru ZLD to set up Mel Wilkins to lay siege on the two athletes ahead. Her fine 11:47 took care of the precocious Steph McCall of SLH but it was Lisa da Silva barreling away a minute ahead who Mel had designs on. With a K to go Lisa's advantage was down to 20 seconds, Mel could do this! Lisa wrote to me later: "It was only coming out of the woods with 500 to go that I glanced behind and saw how close she was…" To which I smoothly replied: "So you were out of the woods but not out of the woods."

But LdS had now become fully apprised of the danger and shifted gears to a 13 second win. But what a race.

The lead that Wasn't… Was… Wasn't… Was… Wasn't

Amazingly, 2015 and 2016 were near reruns. The first was highly bizarre in that a riotous Bracknell in a good lead could not find a third runner. I frantically signalled this to anchor Rose O'Brien, who didn't catch the *minor* plot twist.

I suppose I could have shouted, "they're cooked, they're gone! Vanished! *Disparu*!" But that struck me rather ungentlemanly, so frantic throat-slitting sign language and dancing a merry jig were all I gave to the bemused Rose, who in turn set off running slightly perplexed at not being able to see the lead at any time, not knowing that she was *IT*.

Courtesy of terrific runs from Flic and Jojo, Rose had a good buffer on the rest, but it was the team way back in the 9th who'd carry the day. A lead of 1:05 may seem like a huge

It's the lead! Set up by Jojo, except Rose doesn't know it...

advantage over just 3k, but Steph McCall was now at her fittest, and by half way she could see a blob of claret in the distance. If only Rose could "hang on" for the last 400 then in a kicker's world maybe she could give McCall trouble, but the switch came with about 900 to go, and that was too early, with 17 ticks the final margin.

More punishment

The race was giving us some punishment and it continued in 2016 when Saron was set off on anchor in 4th with Harrow, TVH and Heathside neatly lined up ahead. Well, in shades of the previous year it was *sayonara* to Harrow who couldn't find a third, Saron was immediately into bronze. But alas our girl went off at 4:40 miling, and it was far too quick. By half way it was clear she had severe issue with her cyllinder head gasket and even a medal was now in doubt as a riotous Luton showed no mercy. Just 31 seconds separated the top 4, and for all her undisputed talent Saron needed to stop going

A lactic drowning Zoe sets up her mates in '16 on one

out like a sprinter in races... It was all that was stopping her from being one of the best runners in the South.

We changed tack and started with Saron in 2017 and in a much more composed run she brought us back in a big lead. Hmmm, that was too much front-loading... clearly the spot for her in this one is in the middle. This became more apparent with Katie-Ellen French who thrives on contact being hurled off in isolation. KEF did ok but Sammi had a tough chase on her hands to stalk Chelmsford. All credit to them, as Alexa Joel refused to encourage SA and they ran lock step the whole way. 22 seconds off the gold and the field had now encouragingly grown to 47 teams.

And there's More!

As a reader of this sequence of fine races would you like to guess what happened in 2018? Hmmm, a medal perhaps in a thrilling race, with gold just out of reach? You got it in one. This time gold just 24 seconds away with an unchanged team. Saron was phenomenal on one, but again too much front-loading, while Sam held the position with a very gnarly run indeed, but behind they were queuing up to have a pop. Katie-Ellen ran fine but incredibly she was up against three of the finest runners in the region in GB marathoner Tracy Barlow [mercifully too far back] and Katie Snowdon & Pippa Woolven. Wow! What incredible quality and cruel and unusual punishment for poor old KEF. Snowden would go on to compete in the 1,500 semis at the Tokyo Olympics, and Woolven placed second at the National cross four months later. Anyone who wonders why club athletics is so magical – this is why. The chance to go up against the best.

Scottish hattrick. In a strong B team Kerimac, Mhairi Hall and Steph Hewitt found a suave 10th; but bizarrely and a clear sign of the ever growing depth of the squad, the C team nicked them by 25 secs in 9th!

We finally took a chill pill in 2019, with a steady 8th, but were straight back on a post-Covid gold hunt in 2021. The result? Another exciting race but Wycombe were quite outstanding with ex-Belle Zoe Doyle enjoying three straight wins with them, and Woolven anchoring again. Heathside were amazing too and must count themselves unlucky to lose by 12 seconds with a team like that. Our own Liv, Jess and Grace coped with the significant TVH threat to hang onto bronze. It should be noted that our B's were 8th here and Cs 12th. What depth *Charlie's Angels* now possessed, and much to savour for the future, at his absorbing race.

RESULTS

Year	Team	Name (team pos.)	Time				
2011	3	C Bryson [4]	13:05	Z Vail [2]	13:03	F Cole [3]	13:03
2012	1	S Amend [2]	12:34	F Maycock [1]	12:59	A Hegvold [1]	13:41
2013	6	J Favell [17]	14:22	Z Doyle [9]	12:36	S Amend [6]	12:47
2014	2	K Mackenzie [6]	12:45	Z Doyle [3]	12:23	M Wilkins [2]	11:47
2015	2	F Cole [5]	12:32	J Rhodes [2]	12:35	R O'Brien [2]	12:44
2016	4	Z Doyle [10]	12:44	S Amend [4]	11:57	S Heileselase [4]	12:25
2017	2	S Haileselase [2]	11:43	KE French [2]	12:50	S Amend [2]	12:26
2018	3	S Haileselase [1]	11:11	S Amend [1]	12:03	KE French [3]	12:08
2019	8	E Howsham [5]	12:11	E Barrett [7]	12:57	L Suggitt [8]	13:05
2021	3	O Papaioannou [6]	11:03	J Saunders [4]	11:34	G Richardson [3]	10:57

SOUTHERN XC RELAY - MEN

Is this a great little race, or, in the words of General Melchett, "the illegitmate, backstairs sort of sprog… the spotty squit that nobody really likes…"? Well, I like it and feel it makes for not just a tremendous spectacle of championship athletics, but a great chance for the B team & the engine room to come to the party. To my mind it makes far more sense for this to be the big race and the National cross-relay to cool it on the numbers which are completely wild, while that venue is dreadfully crowded and one slip at the start a man will lose 80 spots.

Anyway, with minimum, perhaps even mute fanfare the race was founded in 2011 and completely passed Belgrave by. It was then rejigged to October of the same year and along with just a dozen or so clubs we set off for a delightful venue in Biggleswade. It was a very exciting race though as the quantity may have been appalling but we still found ourselves *only* 2nd coming into the last leg, with surely minimum chance of dealing with TVH. But Richard Ward then a slammed down a time some 4 minutes better than them, who had to run a filler, as they slipped into 4th, allowing Medway and Bedford to move up, and we came home very pleased with our day's work.

Belgrave's winners: Paskar Owor, James Fairbourn, Will Cockerell and Richard Ward

How do you solve a problem like The Machine and The Pillar?

In 2012 we identified TVH as our key threat in the week and we knew it'd be a close one, after the late Chris Smith warned the author at Battersea during the week that his lads were ready to rumble. So who to select for our 4th, when as so many times over the last decade it was a wee bit of a "face-off" between the animals concerned. For years Richard Ward and I gave Alan headaches about who to put in a relay team, and at least three migraines! The somewhat unpredictable speed but undoubted class of Richard, nicknamed "The Machine" by AW in his mid-teens, or the monomania of the Cockerpillar?

We were tricky to compare as I'd often go long to Rich's short, but here's a summation of our friendly decade-long relay saga of A-team Regional and National relays, when we ran the same distance:

	RW	WC
2003 National 12	**14:48**	15:05
2006 Southern 12	17:36	**17:23**
2007 National 12	15:41	**15:34**
2011 southern 12	**25:58**	26:14
2011 national 12	28:44	**28:35**
2011 Southern 6	**18:42**	19:40
2011 National 6	**18:17**	19:01
2011 seaa cross	**16:09**	16:41
2012 southern 6	20:11	**20:08**
2013 national 12	16:06	**15:53**
2013 seaa cross	15:54	**14:49**

A fine rivalry then, between two very different runners, and precious little in it. For this one I proposed to Alan an idea I'd had some years earlier that Richard and I draw lots for the spot in the team. We were both going well, and could only be separated by 3 seconds earlier in the month, in my favour, but this was less distance. It does become rather personal to give the nod to one or another in a case like this, when the chance is great that it'll be barely nothing in it either way. So Alan acquiesced and asked us both to pick a playing card. Mine was the Ace of Spades. He gave his brand new pack a *looooong* shuffle, and started turning the cards to see who would appear first. The first card he turned was the Ace of Spades. Alan mumbled something about voodoo magic and dark Cockerpillar forces at work, and I had my spot in the team. Who knows what would have happened in a head to head, and we can't base anything on the following year when I prevailed by 65 secs, as Rich was clearly running out of gas.

On the day, I hit my run just as intended, and we nicked a strong Bedford team by just 17 seconds to take the silver, with both *Panthera pardus* [Paskar] and Matthew Graham on electrifying form, whilst Richard Stannard ran well on one; but up ahead TVH were a sensation and screamed home with over 400 yards to spare. Hats off, that was amazing.

In 2013, Wardy was back in play, but had alarming news: he'd outgrown his "lucky shorts", and that an unbearable crush had taken over. Bad luck quickly followed as Richard was around a minute down on optimum – there are some charms you really shouldn't break; although a top Bedford runner did once get disqualified at a major event for indecent attire... it was not a pretty sight. Our luck was not running elsewhere either as we had to settle for 5th.

Gold – The Hard Way

I have had some 'battle royales' with the SEAA over the last decade but our scrap for the 2014 race was one of the worst. As ever the problems with their entry system were dreadful, with a derisory amount of runners allowed into a squad. Clearly a system designed by a non-athlete. Phil Wicks signalled he couldn't make it, I shuffled my pack, then Phil came back in... all the while I couldn't enter a squad for love nor money due to a system that clearly wasn't fit for purpose. Anyway, although there were bugs in the system that took us all beyond the entry deadline, when Phil came back in, a good many days before the race, they point blank refused to accept him, pointing to the deadline. I mean why *WOULD* you accept the finest runner in the South over the last decade who's been such a magnificent ambassador for the sport? Especially in a race that's trying to grow and gain traction...

All's well that ends well, as Kris, Roy, Gus and PO bring it home in 2014

So we went in minus our talisman, but such was the dodgy standard, messrs Gauson, PO, Gus and Royston Maddams performed brilliantly to take the race in comfort. Much ado about nothing? No! It's the principle. Too much officious bureacracy and incompetence and not enough common sense, compassion and remembering the ideal, "we're here to provide competition, not deny it."

More Bling

We were finding our feet and grabbed silver in 2015 in another very entertaining race, my swansong at the event, pushing 42. AJ set us up nicely in 7th, which I held. Some progress would've been nice, but the field had seen a sweet concertina, leaving PO to run amok, and leave only our old friends TVH to go. Roy ran a beaut and Sean Renfer was going to be untouchable, but with some notable strength and calm running, Roy saw off the fast finishing WSEH with 7 ticks to spare.

In 2016, perhaps I front-loaded too much with PO in a 12 second lead. Looking back, what was I thinking? I believe PO really campaigned for it, and on this occasion for whatever reason I caved, perhaps because I didn't want him running isolated. Rather poor management though and it left Matt Welsh at the mercy of the likes of the European record-holder for the mile Dale Clutterbuck*, and he did well to cling onto the medals in bronze. Nick Buckle was on cracking form and also did well to advance us to 2nd, whilst Alex Miller's 14:31 was excellent, surrounded as he was by 14:10 guys and actually outrunning the leader. He only leaked a spot and Herne Hill were kept at bay. The top 9 in the race now were all very good squads with "the small matter" of Tonbridge in 9th.

Onto 2017 and yet again we came to the party with some expert running. 49 squads were now throwing something at this one and Andy Fyfe placed a hard-bitten 12th on one, which a riotous Buckle transformed to 4th. PO surged to 2nd and the duel with both Highgate and Hillingdon was oh so close with the rest rather detached. What would you say the chances are that the four names (first and second) of the last two runners of the winning club being the same? Well, that is what Hillingdon threw at the problem as Mohamed Mohamed & Mohamed Mohamed put the ball away... Ed Auden had a stunning duel with Robert Wilson for the silver, but lost by 1 second, oh so close! Ed was semi-comatose on the ground after the race for a good 5 minutes after that...

*Beer mile that is, but still no joke at 4:47.

RESULTS

Year	Team	Name (team pos.)	Time						
Biggleswade:									
2011	1	W Cockerell [6]	16:41	J Fairbourn [4]	17:01	P Owor [2]	14:59	R Ward [1]	16:09
Wormwood Scrubs:									
2012	2	R Stannard [5]	15:11	M Graham [2]	14:12	W Cockerell [3]	15:30	P Owor [2]	14:05
2013	5	W Cockerell [12]	14:59	R Ward [12]	15:54	P Owor [8]	14:09	M Trees [5]	14:58
2014	1	P Owor [1]	14:19	R Maddams [1]	15:33	K Gauson [1]	15:00	G Upton [1]	15:12
2015	2	A Jaksevicius[7]	14:12	W Cockerell [7]	15:01	P Owor [2]	13:53	R Maddams [2]	14:43
2016	3	P Owor [1]	13:31	M Welsh [3]	14:50	N Buckle [2]	14:22	A Miller [3]	14:31
2017	3	A Fyfe [12]	14:37	N Buckle [4]	14:17	P Owor [2]	13:53	E Auden [3]	14:30
2018	2	N Buckle [14]	15:02	P Owor [2]	14:02	N Goolab [1]	13:57	K Touse [2]	14:47

An All Time Great Race

Surprisingly, 2018 is all she wrote – for now. Our new management have quietly shelved this race, but maybe it'll return to the roster, because it can be a special day, and 2018 was perhaps one of the most exciting races in this tome. Two seconds covering the first three clubs – *incredible*! Let's take it from the top: We kicked off with an unfit and woefully short on confidence Nick Buckle. It was a lot to ask of the lad, but natural ability and fire in a belly will always be hard to ignore. "Only 14th" was the sum of his labour, but the time wasn't bad and had the lion positively drooling in anticipation. "I will feast on the deer of Richmond Park" he once memorably bellowed.

Well, there were a few furry animals up for grabs here, too. 14th became 2nd as he went through 'em like a blowtorch through butter, and now we had none other than Nick Goolab to enter the fray. Like his namesake, Nick was not race-fit and I couldn't bear to put him on last and have him run isolated. I wanted to give him all the help I could. On reflection though, this is a top quality international athlete – maybe I was too circumspect.

Ahhh, the ifs and buts of a relay order, and let's face it, we surely wrung every last shred of equity out of the boy wonder's sinewy frame as he dragged us into a fragile lead. Also, it's not as if I put a lemon on last – Tinos Touse has loads of experience, is very strong and can handle pressure. His run was amazing. Sean Renfer is a classic old hand on the circuit and poor Tinos had the bead on the back of his head, who also cost himself a little by veering off course. It's not nice, but it wouldn't have been nice for Goolab not being able to see the lead, around a minute away, if he'd gone last. We so, so nearly got it right. Renfer caught Tinos with 1200 to go and up behind, some 25 seconds away another Mohamud, this time Aaden of TVH was absolutely flying, turning in a time over 30 seconds better than Nick. So now we had Tinos under double attack.

The last 500 will live long in the memory – it was mesmerising stuff. Renfer had gone too early! And Tinos was finding strength from goodness knows where... And Aaden was slashing away at both deficits. Forget silver, he wanted to win the whole damn thing. With 200 to go, 1st had 16 yards on 2nd who had 16 yards on 3rd. Those gaps came down and down, till the finish line embraced the runners each separated by just a handful of yards.

Highgate	57:47
Belgrave	57:48
TVH	57:49
Hillingdon	58:08

What a race, what a finish. We of course were pleased to hang onto silver under such an assault, but gutted to let that gold elude us.

It all adds value to the 2011 and 2014 wins though, and we can be very proud of a happy sequence on the Scrubs.

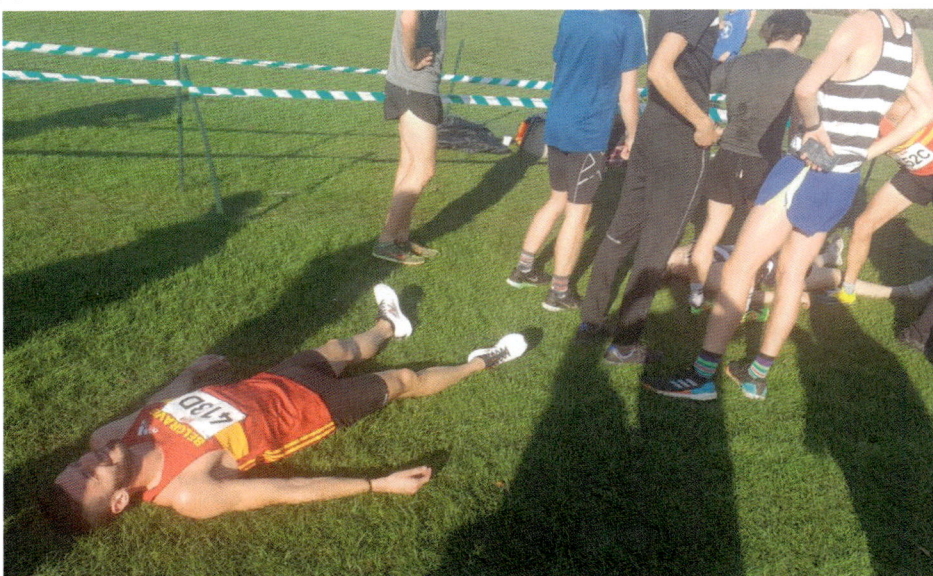

Quite simply, what club athletics is all about. As Highgate hover like vultures over Sean Renfer's prostrate body, Tinos slips into a dream

NATIONAL 6 STAGE - MEN

A simply magical ride

Well, what can we say about this amazing race? One would have thought that with distance and manpower vastly reduced over the 12 stage, that it would be an even tougher nut to crack, but due to a variety of factors we laid siege on it to boss the day in a matter never seen before. Since our amazing heyday of 1999-2013, the race has indeed reared its head and shown just how tough it is. It should be noted that our roots in the race date back to its founding in 1969, when in a very low key start at Crystal Palace, just 9 clubs fought it out. But the action was excellent and a fine Belgrave squad of Piotrowski, Kerr, Gy North, O'Hara, Fairclough & Thresher found a good bronze 50 yards down on Manchester, with Stoke a minute up the way.

We begin with 1999 as it's part of the Millennium season, and it was a return to the fray after 21 years away; and what a return.   ARM collated a remarkable squad, with the only asterisk being they were a little short of fitness. But surely medals could be claimed? With some serious back-loading – the sign of a TM who means business – we hovered in 13th at the half after Paul Freary, Jason Lobo and Lee Hurst's solid but not spectacular runs. We then introduced future relay 'god' Mark Miles, who was also yet to ripen and now we nestled in 10th. Spencer Barden then ran a fine time to add two more bodies to our sack, but 8th was asking too much for Paul Evans, a big City Marathon winner [Chicago] that he was. Paul ripped along to the day's 10th fastest to advance to 4th, but the gap to the medals was 64 seconds. Considering our lads were still a work in progress, we pledged to come back stronger and try again.

2000 was genuinely frustrating as Jason had a shocker on one and could only find 39th. Chas Herrington started the long slog back, continued by a rather circumspect Hursty, before 'Spennyrunner' ripped 24th to 13th. In pretty terrible conditions the slightly built Yacin Yusuf trimmed us to 9th, a marvel he didn't get blown over in the mini hurricane. Finally, Al Stewart with shades of a pretty epic relay career to come, was rock steady against future 2:17 marathoner John Mcfarlane to bump a fine Thames team into 7th and end up just 8 seconds shy of Salford who were in 5th.

Was this the greatest club race of all time?

Belgrave arrived at the 2001 National 6 stage with a team that might have been short on superstars, but what they had was unforgiving consistency throughout. Would it be enough to shoot for gold bullion? Windsor had been simply on another level at the Southern.

We kicked off with Lee Hurst, still pea-green from his gruesome meltdown six months earlier at the 12 Stage, when he took off on anchor with a 35 second advantage over a man he was deemed on par with. The result? A six second loss. A sickener for sure, but Lee was back with the only proviso to get him out the way early. He ran round in a smooth 12th.

Next up was Paul Freary, who in the first of the day's three tremendous duels latched onto Windsor's Ben Whitby who proceeded to rip his team right up into the lead. What a run. But Paul was not to be denied and grimly clung on just a handful of seconds back. It set up new man Steve Sharp to lay the first key marker in his claim a decade hence of being the finest relay man in British history. SS simply blew Windsor away and our lead was healthy.

But then we had to handle the first of Windsor's ferocious assaults – this from the young and dynamic Sam Haughian who creamed the fastest lap of the day to take 34 seconds out of Kassa Tadesse. We were in big trouble now, because we knew what lay in wait…

First up though, a like for like duel, with Al Stewart starting 10 seconds up on Tom Hart. After a mile they were level. Oh dear. But Paul was not fazed: "Al, you've got this," he consoled his mildly panicking teammate. "He's come up that hill way too fast…" Al, a metronomic runner of great intelligence, discipline and composure, plugged away. The gap rose, and rose some more. Sutton Park takes no prisoners to those who go out too quick. By the end Hart was in a world of trouble and stepped off the course and straight out of athletics. That's what this level of competition can do to a man.

Spencer Barden was facing up to 'the eye of the Tiger." The splendid Mohamed Farah, whose silken, light-footed stride and flying hair captivated all who saw him. Spen's answer was enough to give the calmest of nerve the shakes: "I'm not going for a time, I'm going to take it steady. Don't worry if the gap comes down. This is about the win."

An admirable and brave approach. If it worked. At the half, Farah had ripped 20 of the required 35 seconds out of Spen. Did Spen have another gear? Surely Mo must be getting tired? He was still only 18.

As seen in AW. L-R Paul, Al, Spen, Al & Steve. ARM with trophy. MS

The last half mile saw a 10 second 50 yard gap, and the last 400 it was down to 6, which became 4 at the final turn, with the 200 metre slog up to the finish. If Mo had anything left, and if Spen was exhausted, it could well have been curtains. But 4 seconds is a lot to make up when you've been chasing like a madman for 16:20 and have been "all in" for the last mile.

Spen had judged it perfectly and try as Mo desperately did, there were no more incisions. The Bels had won their first major National road title for 50 years. Oh sweet relief!

2002

I all but got into the magnificent '02 team after finishing 6th on the opening stage fo the SEAA 6 stage [a race we won]. But it wasn't quite to be, such was our strength, and I was edged out by the teenage prodigy Richard Ward. It was the right choice as RW's 17:48 on one was around a dozen seconds up on what I could have found.

I roomed with Dave Anderson, who subjected me to his alarming pre-race ritual… clad in only some figure hugging pants on the morning of the race, taking a little run up and then crouching down low into a groin-stretching lunge, pumping in his fist and bellowing, "COME ONNNN!!" Although it was a performance that made me feel uneasy, I felt worse for the opposition.

So, Wardy set us up perfectly in what was to be his last National 6 run for nine years, and Steve Sharp loaded his weapons. He tore through the field, akin to Freary the year before, rising from 10th the 3rd. The Belgrave team was simply scary this day, as 14-minute man followed 14 min man. Spencer took us into the lead, Allen Graffin all but matched the run, Mark Miles felled them both and then the lethal, lunging Dave had something of a thankless task on his hands. How do you pay the blood price with a 2 minute lead? Well, he pattered along in the rain, and all the manager could do was offer him something earlier next time. It could just have been the most dominant performance in not just our history, but anyone's. What a team – and no disgrace to have been first reserve!

2003 was a déjà vu all round. I all but made it again, and doubly so when training partner Marty Dent smashed into a steel post on the Tuesday night before the race in Richmond Park in the dark. He turned round and said to me: "you'll be running Saturday, Will…" He of course didn't do the session, informed Alan that he was in big trouble, but then to all our surprise declared himself fit on the Friday. Quite frankly, the team could afford the risk, although on the flip side, they could have afforded me, too! But Marty certainly wouldn't have run if he felt the injury was going to play up like it did.

Anyway, it was another majestic team with the only switches those of Paul for Rich and Marty for Allen. Paul had one of the best runs in the claret to roar home in 3rd and DA calmly rolled round to 1st, much enjoying heightened contact. David had a shock though when two steps behind him arrived the amazing Chris Davies of Telford who'd gone from, get this, 33rd to 2nd. What a humungous talent this Postie was, although he never quite did transfer his amazing Sutton Park pedigree to the rest of his career. Leg 3 for Telford ran nearly 3 minutes slower. Our victory would've been even larger than '02 if not for Marty soon running into an emergency on leg 5. His "thigh smash"

What an outstanding start from Mr Freary. That could be the race right there

meant he could find no rhythm or fluidity at all and his run was excruciating, the icy rain not helping. But he only lost around 70 seconds and we still had a 59 second buffer over Salford with a fine effort from Bedford in 3rd, albeit a minute back.

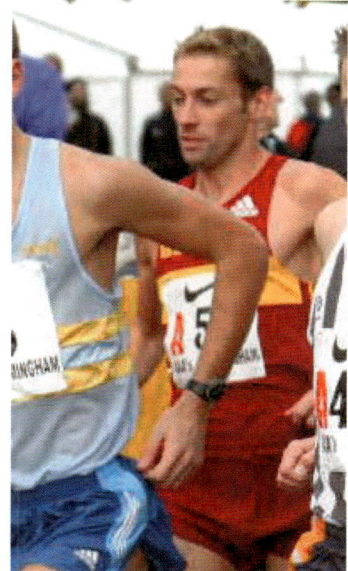

Yet another Dreamteam in '03! SS MD PF SB MM DA

Building on the hat-trick

There was no doubt that ARM had found his metier with this race. It was fast, brutal and bloody and he had the personnel to lap it up. The reason that the 12 Stage presented us so many more problems was its added length both in terms of distance required and men, which meant that randomness and squad depth count for more, and however reasonable our depth, it was always going to be challenged by bigger squads. It was true that we were a team of *Galacticos* at this time, rather like the Real Madrid squad of the same era, and there's no crime in that. Not an easy thing to achieve.

In 2004 we arrived having had a major scare at the Southern, and Alan was determined to have a less fraught afternoon. The consistency of the team was outstanding with Barden, Sharp, Anderson and

Miles once again to the fore. How on earth to you beat a team like that? Well, you don't. It really is that simple. A front and back-loading AFD ran well (2nd after one is a bit frisky and leaving Thommo till last is too wasteful), but the rest were again not too troubling. We worried about Birchfield, but their 20th on one becalmed them, and their leg 2 wasn't much better. Jon Blackledge had a tremendous run

A sodden crew in the gloaming. L-R: MM DA KN JB SB SS

after Gnasher's fine opener and the four heavies simply battered the opposition into submission, with Milesey running a gloriously isolated 17:02. Some just don't mind running with a huge lead, they can still absolutely batter it, and Mark ended up just 1 second shy of the great Keith Cullen.

Five Alive

The mission for 2005 was no joke: Five in a row – wow, that really is getting serious for such a competitive race. Think Bjorn Borg at Wimbledon (1976-1980), or Stephen Hendry at the World Snooker (1992-1996) – that sort of thing. In short, it's rare.

The team was curious in that it was all but identical to four long years earlier. So, no Danders or Milesy, back came Al Stewart and Paul F, and the only switch for 2001 was Wicksy for Hurst. One couldn't then help but feel it was a little vulnerable, not least with one never being 100% sure what Kassa had in store... Well, that question was soon answered as after Paul opened in 12th, Kassa blew the whole race wide open to bring us to 2nd – what an advance and continuing our tradition with *marmalising* the second leg. Al was under the most severe pressure though on his return to the team and did well to leak just a spot, despite interest from all around. Phil then, still a very young man, struggled a touch in the face of a torrid Mo Farah onslaught [who went from 8th to 3rd], and we found ourselves in 5th – which was a problem.

Up ahead Altrincham were having a blinder in the lead, courtesy of the ever fragile but always dangerous Andy Norman [son of '76 Olympian Geoff], backing up Jason Ward, brother Dave and Matt Barnes. Rumour had it though that they were a wee bit short on back-up and so it transpired as they'd regress to 6th. So often a man on a solo mission, Steve absolutely loved having 'rare game' to chase. Panicking furry creatures scattered for cover all over the roadside, as our Sharpshooter [see what I did there?] took aim. Newham had hit Belgrave hard all race, and they only relinquished their lead in the final yards, after Stuart Major's brave and lonely vigil at the front, with Sharpy stalking him for six long and painful 'kliks'. The leg ended with this priceless walkie-talkie parlay:

A quarter of a mile from the finish an excited Gordon Biscoe was shouting over his two-way radio to those at the finish that the leader had just passed him and it was Stephen Sharp just ahead of another runner. "Yes, but Stephen Sharp from whom?" he was quizzed. "Stephen Sharp from Belgrave of course!"

So it was Spencer, in his 7th consecutive run here, against Hellmers of NEB, but the result was a bloodbath, and in what had been a wonderful battle for 85% of it, turned into a procession, although Spen never quite knew what was going on behind, so never relaxed. A team of "oldies but goldies" [loosely speaking], had run a tactical masterpiece to claim that fifth National 6 stage in a row.

Could it be six of the best?! No... our luck finally ran out with a very high injured and unavailable list in 2006. This was my big chance to squeeze into the reckoning but I was carousing in Vietnam, as one does. So, an unlikely line-up did their best, with Wicksy back from a fairly lengthy lay-off in particular excelling. In truth, Newham were untouchable on this day, with a dream team that included a Commonwealth winner Michael East, club greats Warmby, Geele and Mitchinson; and Mo Farah to settle the account. Too good - and it was probably quite a well-timed year to 'bury bad news'. If you call just 28 seconds off the medals bad! Old faves SS, Paul and Phil held us rock steady in 4th, before a still very young Kris Gauson leaked a few, new man Jonesey got us back to 5th and DA had one of the toughest chases of his career on hand. Aldershot soon fell to David, but up ahead were Bristol and the small matter of Rob Whalley, whom a less than fit Dave had to give best to. Still, a fine effort from the boys and all were in agreement on one thing: "next year!"

RESULTS 1999-2006 *courtesy of ARMead belgraveharriers.info*

| 1999 | 4th | 1:44:37 | 30 Oct. Teams: Paul Freary 17:21 (15), Jason Lobo 17:50 (15), Lee Hurst 17:36 (13), Mark Miles 17:46 (10), Spencer Barden 17:14 (8), Paul Evans 16:50 (4). 1 Cardiff AC 1:42:46; 2 Tipton H 1:43:26; 3 Birchfield H 1:43:33; 74 teams started, 73 finished. Fastest: Christian Stephenson (Cardiff AC) 16:28, 10 Evans. |
| 2000 | 6th | 1:47:36 | 28 Oct. Jason Lobo 18:34 (39), Charles Herrington 17:57 (32), Lee Hurst 18:19 (24), Spencer Barden 17:03 (13), Yacin Yusuf 17:40 (9), Alaster Stewart 18:03 (6).
Teams: 1 Morpeth H&AC 1:44:14; 2 Tipton H 1:44:21; 3 Birchfield H 1:46:35; 61 teams finished. Fastest: Mark Hudspith (Morpeth H&AC) 16:42, =6 Barden. |

Sutton Park, Sutton Coldfield, Birmingham – standardized stage length 5.847 km.

2001	1st	1:45:28	27 Oct. Lee Hurst 17:49 (12), Paul Freary 17:30 (2), Stephen Sharp 17:26 (1), Kassa Tadesse 17:28 (1), Alaster Stewart 17:46 (1), Spencer Barden 17:29 (1). Teams: 1 Belgrave H 1:45:28; 2 Windsor, Slough, Eton & Hounslow AC 1:45:32; 3 Cardiff AAC 1:46:31; 65 teams started, 64 finished. Fastest: Sam Haughian (Windsor, Slough, Eton & Hounslow AC 16:54, =10 Sharp.
2002	1st	1:44:24	26 Oct. Richard Ward 17:48 (10), Stephen Sharp 17:31 (3), Spencer Barden 17:12 (1), Allen Graffin 17:15 (1), Mark Miles 17:08 (1), David Anderson 17:30 (1). Teams: 1 Belgrave H 1:44:24; 2 Morpeth H&AC 1:46:24; 3 Birchfield H 1:46:52; 68 teams started, 64 finished inc. 1 n/s. Fastest: Chris Thompson (Aldershot, Farnham & Dist. AC) 16:53, =3 Miles, 5 Barden, 6 Graffin.
2003	1st	1:45:22	25 Oct. Paul Freary 17:26 (3), David Anderson 17:14 (1), Spencer Barden 17:25 (1), Mark Miles 17:09 (1), Martin Dent 18:28 (1), Stephen Sharp 17:40 (1). Teams: 1 Belgrave H 1:45:22; 2 Salford H 1:46:21; 3 Bedford & County AC 1:47:21; 67 teams started, 63 finished inc. 1 dsq. Fastest: Chris Davies (Telford AC) 16:25, 4 Miles, 5 Anderson.
2004	1st	1:44:35	23 Oct. Kevin Nash 17:44 (13), Jonathan Blackledge 17:41 (4), Spencer Barden 17:18 (1), Stephen Sharp 17:23 (1), David Anderson 17:27 (1), Mark Miles 17:02 (1). Teams: 1 Belgrave H 1:44:35; 2 Aldershot, Farnham & Dist. AC 1:45:55; 3 Birchfield H 1:46:49; 65 teams started, 63 finished. Fastest: Chris Thompson (Aldershot, Farnham & Dist. AC) 16:39, 4 Miles, 7 Barden, 10 Sharp.
2005	1st	1:46:30	22 Oct. Paul Freary 17:52 (12), Kassa Tadesse 17:20 (2), Alaster Stewart 17:58 (3), Phil Wicks 18:19 (5), Stephen Sharp 17:36 (1), Spencer Barden 17:25 (1). Incomplete B team: Will Cockerell 18:34 (41), Kevin Nash 18:02 (23), Peter Willis 18:59 (29), Lee Greatorex 19:51 (34), Mark Humphrey 20:12 (37). Teams: 1 Belgrave H 1:46:30; 2 Morpeth H&AC 1:47:48; 3 Notts AC 1:47:54; 82 teams started, 76 finished. Fastest: Nick McCormick (Morpeth H&AC) 16:41, 10 Tadesse.
2006	4th	1:47:29	21 Oct. Stephen Sharp 17:32 (4), Paul Freary 17:55 (5), Phil Wicks 17:52 (4), Kris Gauson 18:40 (8), Simon Jones 17:39 (5), David Anderson 17:51 (4). Incomplete B team: John Kimaiyo 18:44 (45), Malachi Byansi 18:49 (44), Peter Willis 19:29 (44), Mark Humphrey 19:54 (46). Teams: 1 Newham & Essex Beagles 1:44:46; 2 Tipton H 1:46:24; 3 Bristol & West AC 1:47:01; 77 teams started, 74 finished inc. 1 n/s. Fastest: Mohamed Farah (Newham & Essex Beagles) 17:03.

2007 - back on top with a classic duel

A long phone call with Alan on the Wednesday night saw poor old DA succumb to his alarming achilles/calf problem, after a fine tour of Rushmoor the previous month. But we had the exciting new American talent of James Kelly up our sleeve for just such an occasion and felt the loss may only be 20-25 seconds. And the rest of the team was an absolute peach. The lads were hungry for redemption in what was a terrific race. Leeds were at the peak of their powers and hit the Belgrave boys hard. Becoming the 'elder statesman' of the side, we wheeled out Sharpy on one who found a very spicy 4th. JK was in the tumble drier and no mistake but like a limpet he hung grimly on to the chaos all around, before finally having to pay just a pip. Enter JB! Wow, at the peak of his powers and into his 5th relay season, Jon enjoyed himself enormously, and aside from a savage duel with Leeds' Dave Webb, saw off all comers. Similar occurred with Simon Jones, who as ARM notes, "never seems to give us a bad one." He spent 17 and a half minutes to gain us one second on Leeds, to reduce the gap to two seconds, with Frank Tickner going ballistic for Wells and drawing up within a second of Simon.

Now, what could Milesy do about Simon Deakin, a very fine runner indeed? Deakin pumped hard, very hard, to the turn around. The gap over our man grew to 30 yards, then 40 and even 50 yards. Was the elastic getting snapped? Were we losing this?! No. Mark is a superb tactician. Anyone who saw his Surrey league wins at the turn of the Century could see that. He was playing it super cool – perhaps even toying with his tall, dark, swarthy friend. In the final third, Mark let rip. He drew level and when someone like him puts the hammer down all hell breaks loose, as he finally handed a 27 second gift to a terribly nervous Wicksy.

Despite this unusually high state of anxiety, Phil ran it all serenely and against an aging Darren Bilton was simply too good. Not that's Daz's 17:32 was messing around, but Phil calmly ran to the day's 9th fastest and a superb 50 second win was the finaly tally.

Elsewhere the 'Baby Bees' could count themselves as the 38th best team in the land, with such luminaries as Neil Speaight ready to burst into the fray.

L-R JK PW SS MM JB SJ

2008 - " 'Ere! We could Get Medals!"

Thus spake the Sharpster, as Alan memorably wrote, during this marvellous race when so many clubs gave us a very hard time indeed. The aim was seven wins in eight years and we had the line-up to do it. After yet another suave opener from Stephen, it was time to unleash the beast that is Nick Goolab on the world. Yes, we'd seen some of him over the last year, particularly at the Spring's Southern 12 stage, but this was when he did his first major flex on a big stage, as the youngster proceeded to usurp his "Master and coach" [SS] by 3 seconds and rip us from 11th to 2nd. How many times is that where we've nailed leg 2 dead centre? Remarkably, Steve Davies also had a superb run but found himself leaking a little to the leaders Winchester, and see Keith Gerrard (future double National cross champion), Tom Russell and AFD's Ben Lindsay come sailing past. Steve must have have been in some sort of shock at the end after running so well for such a return. But in truth, the field was well bunched up and clubs were front-loading.

Just 14 seconds separated the top 5 and we had the clinical automaton for just such a ride in Jonesy. He loved the drag the leaders gave him, and the feeling of putting men into his sack, one by one by one. Only Newham remained, and we knew Sp8y had the mother all battles on 6 with Moumin Geele limbering up. NEB TM Bob Smith warned that anything under 30 seconds for us would spell doom. "Guess I need to open it up then…" said an always understated Phil on five. It was a mission in which he revelled, ripping past the competent Dan Pettit and then going "full regalia". It was the only choice, Sp8y was a purist 800 man, good in a kick and under pressure, but 6k was into the danger zone.

Tense Denouement – a need to bury

Phil's gift to Neil was 49 seconds, although of course he won't have known that… maybe it was only 35 for all he knew. Neil needed a strategy, and going down the Barden route of 'taking it steady and waiting' was "not his bag, baby". He had another plan: to completely bury himself in the first mile. It was agricultural and probably cost 5-10 seconds but, "I didn't want to give them the slightest bit of encouragement in the early part." As it went Geele instead got into a curiously pragmatic duel with Bruce Raeside of Notts, and they both seemed to forget about the unsightable leader. Toward the end the duo ripped chunks out of each other, and to the surprise of the field it was Notts who edged the silver. But 32 seconds up the road Neil had done his job nigh on to perfection. He never gave them a sniff.

The Magnificent Seven starring: Sharp, Goolab, Davies, Jones, Wicks & Speaight. ARM

Beagles' gory revenge

In 2009 yet another fine Belgrave team came to race. But the impending sense of doom cloaked the day from the outset, with both Geele and Farah lined up and salivating. Such was the strength of our side that we believed we could still perhaps lay a hand on them, and after leg one with SS opening the batting for a 4th year in a row, that glove was being laid with a 2 second advantage. But one couldn't help but feel that Dave Mitchinson had had an outstanding run and three top runners were to come in Chris MacKay, Lee Merrien (of London Olympic fame – and controversy) and Kevin Skinner. We were scrapping mightily only 40-odd seconds down, and still had Wicks and Speaight to come, but they would have to bow to Mo and Moumin by 55 seconds, which is no disgrace at all. The battle with Aldershot was superb and Ben Moreau threw the kitchen sink at Neil less than 10 seconds back, but whatever he tried the answer was the same: "you and I are running lockstep today, and that is our story."

Remembering Patricia

We arrived at SP in 2010 in mourning for Pat Mead who passed away a fortnight earlier. A truly great Belgravian, ex-President, with the Belles since their founding in 1976, and training from the Hall with Selsonia for many years before that. The beloved spouse of our esteemed leader it was a sad day and it simply wasn't the same not having Pat up at the Jamboree Stone, or said vicinity. Pat always had the *mot juste* for an anxious runner, who imagined dark goings on behind him, with just the right phrase to calm the mind. I go into this more in my 2004 stage 11 at Milton Keynes when I was really panicking. As for Pat's teas and in particular her lemon drizzle – it'll always be the best I had. Alan and Hazel were so strong to get through this day, ahead of Pat's funeral on the Monday. Bob's Beagles very sweetly wore claret ribbons on their vests as a mark of solidarity, affection and respect.

The lads were just "off" here, and may well have been rather depressed. It was a marvellous race, an instant classic in fact, and we never gave up and were always "in the mix", but in short, for three men not to break 18 was most unlike us. We switched the order this time and had Nick Goolab on 1, who is too strong for that, but I think Alan felt he was repeating himself with Sharpy, and leg 1 is such good fun. But who then? Maybe Dan Mulhare? But he was also tad strong and Simon Jones was a famously good isolation runner. Perhaps on balance it was time to give Steve Davies a chance at it, who had a rather troubled run on three. Well, SD would get that chance three years hence.

Sharpy had a small cold that affected him, but he only dropped a place, while SD was attacked from all angles to drop to 9th, to set up Dan for a brilliant run. Didn't he enjoy mending all the damage. But as Henry Jones said in *The Last Crusade*: "our situation has not improved…" 5th after two and now 5th after four. Simon Jones then ran well, but could only go marginally backwards for his trouble, but all was still possible for the lion: Tipton led by 10 over Bedford, who had 24 on Shettleston, who had 25 on us. Nigel Stirk [Tip] is one of the great club servants, but he couldn't handle the redoubtable Matt Janes of Bedford who scored a deserved win for them – all credit to a very fine squad brilliantly run by Tony Forrest. Paskar had an oustanding run, but ended up just 5 seconds shy of bronze and 8 of Shettleston. Did this not make us 3rd best

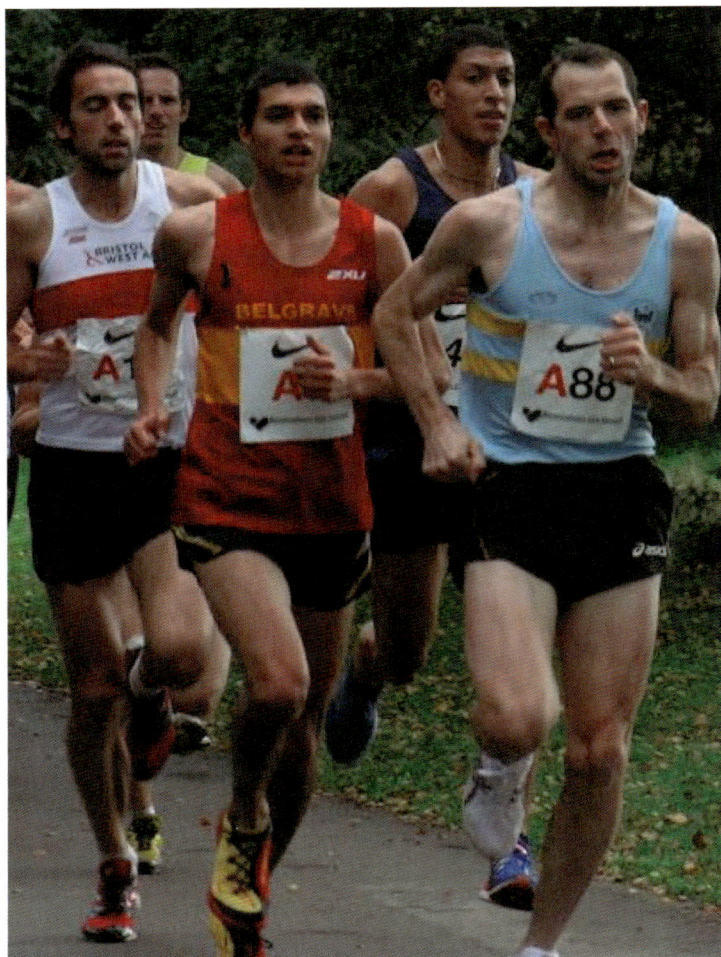

A good mini crash course into the perils of front-loading… basically, when you're strong, try to avoid! Here, the always formidable Ben Whitby leads Goolab but Windsor would end up 40th. Jermaine Mays is being a pest but Kent would fail to finish, whilst Bristol's Jon Wills is by far their biggest threat and they would finish outside the top 10. The Alty boys can be dangerous [Matt Barnes in shot], but surely not to be worried about. Meanwhile the winners Bedford would place 16th, and Tipton 27th who would also catch the Bels for bronze. The worst front-loading though, came from Shettleston who had a simply remarkable squad. They went 1 1 1 1 after four stages, but then slipped to bronze and just held onto silver in the end by 3 seconds. But why start with by far their best runner [17:10] in the race on opener? They could easily have finished outside medals for that little stunt, with the Bels just 8 seconds back in 4th.

English club? A confusing anomaly, but one we're happy to let slide, although I think the ERRA did deal with it thereafter. Aldershot's Rodgers was in turn breathing down our necks, and our work was done. An injured Phil and Sp8y ran the course all day cheering the men on – Jim Kelly too.

An offbeat 2011

If we were a tad depleted in 2010 we had a whole lot more trouble in 2011! Even the author snuck into the team after a decade of trying. It was a gung-ho and merry tribe and our 14th was no disgrace. Up top Aldershot had a brilliant day, in an exciting race, and the reigning champions Bedford finished just up on us. Steve Davies had a very fine run on 2 to take us into 9th, whilst Wardy was solid and Polly fair enough. PO claimed back 4, before I was battered by one of my heroes, Ian Hudspith who had a stunning run to leap from 14th to 8th well into his 5th decade.

Clumber Calls

In 2012 I got blunt insight into how fragile our adminsitrators are. They charge the clubs so much to run the sport, what with the millions they voraciously grab in the registration fee, to goodness knows what end, but then do precious little when times are hard. An outbreak of Ecoli made Sutton Park untenable, so instead of finding another 3k stretch of macadam somewhere in England, they simply pulled the plug. But you don't do that.

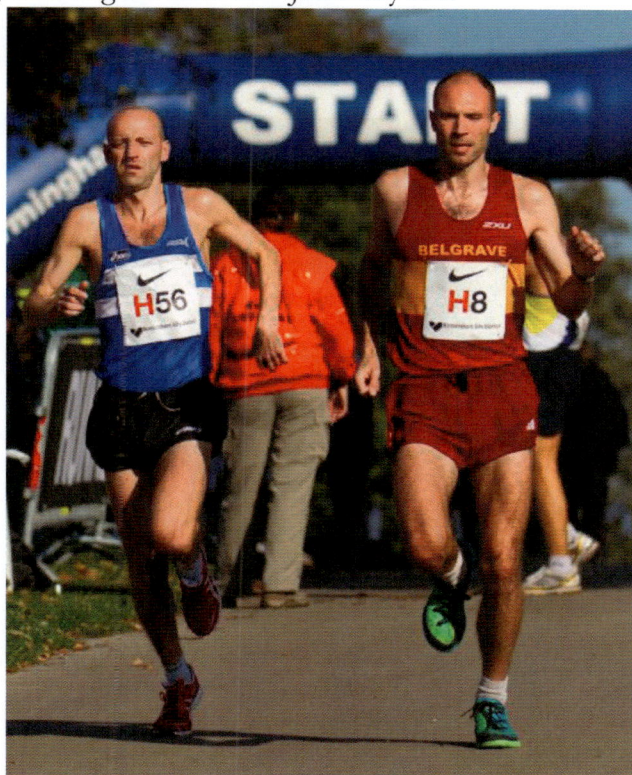

In 2010 I did a huge feature for AW on the top 100 greatest club servants since 1980, and Ian Hudspith quite comfortably won the vote. The author enjoys a 3-second duel with Ian before having to get out the way

This is an historic Championship sporting occasion which hundreds of athletes have busted a gut for. So I called their bluff, hit the phones and found five venues in one morning. I alerted the ERRA to this and they agreed to uncancel, something that the SEAA point blank refused to do nine years later, despite far more notice. Inexplicable. The venue we settled on was glorious Clumber Park in Notts and the event was a great success, with two thrilling races.

I was grateful to Alan for taking on the logistical nightmare of rearranging everything after standing the lads down, but I don't think we regretted it. Matt Graham started us off very nicely and Polly held firm in 11th, with the field well bunched. Time for Stevie D to go to work, but this was still very competitive stuff, and just a single pip was all he could find for his trouble. But on the plus side we were only 41 seconds down on the gold of Liverpool who had gotten Johnny Mellor out of their system. Finally our climb began in earnest with the Kris Gauson having one of his best runs for us, and the lead was 28 seconds away – what a race! Aldershot had it, with Newham just ahead of us.

James Kelly dragged Neil Phillips back to within 11 seconds, but up ahead it was now John Beattie who took the Beagles into a fragile 13 second lead over Liverpool, with us in 4th. The anchor was riveting and after PO disposed of 'the Shots' [only just mind you, Joe Morwood was a right menace] it was just Harry Harper [Liverpool] and Rory Chesser to go. Harper was coming back to Paskar, but in the end we ran out of road, while Chesser took the Beagles to fine win by 31 seconds. It was a lovely race and we all could celebrate saving the 2012 version from the scrapheap.

A timeless classic for Alan's swansong

15 years of thrills and spills came to an end for ARM with this *deelish* encounter. Steve D was solid but not spectacular on 1 to find us in 36th. It seemed an awful long way back, but remember how closely bunched they are and how many front-load. We weren't ready to give anything up, not even the gold. Enter the Rudster, Craig Ruddy, a fine new recruit from north of the border who enjoyed himself greatly, easing us 15 spots up the way, and we were "only" 1:10 off the gold, in the form of Central AC with Brighton just behind. All due respect but we could discount their chances.

The forward momentum continued with PO, although up ahead alarmingly good runs were going down. The order now had normality, and pretty much every club was now a good 'un. The deficit to Sale in the lead was 1:24.

What could Wicksy find? Well, fourth fastest of the stage was his lot, but Matt Bond of Sale had barely given up a thing. It was some sort of nightmare this: we were running well, we knew we had a fantastic squad, but progress was glacial. Was it really possible to win from 8th after 4…? The deficit was 77 ticks, and we had Goolab up our sleeve. Meanwhile with clubs now finally running out of petrol, JK ran a really excellent 17:51 to put away the likes of AFD and draw right up on Highgate, Central and even Tipton. Still though that gap to the lead remained unmoved at a chilling 1:19. It had simply hovered there *ALL* race long!

Nick's almighty chase

Still, if there was one man who could find those 80 seconds it was Goolab. He set off like a man possessed and Ben Noad, Michael Wright and Tipton's Ben Gamble were swiftly dealt with by the surgeon's scalpel. It had been a long, amazing day, of agonizingly hard fought metre by metre progress, but here, with a mile to go, we were in 2nd and "only" 40 seconds down on the lead, who didn't look all that comfy. If James Bailey were to find a 5:20 mile, Nick could just about be in with a breath of hope… But it was simply too much to ask. 28 seconds was the final margin and Sale had played a blinder; and let's be honest, perhaps Bailey had more in the tank if he had come to that. Our slightly dodgy start had haunted us all race long and it was too much to ask. It's the hope that kills you!

New management and another brief thrill

I was now TM and was determined to continue Alan's majestic legacy in some shape or form. We had great fun here – and a real surprise, savouring the lead right up until the final yards of leg 4. What a surprise! Oh for some of that gelignite a year before. Dan Mulhare, with an alarmingly swishing pony-tail, came to test himself against the best and this he did with a terrific 6th on one. We then enjoyed the glorious sight of PO flying into the lead, a 9 second one, over Reading. Wow, this was fun! Craig then had a super run and we had a remarkable 17 second lead and no less than 58 seconds over 4th in the form of Aldershot, who in turn chucked Jonny Hay in the fray. Stephen Trainer did brilliantly well to hang on to that lead until the final 30 yards whereupon Hay took over. It was a lofty perch for hot new find of mine Gus Upton to find himself. One day he's just an anonymous parkrunner, then next he's going out on the shoulder of the leader at the National 6 stage, on 5.

Gus, pictured, had a brave run as Ian Bailey put him through the wringer, but he hung in there to go sub 19, and preserve the top 5. It was at this point that the TM, into his 5th decade finally admitted

he was out of answers and swapped clipboard for flats. It was not a pretty sight and Tonbridge, Leeds, Notts, Newham and Reading feasted on my furry body. But a little way back, Kent, Morpeth, Liverpool, Swansea and Bristol also got a scent of a bloodied Cockerpillar, but to my defence top 10 was preserved and I was pleased to narrowly hold off Kent's flying Greenwood. It had been a splendid day, all credit to Aldershot, oh for a couple more aces! But that's what they all say.

Gus Upton - One moment parkrunner, the next on the leader's shoulder at the National

What a thrill to see nothing but open road behind the leading Bels, courtesy of Craig, at the half-way stage. Enter the Trainer!

2015-2020

It is fairly unthinkable that we would then not trouble the scorers over the next six years, but it all adds to our previous achievements here, and when the race would roll round there were always reasons why SP simply wasn't practical. In 2015 we did brilliantly to get 2nd at the Southern, but that was *our* race and although there's a strong point to be made about turning up when you're weak, the race is a 6+ hour round trip and it's a lot to ask people to only come 40th. Especially when some you are asking have won it multiple times, and in Wicksy's case now a father of two young pups. I was putting out multiple fires elsewhere, like Surrey league survival, and sometimes a race has to "give". We always knew we'd be back and when I stood down in 2019, the new managers had a long hard look and like me said, "not today…"

2021 Belgrave return, low key, but very happy to be there

I think we'd have run in 2020 but Covid put paid to that, and finally, after an almost unimaginable seven years away we were back. It was a squad full of promise and well worth their 30th in what was a humungously tough field, in which AFD were on another planet and carbon plated shoes brought the times down by around 2%.

The Bels hoped for top 24, and were only a minute or so off that. Sam Gebreselassie's gain of 21 spots was superb and we liked TM Arne rising to occasion on

Team medal table since 1969

#	Team	Medals
1	Belgrave H	●●●●●●●●●●●●●●●●●○○●●
2	Bingley H&AC	●●●●●●●●
3	Tipton H	●●●●○○○○○○○○○○○○●●●●●●●●
4	Aldershot, Farnham & Dist. AC	●●●●●●●●●●●●○○○●
5	City of Stoke AC	●●●●●●●
6	Liverpool H&AC	●●●●●●
7=	Gateshead H&AC	●●●○●●
	Swansea H	●●●●○●
9	Newham & Essex Beagles	●●●●●●
10	Birchfield H	●●○●●●●●●
11	Stretford AC	●●●●●●●
12	Cardiff AAC	●●●●●●
13	Shaftesbury H / Shaftesbury Barnet H	●○○○○●
14	Leeds City AC	●○○○●
15	Morpeth H&AC	●○○○●
16	Bolton United H&AC	●○●●●
17=	Blackheath H	●○○
	Tonbridge AC	●○○●
19=	Cambridge & Coleridge AC	●●
	Bedford & County AC	●●
	Sale H Manchester	●●
22	Stockport H&AC	●
23	Salford H	●●●●●
24=	Invicta AC	○●
	Derby & County AC	○●
26	Notts AC	○●
27=	Manchester & District H&AC	○
	Cambridge H	○
	Birmingham University	○
	Cannock & Stafford AC	○
	London Irish AC	○
	Windsor, Slough, Eton & Hounslow AC	○
	Shettlestone H	○
	Highgate H	○
35=	Airdale & Spen Valley AC	●●
	Bristol AC / Bristol & West AC	●●
37=	Sheffield United H	●
	Copeland AC	●
	Central AC	●
	Lincoln Wellington AC	●

40 teams have medalled

anchor to turn 34 into 30. Sam aside, it was a team of engine-roomers, all who will have enjoyed getting a taste of big time competition and we'd surely be a lot stronger in the spring at the 12 Stage.

As for the National 6 stage, it has been a magical ride and we will forever have this as one of the jewels in our crown.

RESULTS 2007-2021   *Courtesy of ARMead www.belgravian.info*

2007	1st	1:44:30	20 Oct. Stephen Sharp 17:18 (4), James Kelly 17:46 (5), Jonathan Blackledge 17:30 (2), Simon Jones 17:33 (2), Mark Miles 17:14 (1), Phil Wicks 17:09 (1).
	38th	1:55:14	B team: Mark Pollard 17:56 (28), Will Cockerell 18:44 (35), Neil Speaight 19:09 (36), James Fairbourn 19:31 (39), Malachi Byansi 19:49 (39), David Mason 20:05 (38).
			Teams: 1 Belgrave H 1:44:30; 2 Leeds City AC 1:45:20; 3 Newham & Essex Beagles 1:45:55; 83 teams started, 79 finished. Fastest: Chris Davies (Telford AC) 16:42.
2008	1st	1:45:18	18 Oct. Stephen Sharp 17:37 (11), Nick Goolab 17:34 (2), Steve Davies 17:40 (5), Simon Jones 17:51 (2), Phil Wicks 17:00 (1), Neil Speaight 17:36 (1).
	35th	1:54:19	B team: James Kelly 18:01 (21), Mark Pollard 19:35 (40), Paul Freary 19:09 (39), Graeme Hyett 19:10 (36), Shaun Moralee 19:10 (36), Will Cockerell 19:14 (35).
			Teams: 1 Belgrave H 1:45:18; 2 Notts AC 1:45:50; 3 Newham & Essex Beagles 1:45:51; 79 teams started, 72 finished inc. 1 n/s. Fastest: Andrew Vernon (Aldershot, Farnham & Dist. AC) 16:49.
2009	2nd	1:44:54	17 Oct. Stephen Sharp 17:28 (11), Nick Goolab 17:35 (8), Simon Jones 17:43 (3), Daniel Mulhare 17:37 (5), Phil Wicks 17:09 (2), Neil Speaight 17:22 (2).
	29th	1:51:10	B team: Steve Davies 17:37 (23), Mark Pollard 18:20 (26), James Kelly 18:05 (18), Paskar Owor 18:14 (16), Will Cockerell 19:20 (20), John Charles 19:34 (29).
			Teams: 1 Newham & Essex Beagles 1:43:14; 2 Belgrave H 1:44:54; 3 Aldershot, Farnham & Dist. AC 1:45:05; 87 teams started, 80 finished. Fastest: Mohamed Farah (Newham & Essex Beagles) 16:33.
2010	4th	1:46:24	16 Oct. Nick Goolab 17:21 (4), Stephen Sharp 18:05 (5), Steve Davies 18:01 (9), Daniel Mulhare 17:20 (5), Simon Jones 18:02 (5), Paskar Owor 17:35 (4).
			Teams: 1 Bedford & County AC 1:45:42; 2 Shettlestone H 1:46:16; 3 Tipton H 1:46:19; 81 teams started, 80 finished inc. 1 n/s. Fastest: Ryan McLeod (Tipton H) 17:03.
2011	14th	1:48:57	15 Oct. James Kelly 17:44 (21), Steve Davies 17:38 (9), Richard Ward 18:17 (13), Mark Pollard 18:48 (17), Paskar Owor 17:29 (13), Will Cockerell 19:01 (14).
			Teams: 1 Aldershot, Farnham & Dist. AC 1:44:51; 2 Birchfield H 1:45:22; 3 Newham & Essex Beagles 1:45:30; 83 teams started, 76 finished. Fastest: James Wilkinson (Leeds City AC) 16:38.

Clumber Park, Nottinghamshire – stage length approx. 5 km.

| 2012 | 3rd | 1:31:16 | 13 Oct. Matthew Graham 14:57 (11), Mark Pollard 15:37 (11), Steve Davies 15:18 (10), Kris Gauson 15:02 (5), James Kelly 15:18 (4), Paskar Owor 15:04 (3). |
| | | | Teams: 1 Newham & Essex Beagles 1:30:36; 2 Liverpool H&AC 1:31:07; 3 Belgrave H 1:31:16; 64 teams started, 55 finished. Fastest: Johnny Mellor (Liverpool H&AC) 14:23. |

Sutton Park, Sutton Coldfield, Birmingham – stage length 5.847 km.

2013	2nd	1:46:24	12 Oct. Steve Davies 18:12 (36), Craig Ruddy 17:50 (21), Paskar Owor 17:49 (13), Phil Wicks 17:27 (8), James Kelly 17:51 (5), Nick Goolab 17:15 (2).
			Teams: 1 Sale H Manchester 1:45:56; 2 Belgrave H 1:46:24; 3 Tipton H 1:46:58; 84 teams started, 80 finished inc. 2 ns & 1 dsq. Fastest: Ryan McLeod (Tipton H) 16:55, 4 Goolab.
2014	10th	1:49:56	4 Oct. Daniel Mulhare 17:26 (6), Paskar Owor 17:43 (1), Craig Ruddy 17:33 (1), Stephen Trainer 18:28 (2), Gus Upton 18:58 (5), Will Cockerell 19:48 (10).
			Teams: 1 Aldershot, Farnham & Dist. AC 1:46:48; 2 Highgate H 1:47:25; 3 Sale H Manchester 1:47:54; 80 teams started, 77 finished. Fastest: Andrew Butchart (Central AC) 17:08; 9 Mulhare.
2021	30th	1:52:40	9 Oct. Neil Wilson 18:47 (58), Tommy Taylor 18:52 (51), Sam Gebreselassie 17:24 (30), Ewan Somerville 19:33 (32), Conall McNally 19:12 (34), Arne Dumez 18:52 (30).
			Teams: 1 Aldershot, Farnham & Dist. AC 1:42:44; 2 Leeds City AC 1:43:47; 3 Shaftesbury Barnet H 1:44:06; 79 teams started, 75 finished. Fastest: Jack Rowe (Aldershot, Farnham & Dist. AC) 16:33.

NATIONAL 4 STAGE – WOMEN

Ever game – always punchy

This is one tough nut to crack as so many clubs can fling four bodies at a 4k problem.

So although the Belles haven't necessarily set the world alight on paper, their returns are terrific in their consistency and willingness to come back year after year. One day they could well creep into those medals – and it'll be because they worked at it so hard for a generation plus before.

Under Catherine Eastham's reign there was a real gung-ho spirit to slog up the M40 every fall, and with Tilly Heaton hitting the race a remarkable nine years in a row, we only had another three to find.

2001 was an astonishing way to start. 7th! And just 1:16 off the bling. It was thrilling to watch the ladies right up there with the best in the land for most of the race. Future National Cross champion Birhan Dagne lit the touch paper with 4th, Juliette Clark leaked just 2 spots, and Maria Sharp held firm. It was then felt that perhaps Anne Hegvold would have to give best to maybe a handful of runners, but not a bit of it, with Wakefield's fast finishing Griffiths 4 seconds back in 8th. And it was only juggernauts that lay ahead. An outstanding effort.

We were bookended by barnstorming runs in 2002 with Getenesh Tamirat giving us 4th, and then Maz turning 24th into 15th on anchor. Marvellous. Maria was such a gifted runner, but the pressure of competition disagreed with her, and she much preferred roaring Steve on to his stunning decade at the top of British road relaying. Still stressful, mind!

2003 saw yet another top 20 return, with some remarkable packing – they were all within 17 seconds – which became 28th in '04.

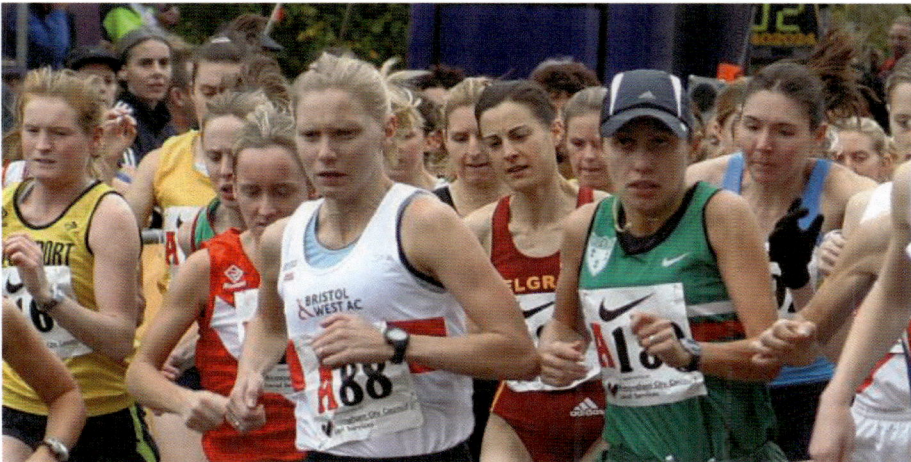

Tilly Heaton, seen here in 2004, pieced together a remarkably consistent and loyal nine runs at the 4-stage. We are indebted. ARM

2005 was a brilliant day: top dozen in the land and all the ladies running spot on to their ability. CE scented their strength and shied away from her tendency to frontload to great effect, as Birhan had one of those magical runs, soaring from 32 to 13 on 3, which is most rare. Smurph then continued the ascent.

None of the girls were *'tripping the light fantastique'* in '06, altho Catherine Bryson had a subtle flex on anchor, taking out six; whilst Birhan was back in '07 [albeit misplaced on one], whilst CB found almost a minute on anchor from her 2006 effort. The danger of burning your best on one was perfectly illustrated in 2008 when in an unchanged line-up, Catherine flopped Birhan and Smurph. And look at the change! Where 7th became 22; now 46th became 17th… Quite incredible, but when all is said and done, that's a team improvement of some 23%. If anyone ever wonders why the order is so important, it's this. Fancy having a 23% influence on your outcome before the gun has even fired. Tilly then had a slightly off day, whilst for the third year in the row Catherine B played Space Invaders, nigh on insisting that we remained top 20. Maybe it was time to let her off the leash earlier.

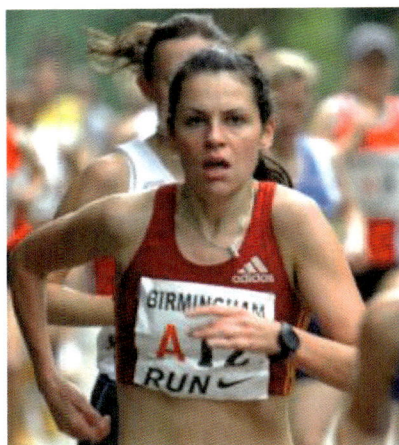

The great switcheroo, starring Sarah Murphy! And evidence that getting your order right can be worth as much as 20% - however daft that sounds

New regime and a huge rebuild

2009 marked my first year of running the Belles ladies on the road and it was great to hear Helen Smethurst say on the phone: "you know what? Let's do it!" I'd had 19 no's and a maybe for the Southern, and had lost a banker when the athlete thought Sutton Park was in, er, Sutton. Although 49th may seem a minor horror, it didn't feel like it on the day. I threw the young and inexperienced Zoe Vail in at the deep end, and although she didn't like her run, she looked at me coldly at the end: "I can do better than that. We're back here in the Spring, right?" "Right!" I replied. But lo, Zoe had a bump to boast in the Spring, and we wouldn't see her again at this one for three years [when she had another bump, but to her eternal credit she gave the nod]. Tilly and Helen ran fine and we must thank Jen Beecroft for stepping up to keep the kettle boiling, and she can always say she's hit the hallowed National macadam of Sutton Park in anger.

A low resolution image for a low key day. We were starting again post-Eastham, and got a top 50 for our trouble. L-R, Tilly, Zoe, Helen & Jen

More building in 2010 was followed by a return to near normality in 2011, where suddenly we had two teams to boast in which the cracking Bs found 42nd which was excellent. A highlight there was meeting Fee Maycock for the first time, who I unearthed by going down the London Marathon leaderboard of unattached runners. I wrote to a friend of Fee's who elegantly swerved my cold call by proffering up this tall, rangy, ever so determined runner from Cheltenham, who would be a mainstay of our squads for four terrific years, and win two London marathon team golds for her trouble, and much more bling besides. The sight of Fee exterminating three or four athletes on the finishing straight was worth the trip to the Midlands alone. Up ahead, I got the team a little wrong [25th] as I allowed the always humble Smurph to talk her way out of the A team after childbirth, and had not quite known what to expect from Fee, but probably only a couple of spots lost.

As discussed in the men's section for 2012, I insisted upon finding the ERRA a replacement venue when they cancelled the event, and we all enjoyed the lush boulevards of Clumber Park. When I saw Emelia Gorecka tearing round for an incredible "Shots" 10-second win, I knew it was right to keep the race on – and no-one could say it was devalued. Any race with Emelia was serious business. We kicked off with Fee in a fine 27th and then 'unleashed the beast' in new find Tish Jones who ripped us up to 13th which was expertly held by Jojo. This left the returning Zoe Vail Smith to anchor us home, albeit running steadily with baby on board, who I waved on through. The bump would enjoy the ride, and knowing the bouncing fireball of pure energy that is Evie, I was right. Only four spots leaked and we could be well satisfied with 17th, our best for seven years.

In 2013 I broke a lot of my own rules and started with Tish. It was pretty naughty, but she was going through an absolutely purple patch and we all wanted to see what she could do in a straight race. We took a step back and enjoyed the fireworks as she narrowly had to give best to Lily Partridge and the evergreen Juliet Potter. But what a performance which stood up as the day's 6th fastest. But it was then pay the piper time as Sammi had to spend a quarter hour and more in a tumble drier and Mel was below her best, struggling with the cruel slopes of SP for the first time. Lou expertly dug in on anchor, to the surprise of many outgunning both Mel and Sammi, whilst in the B's Fee also warranted a spot in the As with her outstanding 16:15 which gained 11 on two. That's at least three occasions that Fee missed out on a spot in the Sutton Park A team, but one she was sight unseen, and once she got into the SEAA squad when someone was quicker in the B's, so all in all, maybe we were just the one blob down for her. And both times we were putting in someone quicker from the previous month – but SP is all about strength and the 'toughees', like Fee, thrive.

So it was a good 15th in 2013 which slipped back to 17th in 2014. We were greatly entertained by Sophie Carter on one, Fee made the cut this time to leak 3; Mel won't have liked losing to Sophie, but still gained 7, whilst the irrepressible Zoe Doyle found another spot, which became two with SBH's DQ.

What consistency, as 2015 found 17th again. Sally Underhill did well to find a spot in the A's and although her 52nd looked pretty torrid, they were all lined up for Mel to have a crack at. 24 spots were claimed but Mel was exhausted from a training camp where she'd overdone it and picked up a bad incoming injury which would land her in hospital a fortnight hence. Little did we know it, but this would be the last we'd see of her near her best in the claret and gold, with her incoming season wiped out, save for a January Surrey league, and a brave but excruciating run at the Southern cross. It was swift and tragic conclusion to a tremendous Belgrave career. She briefly opted for a fresh challenge at Winchester, before settling at Wycombe where she is reunited with 'bestie' Zoe Doyle. ZVS hit the oppo for 9 more – what progress she was now making in her running – whilst ZLD continued the ascent with a time 13 seconds quicker than last year.

RESULTS
Clumber Park

Year	Team	Name (team pos.)	Time						
2001	7	B Dagne [4]	14:34	J Clark [6]	15:40	M Sharp [6]	15:29	A Hegold [7]	15:49
2002	15	G Tamirat [4]	14:51	L Cooper [25]	17:34	V Edwards [24]	16:50	M Sharp [15]	15:26
2003	20	A Walker [35]	16:04	B Dagne [24]	16:00	R Powell [18]	16:11	M Heaton [20]	16:17
2004	28	M Heaton [46]	16:03	V Edwards [47]	17:13	L Cooper [36]	16:39	J Clark [28]	15:55
2005	12	J Clark [37]	15:52	M Heaton [32]	16:14	B Dagne [13]	14:24	S Murphy [12]	16:06
2006	26	S Murphy [44]	16:06	S Gailey [42]	16:57	M Heaton [32]	16:14	C Bryson [26]	16:00
2007	18	B Dagne [7]	14:27	S Murphy [22]	15:47	M Heaton [22]	16:50	C Bryson [18]	15:07
2008	20	S Murphy [46]	16:07	B Dagne [17]	14:51	M Heaton [26]	17:19	C Bryson [20]	15:10
2009	49	Z Vail [49]	16:15	M Heaton [45]	16:55	J Beecroft [51]	19:16	H Smethurst [49]	17:45
2010	42	L Blizzard [54]	17:12	A Linford [48]	16:55	M Heaton [43]	17:46	V Goodwin [42]	17:59
2011	25	S Amend [35]	15:45	N Quispel [23]	16:04	C Bryson [23]	16:29	M Heaton [25]	17:43
2012*	17	F Maycock [27]	12:54	T Jones [13]	12:14	J Rhodes [15]	13:41	Z Vail Smith [17]	13:49
2013	15	T Jones [3]	14:19	S Amend [13]	16:17	M Wilkins [15]	16:27	L Blizzard [15]	16:15
2014	17	S Carter [23]	15:34	F Maycock [26]	16:22	M Wilkins [19]	15:42	Z Doyle [17]	16:16
2015	17	S Underhill [52]	16:35	M Wilkins [28]	15:32	Z Vail Smith [19]	15:52	Z Doyle [17]	16:03
2016	23	S Amend [20]	15:13	R Prince [29]	16:27	Z Vail Smith [20]	15:58	J Rhodes [23]	16:43
2017	10	S Harris [2]	14:17	S Haileselase [2]	15:19	N Quispel [11]	16:40	J Vongvorachoti [10]	15:39
2018	7	S Haileselase [3]	14:39	S Amend [8]	16:14	J Vongvorachoti [9]	15:42	S Harris [7]	14:46
2019	25	O McGinley [43]	16:38	F Maddocks [37]	17:01	M Hall [32]	16:52	R Brown [25]	16:13
2021	9	S Astin [4]	14:12	S Hewitt [8]	15:38	G Richardson [7]	15:42	O Papaioannou [9]	15:56

CD era begins

I remember the CD era beginning in 1988, the compact disc era that is. All shiny and futuristic. Well this CD era boasted similar. Charlie loves the challenge of the relays and insists on making the pilgrimage come feast or famine. His management era began with Sammi in a superb 20th in 2016 – one of the best runs of her career for sure, before one of my "parkrun pick-ups" Rebecca Prince [O'Kill] leaked a few but held us steady, whilst Zoe VS, right, claimed back the 9 leaked spots. Jojo wasn't quite at her best but kept Cambridge, Stroud and Serpies at bay to only lose 3.

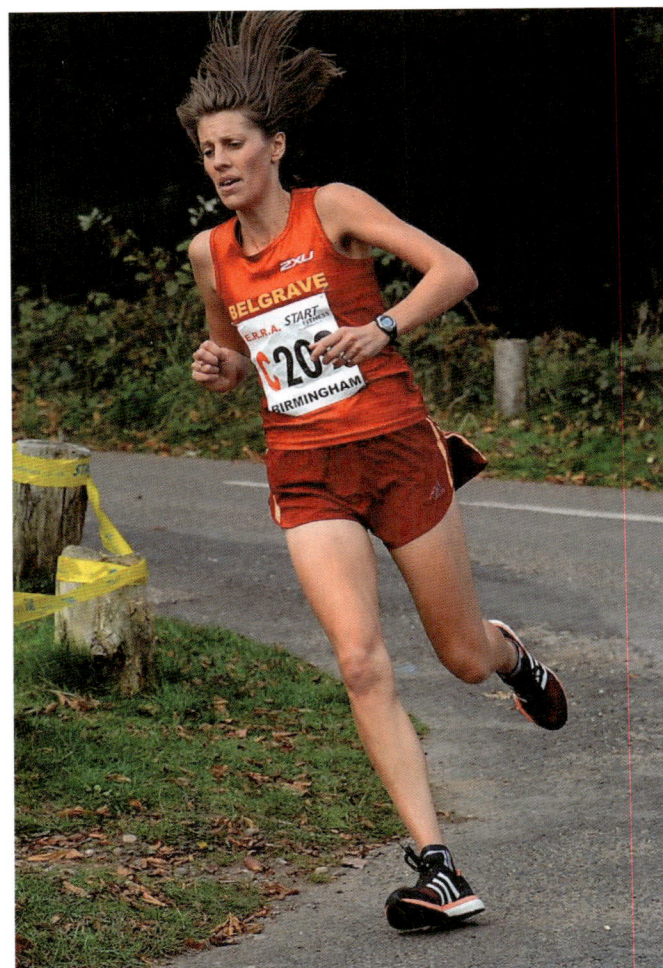
Sam, Jojo, Becky and Zoe notch another tough return into the annals

Up 9 in 2015 on 3, up 9 in 2016 on 3. That's some Zoe magic for ya'

A team bristling with talent and intent turned up in 2017 and Chas couldn't resist front-loading the living daylights out of the day. It did make for half an hour of thrills though as first Sophie Harris [2nd], then Saron brought us home in 2nd place at the half. Epic stuff, but it threw a jet-lagged Nelle Quispel to the lions. Over in the B's Katie-Ellen French travelled some 39 seconds quicker. But only 9 spots were leaked, before we welcomed Thai Olympian Jane Vongvorachoti to steadily anchor us home in the top 10.

Charlie front-loaded less in 2018, but still couldn't resist Saron on 1. Despite her unpredictable nature and love for a pack, she's too good for it, especially for such a super team, and it meant that Sammi – now an ultra-runner - on 2 - couldn't do any real drafting. Maybe Jane to open, Saron on 2 and Sam on 3? Sophie, who craved opener again – it can be addictive - then had a very good run on 4 to grab us our best equal finish, and see off the fast finishing Bristol. But it all meant we were just 3 seconds off Swansea in 6th, highlighting the importance of getting Saron in the right place.

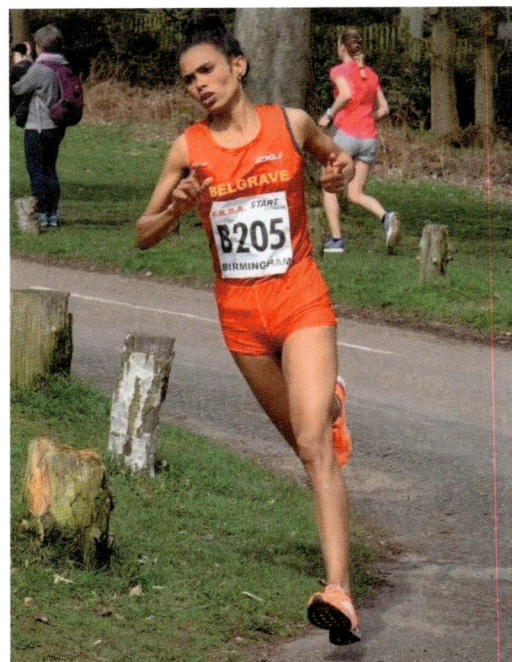
Saron hooooolds Sophie's magnficent 2nd

How do you lose a gem like Sophie?

On the subject of Swansea, Sophie was alerted to their prowess… We couldn't have dreamt it at the time, but this was to be her last appearance in the claret and gold, as she switched to them. It was gutting, but what a magical two years we enjoyed from the great SGH – from pavement plodder to superstar – and a testament to the tireless hard work of Charlie, running those Battersea sessions for over a generation. Once every 5-10 years a gem would appear there, but now, it's once every 5-10 months!

The question of how a club as fine as Belgrave can lose such a magnificent runner after two years is a thorny one, but one that should be addressed. To say that Sophie switched to a club 3 seconds up on us at the National is of course a cover-up and would reflect poorly on her. The truth is always far more complex. We can do no better than let Sophie pick up the story which she told me in the summer of 2022:

As my results continued to improve, I felt caught in the middle of a conflict between my own personal progression, championed by Matt [Welsh, also now her partner], and my desire to be a team player and club representative, championed by Charlie. In the latter stages of 2017-2018, I tried to do both, running every race I could, including when I wasn't in peak condition and ultimately I began to burn myself out. Unfortunately, the conflicts escalated with each party also vying for recognition for their contributions to the rapid rise I'd experienced in the sport, which manifested itself when an article only recognised one of those contributions. Both Matt and Charlie made important contributions to my journey, but ultimately, I loved being a part of Belgrave and really just wanted to do the sport I loved, but instead found myself getting dragged down by the politics that surrounded my progression.

Ultimately one influence became the stronger of the two and this lead to increasing distance from the club, something that was exacerbated by the formation of a Belgrave splinter group known as the 'Battersea project'. The group continued to train on the track in winter, running different sessions, which created a deeper rift within the club. The atmosphere between the two groups became difficult to manage and the acrimony became overwhelming.

As 2018 came to a close, I suffered a big injury which put me out of running for 5 months. When I returned, I was advised to train all my sessions alone, which I did. I'd become isolated and despite running well, I no longer had the community and support which made me join the club initially. I knew something had to change and ultimately this drove a lot of the decisions I made over the coming months, leaving Belgrave and beginning a new leg of my running adventure.

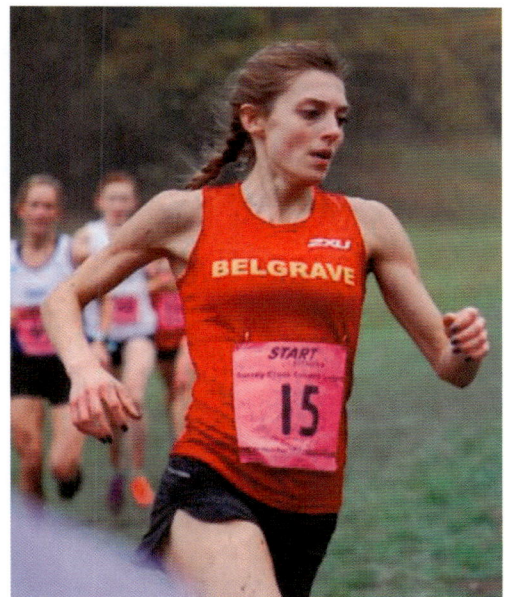

Sophie en route to her "World Record" Surrey League Grandslam

This was my first club and always has a place in my heart.

In short, Soph has nothing but positive words for us as a club in general, and almost rejoined a short while later. Belgrave could have done better and dropped the ball here. But as noted elsewhere, negative things happen to great sports clubs and this was one. We move on and learn from our mistakes, and hopefully such a sad end to a wonderful Belles career will never be repeated.

Sophie continues to run well and is recently married [to ex-Bel Luke Pikett, a National cross scorer no less] and now lives in the North, but occasionally tours Battersea Park. She knows we're always delighted to see her, and will never be forgotten.

Steady as she goes in '19 and post-Covid leap

After that tremendous shimmy of form we savoured a good, tough no-nonsense performance from the engine room in 2019 for 25th. Orna McGinley was rock solid on one, Fi Maddocks turned 42nd into 37th, Mhairi Hall also grabbed 5, which left the gifted Rachel Brown to rip us into the top 25.

After Covid struck, we were happy to show that our training group had gone from strength to strength. Four fresh faces brimming with menace came to race in 2021. Sarah Astin, by far our quickest, placed 4th, with Steph Hewitt doing very well to only leak four. New star Grace Richardson actually had to bow to Steph by 4 seconds, whilst gaining a spot, with Liv Papaioannou only slipped a couple of notches to 9th. If that running order was tricky to find for Charlie, with Sarah a slight unknown and opting for the safety of giving her a real race [as was his wont with Sophie then Saron]; he also had a selection conundrum, as the slick Alice Reed languished in the B's with a 15:23. What riches indeed, and we would have been 5th if only the solution to that little riddle had been clear. But it doesn't work like that, this is far too layered and complex a business.

The B's had a screamer to place 30th, and we were clearly well set for some fun at this highly entertaining and rather ferocious race.

NATIONAL XC RELAY - MEN

Headfry incoming...

What a bonkers ride the Bels have had at this barnstormingly bonkers race. Its ferocity is cruel and unusual, and the drama it's been known to produce, seering. In a moment of real gung-ho spirit Alan sent a team bristling with intent to Mansfield in 1996 in the very early days of his tenure. Messrs Gerry Adams, Matt Yates, Darren Mead and Gary Staines were eyeing up no less than medals and came away a tad deflated in 5th. Not bad though!

But then a long 7 year break, before Alan had another whirl, this time with the eye-watering group of Sharp, Barden, Freary and Anderson. What were the rest going to say to that?! Very little. Both Aldershot and Morpeth were good value but the rest were nowhere, and after Stephen bolted round in 2nd, there was going to be no stopping us.

And is this the 2nd greatest race of the book?

We're pretty certain we've flagged the finest race of the book elsewhere, but 2004's Mansfield could just be the bridesmaid.

Do not be deceived...This is one fiddly fish to fry but Paul Freary, David Anderson, Stephen Sharp and Spencer Barden were electric on our return to the fold

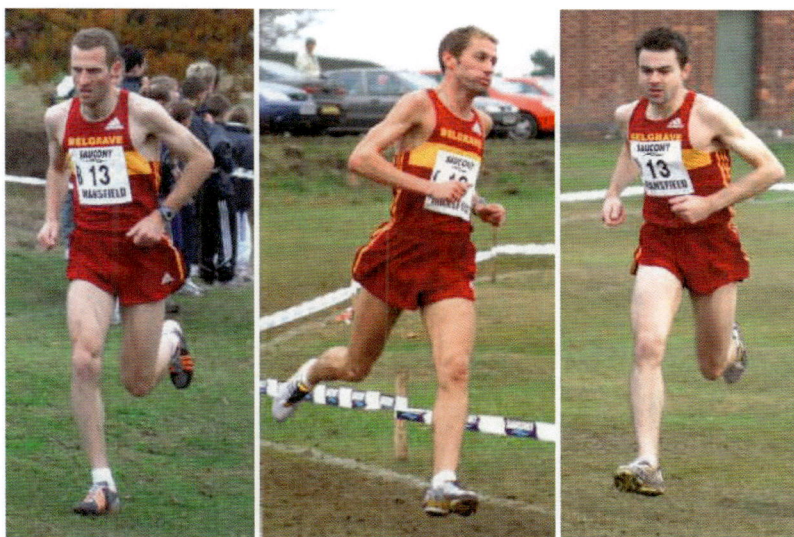

Spen, Paul and Danders ran amok in '03. ARM

It was another stunning line up of Nash, Blackledge, Sharp and Miles. Had we lost anything? Yes, maybe 45 seconds as Barden and Anderson were no slouches. 9th was our lot at the 'half', and we can do no better than hand you over to Alan's sharpened pencil for the thrilling denouement:

Leg 3

It was beginning to look as if we would find it very difficult to get to the front but Stephen Sharp is going through a superb spell at the moment and is brim full of confidence. Immediately disposing of Tipton and Altrincham, he floated up to Windsor and they too fell away.

"Who's that!" gasped Morpeth's team manager Jim Alder. "Stephen Sharp," came the swift reply from a Belgrave supporter. "Whor! Of course. Thanks Lass" Still described as a "great club man" in the athletics press, Stephen's fame is beginning to spread.

In front, Ian Hudspith for Morpeth was also going well and as leaders Blackheath, Sale and Derby sagged, the whole field became prey to Stephen who was a man on a mission. Morpeth and Belgrave colours were side by side during much of this battle but eventually it was our man coming out on top and as the final hand-over was reached only Harrow were a stride or two ahead – and incredibly did not have a fourth man.

Leg 4

Hero of so many races, Mark Miles set out at the head of the pack with Sale seven seconds in arrears and Morpeth, in the form of Nick McCormick who ran so brilliantly in Sutton Park a fortnight earlier, just two seconds further back. What pressure for Mark, not feeling too confident after a disappointing 8th in Birmingham seven days earlier.

McCormick ripped into Sale's advantage and within half a mile was a few strides behind "Milesy". They were locked together as the first lap was completed, and setting out again the advantage now swung towards the Belgrave man. McCormick had definitely overcooked his initial charge and with spectators racing from one side of the course to the other to witness this titanic struggle, Mark went ahead. Two metres became ten ... ten became twenty ...

The Tipton lads were screaming their training partner Milesy on as the pair raced through the woods. The Newham boys back at the finish felt that Mark would have the edge; but with this race proving to be a thriller to the end there was more drama to come. Already, poor Mark was running close to the edge. McCormick overcame his bad patch and the gap came down ... and down ... until 50 metres out on the short sharp rise towards the finish, Morpeth's blue and white colours went ahead. Mark's legs had gone. It was pure memory and will power that kept him moving over the last few metres until, with legs buckling, he sank to his knees as the line was crossed.

Minutes passed before he could get up. Mark had given everything, and the respect he had earned (yet again) from the rest of the team was immense. It was a terrific run when he hadn't felt at his best – and yet he was our fastest man. Such is the talent and courage in young Mark's frame that one of these days he is going to do something unbelievable.

What a race!

Teams: 1 Morpeth H&AC 1:01:06; 2 Belgrave H 1:01:12; 3 Altrincham &DAC 1:01:44; 4 Aldershot F&DAC 1:01:57; 5 Blackheath & Bromley 1:02:24; 6 Sale H Manchester 1:02:50; 150 teams started; 120 finished.

A - K.Nash (11) 15:31; J.Blackledge (8) 15:35; S.Sharp (2) 15:07; M.Miles (2) 14:59.
B - R.Alsop (57) 16:50.

Fastest: 1 C.Thompson (Aldershot F&DAC 14:30; 2 M.Skinner (Blackheath & Bromley) 14:42; 3 N.McCormick (Morpeth H&AC) 14:43; 5 M.Miles (Belgrave) 14:59; 6 A.Bowden (Harrow) 15:04; ... 8 S.Sharp 15:07.

Back to back stunning duels. Hudspith vs Sharp; McCormick vs Miles... Juggernauts all - where's your money?! ARM

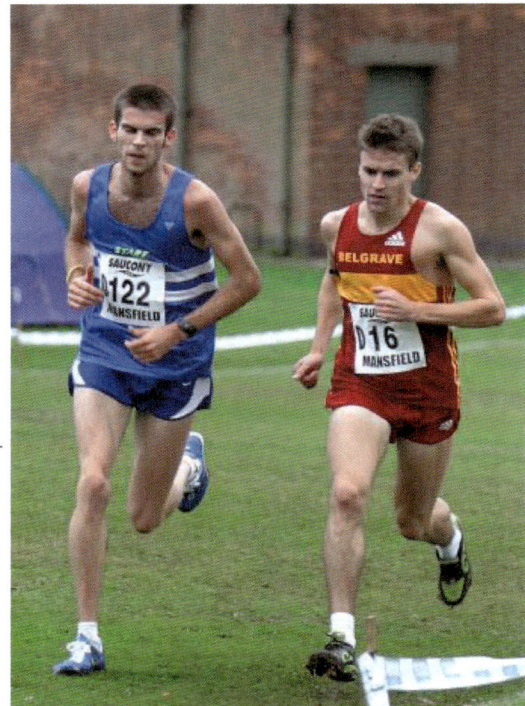

More fine teams came along in 2005 & 2006, but remarkably they could only manage "a pair of eighters". It was not a poor show from the lads, this is just a bloodbath of a race, narrow in parts and so little room or time to correct errors.

2007's Absolute Stunner

It appeared that there wasn't a huge uptick in the squad for 2007 as it's hard to choose between Anderson, Speaight, Wicks & Sharp, versus Sharp, Pollard, Miles & Wicks. But that latter squad is not only kicking like a mule, but in Polly it had one of the great XC purists (and a double Scottish champion). It's clear Mark's was the best run of the day for us, getting withing 4 seconds of his namesake. The lads grouped their efforts so well, and after SS's fine 6th, it was a great surprise to turn that into 4th. Milesey drove hard on 3, and immediately Leigh gave way, and MM then enjoyed a remarkable duel with Notts' Billy Farquaharson whilst also becalming Bedford and Harrow. What a battle and now it was Phil one second behind Ian Boneham, who was swiftly dispatched.

What pressure for Phil! But he loves it, and although Dave Webb was going a mite quicker for Leeds, Neilson Hall always to be respected, and Frank Tickner scoring the day's fastest for Wells, Phil's ran the perfect race. What a leaderboard, with six clubs within 34 seconds. An epic and surprising coup.

RESULTS

Year	Team	Name (team pos.)	Time							
2003	1	S Sharp [2]	14:46	S Barden [1]	14:46	P Freary [1]	15:15	D Anderson [1]	14:42
2004	2	K Nash [11]	15:31	J Blackledge [9]	15:35	S Sharp [2]	15:07	M Miles [2]	14:59
2005	8	P Freary [23]	15:41	P Wicks [13]	15:12	A Stewart [9]	15:38	S Sharp [8]	15:16
2006	8	D Anderson [9]	15:14	N Speaight [6]	15:29	P Wicks [10]	15:43	S Sharp [8]	15:14
2007	1	S Sharp [6]	15:05	M Pollard [4]	15:08	M Miles [2]	15:04	P Wicks [1]	14:45
2008	7	P Freary [75]	16:47	S Sharp [34]	15:45	N Goolab [17]	15:22	P Wicks [7]	15:01
2009	8	S Sharp [34]	15:56	N Goolab [16]	15:24	S Jones [9]	15:24	P Wicks [8]	15:14
2010	5	N Goolab [1]	15:04	S Sharp [12]	16:12	S Jones [7]	15:33	P Owor [5]	15:29
2011	8	M Mulhare [2]	15:31	J Kelly [14]	17:27	P Owor [14]	16:19	D Mulhare [8]	16:19
2013	5	N Goolab [1]	15:24	M Pollard [8]	16:51	P Owor [6]	16:22	K Gauson [5]	16:08

And back to the boondocks

Well, they're hardly that, but such were our lofty ideals for this race it was always a surprise to finish outside the top 6 – which we frequently did.

Long chats with ARM occurred for 2008 as we found ourselves one short of a great team. It was between myself and Paul for the final spot and he got the nod, although 75th was a wee bit profligate. But the boys loved the chase. A rise of 41 spots must be close to a record in any relay ever for Steve, whilst 34 to 17 was equally tangy for Mr Goolab, with Phil's 17-7 on anchor even better! A very fine effort, but we were 1:48 off the win, so it would have taken a very special runner replacing Paul, to get close to the 'Bedford Massive'.

Another outstanding team came to race in 2009, and 8th would have been quite unthinkable at the start. Our perceived weakest man ran the same time as Nick Goolab. Whew, some depth. But our problems here started on the B of Bang. I'll let Alan describe the chaos:

Nightmare on Berry Hill

When we discovered that of the 208 teams entered for the senior men's championship at Berry Hill, Mansfield, we had been designated team no. 13, we laughed. "Unlucky for some," we said, "but not for us!" The talk was of teams that were likely challengers for the title and whether we could get the better of Bedford & County AC, a feat, we felt, that if achieved could earn us the win. But some evil Hallowe'en witch was at that very moment concocting a spell to thwart our hopes … and when the starter fired his gun she cast her curse down on the assembled field to cause mayhem.

The start area seemed a little narrower than normal as the organisers had tinkered with the take-over arrangements. As a result the eager first leg men were packed ten deep or more. There were numerous pushes and shoves and on the front rank, down on the deck went Sharpy. An attempt to get to his hands and knees failed as a man behind ran over him. A second crack at getting up was no more successful, a hurdling runner's knee striking him in the back and expelling every last gasp of breath; but up he got, eventually, in his own words, "stone bonkers last." Certainly he had, perhaps, a hundred men ahead of him.

"I did bring a few others down," he later related to his team mates, as if that was some saving grace. "Yeah", muttered Phil with a grin, "not the right ones though." Not the right ones indeed, for most of the likely contenders were already well to the fore as the multi-coloured stream of vests were now strung out over more than 200 metres as the leaders entered the narrow paths in the woods. We say 'most' because although Sharpy ploughed on manfully, receiving apologies from unfamiliar rivals as he overtook them ("Sorry I trod on you mate!"), Blackheath continued to languish down the field, ending the stage in 44th – and look what they achieved.

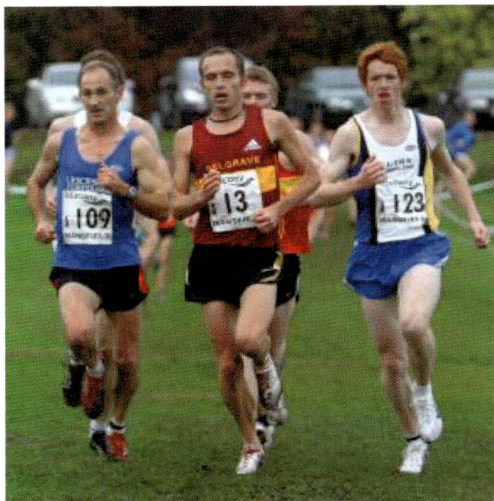

Stevarino makes new friends in midfield. ARM

So there it was, a fine and noble chase, but the damage was too great and it left Phil too much to do on anchor, overcooking it on lap 1 as he had to.

2010 was yet another fine side, but as with the National 6 stage, medals a little out of reach in 5th. Perhaps Alan was wasteful with Nick Goolab on 1 who flew round in the lead and Jonesy may well have been the man for that job. Steve had a very off day indeed as 1st became 12th as he came down with a cold shortly after which was probably weakening him. Simon and PO had excellent runs, but the ferocity of the race was perhaps finally catching up with Steve.

And more déjà-vu

What could a brace of Mulhares, JK and PO find in 2011? Not a lot! Ha, well this time it was the mud that killed us. Michael was a sensation on 1 [2nd], but then James and then PO got completely stuck. James is such a tall, elegant runner, but could only shake his head in disbelief at the horror of it all, and PO was little better. Like Bambi on ice for our 800 star. Dan had come via Kenya which entailed an early morning Heathrow pick-up by the author who dumped him at St. Pancras. He ran well to dispatch half a dozen, but in short it was "one of those days". In fact that was four 'iffy days' on the trot since the win, and 6 out of 7. But in the middle, that complete gem.

We then 'won' in 2012, but in reasons gone into detail in 2013's National 12 report, withdrew ourselves from the race; and turned up in 2013 to score an immaculate 5th. Medals were nearly a minute away, but another win by Nick on 1 (hold him back Alan, *hoooooold*!), Polly got savagely devoured by eight clubs with a time some 1:45 off his 2007 epic. Paskar had got the day wrong, and was in the bath when ARM checked he was on the train. Manic travel action followed on bikes, buses, tubes, trains and cabs and PO arrived 45 mins before his stage. He ran smoothly and 9th became 6th before the talented Kris Gauson, who made his relay debut a decade earlier as a 17 year old, held us there before a DQ for Bristol meant a laudable 5th.

And that's our lot at this one – for now. I all but raised a humdinger in 2014, but it was the unlikely figure of PO who collapsed a few days out and I had to call off the dogs [Wicks, Goolab & Auden]. My tenure couldn't justify the race thereafter, rebuilding as we were, but perhaps this is a race to be revisited with our refound depth.

BELLES

And for the Belles, it has also been deemed a trip too far. It is an awful long way to go to zap a top 40, with only 3 kliks of running on offer. We tried it once though and an unofficial squad of Rose, Jojo and Fi Maddocks ran nicely to place 33rd in 2013. [We were unable to register Fi in time to make us 'real'].

But with only three required – who knows. And perhaps the ECCA might consider bringing the race a tad further down the motorway, or even follow the National cross's model of going South, Midlands, North. There is a certain lack of imagination and flexibility there, but the ECCA would no doubt rebuff me and point to how popular the event is, although that's a bit of an illusion as there are a great many B and C teams. Fact is, only 10 Southern women's clubs make the trip, and the venue is a key reason for that.

SOUTH OF THE THAMES TEAM RACE - WOMEN

Bish, Bash, Bosh

What fun the Belles have had at this one after quiet beginnings. It was (for reasons unknown), not a race for women until finally they started to creep into it one by one in the early years of the century, and the 4 to score system kicked in over 2001/2 [when Tanya Sturton grabbed a fine silver], and the race was nice and entertaining to see a mixed field over the country, which is comparatively rare. Mob matches of course are also mixed.

The Belles nailed their first hardware in 2004 at Petersham, when in a delightful battle with Walton, they sneaked out a set of bronzes 70-72 – with a team of Tilly Heaton, Lou Cooper, Sarah Gailey and Vicky Jones. Good going.

Tilly repeated her silver the next term, but insufficient back-up, and I almost raised a crack squad in 2011 but multiple drop-outs floored us to 3, so I called the athletes off. Tish Jones kindly ventured to Reigate in 2012 and stormed to a riotous win, placing 23rd/215 overall.

Twin 29s

Right, enough of the shadow-boxing, this was clearly a race to be plundered and we started in the hours before my 40th birthday party, at Streatham. A great team came to race and they didn't disappoint. Keri Mackenzie has startling gifts in her armoury, but fragility often comes with astonishing speed. A workout with her on a hot summer's night is lethal to handicap because in that last 500 of a pyramid session, she will break 1:30 and will slam everyone in sight. Here, Keri was very good, if surprising, value, for 3rd, but such is the quality of the beast. She was just 28 seconds off the win. The next cab off the rank was ZLD in 6th, and our scoring quartet was completed by Fee [8th] and Flic [12th]. It all meant 29 points and a strong win over all our close Surrey League rivals SLH.

It was an excellent and clinical defence in '14 on HW's always entertaining course. We were led home by Mel, who had to give best to the excellent Stacey Ward [HHH], whilst Zoe held onto her 6th from 2013. Catherine Lovegrove shone for us very briefly, and was always a delight, and has now qualified as a doctor. This was probably the peak of her Belles career in 10th, whilst 15 ticks back, Kerimac fought her way back into the scoring squad, pressed hard by Jojo Rhodes and Genia Marek. Our team score? You guessed it: 29 points again, incredible consistency.

A remarkable day's bounty hunting on the Common with Individual gold and silver for Paskar and Mel, and gold and silver for the Belles and Bels, with the Bels also winning the 8 to score. Clockwise TL: Imogen & Will Cockerell, TO'N, PO, Gus Upton, Nick Bundle, Matt Welsh, Taras Telkovsky, AJ, Roy & Reece Maddams, CD, Genia Marek, Mel Wilkins, Catherine Lovegrove, Keri Mackenzie, ZLD, Jojo Rhodes, Hannah Hegvold [in lieu of Knut]

Lots of medalling – but this ain't so easy

We seemed dead set on a hat-trick in 2015 at the glorious Polesden Lacey course – what a cruel and unusual mistress that is. Amend. Vail Smith. Rhodes. What a trio of trouble. We were on 16 points after 3 runners. Another 29'er incoming perhaps? But that's not how this works – you can't assume anything. The hows, whys and '*do you mind if I don'ts*?' presented a gaping hole in the squad – time for a hero to step in, and it turned up, as it did more often than one might recall, in Megs Bailey. We had to wait till 51st but we were operating with zero back-up, so a deserved Championship silver for MB. It just shows how when you think you may not be required, the call often comes. I would have said that of my 18 scores at the National, I wasn't slated to score in half of them either the day before, race day or during. In short, there's many a slip.

2016's thriller

Back to Polesden and Zoe VS has now hit the form of her career. She's such a talented runner and we've not given up on seeing her in the vest again. One of my favourite recollections was trying to pace her to a sub 18 at Bushy. She got 18:15, went home and cried in bed. I chided that this was one race and we'd try again in a fortnight. We headed to Fulham Palace, and whammooo, 17:15! It was an electrifying romp which I could only observe from some way back due to its pace. (I was supposed to pace her again – no chance). Anyway, as we say, such a talent, who once won the Wedding Day 7k in a time quicker than a winning Julia Bleasdale once posted. Zoe's focus on her family then took over, but she remains on close terms with the club. Just 19 seconds off the win here, but who for back-up, with Charlie now soloing at the reigns, as I was massaging the men to a brutal 23 point tally to destroy Kent?

Well, we packed a beaut, with the up and coming Sophie Harris in 12th, Iona Cousland 14th and Helen White 18th, but would it be enough? The scores came in: Belles 46, Ranelagh 38 and Kent 35. Fair play, and a brilliant race.

We stepped off the gas in 2017 with newbie Mhairi Hall fighting a lonely vigil, but were right back "on it" in 2018. In yet another wonderful day's racing, Saron blasted to a dominant win, Mhairi covered well in 8th, tracked in turn by Emma Howsham, and another fresh name in Steph Hewitt in 17th. 35 points was good, but Dulwich had looked hot out there with a 2nd and 5th, so we had some ground to make up. But they finally closed in 19 and we had the day by 4 points, sweet relief!

This was a wicked little smash and grab for a team that sailed under the radar. L-R, Saron, Mhairi, Emma and Steph

We were missing stars in 2019, but our packing was impressive: 21, 22 & 23. Kent were vulnerable with 56 points but even with Emma's excellent 8th, we had too much to do. We were sad to lose Emma to Reading who became a fine sub-4:30 1500 runner. Those packers were Mhairi, Iona and Flic [described in dispatches as our "resident badass", and indeed some of the *Wipeout* style fitness competitions she does, makes that handle very apt].

Had the squad held through Covid we asked? Oh, you better believe it! But in an unusual trick of the calendar, which decimated the race of numbers, it clashed with the London Champs, which the Belles attacked instead (and duly won). Hopefully 2022 will see matters untangled.

RESULTS

Year	Team	Athlete
2001	-	7 T Sturton
2002	-	2 T Sturton
2004	3	2 M Heaton; 13 L Cooper; 24 S Gailey; 29 V Jones
2005	-	2 M Heaton; 20 C Eastham
2012	6	1 T Jones; 6 J Rhodes; 44 H Barsham-Rolfe; 56 V Goodwin
2013	1	3 K Mackenzie; 6 Z Doyle; 8 F Maycock; 12 F Cole
2014	1	2 M Wilkins; 6 Z Doyle; 10 C Lovegrove; 11 K Mackenzie
2015	2	3 S Amend; 5 Z Vail Smith; 8 J Rhodes; 51 M Bailey
2016	3	2 Z Vail Smith; 12 S Harris; 14 I Cousland; 18 H White
2017	-	9 M Hall
2018	1	1 S Haileselase; 8 M Hall; 9 E Howsham; 17 S Hewitt
2019	2	8 E Howsham; 21 M Hall; 22 I Cousland; 23 F Cole

SOUTH OF THE THAMES TEAM RACE
[SOT JUNIOR] - MEN

A curious creature, but still something to love

It's hard quite to what to make of this race. A little gem, or a damp squib? A terrific way to spend a Saturday afternoon, or one to quietly pass by – no-one will notice?

From personal experience it was a race too far for me and when looking at the season would be the one I'd skip telling the gaffer – 'but you can put me down for the rest'.

The key problem started *waaaaayyy* back over 100 years with a dreadful, hoity-toity, patronising, mangled, bastardised moniker that is never going to set the pulses racing.

"Junior". What on earth does that even mean? Well to 99% of souls it means a race for the youths. But it actually meant the lesser runners of a lesser club. Don't believe me? These are Alan Mead's excellent notes on the association, and happily now all the snobbery and silly clarifications have been done away with and the two races continue to thrive in the calendar, although as an ex-TM I wonder if one might be enough:

In the late 1880s athletics experienced its first boom. The established clubs of the time, south of the River Thames, were Ranelagh Harriers, Thames Hare & Hounds, South London Harriers and Blackheath Harriers. These clubs were extremely careful in accepting new members and this led to many further clubs being formed. Often these newer, minor, clubs were attached to Public Houses. Their fortunes were very mixed: some continued but many died, amalgamated, or were absorbed by others. The standing of the established clubs seemed unaffected by the boom. The newer, clubs accepted the 'Junior' or 'Second-Class' status put upon them by the established clubs and they had no opportunity of competing against them.

In November 1887 a group of the newer clubs from South London, led by Reindeer Harriers, asked the Southern Counties Cross Country Association for permission to run a South of the Thames Second Class Inter-Club Race. Similar clubs North of the Thames requested that the race be extended to include them but this was turned down by the South of Thames clubs and so the North of the Thames clubs formed their own association.

On 14th January 1888 the first South of the Thames Second Class Inter-Club Race took place on Wandsworth Common and the venue continued to be used up to and including 1894. A formal constitution was written in 1893 but the true start of the Association was, without question, 14th January 1888.

In time the Association expanded from a South London Association to a truly South of the Thames Association with clubs from Surrey, Kent, Sussex, Wiltshire, Berkshire and Hampshire (including the Channel Islands). Subsequently, the 'established' clubs all, over the years, affiliated to the Association and have very often hosted its races.

In 1910 the Association started the annual 'Junior' (by standard) races in addition to the Championship race. Initially the 'Junior' races were on a County, or group of Counties, basis but changed to one race only in 1933. The 'County idea continued, however, with the 'County' Medals given at these races.

Belgrave has loyally supported the race and have claimed 10 titles since 1925. Here's Bill Lucas winning in 1946 (and leading Belgrave to the title at Nonsuch park). 70 years later he'd celebrate his 100th birthday at Belgrave Hall [inset].

In 1984 we peeled off one of our finest cross-country performances of all time: 16 points! Quite incredible for a race of well over 200 souls. So a special shout-out to Ollie Foote (1), John Gladwin (2), Mark Sinclair (6) and Dave North (7). It was noted that Ollie added his name to such winning luminaries as Chris Chataway and Dave Clark [triple National Cross winner]. Hardly second-class runners.

Renewed Ambition and the wonderful Chataway

We commence this race's remit in fine style with a set of silvers in Nov 1999. We'd lost by just a point in '98 so Alan sought to rectify that by raising a devasting team. He envisaged five in 10... But then injury, illness and no shows suddenly made things fragile, and it was all Brighton needed to pounce. Geremew Wolde won it (over Michael East no less), with Gnasher in bronze. We then dropped back to Kev Quinn and Bruce Barton [BB was still a near ever-present in *Charlie's Runners* nearly a quarter of a Century later]. On the subject of durability though, how about Chris Chataway returning to the scene of his win from a half-century earlier and still taking care of 17 runners?

No fewer than four 4th place finishes followed in the next five years which was a mite frustrating and we were generally that ace in the pack short of much better; then three quiet years followed before a very good third in 2008, where we tied with Epsom but closed in before them. Phil had a glorified training run for the comfortable win and old faves Willis, Trees and Byansi followed in.

RESULTS 1999-2010

1999	2	1 G Wolde; 3 K Nash; 18 K Quinn; 24 B Barton
2000	4	7 J Wolf; 15 W Lynch; 25 R Harding; 36 J Curtat
2001	4	1 S Kennefick; 7 J Blackledge; 16 A Jones; 45 W Lynch
2002	4	2 P Buckley; 5 R Alsop; 6 W Cockerell; 62 D Anderson
2003	-	3 R Alsop
2004	4	15 T Ellacott; 17 R Alsop; 22 J Wolf; 30 B Barton
2005	14	32 W Lynch; 33 M Whiting; 46 F Ward; 144 L Rehn
2006	9	5 M Byansi; 20 W Cockerell; 40 M Humphrey; 110 H Corbett
2007	-	11 K Hegvold; 52 F Ward; 108 D Anderson
2008	3	1 P Wicks; 10 P Willis; 25 M Trees; 26 M Byansi
2009	-	158 D Anderson
2010	5	10 C Sweeney; 17 W Cockerell; 19 L Eguia; 48 P Bogues

Electric Decade

There was more good bronze in 2011 as Wardy (3rd), was trailed by myself, Morten Holm and Lander Eguia in another very hard fought race. More quietness followed, but I found the race really alluring with my TM hat on in 2014. Come on, surely we can throw four bods at this baby. It began an outstanding streak of performances where for five years we medalled with terrific teams. I wanted to score in 2014, but the lads were having none of it. A victim of my own success perhaps, as recent recruitment had found us enjoying the skills of the great natural talent that was Gus Upton, the self-made workhorse of Andrius Jaksevicius, and the charming Taras Telkovsky. Up front, Paskar was on riotous form and I believe this was the famous occasion when he uttered the immortal line on email to the gang: "the lion is hungry and will feast on the deer meat!"

To have Nick Bundle not scoring in 24th seemed almost wasteful, but to show how strong this team was, Nick would go on to score in the Southern in January, for a set of team silvers. Alas here, the outstanding Tonbridge pipped us by 8pts.

We ventured to Polesden Lacey in 2015 which is an amazing venue for cross-country running, and some real initiation from the SOT to unearth such a gem. Indeed, my advice to the governing bodies who struggle to find us venues is often this: go private and get the heck away from the councils and the red tape.

We had Wicksy leading our lines who in turned was stunned to get assaulted by a relative unknown from Kent called Alex Yee. 'Too good,' Phil muttered at the end about the young tearaway who'd score Olympic gold six years hence. Kent were phenomenal with four in 8, but we did really well to see off evergreen Tonbridge by just 3 pips; with Andy a strong 7th, Alex Miller having a terrific run – what an understated signing he was from the Datchet Dashers – and still basking in the glow of that Southern silver ten months earlier. And to see us home was the oaklike Roy Maddams, with thighs like Australian gumtrees, that saw him clear of the close attention of Matt Taylor.

So, two hard fought silvers and we were back at Polesden again the next year, with yet another super team. I'd taken "early retirement" from the sport, but after 6 weeks or so realised that this is a life sentence and was re-lacing the spikes by Christmas. As Dan Wallis pointed out to me: "my lay-offs are longer than that!". This time Wicksy got that gold he was after, but Andrius, with marvellous spirit, was a right pest all day, to keep Phil very honest.

How incredible for such a self-made grinder to push 'the ledg' so close. But that's what makes running so great. Put in the work and amazing things are possible. Surely with a one-two the title would be ours, but who to settle the account? Well it was the gifted Ed Auden who grabbed 7th and then we enjoyed an outstanding 'breakthrough' run from Arne Dumez, who was perhaps deemed too young and 'wet behind the ears' to flourish on such a cruel and unusual course. But AD, surrounded by purist cross-country experts like Alan Barnes and Ollie Garrod held firm for 13th and Nick Bundle again had to give the nod and say "too good."

Both Kent and Aldershot was hot and ready on this day, but Belgrave carried the race by a whopping 30 points – an outstanding performance.

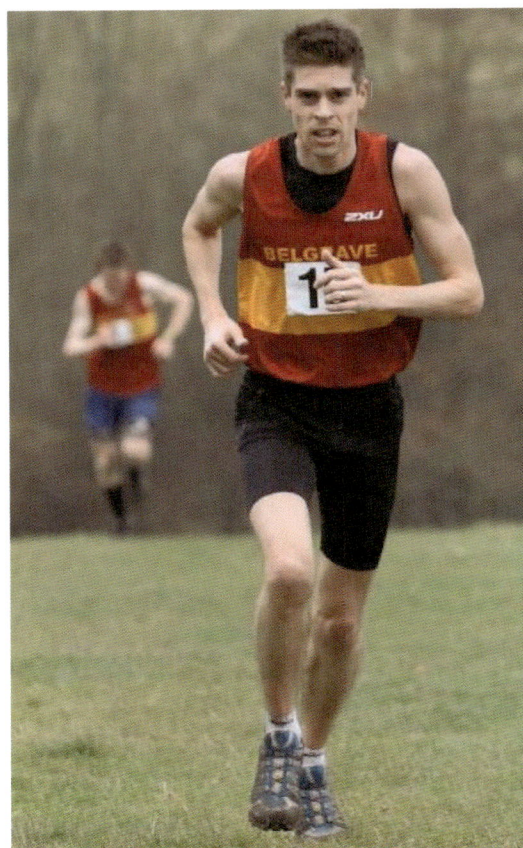

The late climb at Polesden Lacey is in the words of John Arlott, "a freaker". It takes a lot to get Phil to furrow his brow. Photo by 'Papawicks'

We were absolutely bang on form for this race now, and we yet again found four good men, with plenty of back up, in 2017, this time at glorious Beckenham Park Place.

Numerous times the bridesmaid to score, but goodness didn't Nick Bundle get it right at the 2015 Southern. SW

Team Gold for ever reliable Ed Auden. SW

What a run from a young and rising star in Arne. One felt that the elder statesmen just behind would have had too much, but not so. SW

Up front, Paskar had one of those runs that singles him out as one of the greatest Belgrave 'entertainers' of all time; with certainly one of the finest kicks. PO's racing brain was so pragmatic, measured and assured, and as he aged, more than ever, he used it. The lion understood intrinsically, it's not HOW you win but IF. Many runners would harbour frustration toward him over the years for his limpet-like, leave-it-late tendencies, but that of course is the secret to great racing. A close friend of mine, the American Jack Fultz, wasn't in possession of the outstanding gifts of a Frank Shorter or a Bill Rodgers, but goodness did he have his head screwed on. At the 1976 Boston with the mercury topping 90, Jack hunkered in 12th at the half. And the result? A win! At one of the world's great marathons. Two years later Jack ran the race of his life for 4th in 2:11 and as he overtook the more talented – but hot-headed Randy Thomas – the word "chickenshit" was uttered as Jack came by. Thomas despised Fultz's wait-and-see strategy of not going bravely with the leaders, but this is a results business, and Fultz understood where the buck stopped.

Ever obdurate, ever ready Royston Maddams, a score and multiple key back-up runs at the SOT team. SW

So it was that Paskar leached off Chris Greenwood and Jordan Weaver all day long. Many times they tried to surge away from the old warhorse, who had attended his first Major Championships [the '98 Commonwealths], 19 years earlier. But PO is as stubborn as they come, and it always helps when you know that if you hang in there, you'll probably win. And that's how it transpired, with PO stealing valuable yards inside the last 400 for the 1 second victory. AJ kept his marvellous sequence in this one going for 5th, whilst Nick Buckle found a terrific 9th and the in-form Andy Fyfe got 15th. And fifth scorer? You guessed it – Nick Bundle. Our team score was an eye-watering 29 points, pick the bones out of that. Well, it was enough to crush Tonbridge, but Kent said "hold my beer' for 23. Maddening! But we couldn't have done any more.

In 2018 we started with yet another incredible one-two gut punch of 1-3 for Phil and Andy J. This meant AJ's five year canvas for the race was an imperious 18, 7, 2, 5 & 3. Amazing stuff, and we could sit back and enjoy what would surely be another set of medals, but what colour?

Well, our boys had a different look and feel to them, and the wait for bods was longer than comfortable. Finally, the ever dependable Arne popped up, and the perhaps unlikely, but always elegant Ross Finlay settled our account, with Ben Hurley scrapping at his heels. Kent were just 4 points away in silver, but Guildford proved what a good system they have up there, with just 33pts for the win. Congrats to the boys in green.

Down to a workmanlike 5th in 2019 although technically 3rd as Kent put three teams ahead of us. But all credit to Callum (8th), PO, Ben H and Will Johnson for getting stuck in. Always nice to welcome unlikely championship scorers into the fold, and both Ben and Will train bloody hard.

Post Covid, Wicksy was back but pulled a calf escaping the advances of an amorous hound, and otherwise it was just Ben, with the TMs getting their Surrey league and post xmas blinkers on. They'll tell you that wrapping the squad in cotton wool isn't a bad idea for the lesser races as evidenced by Phil's tough day here. Still, it had been a superb decade or so at this charming and under the radar race, which gave us many enjoyable days and a crucial taste of the big time to many developing athletes.

Andrius Jaksevicius had a remarkable sequence of results at this race - read them and purr. SW

RESULTS 2011-2021

2011	3	3 R Ward; 10 W Cockerell; 16 M Holm; 23 L Eguia
2012	12	31 C Scott; 53 R Norville; 64 T Weeks; 79 M Foord
2013	5	1 P Owor; 26 R Maddams; 28 W Cockerell; 29 J Browne
2014	2	1 P Owor; 11 T Telkovsky; 16 G Upton; 18 A Jaksevicius
2015	2	2 P Wicks; 7 A Jaksevicius; 14 A Miller; 26 R Maddams
2016	1	1 P Wicks; 2 A Jaksevicius; 7 E Auden; 14 A Dumez
2017	2	1 P Owor; 5 A Jaksevicius; 9 N Buckle; 15 A Fyfe
2018	3	1 P Wicks; 3 A Jaksevicius; 20 A Dumez; 30 R Finlay
2019	5	8 C Stewart; 12 P Owor; 46 B Hurley; 51 W Johnson
2021	-	4 P Wicks; 29 B Hurley

SOUTH OF THE THAMES CHAMPIONSHIPS - MEN

An old world charm since 1893

1897

A tight corner.

The leaders tackle a barrier during the South of the Thames Cross Country Association's Championship at Oakley Park, Bromley Common.

Published in The Illustrated Sporting And Dramatic News, 13 February 1897.
© British Library.

Source ARMead www.belgraveharriers.info

It is undeniable that there's an offbeat, nostalgic charm about the SOTs and the race will always have a special place in my heart, and it's worth retelling why here, albeit a tale not strictly in this book's remit.

The 100th running of the race was in February 1999 and I had no idea of what I was going to when I set off on the fiddly journey from Shepherd's Bush to Sparrow's Den by rail. Alan's fixture card from the previous autumn, my first season with the club, confused me in parts, as I didn't really understand what several of the races were about – and this was a case in point. A bit of a funny title for starters.

Anyway, I arrived at the partly benign yet quietly ferocious course in heavy marathon build-up and not, it must be said, particularly 'in the mood.' Maybe I was 50th after two of the three laps. But I then became aware of our supporters, who were multifold, urging us on frantically. Apparently the race was close… I was some way off the scoring 6, but someone, somewhere lit a fuse under me and I joined in the action. 50th became 40th and I was acutely aware that it was the dark Blackheath shirts who needed to be zapped. But then a minor 'Groundhog Day' nightmare transpired. Every time I took out a Blackheath man another popped up in his place. It was like some ghoulish game of *whack-a-mole*. And the harder I ran, the more the supporters yelled at me that I needed to work harder, much harder. It later transpired that our most vociferous supporter [Bill Lucas] had first scored for the club in 1936!

Some Bels started to give way to me too, and then a spectator hollered, "you're scoring! Keep going!" I was transfixed by the euphoric, heady atmosphere now and dispatched our captain in the last mile, Gerry Adams, who was having none of it, and zoomed back past on the sharp descent to the finish. Here's the climax of Alan's report [right]:

So, a slightly lucky win, but what a fantastic day. Everything about it had been brilliant and as I examined the pretty gold medal on the train home, I thought, 'I could get used to this.' In some ways I think the Bels never looked back from that day, and we never really stopped winning again for the next dozen years.

2000 Hat-trick

In 2000 we won again, in another outstanding race, all the more admirable due to old-fashioned barring clauses which meant that team winners got banned for life. [1998 was termed the St. Valentine's Day Massacre for a team one gets together once in a generation, with a top 3 in the race of Tadesse, Staines & Estall. Smoooooth.]

The 2000 team was Dinku, Herrington, McHarg, Stewart, Nash and Quinn and defeated Brighton by just 6 points.

Much more magic 2004-2009

The final circuit saw Will Cockerell come charging through, displacing Saul Armanini as sixth man and all but getting the best of Phil Carstairs as well. Both were breathing down the neck of Captain 'Gerry' Adams who in turn had his sights on Roger. Paul Coughlan's recent heavy mileage left him unable to jump the bunch ahead of him which included several black vests of the home club. Meanwhile, towards the front Najibe had been caught by Thames's Oxborough and then by Dover of Herne Hill, but he was hanging on grimly to his 4th place.

A good crowd of Belgrave spectators including former Team Managers Bill Lucas and Gordon Biscoe were desperately urging on their men but it was going to have to be left to the man who currently does the pencil and paper work to tot up the numbers on the discs. While Team Manager Alan Mead came up with a Belgrave score of 95, John Jeffery was looking over the shoulder Blackheath's John Baldwin — and then came scuttling back with, "They've got 103." The Portsmouth man was bemoaning the fact that one of his forward placed runners had dropped out of the race with stitch, and they would have won it otherwise. News hound Martin Duff picked up on this in his *AW* report — but isn't having sound wind and fitness all part of the race?

We really were all tapped out now with 18 runners unavailable for 2001-2003, but then the barring clause was scrapped and another super race ensued in 2004.

This time messrs Watson, Hegvold, Cockerell, Ellacott, Lyne & Trees packed in 23 to see off Kent 80-97. A silver next term was followed by an almighty shellacking in 2006 with a pretty scary team of Wicks, Anderson [1st & 2nd], Trees, Willis, Kimaiyo and Bodin. That was 75-144 over Herne Hill in silver. Here are Dave, Pete Willis, Mike Trees and Phil at the start:

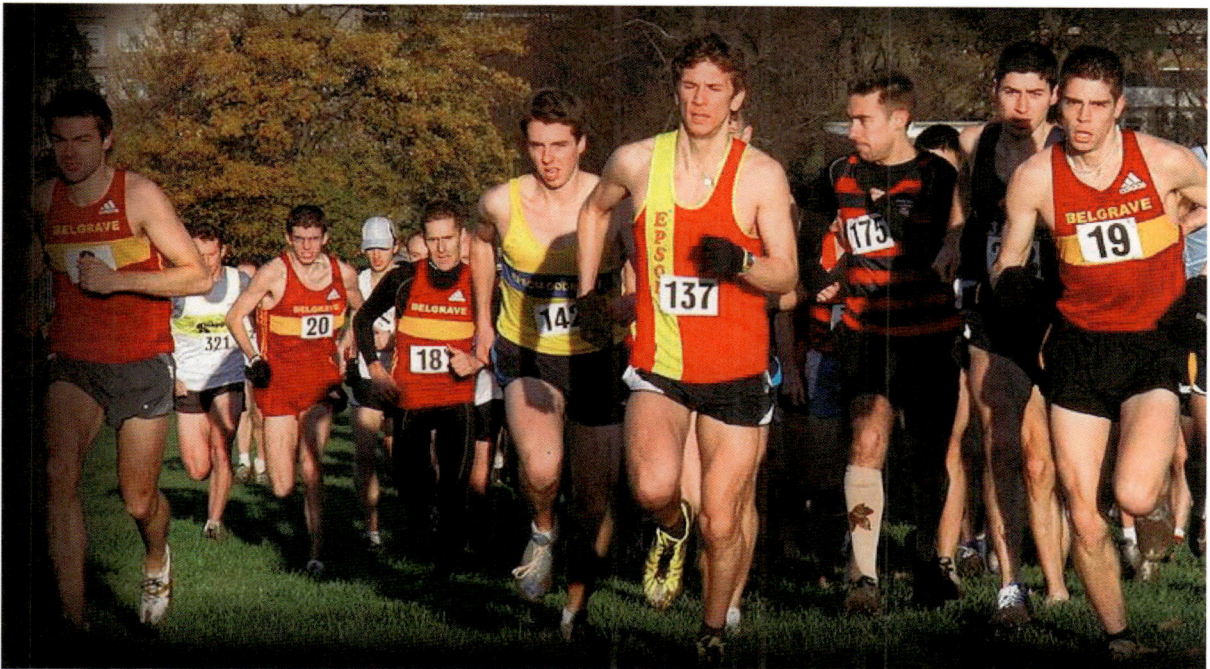

And some other non Bels luminaries include: Nic Gould [cap], the great James McMullan in his Oddball days, Will Clark 137, Alan Barnes & ever ready James Connor of Kent

Down to 2nd in '07 before two more superb wins in 2008 and 2009. First we were led out by a startling trio of Dessaix-Chin, Kelly and Speaight – pick the bones out of that! With the back up from Cockerell, Willis and Byansi, to edge Herne Hill by a dozen points; and then a marvellous duel with Kent in 2009. Just nine points separated Kelly [1st], Owor, Cockerell, Fairbourn, Byansi & Stannard from the Garden of England.

2010-2021

We've had to sing more for our supper since those heady days of seven wins in 12 years, but this has still been an enjoyable day out and a fine preparation race for the three big championships after Christmas. We would almost certainly have won in 2010, especially as ARM parachuted in Polly from Scotland, but heavy snow cancelled the race, and our dream team could not return for the rerun in March, where an unlikely set of lads almost picked up medals.

Wicksy won [again] in 2011, but 5th was our lot, and 5th again in 2012 after a great win by PO, who repeated his win in 2013 but the Bels slipped to 7th. Back to 5th in 2014, before back to back bronze medals behind awesome Tonbridge and Kent squads who were far too strong – no business to be done there! In 2016, a dominant Phil Wicks won yet again a decade on from 2006 with some really tremendous packing in both years from a good variety of hardy souls denoted below. 5th, 6th and 8th then followed, which is consistant, but all adds value to that tremendous streak of form from above.

An image to capture a squad and a club smoothly evolving in December 2016... L-R: Tom O'Beirne, Alex Miller, Nick Bundle, Phil Wicks, Steve Gardner, Alex Mills, Arne Dumez, Ben Moores, Alex Luce, Sophie Harris, Lizzie Goldie-Scott, Justine Lynch, Andrius Jaksevicius, Christina Pennock, Megan Bailey, Flic Cole, Gemma Farrell, Vicki Goodwin. Front: Sammi Amend, Becky O'Kill, Helen Auden [White]

Our new regime then let the SOT slide as they focussed on getting our mojo back in the Surrey league, which let's face it, did need a little TLC and I'm sure we'll make a return to the race in the future. It has been good to Belgrave and Belgrave has been good to it and we are currently custodians of its historic archives and Alan has done up a complete document of our history at the race, of which the 21st Century looks like this:

2000	1st	95 pts.	**Tilgate, Crawley** — 4 Y. Dinku, 8 C. Herrington, 10 R. McHarg, 16 A. Stewart, 24 K. Nash, 33 K. Quinn, 48 B. Barton, 49 M. Kazimierski, 57 R. Harding, 67 D. Ochse, 69 A, Jowett, 74 Don Anderson, 83 J. Mather, 102 A. Cowmeadow, 141 finished; 12 teams closed in.
2001	-	-	**Roehampton, Wimbledon Common** — 62 S. Zealey; 177 finished; 13 teams closed in.
2002	5th	172 pts.	**Wimbledon Common** — 2 M. Trees, 3 S. Kennefick, 24 L. Catley, 39 S. Nelson, 44 M. Kazimierski, 60 W. Lynch, 152 E. Assiedu; 162 finished; 13 teams closed in.
2003	-	-	**Farthing Downs, Coulsdon** — postponed race? No Belgrave runners; 110 finished; 7 teams closed in.
2004	1st	80 pts.	**Wimbledon Common** — 5 T. Watson, 7 K. Hegvold, 9 W. Cockerell, 15 T. Ellacott, 21 E. Lyne, 23 M. Trees, 67 M. Kazimierski, 81, T. O'Neill, 112, H. Corbett; 152 finished; 11 teams closed in.
2005	2nd	135 pts.	**Wimbledon Common** — 5 S. Omar, 15 W. Cockerell, 19 T. Ellacott, 23 M. Trees, 26 E. Lyne, 47 T. Hadfield, 63 S. Zealey, 70 M. Humphrey, 78 F. Ward, 84 T. Fordyce, 88 T. O'Neill, 95 S. Ryan, 133 M. Taylor (1), 140 J. Lynch, 168 L. Rehn; 188 finished; 15 teams closed in.
2006	1st	75 pts.	**Brockwell Park** — Colman Cup winners 519 pts. — 1 P. Wicks, 2 David Anderson, 13 M. Trees, 14 P. Willis, 21 J. Kimaiyo, 24 A. Bodin, 34 W. Cockerell, 50 J. Fairbourn, 64 T. Fordyce, 88 M. Humphrey, 103 R. Poulter, 105 H. Corbett, 113 C. Moynihan; 137 finished; 11 teams closed in.
2007	2nd	98 pts.	**Nork Park, Banstead** — 1 P. Wicks, 4 J. Kelly, 12 J. Fairbourn, 25 K. Hegvold, 27 M. Byansi, 29 T. Weeks, 65 S. Zealey, 80 C. Hobbs, 85 R. Merrick, 135 finished; 11 teams closed in.

2008 1st 76 pts. **Wimbledon Common** — Colman Cup winners 444 pts. — 1 R. Dessaix-Chin, 4 J. Kelly, 8 N. Speaight, 13 W. Cockerell, 14 P. Willis, 29 T. Elsey, 36 M. Byansi, 39 K. Hegvold, 52 A. Sentence, 58 B. Hurley, 63 R. Stannard, 77 T. Weeks, 79 M. Humphrey, 111 T. Hadfield, 173 finished; 15 teams closed in.

2009 1st 105 pts. **Wimbledon Common** — 1 J. Kelly, 2 P. Owor, 15 W. Cockerell, 16 J. Fairbourn, 29 M. Byansi, 42 R. Stannard, 55 A. Marek, 89 R. Norville, 119 T. Kingston; 152 finished; 14 teams closed in.

2010 - - **Farthing Downs, Coulsdon** — Race postponed to March 2011. 4 W. Cockerell, 31 W. Ireson, 33 E. Egelie, 39 A. Lang, 40 R. Harding; 52 finished; 3 teams closed in.

2011 5th 206 pts. **Roehampton, Wimbledon Common** — 1 P. Wicks, 11 R. Stannard, 24 W. Cockerell, 44 D. Mason, 45 L. Eguia, 81 B. Barton, 83 M. Byansi, 92 R. Norville, 99 P. Carstairs, 122 N. Dilley; 154 finished; 12 teams closed in.

2012 5th 196 pts. **Kingston Gate, Richmond Park** — 1 P. Owor, 19 W. Cockerell, 27 M. Trees, 38 K. Hegvold, 45 R. Maddams, 66 A. Luce, 67 M. Foord, 69 R. Norville; 138 finished; 14 teams closed in.

2013 7th 305 pts. **Wimbledon Common** — 1 P. Owor, 28 W. Cockerell, 35 R. Maddams, 67 K. Hegvold, 86 M. Young, 88 R. Norville, 90 F. Logan, 103 A. Luce; 189 finished; 22 teams closed in (including 'B' teams from here on).

2014 5th 166 pts. **Farthing Downs, Coulsdon** — 9 A. Jaksevicius, 12 T. Telkovsky, 24 N. Bundle, 29 M. Taylor (2), 31 E. Auden, 61 M. Welsh, 102 P. McDougall, 148 T. O'Neill; 208 finished; 23 teams closed in.

2015 3rd 117 pts. **Somerhill School, Tonbridge** — 5 A. Jaksevicius, 7 P. Owor, 16 A. Miller, 19 P. Lowe, 20 Z. Abery, 50 N. Smallwood, 63 W. Cockerell, 83 J. Goymour, 117 R. Norville; 177 finished; 19 teams closed in.

2016 3rd 125 pts. **Beckenham Place Park, Beckenham** — 1. P. Wicks, 6 A. Jaksevicius, 13 A. Miller, 18 N. Bundle, 34 A. Dumez, 53 T. O'Beirne, 64 S. Gardner, 65 A. Mills, 81 B. Moores, 111 A. Luce; 198 finished; 21 teams closed in.

2017 5th 196 pts. **Wellesley Woodlands, Aldershot** — 16 P. Owor, 17 N. Buckle, 22 A. Jaksevicius, 38 G. Lee, 43 A. Miller, 60 T. O'Beirne, 63 R. Finlay, 67 M. Trees, 70 P. McDougall; 159 finished; 18 teams closed in.

2018 6th 208 pts. **Beckenham Place Park, Beckenham** — 7 A. Jaksevicius, 14 P. Owor, 27 A. Dumez, 37 B. Courtney-Pinn; 46 R. Finlay, 77 O. Young, 87 R. Norville, 93 C. Warren, 97 P. McDougall, 135 J. Morris, 141 A. Luce; 223 finished; 19 teams closed in.

2019 8th 321 pts. **Lloyd Park, Croydon** — 16 P. Owor, 32 A. Cumine, 62 M. Edgar, 66 N. Buckle, 67 B. Hurley, 78 O. Young, 135 R. Norville, 151 J. Morris; 241 finished; 29 teams closed in.

Elsey in 2008 should read M. Byansi

SOUTH OF THE THAMES CHAMPIONSHIPS - WOMEN

Flagellation Devoured

The SOT committee, perhaps as part of the *Everyone's Invited/Me Too* Movement decided in the early part of the millennia to make the women's 12k race 6 to score. That's a big ask over the only race in the calendar when the women travel so far, which I concur I've questionned… But you know what? They've sort of got it right in that some teams *do* close in, and the Belles have made an exceptional go of things. Usually we'd only have one or two in the fray, and notably Chrissie Wellington of World Ironman fame won it for us in 2006.

After I took over as women's TM the challenge of getting so many of them out for so far led to some very funny email exchanges, but succeed I did, even though some chided me for cruel and unusual demands on a bitterly cold day in 2011. But marathoners Sammi Amend and Fee Maycock were happy as larks, unlike bemused 800m specialist Nellie Quispel next up. But the run served her a treat for the following month's amazing stuntwork at the Southerns. Next up the lesser sighted Kerri Renshaw who arrived minutes before the gun, and closing in the ever reliable Vicki Goodwin and purist race-walker Maureen Noel. What a deliciously unusual and gung-ho team to take a pleasing set of bronze, a tantalising single point behind the canny Saltires.

The following year, six more bally heroes! A masterful run by Tish Jones, just 7 seconds down on the win (by her fabled rival Ruth Clifton), and then Fee returned and 3rd scorer went to Mary Grace Spalton, who ran against all wisdom with a heavy cold. We knew MGS's drop-out would cost us dear, so hit upon the adorable plan of her soaking in a long, hot bubble bath before the race, hoping the fever would lift. "It didn't work," she wrote, "but coming anyway." What a run for 10th! Samantha McClary, Hester and Yankee Laura D'Albey saw us home. Another highly unpredictable team, but troopers all.

2013-2018   Goldrush

Right, time to up the ante on the precious metal stakes?! Oh you better believe it. 2013's dreamteam was amazing and clearly now we were one of the best squads in the country. Amend [2]! Wilkins [6]! Doyle [7]! Bish, Bash, Bosh. Throw in a bit of Mackenzie, Vail Smith & HBR [again] and we were all kit and kaboodled by the 28th lady, for a huge win over Tonbridge 80-155. One recalls Jojo Rhodes' dramatic report where a runaway horse joined the race. It is apocryphal that Sammi mounted it and rode the final lap to the finish.

A superb defence of the title came on the very long and demanding Coulsdon course in 2014. Mel Wilkins won a great duel with Lucy Reid of Tonbridge, and ZLD found 5th, going some 7 miles over preferred distance. Keri and ZVS returned from the previous year but then a tense wait to see if we could close in. Did you ever doubt them?! Celine Duraffourd and Vicki Goodwin kept their cool [there was no back-up], to see us home with 46 points to spare.

A hat-trick was not to be in 2015 but the medal streak continued with more bronze, before an absolutely magnificent team rocked up in 2016. Goodness, how this race captured the imagination of our girls. For an image of the team, consult the men's section. Yet again Samantha took a individual podium finish, and then Sophie Harris, Christina Pennock, Justine Lynch, Becky O'Kill and Lizzie Goldie-Scott handled Kent 81-98.

At Aldershot in 2017 our gold rush was narrowly broken in a vintage duel with Kent, losing by just 9 points. But Sophie Harris, 12 months on from the above, took a dominant win.

Lizzie G-S put together a hat-trick of telling runs at the SOT Champs

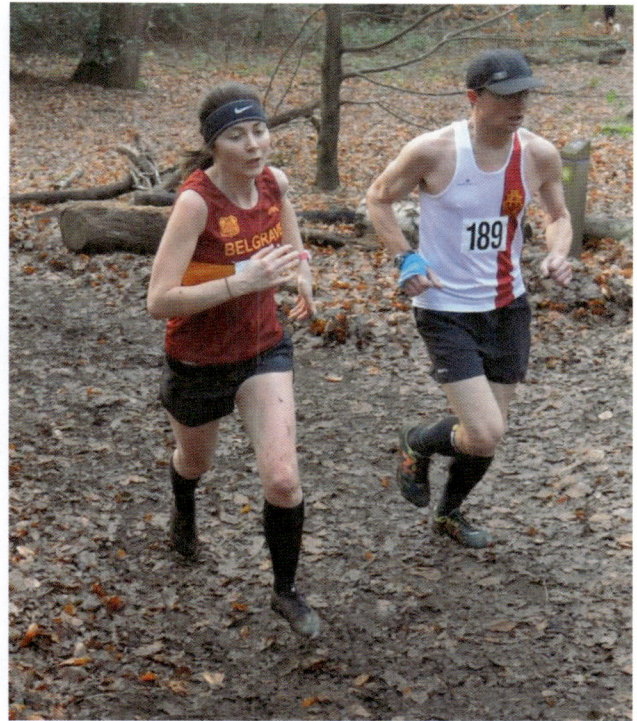

New face Mhairi Hall [14th] ended 2017s wild ride in Aldershot requiring medical aid for numerous ailments. Hypothermia and losing a fight with a bramble bush, to name two

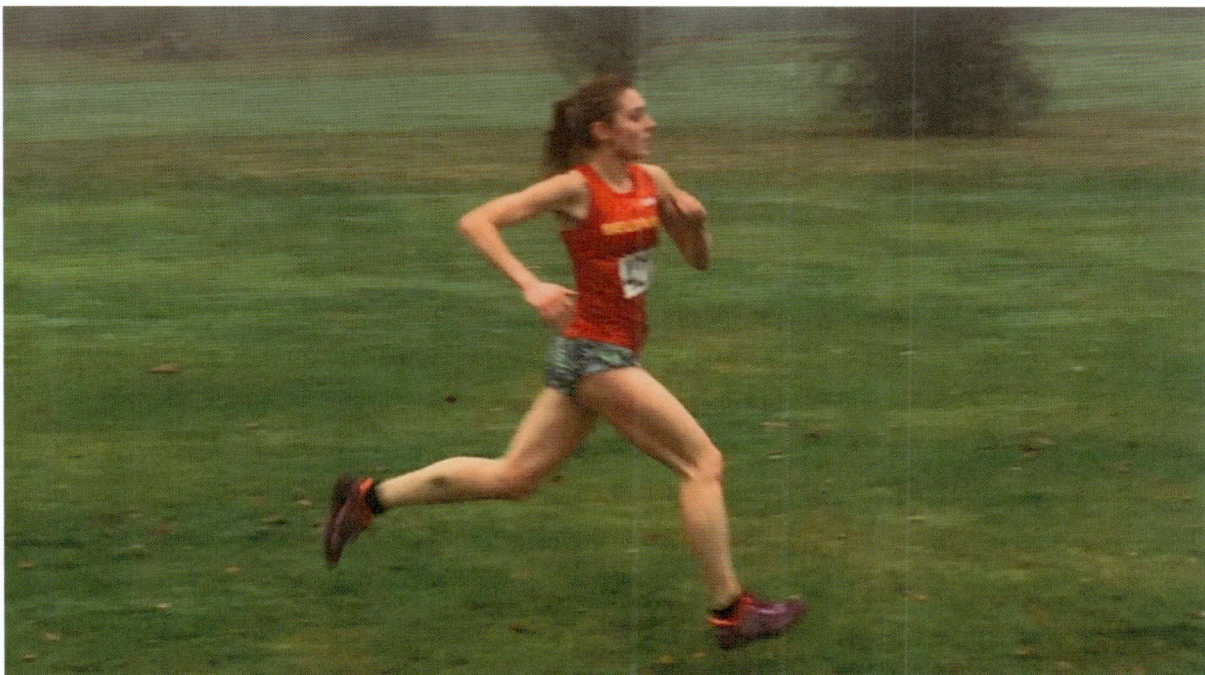

Blurry, but you get the picture. It was early days but we were seeing "something to work with" with Sophie Harris in 2016

But back to GOLD in 2018. Some superb packing by some new names in Georgie Fenn, Saron Heilesalase, old fave Amend, Mhairi Hall, Emma Howsham & Justine Lynch. Tremendous stuff, in a wretched storm, and an eight-year medal streak now with four golds.

Saron gave her absolute all in foul conditions in 2018, but now her "Knight McDougall" in shining armour, must carry her to the waiting carriage [van]. Jojo Rhodes and Sammi help prepare the patient, whilst Medusa [Chris Warren] would do more if not frozen into stone

A blob, a pandemic, and as you were

Occasionally of course everything just misses and the streak must end. Not that we were dreadful in 2019, just a little short of bullets. Camilla Barden, Mimi CL and Ellen VdV nobly flew the flag though. However, post Covid the Belles were monumentally back. All the signs were in the preceding 18 months that this race was going to be one to inflict mayhem given the incredible strength and depth of the squad.

Little did we ever imagine 6 in 12 though! That must be one of the finest returns in Belgrave history. Yes, there were "only" 84 finishers, but all the same… Kent could only find three of the top dozen, Dulwich two and Herne Hill the other. The wonderfully talented Rachel Brown took the win in a very solid 55th overall. Sammi was rock solid as ever in 3rd, newbie Jess Saunders a mere 30 yards back, ever reliable Nat Beadle in 9th, and evergreen Mimi 11th – her patience for two years earlier rewarded; and then Laurel Bray bravely hung in there for 52 minutes – more of a speedster that she is.

Laurel was presented with her medal at training around a month later and the look of delight on her face was a pleasure to see. I was able to regale her with the story of when I won a surprise gold at this one 23 years earlier and how I never really looked back with the thought: "I could get used to this!" I expressed the hope to Laurel she'd still be part of our affairs in the year 2045. With nerveless moxy, CD had gone into the race with no back-up. Dicey, but on this day – fine.

2004	-	-	**Wimbledon Common** — 4 M. Heaton, 17 R. Takayasu; 27 finished; 1 team closed in.
2005	-	-	**Wimbledon Common** — No Belgrave runners; 41 finished; 2 teams closed in.
2006	-	-	**Brockwell Park** — 1 C. Wellington; 4 M. Heaton; 20 finished; 1 team closed in.
2007	-	-	**Nork Park, Banstead** — No Belgrave runners; 42 finished; 2 teams closed in.
2008	-	-	**Wimbledon Common** — No Belgrave runners; 39 finished; 3 teams closed in.
2009	-	-	**Wimbledon Common** — No Belgrave runners; 37 finished; 3 teams closed in.
2010	-	-	**Farthing Downs, Coulsdon** — Race postponed to March 2011. No Belgrave runners; 27 finished; 1 team closed in.
2011	3rd	123 pts.	**Roehampton, Wimbledon Common** — 7 S. Amend, 10 F. Maycock, 12 N. Quispell, 24 K. Renshaw, 33 V. Goodwin, 37 M. Noel; 60 finished; 5 teams closed in.
2012	3rd	97 pts.	**Kingston Gate, Richmond Park** — 2 T. Jones, 8 F. Maycock, 10 M. G. Spalton, 12 S. McClary, 29 H. Barsham-Rolfe, 36 L. D'Albey, 45 H. Gathercole, 52 H. White; 66 finished; 6 teams closed in.
2013	1st	80 pts.	**Wimbledon Common** — 2 S. Amend, 6 M. Wilkins, 7 Z. Doyle, 15 K. Mackenzie, 22 Z. Smith, 28 H. Barsham-Rolfe, 31 A. Friday; 68 finished; 5 teams closed in.
2014	1st	92 pts.	**Farthing Downs, Coulsdon** — 1 M. Wilkins, 5 Z. Doyle, 10 K. Mackenzie, 11 Z. Smith, 30 C. Durraffourd, 35 V. Goodwin; 74 finished; 6 teams closed in.
2015	3rd	106 pts.	**Somerhill School, Tonbridge** — 3 S. Amend, 8 M. Wilkins, 11 Z. Vail-Smith, 16 F. Cole, 30 L. Goldie-Scott, 38 V. Goodwin, 41 M. Bailey; 65 finished; 6 teams closed in.
2016	1st	81 pts.	**Beckenham Place Park, Beckenham** — 3 S. Amend, 8 S. Harris, 15 C. Pennock, 16 J. Lynch, 18 R. Prince, 21 L. Goldie-Scott, 23 G. Farrell, 28 H. White, 34 F. Cole, 65 M. Bailey; 89 finished; 8 teams closed in.
2017	2nd	123 pts.	**Wellesley Woodlands, Aldershot** — 1 S. Harris, 6 S. Amend, 14 M. Hall, 16 C. Pennock, 39 L. Goldie-Scott, 47 M. Bailey; 69 finished; 6 teams closed in.
2018	1st	68 pts.	**Beckenham Place Park, Beckenham** — 4 G. Fenn, 5 S. Haileselase, 9 S. Amend, gst R. Brown, 12 M. Hall, 13 E. Howsham, 25 J. Lynch, 64 E. van der Velden; 109 finished; 10 teams closed in.
2019	-	-	**Lloyd Park, Croydon** — 18 C. Barden, 34 M. Corden-Lloyd, 57 E. van der Velden; 108 finished; 11 teams closed in.
2020			No race due to coronavirus pandemic.
2021	1st	40 pts.	**Beckenham Place Park, Beckenham** — 1 R. Brown, 3 S. Amend, 4 J. Saunders, 9 N. Beadle, 11 M. Carden-Lloyd, 12 L. Bray; 84 finished; 7 teams closed in.

2004's Takayasu is now Trees; 2011 should read Quispel; 2021 should read Corden

THE WORLD OF MANAGEMENT

Where a team starts and finishes - and lessons learned from a decade in Team management

Plus: A Day in the Life essay by <u>Alan R Mead</u>

Author's note: this chapter is a strictly personal take on the 16 years I spent in club administration and around a decade in management. They are my views alone and I absolutely concur there are certainly plenty of ways to skin a cat. Throughout the pages of this book I've emitted firm views on relay strategies, selection and running orders, because to be sure they're complex things; and of course having served in the Belgrave committee for so long, and seen so much incredible success, I picked up a thing or two along the way. So what follows isn't Gospel, merely personal opinion.

There is no better example in team management of the difference the gaffer makes than Sir Alex Ferguson. It was clear by the 1989-1990 season that Ferguson had 'a bit about him', and a pal and I tried everything to secure tickets for the rematch of the 1990 FA Cup final against Crystal Palace. I didn't even support Man U, and technically should have been supporting Palace as a Londoner, but such was the allure that Man U were starting to build, one couldn't help getting sucked in. And it was all down to Fergie. Then the assaults on the league title started. Slowly at first, getting pipped by Leeds in '92, but once they started, they barely stopped – for a generation. Quite incredible. And since 2013, well we know what happened – it has been largely dreadful, as manager after manager has got a bloody nose. How can it be so hard, with a stadium and a budget like that? I attended the game at Old Trafford vs Liverpool in November of 2021 and it was like watching a spectacular car wreck and the Red Devils were carved to pieces and soon found themselves 0-5 down. Oh how the mighty have fallen.

The same holds for managing a top Road and Country club. Yes, there are different disciplines required, but right at the very top is rallying the troops and convincing them to spend their Saturday afternoons with you. There are an absurd number of clubs in the country – around 1,850, which really isn't necessary. Far better to have 1,000 pretty good ones than a vast majority of which can't hope to succeed on any objective level. But splinters occur and people fall-out, and a spirited brainwave is had and another club pops up. How many are there in Clapham alone now?! Goodness I've lost count. And in [Greater] London maybe over 40? Maybe 60! Surrey has at least 55.

All this though makes it harder to have a really good club due to the amount of competition around. However, Belgrave can hold its head high that through good times and bad, through two World wars and three different Centuries we've been there or thereabouts for a majority of that period. The 1930s-1950s saw the exceptional leadership qualities in Bert Footer and Tom Carter and their fearless leader Ernie Duffett, Road and Country secretary for some quarter of a Century between 1928-1953; thereafter "Bomber Bill Lucas" took over for another great period between around 1953-1972. WEL just had to make a one-sided telephone call to an athlete and he'd largely done his bit:

"Hello?"

"Surrey Cross-country League. Saturday, November 12th, Farthing Downs, 3pm."

"I'm sorry, who is this?"

But the line was already dead. Such an approach worked back then – hey, we won the league seven years in a row, but nowadays, the athletes require more gentle persuasion. It's a whole new world. There's huge competition from road races, big half and full marathons, parkrun and a sharp reduction in how much athletes are willing to race. And yes, athletes are somewhat more 'precious'. Runners nowadays turn down the National cross if they have a Half the following weekend. Why?! Because they may still be fatigued. But of course, the National eight days out from a half is nigh on the perfect prep. Then I'd also get the excuse that due to a Half the weekend before the National that the athlete would be fatigued, so no National.

Athletes have even turned down races with a mere 10k to come eight days after a relay. It's nigh on impossible to rationalise with as there's no doubt they'll bash out a hard session instead of the race, and a hard session (ca. 50 minutes) can batter the body a lot more than a relay leg.

It's like you're hemmed on either side… But my view is, ok, so you're fatigued, it may cost you 40 points but 280th at the National instead of 240th is still hugely useful, and perhaps worth 450 points to the club – something that will be in the club's history books forever. Compare this to Thames' Ben Reynolds before the brutal National cross of 2022. As an M55 he had the final of the European Masters 3k indoors in Portugal on the Thursday 48 hours before, which he described as "less than ideal'; but he still placed an immaculate 430th at the National, having medalled in Braga.

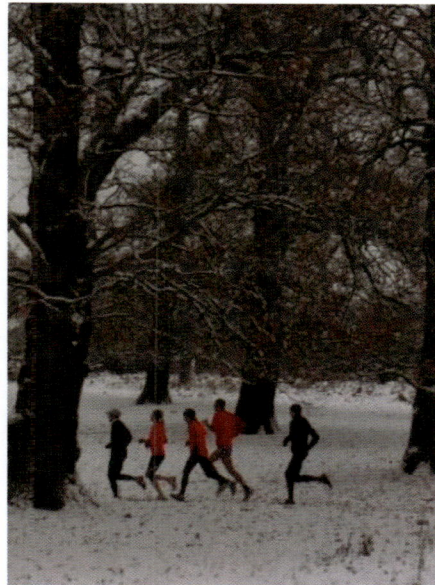

A great image from Richard Xerri which shows how the dovetail between the individual and club can been seamless. All these are marathoners with great focus on their personal running, hence a gnarly 18-20 miler in these conditions. John McFarlane [left], and Huw Lobb [centre] were Team GB for the marathon and Lucy Macalister a big City marathon winner at Houston. The author had a top 36 at London and Dave Alcock, right, a top 33 at Amsterdam. But did this affect their club careers? No; the two went hand in hand. Lobb was a juggernaut for Bedford which included two Southern Cross wins, McFarlane was prolific for Thames, and Lucy has the most Surrey League wins of all time. RX

A creeping, insidious problem

In some ways it really is all in the mind: if one looks for perfect racing conditions, one can wait an awful long time.

The obvious solution of using club races as training runs and tempo efforts is often lost on today's crowd, when in the past the likes of our own Gary Staines would belt out a Surrey league when still fatigued from the Tokyo '91 World Champs. Sorry, but when you have Gary setting an example like that, some excuses do become a little bit hard to stomach. Two of our biggest ever guns, John Bicourt and Alan Black, hammered out a whopping 67 Surrey League scores for us, and made no secret they'd do them more as sessions or tempo runs. Was it a problem for the team or manager? Course not. Just a case of scratching each other's backs. Bicourt's priorities were the '72 and '76 Olympics, but between the 1960's up until the '90s he scored when he could, which was a lot: our 5th highest league points scorer.

This problem is creeping into sport everywhere. The West Indies cricket board don't have the first clue who they can pick for the upcoming World Cup because the players won't commit. Playing for them used to be everything, now it's all seen as a bit "*meh*". And look at the Ryder Cup – in danger of becoming simply an exhibition match, and could the golf Majors be following suit? 170 years of golfing history are in grave peril due to the Saudi financed LIV tour.

Tough old trade then

In short, team management can be a pretty unforgiving trade, and a rough estimate these days is that there's around a 40% chance that any given athlete will be able to do any given race. Back in the day – call it 1965 – that attendance figure was more like a 75% strike rate. It's a huge decline, but club athletics has changed. It's still a marvellous and exciting world to be in though. But the art of *Getting the Buggers Out*, the title of the great Newhan boss Bob Smith's memoir, is never more relevant.

After Bill Lucas stood down in the early 1970s, Belgrave began a slow, somewhat tortuous decline than lasted nearly a quarter of a Century. By around 1995 it was written that our roots as a Harriers club had been all but forgotten. As noted elsewhere, in an editorial by Alan, there were: "No easy answers". But my goodness, were answers found! Mainly by the scribe of those words.

WVLCs management journey 2009-2019

The purpose of this book is to entertain and inform, and it would be remiss of me not to pass on what I learned about management, firstly through the halcyon days in those great squads of 1999-2013, and then my own management journey of some ten seasons. In ARM I did of course have the perfect mentor. Here then are some key markers to get the most out of managers:

Back Me or Sack Me

The committee must be *right behind* the TM, there is no other way. With the committee's backing, the tailwind is huge, and for Alan's reign the committee made the collective [and of course correct] decision to: "back this guy." Alan had worked his socks off for the club since 1958, and now 37 years on was offering to have a go at the Road and Country, something of a poisoned chalice since that last League win of '72. It was trusted implicitly that he had the best intentions for the club in his heart; and that he would never dream of defrauding us, or spending frivolously.

An early foray into caretaker management at the 2007 Surrey relay. We won, but a millimetre or so of fingernail was removed. RX

Defrauding a club is very difficult to pull off anyway, as expenses are granted upon proof of funds spent. Ie, £390 for entry into the National cross? Well – the National publish the entered runners far in advance. If there aren't 39 runners listed, there will be blood, and quite right too. The high expense that came with ARM squads for travel, hotel and perhaps a club meal at "The Big Ones" was deemed a good investment: it attracted sponsorship, the warm feedback of a benevolent patron, and some extremely generous bequests. After all, members are <u>far more likely</u> to bequest to the club if they see Belgrave fighting hard at the sharp end, and keeping the Claret and Gold flag flying high, and preserving Belgrave as a renowned force both at home and indeed overseas, where we enjoy great interest as well. In short, if the club is flourishing on the field of play, it's remarkable how everything else slots into place – including social. People are much more likely to wish to imbibe in the *amber necter* after a great day's competition, than a limp, insipid one.

Stormy Starts

I came into both of my management roles for the women, then the men, by less than ideal routes. For over half a dozen years Catherine Eastham had done a superb job with the Belles, but by 2008 was running out of steam. To be sure, this happens in what can be an onerous role. I raised the idea of taking the weight of the road section off her – around five major relays and of course the

Marathon where we had the potential to excel, and the odd piece of shrapnel – a National 10k or half-marathon etc. Memory does not relate to whether this was contentious at the time, but it was clear I'd taken on a tricky venture, with 19 no's and a maybe for my first race in charge, the 2009 Southern 4 stage. It may be that CE didn't like losing the road section, but the next two cross-country seasons were rather modest and her reign ended with Surrey league relegation and only around three regulars. It was a dark day on the Common and I did wonder if the Belles could anticipate any sort of future. In retrospect, Catherine was probably *too* loyal to the cause. Her life had gone in another direction, but she hated to let her beloved Belles down. But of course a TM whose heart is no longer in it is far more dangerous in the long run than having no-one at all, as the severity of the problem is camouflaged.

It did all mean though that I could start largely from scratch and things took off the very next month with bronze at the inaugural Southern XC relay and then a terrific 4th at the SEAA 6 stage. So not quite dead after all! I recall Vicky Filsell of Thames coming up to me at Milton Keynes and asking, "Hey! What have you done to your women?"

The journey over the next few years was a real thrill, even though it badly coincided with the last embers of my trying to be a decent runner. I needed all the help I could get as I was turning 40, but instead I was rocking up to the men's races dehydrated, distracted, unfed and sometimes with under 5 minutes to pin on my number and lace on the spikes. Madness. I recall anchoring a strong men's team at the 2011 National 6 stage and Alan saying: "there's only one person I'm really worried about today…" "Who?" I asked confused, as the tribe seemed merry. "You," he replied, not liking the way his anchor had been running around like Coco the Clown on acid for two hours organising the women.

Now for the Men!

When I came in to manage the men in the summer of 2014, the *brouhaha*, if I may invoke a little… *French*?, about the Lozano scandal was still hot off the press and there were some very upset people, a few of whom were on committee. I was also deemed with suspicion from the old guard as too young, and by the young guard as too old. So in some ways at the age of 40 I found myself with few friends. The women's squad was flying though and no-one else had come forward to take over from Alan *as far as I could make out*. But my error in hindsight was not waiting to be asked. In short, I panicked that my beloved team, that I'd fought and sacrificed so much for the past 16 years, were leaderless for a few months, and it was my eventual undoing. The reason I wasn't asked is that the committee probably didn't deem me to be the right fit, but were unsure who was. I never did learn of another contender, and no-one challenged me for the role.

I expect too, as I was still competing at a fairly high level, and doing so nicely with the Belles, it was felt prudent to leave me unmolested. I think if these concerns had been relayed to me, with a nice note like: "you will be perfect – *one day*!" we would all have side-stepped trouble down the road. But I had found managing the Belles fairly straightforward, and they were only going to get better. They had just won the Surrey league and placed 2nd at the Southern Cross and 4th at the National. How hard could this be?

Frantic Times

I was about to find out. *Very*. And of course what happened was the worst of both worlds: as I frantically tried to stabilize the men into a new era [I got a miserable five yesses for the first Surrey League], the Belles noticed that I wasn't quite so loquacious and loving in my dispatches and they in turn started to cool. Not a lot. But a little is all it takes for the House of Cards to collapse. Not that I didn't have my moments managing both squads: in January of 2015 I guided both the Bels and Belles to Silver at the Southern Cross on the same afternoon. It was a wonderful day, and the first medal for the men there since 1971. However, I didn't know it at the time, but the knives were sharpening, and I would never quite be the same manager again.

Peaks and Troughs

More success followed with the men securing a surprise but well constructed silver at the Southern six stage in September 2015, but my depreciation took hold and peaked in the winter of 2015-16 when I had to suddenly stand down from the Belles because I realized both squads were creaking badly. The Belles were not even finding five runners in the league – and they had won it the last two years. It was a scarily sudden decline. But I was still too late. Although the salvage mission to get the men back on an even keel nearly worked, we were relegated from the Surrely league, scoring identical points as Clapham but going down on goal difference. A dreadful day, yes, but hardly the end of the world, as some opined in saloons and funeral get togethers. It was fed back to me that we were "cooked, finished & kaput". Ahh, what nonsense – indeed we'd be back in the top 8 of the National 12 stage the following year.

Money matters

The confrontations I faced with committee were varied and complex but some can be fixed in a heartbeat, and one was finance and budget.

Quite simply: give the TM a sober and pragmatic budget and let them spend it. I descended into all sorts of *Kafkaesque* nightmares where the financiers were trying to spend the TMs money for him. But the moment finance are dictating the specific and complex spends on squads, it is *they* that become the managers. Enormous confusion arises over who is driving the chariot. I always used to come in under budget and spend a lot of my own money each season on the squad myself. But the rows were terrible.

One-Trick Ponies

The membership secretary too must also dovetail amicably with the team managers, because there will always be late-comers, late-payers, and yes, one-trick ponies. My own daughter got slung out the club the other day for shortfall of subs, which she found mildly brutal. Of course I'll take care of it, but starting from scratch when the club know all about her, will be a surreal piece of admin. Better to deal with cases like her with a tranquiliser dart not a gallows.

The Kate Rennie saga was a key early marker in my time at the helm: a fine, talented runner, who would surely help us win the National Vets relay. But without her, no team, due to the pricey losses of Sammi and Fee Maycock. She was Zoe Doyle's training partner and a busy mother of three who lived a ways away. To ask her to ship us £65 for subs, reg and vest just to do what may only be a single race we were desperate for her to do, made no sense. But it was clearly unthinkable that for the sake of that 65 quid we would sacrifice the National, which would get a page write-up in AW, with a big photo and loads of social media exposure. But the committee were unmoved: she cannot run. Could she borrow a sweaty vest off a teammate? "Yes." right, so down to 50 quid to find. Concerns were raised about whether she was a *real* Belgravian.

What does it MEAN to be a Belgravian?

When and how are you a Belgravian? You are a Belgravian – **for life** – if you pull on the vest in competition. It is that simple. If you're trekking in Nepal and you spot someone up ahead in a Belgrave vest, do you not offer them a hearty greeting? Of course you do. Do you ask if they've paid their subs? Of course not. As Alan wrote in his President's notes: "We are family."

The notion of subs is important, yes, but only to keep the books stable. In recent times the club got a big Covid grant, we have a wonderful Victorian clubhouse in Wimbledon village, a membership on the rise [with heavily appreciating subs], and still receive extremely generous bequests. Does all this mean that one day we couldn't fiscally fail? Absolutely not, but before that occurs, we have the mother of all buffers. Some of our finance chat from the 1960s is quite unthinkable today... Stuff like: "£271 in the bank, a £79 deficit for the year, going broke in three and a half years." Suffice it to say, we've come on a bit.

The Rennie affair was about treating matters such as this on an <u>individual, bespoke basis</u>. Sometimes the odd "one-trick pony" will come along. Six long years after his time with us, Marty Dent returned to these shores to do the elite London Marathon. Alan pounced for the 12 Stage... it was a tad brutal on me as I'd put in a full season and was in good shape and was knocked out the side, but it was fair enough. We knew Marty well and had the link to him from years gone by.

Without this outlet and breathing space a vital resource is closed off to amateur sports clubs the world over. How many "one-trickers" have Belgrave had down the years? Perhaps around a 1,000, and we've had 158 in the Surrey league alone... and that's just to score. Treble it for those that didn't. I have been a one-trick pony for at least a dozen cricket clubs up and down the land. I turned up to watch the elite, closed shop John Paul Getty XI in 1993 but they were one short. The booming voice of BBC commentator Brian Johnston called out: "Cockers, CMJ's got a spare pair of whites, you're playing." Whew... we had five Test match stars in the side, and Angus Fraser charging in on his long run, who would take 8 Ashes wickets in the Oval Test that month. Three of our team would play for England that summer. But I was a happy little one-trick pony and had a tangy last wicket stand with Indian star Dillip Doshi.

One-trick pony nirvana! The author hobnobs with two England captains and five Test match cricketers when John Paul Getty came to me cap in hand. Front row L-R John Emburey, Dilip Doshi, Clive Radley, Mike Gatting & Angus Fraser. Doyens of Test Match Special, Christopher Martin-Jenkins [centre L] and "Bearded Wonder" Bill Frindall also on show

Oh - and what became of that Rennie squad?! A big, booming, comfortable National Vets win duly ensued, but only because I fired off 50 quid to the club. [Consult *Miscellanea and Vets* for a report and image of the fab four.]

Perhaps my favourite "one-trick" story concerns the cricket grudge match between those doyens of British literature Harold Pinter and Sebastian Faulks. But Faulks was one short, so had to raid the crowd… A while later and a tall, whippy fast bowler from *The Guardian* print room observes his Fine Leg, hopelessly out of position. He beckons Faulks over, pointing at the fielder: " *'Ere* Seb, I have to ask… is *that… is that Salman Rushdie*?!"

"Umm… yes, as a matter of fact it is."

"Well could you ask him to move a little finer?"

The Art of Recruitment

Full many a flower is born to blush unseen,
And waste its sweetness on the desert air.
Thomas Gray - Elegy Written in a Country Churchyard

I once borrowed a great line from *Mad Men* about Manhattan and refined it to the claret and gold:
Belgrave is a marvellous machine, filled with a mesh of levers and gears and springs, like a fine watch wound tight, always ticking.

And at the heart of this ticking is recruitment – a 24 hour job for sure. It really is the be all and end all of any club. No people, no club. How do you recruit? Well, there are dozens ways, and I've tried most. Just walking to Gloucester Road tube this morning a runner trotted past looking absolutely ripped. It was all I could do not to approach, but the person I was with said: "don't bother, look at those muscles, definitely with a club." How does one know? Was that the 'lightning in a bottle signing' that clubs dream of? As I stood there hesitating, the runner disappeared into Waitrose, and that was that.

And once that athlete is hooked on the line, getting the vest on them in competition is the next hoop to jump through. Committee plays a huge role in this, the wheels must be fully oiled, and action must be rapid. I had given up on Belgrave after I applied in the spring of '98. Nothing back for some seven weeks. I had forgotten all about it. But that's the way it was back then. If you just missed committee, it was a long wait till the next – they were once every two months. Things are mercifully swifter now, and computerised, it can all be done overnight, but the membership secretary still needs to be on 'cutting edge'.

Before I became women's TM I was once after a very strong South African athlete for a year, but Woodford wanted her too. It became some sort of an arms race. Surely her locale near Wimbledon was hugely in our favour. One glorious day I bumped into her on the Common: "Will! I wanted you to know I've signed my Belgrave form and am taking it to the postbox today…" I was so pleased. She was going to be worth at least 5,000 points to the club, probably a lot more. I promptly emailed the club to celebrate, cc'ing her in, and then waited for her to appear in Belgrave colours. But the club never did acknowledge the email, the athlete noticed, and Woodford scenting the delay, pounced. She barely missed a race for them for seven years, and then in the autumn of her career switched to Ranelagh. But it can't be denied – we had our chance.

With these huge signings, there can be simply no weakness, iffyness, flakyness, or half-heartedness from the club. And point-blank *zero* talk of: "this is Belgrave, if they want to join, they'll join."

Hmmmm, maybe in 1932, when cigarette cards were saying Belgrave were the greatest athletics club in the world, but it's not 1932 any more. Competition from other clubs has arisen. Some 1,850 of the little blighters.

Our Spooks Land the Greatest

The story of us getting Gerry North, the finest Road and Country signing in our history, is straight out of John le Carre. A Bel spotted him in the back of the smoky recesses of a West London diner… what was this Bolton goliath doing in London? The Bel could have let it go. Instead, he hit the phones. Word spread, meetings were had, a letter drawn up, proofread, finessed, and dispatched. The reply from Gerry came in: "Sorry, I haven't moved to London… was just visiting. But I'm thinking about it…" and the rest is history. When he did relocate a short while later, the Bels were his first port of call after that flattering approach.

All of us at Belgrave can do our bit. It's a ferociously busy world out there. Finding would-be-competitive runners is one thing. Finding those not already snapped up quite another. All we can do is keep our eyes peeled, offer a terrific product and be ready to be all singing from the same hymn book when opportunity knocks. One regular "ace" can completely transform the fortunes of a club. We did superbly to land "pavement plodder" Sophie Harris in 2016 when resident "spook" Terry got wind of her, but then disastrously lost her after a couple of years. Both sections in this book are currently thriving, but just when you think you've got it sorted? Bang! It's just the moment when the slippery slope starts. Careers are so incredibly fragile. We're all a hamstring injury away from oblivion. As Alan Black points out: "the problem with the 1970s is that we all got old at once."

The holistic & flexible approach

Belgrave works best when it shows imagination, flexibility, pastoral care and the holistic approach. The moment any institution such as ours becomes regimented, autocratic, hostile or unfeeling it is doomed to fail. I picked up the sub-15/sub 4 runner Kieran Gilfedder second-claim who is partially-sighted. As you can imagine, cross-country was a "bit of a mare" for him, but he grimly gave the nod, because I wrote him a sob story. He'd go into the woods in the Surrey League in 20th and come out 80th. The snag was that three of the races that winter were on Wimbledon Common, where it doesn't get much murkier or littered with furniture like tree roots. I asked the club if we could give him a gratis vest as a mark of our gratitude, but was told, no, everyone pays, and that I "couldn't see the woods for the trees." A somewhat unfortunate response.

Another great example of a rule where flexibility is so important is: "no taxis to a venue of under a mile". Ok: what about a TM of a ripening age, with a tent, in the lashing wind and rain, with a massive hill? Still no taxi? Guidelines are fine, but what's crucial is to *trust* people to behave with judgment and honour, because without trust relationships can be ruined – sometimes forever. There was a horror rule about no travel expenses within the M25, but that means you could get travel for 1 mile of 2 minutes, but not for a 2 hour journey of 40 miles. In short, to quote from *Indiana Jones*, "X never, ever marks the spot." Flexibility is key.

The "P" word

The capacity to offer assistance in physio to the needy is another contentious issue and was probably the straw that broke the Cockerpillar's back. We tried having a hardship kitty, but it didn't work. My approach was to treat every case on its merit, but an opposing one is to treat every athlete the same, which of course means zero physio for anyone. The rub though is that not every athlete's *contribution* to the club is the same. You could have an Olympian and a great ambassador who still competes regularly and turns our teams upside-down. Or you could have the Vice-president of a major bank pottering along doing 27 minutes for 5k and enjoying the gentle exercise. Now, both get plantar fasciitis. Who to grant a little physio aid to? The reason to deny both cases because it could: "open the floodgates," doesn't stand up. Not if you have the correct checks and balances in place.

Chasing Shadows

There was a surreal row at the club about who would pay for the tea-party to celebrate Bill Lucas' 80 years as a Belgravian. Could that also open the floodgates? I wrote to the Chairman to suggest we pass a resolution to pick up the tab for a tea-party *for everyone* who reaches 80 years of service with the club. I believe this is now club policy, and I'm not worried about it fiscally crushing us. My tea-party is slated for June 2078; I'll be 104, and I'm going to push for The Savoy.

We then had to revisit the matter when Bill turned 100. "Why are we having a party for an old man?" a senior bigwhig asked... well, I think the investment was justified – the party made news headlines all over the world:

↻   🔒 bbc.co.uk/news/uk-england-38633035

An evening whisky is the key to a long life, according to Britain's oldest living Olympian on his 100th birthday.

Bill Lucas said a glass of wine or sherry before lunch also kept him strong.

Mr Lucas, also the country's oldest living Bomber Command pilot, competed in the 5,000m track event at the 1948 London Olympic Games.

He celebrated his birthday at a party organised by his athletics club, Belgrave Harriers.

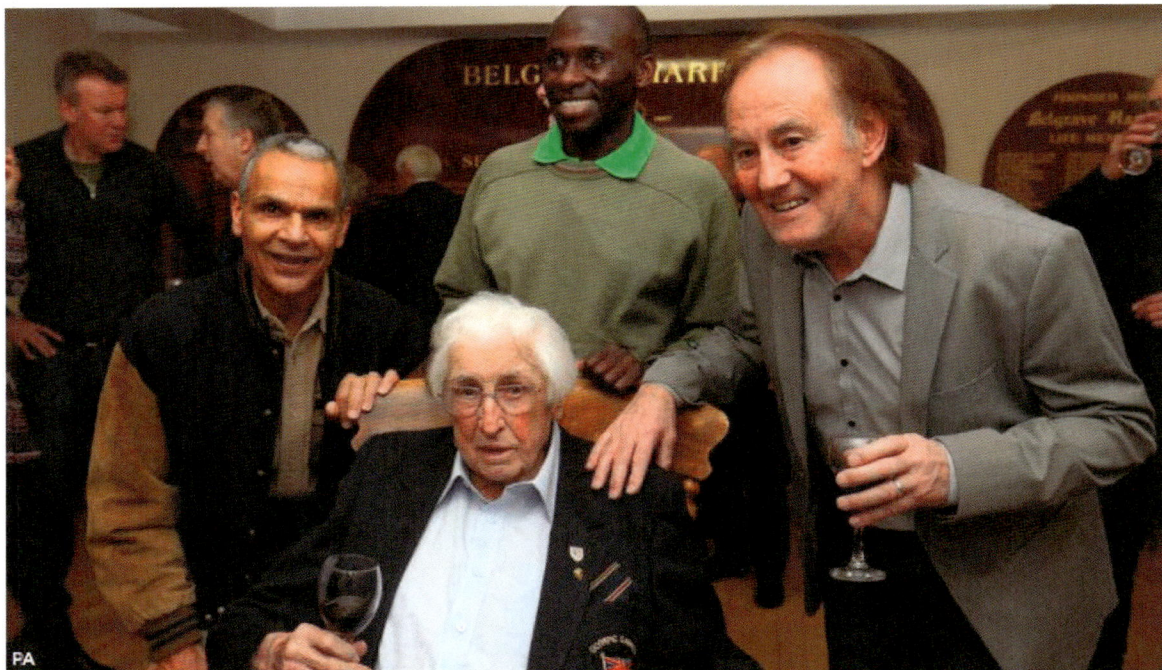

Bill Lucas was joined at his 100th birthday at the Belgrave Harriers club by fellow Olympians Snowy Brooks, Paskar Owor and John Bicourt

Whilst John Gladwin converses with Dave McMillan in the background

The three Holy Grail Questions for TMs

In summary then, problems with TMs will arise with a lack of trust and second guessing their leadership, strategy, tactics, approach, and fretting about minutiae. Keep a close eye on your TMs for sure, but **trust** them, don't interfere [and try to do their job for them], and then at season's end look for three sacrosanct things:

1) Results   -   as a competitive sports club, we're in the results business.
2) Budget granted vs Budget spent
3) Squad size at the beginning and end of season.

There really is nothing else. Stuff like, "are people happy and having a good time?" will all be answered from the above questions. And committee should be acutely aware that the *more* a TM is spending is <u>not</u> a bad thing, in fact, it is the best of things, because it means there's some *action*. <u>And no action, no club.</u> The TM who isn't spending on race entries and the like, is the one you need to worry about.

When I stood down, the two-headed monster of Steve Gardner and Arne Dumez took over. Some of their stuntwork has been incredible [and certainly pioneering], and due to their improved diplomatic relations with committee, and perhaps their youth, not to mention their hunger and ferocious competitive spirit, things have taken off and they can only be applauded. There have been some tough, executive decisions by them, and numerous Championship assaults sacrificed for "the Big Picture"; but one can't argue with what they've produced. Covid also stopped them in their tracks, but far from flailing they seemed to flourish in it, and just kept on building.

December 1991

CHARLES DICKINSON reports on the early season results

Building on the success of the Belgrave Track and Field team over the summer there are some very encouraging aspects of the Cross Country and Road team

That's several decades now that CD has looking for "encouraging aspects"... he is good value for his success

Derby double for Charlie Dickinson

A CARPENTER by profession, Charlie Dickinson crafted a one-day distance double at Derby in the British Masters' Championships using tenacity and fortitude as his tools, *writes Pete Mulholland.*

On a windy weekend that almost saw the Bourne Sports marquee go off into orbit, the first title to come Dickinson's way was the M55 1500m.

"It was a quiet year for me as far as international events went," said the Belgrave Harrier journeyman athlete and former European M50 5000m champion, "so I went for the 1500m to see what I could do.

"I couldn't believe the early pace, we were lapping in 82s. It was more like a 10,000 metres," recollected Dickinson, "but the tall figure of John Potts was my priority."

Then came the bell and pre-race favourite Potts took off. "I was blocked in and remember shoving someone out of the way to hammer after John. The final bend saw me two to three yards adrift and then he began to 'tread water' and I edged clear just before the line."

Referring to his coach, Arthur Bruce, Dickinson admitted: "He told me my strength from the longer events would be a factor – and so it proved."

Four hours later came the 5000m. "I felt relaxed as I had my gold medal. I sat way back off the pace way before easing through the field."

Over the final stages Brian Hilton led M50 competitor Archie Jenkins, with Dickinson now third. "I knew Brian was the main threat to my title so I concentrated on him.

"With 300 to got Brian began to sprint so I opened the throttle and went for him. I went past Archie to close down on Brian and eased by just yards before the finish."

♦ WHAT were your personal memories of 2003? Write to Memories, *Athletics Weekly*, 83 Park Road, Peterborough Cambs. PE1 2TN

And as for Charlie and the Belles, his build [mostly behind the scenes until 2015] has been around 30 years – count 'em. I think Arne and Steve have also pointed the way for the future of the men: two is infinitely better than one. The men's Road and Country role is too large, layered and complex for just one soul – unless your initials are ARM. And when one of them gets too busy or distracted, the other is there to keep the kettle boiling. The perfect precedent for this was set by Bill Laws and Leo Coy in the BAL, which became the equally strong Laws and Jeffery.

Chas had a quality career as a Vet, world class even, and brings this experience to his coaching and management

A DAY IN THE LIFE, *by Alan Mead*

It is 1963, and the match versus the German club Turnverein 1862 Langen, at Battersea Park. Alan holds the curb before launching a long kick for victory. Photo by Alan Black

Here's an absorbing essay from Alan Mead to the website *Runnerslife* about the enormous sacrifice and logistics that being a TM involves. His results speak for themselves and it's only right and proper that such a soul should be left to get on with the job in hand. More than anything, this marvellous piece states very clearly: don't get bogged down in the minutiae, look at the big picture.

Getting into team management

It started early. I became Belgrave's track & field captain in 1962 at the age of 18 and did that for four years. Then in 1975 became T&F Team Manager for three years. There were a few other team management jobs – veterans T&F in my last running years, the British League for a couple of years, jointly with Bill Laws, during the period when we won the Premier Division for the last time, and also the National Junior League, again jointly with Bill. But although my background was in 440/880 I was always lured by the magic of middle and longer distance running and in 1995 when we hadn't won anything much for decades I thought I'd have a crack at organising the endurance teams. It's never been about the need to 'be the guy in charge' – which I rather shy away from – always it's been a pride in and loyalty to the club I belong to that makes me want us to do the best we possibly can.

Sutton Park

Wonderful place! The long line of clubs and individuals recording wins and losses going back over nearly 50 years has built up an atmosphere that cannot be beaten. Dynasties of powerful clubs have risen and fallen in that time. I love the fact that the course has remained unchanged (we are led to believe) since 1974 and the runners out on the road not only test themselves against each other but against the ghosts of runners from other eras. It's a place where the north meets the south and old timers whose feet no longer pace the long and winding road continue to meet up to carry on the old rivalries as team supporters and managers. I hate it when a course or venue for a favourite event changes

Picking a line up

This is the hardest part of the job for any manager. It includes the heartbreak of having to tell a runner that he is not in the final squad, the frustration of seeing a team disintegrate over the week before the race, the tensions caused when a man comes out the night before or even on the day itself and a re-shuffle is required. The only way to do it is to attempt to be absolutely fair and remove any bias whatsoever from the equation. If a guy's been running really well then he must be considered ahead of someone who has the potential to do better but hasn't done anything for ages. This can be the most difficult thing of all – especially when the latter might then run in the B team and go faster than the man selected. I always try to bear in mind that whilst being fair I could also be wrong. If I am doubtful over the last few men into the team I delay as long as possible to ensure that I don't upset a man who subsequently gets the call up anyway because someone else drops out late. I try not to name names in anything that can be construed as selection sequence – this can really annoy some men right at the time I want them to run well. Where there are obvious differences in ability then I'll name men in groups. To add to all these difficulties, some runners talk themselves up much more than others and some take being left out much better than others (see worst moments below). In a six stage I once left out Paul Evans – he hadn't done much for some time, but let's face it he was a 2:08 marathoner. He was very gracious and thank goodness we won.

Medal haul

Since 1995 (in fact since 1999) – in the four area and national road relays:
Southern 6 Stage – 6 gold, 2 silver, 2 bronze.
Southern 12 Stage – 7 gold, 3 silver, 2 bronze.
National 6 Stage – 7 gold, 1 silver, 1 bronze.
National 12 Stage – 4 gold, 2 silver, 3 bronze.

Belgrave Harriers

The club has been a huge part of my life since I joined aged 14 in 1958. I had been a real rebel at school, always in trouble. That trouble spilled out onto the street outside of school. I had a natural antipathy towards 'those in charge' be they teachers, policemen or whatever. The one time I shone at school was when sports day came around each year. I found that the excitement of running fast at the school and district sports was not enough for me so I searched for an athletic club where I could do it more frequently and, finding such a club, my life changed. Mixing with adults who treated an adolescent as 'one of them' was what I needed. Whilst most of those adults have now passed on, I have acquaintances within the club whom I have known since we were teenagers. Luckily my family have always been supportive of my strong connection to the club, becoming as much a part of the athletic community as I have.

Rivalry

I was always impressed by the clubs who, in my younger years, regularly did the business at endurance events – among them Coventry Godiva, Gateshead, Bingley, Birchfield, Morpeth, Blackheath … and running through the last 50 years like a thread and still right up there - Tipton Harriers. I wanted us to emulate these clubs and for them to view us as rivals. Most of them we have equalled although Tipton's record is quite outstanding. But as we did it, other teams also rose to the challenge. Our rivalry with Newham & Essex Beagles has been very healthy and at the same time respectful and friendly. That's the way it should be. This might sound rich, coming from a Team Manager who has pushed hard for team wins, but in actual fact I usually walk away from a race whether we have lost or won with emotions that all fall within a narrow spectrum. I don't get over elated by a win and I cannot abide the team or manager that crows and flaunts their victory in the face of those who have lost. I feel good for a team that has beaten or been beaten by us – particularly if they if they have fought well. It is most important that we do our best and attempt to rise to any challenge. For me running, even though I am long past doing it any more, is a spiritual thing; but the race is, in spite of the passions aroused during its course, at the end of it all, a game.

12 stage vs. 6 stage

The six stage race is very much more open and should, therefore, be harder to win, with no time to recover from a below par run and more clubs being able to pull together six good men. However, it is here where we have been most successful, and that shows that we have been fortunate in having a core of six to eight really strong runners of like mind who have enjoyed the success and the fact that they can come together and run for each other. The twelve stage on the other hand is, for me, the traditional event, harking back to the old days on the London-Brighton Road. To be regularly successful certainly requires a strong base of eighteen or twenty men to choose from and a club without that base can find it a daunting task to be on the road for 4 ½ hours

Best and worst memories

There have been many really good memories. Just a few and not in any order:

- Getting a national 12 Stage team together in 2000 to place 17th after 25 years during which we had only finished a squad five times and mostly hadn't even qualified.
- 2001 and placing 2nd after a disastrous start, getting to the lead and then losing it in the last half mile – people really knew we meant business after this. (This was also one of the worst, to lose at the very end!)
- Later in 2001, winning the six stage for the first time.
- 2002 and making up for the previous year's 12 Stage loss by winning in one of the fastest times in the modern era. It was the first time we had won since 1951 and the margin of victory was the greatest in the history of the race – 6 minutes 26 seconds.
- Getting a 12 Stage bronze in 2008 when everyone thought we were on the slide and then coming back the next year with our fastest ever team – the guys were so pleased to have collectively run faster than we did in 2002.
- An oddity this one – during our period of real dominance when we had won the 6 Stage five times in a row and held just about every single national endurance title including National Cross, Cross Country Relay, half marathon, 10k, etc., it was generally assumed that we as a club paid our athletes to run and paid athletes to come and join our team. It was even reported as such in *Athletics Weekly*. The Tipton Team Manager came up to me and said, "Alan, I want you to look me in the eye and tell me that you do not pay your runners." Of course I *was* able to look him in the eye and assure him that we and I did not, and that if he wanted to he was welcome to ask them himself. It was great to set the record straight, to be believed by someone at last, and to see the relief on his face.

Worst memories:

- A selection problem. I omitted a runner who could be good but occasionally wasn't, in favour of a man who was rock solid. I could have been wrong but I had to make a choice. The man left out took it very hard and immediately wrote a letter of resignation even though I pleaded with him not to. Two days later a man came out of the twelve with injury. I returned to my omitted runner and asked him to change his mind but he told me his heart was no longer in it – and he did resign.
- 2006, and for some inexplicable reason I left Paul Freary off the entry sheet, not noticing this until I was giving the numbers out. At the same time the organisers had left out Richard Ward, whom I had entered. My pleading with the Referee, pointing out that both sides had made an obvious mistake, cut no ice. Richard was allowed to run (their mistake); Paul wasn't (my mistake). The subsequent rejigging of the team when the race had already started, retrieving race numbers and reallocating long stages to those expecting short, brought me nearer to mental collapse at a race than anything else I can remember.
- At a National 12 Stage, those dreaded words: "Will the Belgrave Team Manager please come and see the Referee" were followed by an accusation that we had not legitimately qualified for the race because we ran a non-cleared athlete at the SEAA race. Apparently some other club had done this and their reaction was to say that we had done the same. This was totally incorrect. The Ref decided to allow both teams to run but gave us a warning – in our case unwarranted. I was livid.

The athletes

There have been some amazing characters in my teams over the last 18 years and it would be invidious to mention some and not others. An article like this makes one look back down the names and realise that there has been a complete turnover. Young men that I welcomed into the team have long finished their days as runners and today's team might not even know who they were. But they all have something in common. They have been a really nice bunch and when they get out on the road in Sutton Park it's not for themselves as individuals – it's for each other. They have always got on so well together and appreciate what each of the others is bringing to the team even if it is not 'star-like' quality. This is probably something that is not often recognised in us by our rivals. The banter before the race continues through race week and long after … even years later, incidents that occurred whilst out post-race 'clubbing' in Brum get brought up and embroidered as time goes by.

A day in the life on relay day

The extraordinary thing about race day is that it lasts for about 40 hours! The following are genuine incidents from over the years. We tend not to stay at a hotel en masse now and as we are not all together, the tradition of the team talk has slipped away.

The day before: 7am   Collect a runner from Heathrow. He has just flown back from Kenya. I feel I should be holding a card so that incoming passengers can read BELGRAVE. I get him to his home in South London to dump his luggage and collect more kit, then back to mine, to load the car with tent, race trophy, spare kit, post-race refreshments and drive to the hotel at Lichfield. Perhaps stopping en route to collect someone from Birmingham International.
2pm   An hour's rest before runners start arriving at the nearby station over the next four or five hours and I ferry them to the hotel; perhaps as many as four trips.
7pm   We go for a meal. In the past we have put the 12-Stage Cup, bedecked in claret and gold ribbons, on the table at The Bull. Nowadays it tends to be Frankie and Benny's. With supporters there might be two dozen of us. The talk is all of times run in the past and what we might achieve tomorrow and what news is there of our rivals. The team drink to success on the following day – the runners mostly downing lemonade and blackcurrant. Wardy will recount again the time he broke the World Record for the 'Chunder Mile'.
11pm   The lads are in their rooms. I keep a closer watch these days – there once being a suspicion on my part that a couple slipped into Brum for a night out. The 'old sweats' sit in the foyer drinking coffee or something a little harder and talking of old days and old characters.

On the day: 7am   Four of us meet in the foyer and drive to Sutton Park to put the tent up. As we leave, already one or two runners are setting out for an early morning loosener.
8:15pm   The tent is up. We always time ourselves and this time we were just outside the record! It's the only tent there at this hour and this year we've beaten the burger van and the toilet truck. The first AAA official, usually Ted Butcher, is arriving as we leave. "Hope you've engraved and polished that cup" is his normal offering.
9am   Breakfast at the hotel. Most of the lads have run and are now following their pre-race eating ritual: everything from cornflakes dropped singly into a bowl of milk and eaten one at a time, through porridge, fruit, muesli … and in one case a 'full English'.
10am   We meet for a team talk. These can be quite intimidating as each man envisages his stage on the road and the job he has to do. The boys quietly walk away now looking drawn and nervous. Some of them are now really fired up.
11am   Arrive at the Park again. Our tent is now surrounded by others with many more still going up. I collect the race numbers and pray that everything is in order; it is. Rival team managers exchange nods and perhaps a, "Got the boys out today?" or "Had a great team on Monday"; but nobody believes the stories told by any of them. The early stage runners are now here and the supporters are arriving – there's as much banter between the supporters as between the runners as they set up their Welsh or Scottish or English or favourite football team fold-up chairs.
12 noon They're off. And over the next hour more runners check in, lying in a corner of the tent or relaxing in a chair outside. One man is driving up on the day; he's totally reliable but I haven't heard from him for nearly a week; I avoid the temptation to call him.

2pm.   The race is going well. I return to the tent in between taking race splits to find the last athlete now present and sitting in the sun with his shades on. The pressure is pretty much off for me now. I used to worry about where my next man was for every single stage. I always lost him in the last five minutes before takeover but invariably he'd disappeared into the woods. I try not to worry about them now and attempt to enjoy the race ... but can I ... ?

2:30pm   I spot our next long stage man ambling away from the ice cream van. "You're on next!" He looks shocked and then counters, "No I'm not, they're only doing stage 6 now aren't they?" My assurance that stage 8 is going out and he's meant to be on 9 at last gets through. The ice cream cornet is dumped and he scrabbles in the tent for his racing shoes.

3:30pm   We've moved into the lead but it's not by as much as I was hoping. It's going to be tight.

4:05pm   We're going to do it!

4:30pm   The tent is packed and steamy and it has started to rain outside. A sudden squall threatens to take the tent into Sutton Coldfield but the taller runners are quick to react and are inside, laughingly hanging on to the frame with 'Spenny' organising them. Everyone's in good humour. Tea and cakes are being dispensed ... and we are called up to the presentation.

5:00pm   People are leaving now; just need to make sure that everyone's got a lift to the station, London, the airport. There are many offers to help take down the tent but really I just need to sit down and do it in my own time. However, the lads are at work and in a twinkling it's down, wet, but packed away. There's no way anyone can get out of the car park but I manage to squeeze the car between some bollards and drive up the other way to load up.

6:00pm   We're on the toll road, on our way: tired, sweaty, damp and hungry ... but relaxed. Cherwell or more recently, Oxford, service area is next stop where we grab something to eat, natter with our supporters who have stopped at the same place and start poring over the result sheets... and perhaps fall in with Bob Smith of the Beagles [now deceased and greatly missed] and a couple of Newham lads he's driving back to London.

9:00pm   Home. A cup of tea and then put the basic facts together and upload with a photo to the website. Totally knackered!

Best Team

We have had some truly great teams and they can't all be measured simply in terms of winning medals. The 12 Stage line-ups of 2002 and 2003 were absolutely awesome. Our Club Record breaking 6-Stage team of 2002 saw Wardy, Sharp, Barden, Graffin, Miles and Anderson in action together and then just six seconds behind them, in 2007, came Sharp, Kelly, Blackledge, Jones, Miles and Wicks. The 2009 12 Stage team ran even faster than the 2002 squad. I was truly impressed by the way we fought for a medal of any kind in 2007 and 2008. Then our 2013 12 Stage team rose to the challenge to run above themselves in poor conditions. But maybe the best team is still waiting to come together ...

The future

Who knows? I would like to think that as long as we as a club go on doing our best and attending these relays, keeping the tradition going, then we are achieving what we should. Even if we don't medal and even if we can't expect to medal we should always support the relays and contribute towards the great harrier tradition. But looking at the men who are team members now I feel that we have a lot that we can still achieve. A wild dream of mine all along has been to try to match the teams of old. Bingley in '96 ran a 4:02 for the National 12-Stage. We are the only team to have come near that since then, with a couple of 4:04s, but way back in 1980 Bristol turned out a dozen who neared 4 hours flat. Now wouldn't a time like that make people sit up. Of course the conditions would have to be perfect because we are talking about an average of 25:30s and 14:30s all the way; but if everybody was fit and had this as a target then we might not be so far away from achieving it as you might think. Just go through the names yourself ...

THE SURREY LEAGUE - WOMEN

Some superb eras

Unlike their male counterparts, the Belles have been by and large outstanding in the league. Six wins is a very good return with many 2nd and 3rd placings too.

We built oh so slowly throughout the 1980s with Rosemary Honeychurch striking a rather lonely vigil, and Jacinta Moore keeping most regular company. Who was Rosemary? Here's a good little blurb:

'DYNAMITE' ROSE

ROSEMARY HONEYCHURCH: Alias "Dynamite Rose" is "Belles" leading middle distance star, and is a 21 year old student at Whitelands College where she is studying for a degree in sociology. How many of you have taken 32 secs. and 65 secs. off your P.B.s for 1500m and 3000m in one season? "Dynamite" did just that!!

At the start of the 1984 season her best 1500m was 5.17 - at the end - 4.45. Her best 3000m was 11.07 - at the end - 10.02. Her coach (since last April), Derek Crookes says she is a "Dedicated trainer" who does everything laid down in training schedules, and is an out and out fighter. 1984 saw her win the Surrey County Senior 3000m and this was followed up by representing Surrey in the same event. Her winter "hobby" is trying to run her coach into the deck over a hard 3 to 4 mile run most Saturdays at Wimbledon. She represented Surrey in the Inter-Counties C.C.Champs 1985 but her best run was to chase Ann Ford in the C.P. 6km road race at the end of December.

12th JANUARY 1985   WIMBLEDON   SURREY WOMENS CROSS COUNTRY LEAGUE MATCH 3

A good run in the Girls from Jackie Stone and the Seniors and Inters pulled out all the stops to record our first win in this League and Rosemary was our first individual winner. We were lucky with the weather as the day was sunny but cold and the course was very icy and had to be changed at the last minute.

Girls 2000m: 1.A.Cox (Downland) 10.07; 3.J.Stone 10.26; 52.C.Gauge 11.30; 69 Finished.

Team: 1.Mitcham 25;   2.Epsom & Ewell 47; 3.Woking 50; 9.BELGRAVE 141.

Juniors 2500m: 1.K.Sutton (Croydon) 10.31; 48.N.Christou 14.23; 49.J.Palmer 14.41;
                51.A.Abrams 15.11;

Team: 1.Epsom & Ewell 56; 2.Camberley & Dist. 65; 3.Walton 76; 13.BELGRAVE 166.

Inters/Seniors 3000m: 1.R.Honeychurch 12.25; 17.V.Mitchell 13.33; 18.J.Webb 13.33;
                35.D.Hawkins 14.10; 36.G.Porter 14.14;

Team: 1.BELGRAVE 69; 2.Croydon 72; 3.Ranelagh 83.

A nice record of the Belles' first ever Surrey League win. They were still at an embryonic stage in their development and only 9 years in existence [and the league just 6], but this showed the project was on the right path. Just a 3 to score race here.

By the 90's at the league, it was still a brick by brick affair, but then suddenly, straight out of the clear blue sky, a tremendous win in 1993-4. The scoring back then was terribly simplistic and even rather babyish, and I think leagues should grow out of it. The Hampshire league perseveres with it. Basically, if you win the day, you get 1 point, and lowest points for the season wins. Pah. It ignores the individual athletes efforts and really dumbs things down. It is a system designed to keeping things as close as possible, but things would soon change in Surrey.

By 2002 the scoring system was as we know it today, which in a word is, "savage"! Every runner counts, and if your 5th athlete is cut adrift, or god forbid AWOL, the price to be paid is last in the entire race, with a 10 point gas bill through the neck. As is well known, the men's system opts for something far more gentle: 90 points for last scorer is as bad as it gets. But I once only raised four ladies so their scores went something like 7-14-25-35 & 240. The horror, the horror. Anyway, the system seems to work fine and the question now is whether to boost the scoring five to 6. I think they should; 5 is too far 'out of whack' with the men. Yes, about 6-8 clubs will squeal for mercy, but perhaps instead, they should take it as inspiration to bump up their squads.

The millennium season kicked off with the following rain soaked souls: Karen Fenner, pentathlete Kate Houston, Tanya Sturton, Cathy Eastham and Kate Dillane. 8th in the first match became 7th in the second and a fine 3rd in the third, with Helen Maskrey [Alsop] enjoying a terrific season, just 32 seconds behind ex-GB junior Dorchie Lee in 1st. They completed their work at Brockwell with Rachel Weston in 5th, the team placing fourth and an overall and hard fought 6th.

There was more 'Weston magic' for the 00-01 opener but then we were relying on Tanya and Syreeta to hold us together. It was insufficient and now relegation was a possibility. Lightwater didn't help with a disastrous turn-out, just Debbie Hearn as far as we can see, and the team had suddenly collapsed. The future didn't look too rosey. A super turnout could just have saved the day, but it wasn't there and it was back to life in the second tier.

Straight Back – With a Stone Cold Bonkers Team!

Things can change so fast. A couple of strong runners and suddenly you have a real going concern on your hands. It's what makes women's club athletics so exciting and full of possibility. Our roll of honour for the season opener read: N/S winner (by 1:40), 1st, 2nd, 4th, 5th & 9th. What a difference 8 months makes. And look at those runners: Tamirat, Sharp, Hegvold, Sturton and Weston. It was no surprise that such a squad decided to dash up the M40 to the National 4 stage, where they promptly placed 7th. *Formidable.*

Things improved further when a very fit looking newbie named Mathilde Heaton placed a non-scoring 3rd. Little did we dream of the ledg that we had unearthed. Vicki Goodwin was another we liked the look of, and although Stragglers pipped us by 4 points, promotion was all but assured. And that was certified with just 34 points in match 3 with Anne in 3rd and Jules Clark now also packing a punch. Promotion was gained in the last with hundreds of points to spare, and now it was just one thing on our mind: we've won this once, we can win it again.

2002-03 What a thriller to start!

Did Epsom Downs ever see such a horse race, let alone running race?! A team bristling with intent hit the 'Irrepressibles' [SLH] so hard, and we were one strong runner short of a phenomenal team, as Tamirat, Sharp, Sturton and Walker is no joke. The score after round 1 was 82-83, all to play for. Some leakage occurred in the next but at least Tilly was finally scoring after some absurd draconian transfer ban had been served. Goodness, those days were harsh. Lou Cooper was another welcome pillar of strength to arrive on the Belgrave scene, and another stunning career in the claret and gold just starting out – audaciously here, still pinning on her number with the runners streaming off down the field. She opted it was thus a trainers day and forgot about her spikes and still made the scoring 5 out of 11 runners with both Tanya and Syreeta having to drop out. Expensive.

An excellent 2nd then followed at Petersham as the blueprint for future success was becoming clear. Ranelagh 56; Belgrave H 70; THH 72, SLH 97. One day… But despite their poor race, South London surely couldn't be caught this time around. That transpired, but another strong showing meant the planning for '03-04 started right away.

Champions!

The important thing with league athletics is to start with intent. It's so hard to reel in a clunker. 10 starters was key, meaning an heir and a spare for all… And those spares were hardly jogging. With luminaries such as Clark, Alsop and Smethurst not required, this had clearly become a wonderful squad. Rosie Powell was a terrific new find, in 7th, and with Ms Walker at the peak of her powers in 3rd and new signing Birhan Dagne in 10th (and four months off winning the National Cross), it was a stonking side, rounded out by Lou and the ever loyal Syreeta.

We topped the lead at half-way, but it was fairly fragile: 92 vs 119. SLH weren't going away. It was a wonderful race with our rivals scoring 45, but we replied with just 36 and five in 12. Rachel Weston made a return to our affairs and Erica Fogg was spicey in 9th.

An Astonishing Race

Match 3 – moving day, in golfing parlance, where the league's winner would probably be confirmed. What drama! SLH 82, Ranelagh 81 and Belles 79. It was all about the packing here as Jules, Tilly, Anne, Vicki Edwards and Helen Smethurst ran around like a sniper's unit, with no fewer than 4 more backing up closely. We had a 30 point buffer, so not quite sorted…

CE sets the scene:

"Going into Match 4, with 3 wins out of 3 under their belts, the Belles were by no means complacent. Not only did they want to win the league, but they wanted to be the unbeaten champions. With a few athletes out of action as a result of injury, every point from every runner would count. And so, with typical dogged determination and winning focus, the Belles set out to tackle the mud and puddles of Lloyd Park for the final time."

With a nerveless Tilly leading the line in 7th, back-up cames from Jules (10th), the talented new member Vicki Clarke 11th, Vicki E in 13th and finally Lou stopping the clock in 18th. SLH would require 29 points to handle that, which is all but impossible. As it went they landed on 73. Anne Hegvold would have been in there somewhere but dropped out with a sinus infection, and look at the back-up from Stracey 20th, Powell 26th, and Alsop 33rd, who had been a member of the squad which last won the league a decade before.

The Belles' league winning squad at the final league match, Lloyd Park, on 7th February 2004.
Standing: Anne Hegvold, Tilly Heaton, Nina Mills, Juliette Clark, Vicky Clarke, Vicki Edwards, Helen Alsop.
Kneeling: Rosie Powell, Louise Cooper and Syreeta Stracey.
Photo by Louise Williams, Sporting Photos.

It's not a crisp image but it is an important one. Congratulations to all

And Now For Defence!

Incredibly, we raised a sweet sixteen on the Common for the new campaign. It's at times like this one gets delusions of grandeur and can't envisage a time when, "we won't be fine". But it doesn't work like that. Six debutantes was also a thrill and of those a complete gem was found in Sarah

Murphy, one of the greatest Belles of all time, and only stopped in her Belgrave tracks by those perilous 'Charlie's Runners socials', which in turn triggered three new men in her life, and a relocation to somewhere more convenient to the BBC's Salford base.

It's quite scary to think of the scoring records that Smurph might have set, but we got half a career out of her, which is worth about eight normal careers! Anyway, although the team were superb, Ranelagh were phenomenal and blitzed all and sundry in match 1, it was going to be a tough defence.

Note from a Small Island: another diamond unearthed

Remarkably, we won the 2nd fixture, and enjoyed the great sight of Catherine Bryson, a past superstar in the States, now based over here with

Two Belles nuggets - Helen Smethurst moving into a new age group, but no sign of slowing, and the great Smurph on debut. Little did we dream of the value incoming... JH

her family, with father Bill in the midst of penning some of the world's best-selling books. Syreeta Stracey still continued to score heavily, and with Tilly, Jules and Rosie, it was no wonder the squad scored just 51 points. At the half-way stage we'd broken free of Thames and eyed up the Greyhounds just 22 points away – nothing really.

Five of those points were gained in match 3 with a classic line-up of Murphy, Heaton, Smethurst, Bertram and Clark. 18 more to find! We couldn't have done too much more in Ewell with a large injured and illness list, and then Jules was lost to the race on the second lap. It was Ranelagh's first win in the league in its 26 years and all credit to them for a stellar season.

The Slugfest Continues

This cracking head-to-head rivalry continued with 2005-06's openers, featuring a fine new find in Heidi Cayzer, and a deepish squad did ok at Reigate, but half way saw Ranelagh on a mere 110 to our 164. Another long slog was in store. And that's how it panned out. The team never gave up, and packed well all season, but Ranelagh dipped below 200 for the entire year. They were on fire.

A global sporting icon comes to play

The Belles turned up to Epsom for 06-07 with a quite astonishing team. Fogg! Heaton! Bryson! Murphy! It's a stunning quartet, but then the cherry on top of the Black forest gateau, none other than Chrissie Wellington, the recent World age group Triathlon champion – winning over all age groups. Global domination at Ironman was looming large, and no better place to prep yourself for that than a Surrey League. Chrissie overtook one of the league's great runners in Emily Nelson at the half, and only fell short of Lucy Hasell [Macalister] en route to one of her 10 league wins – a record that may well never be beaten.

But Ranelagh weren't taking it lying down and after that breathless day had only given up 5 points to us. A truly magnificent squad came to race at Lightwater, and finally, after well over two years of not giving an inch, Ranelagh cracked and the Belles pounced.

You have to say that's magnificent! What a squad, and good excuse to finagle the 4 time Ironman Kona winner into these pages. Chrissie Wellington warms up for her debut win at Hawaii, less than a year away with the equally testing environs of Lightwater, whilst Sarah Gailey, Smurph, Catherine Bryson [2nd], Vicky Clarke, Lou Cooper, Helen Smethurst and Tilly back up the winner. [Junior Galley]

Fine athletes like Erica Fogg and Sarah Gailey were getting shut out of the reckoning as this time we score a 1-2 with Chrissie and Catherine. A wrong turn didn't derail Chrissie too much, although it played havoc with the talented Aussie Saltire Naomi Warner. CW was in no mood to let that bother her though, and in a superbly judged race, CB picked off bodies all the way through to finally finish in silver. Our lead was 74 over Thames, and league winning chances hovered at circa 90%.

Fresh from winning the County Champs, Thames then imploded on the Common, but Ranelagh launched a last ditch fightback. All credit to them for not giving in, but it meant a 69 point lead going into round four. Up front Catherine unleashed that famous, deadly finishing kick to take the day by just 4 seconds and score her debut league win.

Petersham was the venue for that denouement and "only" 7 Belles came to play, and one of them a rear-gunner. But the other six were all top 30, and they were 7 Murphy 16 Heaton 19 Clark 24 Gailey 25 Fogg and 30 Smethurst. What a team. However, there were two things to note as the league was secured by 75 points. One was the thinness in quantity of the team, the other that CE did not produce reports for either of the last two fixtures. It may have been that this was the moment that her reign started to come down the other side of the mountain. Time would tell.

2007-08

The new season began with more of the same. "Catherine the Great" winning with that fearsome kick, Heaton, Murphy and Fogg to the fore, but then the gaffer had to discard the clipboard and shepherd us in. We were suddenly on absolutely zero back-up and despite being 14 points off the win, something had to give. That crash duly arrived in the next fixture with a dreadful return of 332 points and just 4 runners. It was clear that the squad now had a big problem and something serious was afoot, but what to do? Well rock bottom hadn't hit yet as 527 points was our lot in the next – was that even mathematically possible?! And that's with Smurph coming 4th, but she had just the Vixster and Jen Beecroft for company. Could we save relegation? Yes. That good start had done the trick, and we had a ok finish too, with Tilly back and a strong run from Sarah Gailey. Perhaps it was just a horror season and we'd be back in biz next term.

2008-09 started with Catherine Bryson outkicking the legendary Sonia O'Sullivan in the home straight. What a scalp! That was 3rd, and with Tilly and Smurph we were off to a wonderful start. Anne Hegvold slipped back into the team like an old pair of comfy slippers, but we were still relying on CE back in 170 to see us home. Oh for a couple more engine-roomers. There's no report for race 2, but there is, somewhat remarkably, a win. It's no surprise, as Murphy, Vail (hot off the printing press, so to speak), Hegvold & Goodwin is a super little team. We were even back in the league, 80 points off SLH. The final fixture saw a classy run off between two of the greatest in the league's history in Julia Bleasdale and Lucy Macalister, whilst the Belles did their party trick of fielding a strong 5 with no back-up. But it all meant 2nd in league and a noble act of defiance after the previous year's funk.

2009-10 was the calm before the storm. A final aria of a stunning period of forceful, feisty league competion. It had been the era of Murphy, Heaton, Bryson, Hegvold, Clark and many other fine supporting runners. They had achieved so much together and there was still time for a swansong. Three of those "old-stagers" were at Reigate, with Jen Beecroft continuing her peppy form from last term in 84th. Just behind was Maureen Noel, so loyal to the cause but as a W45 race-walker, we shouldn't really be relying on her to hole the closing putts.

A quite brilliant performance

Denbies of Nov 2009 was an amazing day that I remember well. Horizontal, lashing rain, and trying to push a baby's buggy through the sludge. If Smurph's 3rd was as brilliant as we might expect, Zoe Vail's 7th was a revelation. We knew she was useful, but this took her straight into the top drawer. And with due respect that elegant, leggy frame was not built for this muck. Anne rolled back the years for 13th, Tilly was solid as ever, which just left Vicki to see us home. Every point counts?! Oh you better believe. Belg 74, SLH 75. Bootiful.

It was the last great race of this team though as in the much kinder climes of Petersham, another disastrous DNF occurred, with CE closing in 4th. Oh dear... the season's climax was an interesting day though and we all loved to see Jules Bleasdale running riot. A top 8 runner in the world incoming. But it was the bare minimum for the Belles and 6th in the league flattered to deceive.

Darkest before the Dawn

The 2010-11 season was a dead cat bounce. After an horrific opener, we got a look at Sammi Amend at Denbies [13th], followed in by Catherine B. With with Tilly and Smurph for once bang out of form in the 70s we were still a grisly 16th in the league. At least we did have a few teams now lined up to have a pop at. Ham Lands was a fun race and we finally got to see the best of Sarah Gailey who had threatened such a forward placing for years – 6th. With Sammi in 8th it was a great start, but then a big gap before Tilly and Rieko slogged in and we then turned to Rosie Dickinson, daughter of Chas, to see us home. The position was grim, but not untenable. 90 points to pull back on Epsom to save relegation. Surely the girls would respond, no? But CE had gone to the well once too often and the Common felt funereal and we were thumped out of the league. A once great team now existed only in name, and was no longer in the top 18 clubs in the county, over 1,000 points off the winners. Oooofff.

Change in Leader

Having taken over the women's road section 18 months earlier, I offered to take on the cross-country as Catherine was completely out of gas. Out of sheer loyalty she had stayed for two, perhaps three years longer than she might have chosen, and the committee needed to be far more attuned to when a TM is no longer happy. Rebuilding a broken squad can take literally decades, so it's the committee's job to anticipate these problems before they get fatal. The women's road and country job probably came too early for me as I was only 35 when I took on the road section, and now at 37 still needed for top 20 league returns with the men. What followed was years of bonkers Surrey league days for me, of running the women, then a mad dash across the county to sometimes make the men's with just minutes to spare. Looking back, it was too much, but at the time, it was an absorbing challenge, although I started to race a lot with no warm-up or mental preparation and my performances started to become alarmingly erratic.

It was clear that the Belles desperately needed some more personnel, and I got to work... a lady was picked up in the queue for the powder room on a flight back from the Athens Marathon (so not quite perhaps as random as it sounds); and although we only got her out once, she pointed me to a wee nugget in Hester Barsham-Rolfe who was not only a strong, gung-ho runner, but more importantly a great tub-thumper and ambassador, who would be out there racing after all-night benders or when baby Roo was home sick in bed.

I also started writing to competent but unattached London Marathoners. It's only around a 3% strike rate, but one gem can be worth 1,000, I repeat 1,000, points to a club over just a few years. Maybe a lot more. A lady called Georgina wrote back with a, "errr, thanks but no thanks. Try my friend." The friend was in Cheltenham, hardly ideal. But she said "ok, I'll do the marathon in your colours and maybe, just maybe do the odd race for you." That lady was called Fiona Maycock, and the rest, as they say, is history, and her name sprinkles these pages with a special kind of magic from a special kind of person.

Such signings were all we needed to get going again. Then Catherine Bryson renewed her subs. I suddenly had high hopes for the future. A platinum blonde fitness junkie called Felicity Cole turned up to Battersea, and I pointed her to Charlie and not my group at Frank Horwill's where a good runner was liable to get poached. I got one South African girl from there to join, she emailed the club to ask about the process, she never heard back from us, and so joined Woodford instead. Yikes, that wasn't a 1,000 point loss, it was 3,000+! I ensured to place Flic into Charlie's arms and told him not to let go.

In the spring of 2011, we grabbed a bronze at the inaugural SEAA cross relay [with Cole, Bryson and Vail] and then a terrific 4th at the Southern 6 stage. We existed again with some force, but first, get the heck out of Div 2 of the league! There was a lovely atmosphere among a select group at Lightwater and my headline said it all: "Slam Dunk". Bryson, Quispel, Heaton, HBR and the promising Amy Linford, with Vicki standing guard. In their junior days CB was New England's no. 1 cross country runner and Nelle Australia's no. 1 sprinter. Here they were 5th and 6th and our meter was stopped on 44 total points, with Walton at 136. Promotion already a huge odds-on.

"All but released from the shackles of the naughty chair" I opined after Petersham. Sammi came to race (superbly in 4th), with Fee commuting in for 5th to start an explosive Surrey league sequence for her. Nelle, Tilly and Anne saw us home and we were going straight back up. Four were backing up the scorers too – nice!

A fortnight out from their incredible bronze at the Southerns, another low score was notched, altho a surprising defeat came via the Oddballs. Good for them, but we had a cool 187 buffer going into part 4. However, on the Friday night I only had about four runners! But Catriona Knox responded to the call, and despite Maureen missing her train (not a first for her) we would be ok, as long as everyone finished. Rieko Trees was particularly noteworthy in 15th. We were back in Div 1, and I had one thing on my mind: We were going to try and win it straight off the bat.

Absorbing Saltire battle

Relegation... promotion... and now nothing short of the Div 1 League win eyed up, and with a squad like this, why not? Tish, SA, Alison Heydenrych, ZVS and Fee get ready for the off in Oct 2012

I was pretty sure we'd win the first fixture of 2012-13 as we had a super squad, but I didn't quite reckon on my THH comrade Nic Gould who is as uber competitive as me. New signing Tish Jones was magnificent and won the first of an epic rivalry with Ruth Wallace for the win. There was then serious bamboozlement is tailend runners came in with the leaders on the figure of eight course. The first of three major snafus Thames would have in laying courses in the coming years, the worst of which was a dreadful cock-up at the Varsity match. With Sammi 13 and Fee 18th, dear old Maureen still lies in 19th on PO10, but instead we looked to ZVS and Sally Underhill to see us home. It was a good start, but we had some 51 points to make up.

11 of those came at Nonsuch Park in a tense win with a very surprising runner's up spot going to W4H – the sort of flash in the pan result that makes the league so entertaining. This time Tish had just a second to spare over Ruth in another cracking win.

The start of a magnificent season long rivalry between Ruth and Tish. Here Tish just gets the edge at Nonsuch

But the following race, Ruth exacted ruthless revenge as Tish's valiant push for the line would be undone by a venomous Wallace kick

After Sam and Fee, we welcomed incoming master-blaster Jojo Rhodes to our lines, a former child star over the 1,500. Anne Hegvold nostalgically scored again, over a decade after first doing so. We then defeated Thames again at Mitcham, but by just a couple of points. This time Tish was just outkicked by Ruth in yet another stunning race long duel, with the team identical to last time.

With a rescheduled Southern and major assault on the National in Sunderland planned, something had to give, so I largely give the A team the day off the for the last match. They were pretty exhausted and ran superbly to get us a brace of 6ths at both the Southern and then National. It meant we slipped in the league to 3rd, but I didn't mind – it was the win we were after, and Thames were too strong - this time!

Two classic league stalwarts in Jojo Rhodes and Anne Hegvold, with over 30 scoring runs between them

Golden Days

The blinkers-on look on the runners' faces said it all at the cramped start before the Lightwater opener for 2013-2014, pictured below. A marvellous squad had come to race and that was despite losing no fewer than eight in the build up. Intent was shown as Rose O'Brien showed Julia Bleasdale a clean pair of heels for the first few hundred of the race. It was kamikaze stuff and JB would charge Rose a 7:16 tariff for that little stunt, but when you've got your back-up landing pot-shots it sure inspires the heavy mob. Tish had to say "fair play" to Jules, but elsewhere we were on great form.

Game faces on. The Surrey league is designed to give club runners a 'taste of the big time' and by the looks of concern here, trepidation is afoot. But they have the league win on their minds, and a top-eight runner in the world is just up the line. But Rose O'Brien [27] has a plan to beat her – and indeed everyone – to the narrow first turn… Also pictured L-R: Fee Maycock, Tish Jones, Hester Scotton, Jojo Rhodes, Zoe Doyle & Keri Mackenzie

Not only was Fee up to 11th, but a second behind was a runner I met on a hot summer's day on a training course, with calves that would have had Michaelangelo beating a path to her door in Renaissance Florence. Her name was Zoe Doyle [ZLD] and the month after I'd signed her, she was run over by a Range Rover in a badly signed race, and the docs were worried as to whether she'd awake. Terrifying stuff, but here she was in her 3rd race for us after a couple of good relays. Some signing, and she'd only get better. In 18th another newbie: a young Scot named Keri Mackenzie whose laconic demeanor masked an ice-cold drive. "Kerimac" took care of Jojo by 10 seconds. We enjoyed a 49 point lead at the close of play, and we needed it, because the teams were stacked thereafter.

Tish did her best to deal with Jules Bleasdale, but it was not to be as Seb gazes into the distances after the Saltire. Imogen bides her time before placing in a top 20 team at the National for the Belles nine years hence

The late withdrawal of Tish was well absorbed by the gang in December of 2013, and the league lead extended. L-R: JJR, ZLD, MJW, Flic, Fee, HS [B-R] & Helen Brown. Front row, Roo.

Another signing had appeared in the summer via Matt Whiting up in Marlow, that of Melanie Wilkins, in whom we instantly saw strength and stamina at the Autumn relays. Mel was gutted with her turn at the National 10k in Leeds, a little tearful even, and took herself off to Egypt of all places where she flogged herself in training. After ZLD brought us back in 6th at Coulsdon, Mel found a fine 9th and JJR, Flic Cole and Fee saw us home by 23rd. The league was up to 80% chances now, but no room to relax as Herne Hill were no slouches.

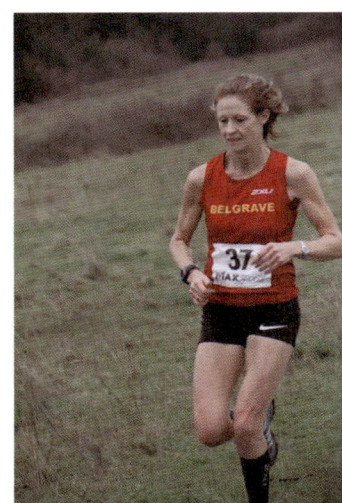

Mel, left, with a huge breakthrough run after big disappointment, the Vixster with so many telling runs over so many years, and the spine of our affairs, Fee

Dreamboat Squad, and yet still Chaos ruled

11 Jan 2014 was one of the peaks of my management career. We scored 33 points! It was total decimatiion of the opposition and the B team were third. It was one of those matches where all the 50-50ers came through. For instance, in the last match we lost Tish [worried about the car's MOT], plus a neat new catch by me, that of Olympic triathlete Michelle Dillon who made it to Coulsdon and turned straight back. I'd neglected to mention the hill. But I got both this time. However, even with such a dreamteam there was still chaos. Thames botched the flags again and the leaders went off course by nearly a minute – about a dozen of them. It happened quite early so Tish had some 20 minutes to rectify matters which she did – with nearly a minute to spare. Incredible stuff, and this athlete was well on the way to becoming one of the top handful or so endurance runners in the country. We'd "hooked up" as coach/athlete the previous summer, and it was such a pleasure to see this talented gem literally soaring. She had the Southerns incoming - could she even win?

There was no way we could be caught for the lead, so I relaxed a lot for the last fixture, which got us a little panicky with the small group that assembled round the flag. But Mel and Zoe D is a heckuva' gutpunch especially with MJW claiming the bronze. Jojo also wasn't going anywhere [but the top 15], and then good old Vicki G was there to score in 4th. ("Are you *sure* you know what you're doing?" she anxiously asked during the week). Headline writer's dream and friend of Hester's, Abbie Friday ["TGIF!"] finally stopped our clock on a luxurious 148 points, but it still meant a 145 point league win.

Back for [Much] More

With poor Tish now battling injury after a magnificent 3rd at the UK Bupa 10,000, we had quite the hole in our ship, but the ladies shrugged off the loss for 2014-15. A chance for another hero to shine. There were many. But first off a team of now old faves. Mel [4th], Zoe D, Kezza, JJR and Fee was such an impeccable line-up, and we had new signing Catherine Lovegrove having one of her best runs in 25th/222, which didn't score! Five more also stood guard and we had 41 points over Guildford, and Thames were off the radar - for once.

Nonsuch a team performance as this

We had a quite remarkable turn-out for the next. 14 athletes, but more than that, all highly competent. Check this out for a possible 5: Lovegrove, Underhill, Cole, Hegvold, Vail Smith. All through in the top 50, and that's the B team. Up front Mel was in the form of her life for 2nd, pushing the redoubtable Hayley Munn hard, Zoe D, right, was terrific in 5th, La metronome Fee in 11th, Jojo 14th and Keri again in 18th. Clapham had a remarkable day to score just 62 points – and a clear sign of intent for the very near future. But it was surely too late for this term, although with such close attention, I signed off my report: it's pedal to the metal ladies.

Rockabye Baby

Champagne leader to Champagne section. Commence dive... now. Ready for Rockabye Baby. Commence spray on countdown. Three, two, one, zero. Champagne leader to Grand Slam task force leader. The baby is asleep. I repeat, the baby is asleep. We're going home now. Out.

And that was just about the gist of it as again, as I quoted Pussy Galore's Flying Circus in the report for Match 3's excitement, as we put the league out

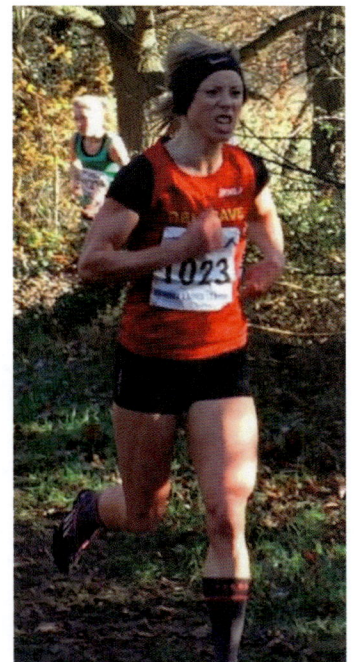

Was it something I said? Still waters run deep and Zoe belies her soft-spoken nature on the racecourse

of sight with a match to go. Clapham had a bit of a horror and there was no way that anyone was taking 115 points out of us in the last match, not when we were scoring around 60 per fixture, and the runners were packing so very deep. Fee couldn't score here, nor could Niki Cahusac in 21st. Sarah Gailey [now Lewis] made one of her oh so rare sojourns and blasted a top 20 return. Zoe D, Keri and Jojo all rock solid as ever and up front Mel and Cathy Ansell had the mother of all duels. Cathy won but not without a near race long struggle.

We'd never call winning the league anti-climactic but with such a loyal and talented squad there was little mystery to be had at Coulsdon, and there was to be no relaxation this time round. The four ever-presents were all right on the money (Mel again getting narrowly duffed up by Cathy, but in the meantime had take her *down* at the Southern]; and we were heartened to see Zoe Vail getting back into her running, such a trooper for us years earlier. For Fee, she had now scored in 12 of the last 15 league races. Amazing stuff. The final league score was Belg 263-CC 427. Bring on the hat-trick assault!

Assault becomes assaulted

The 2015-2016 campaign start disastrously – and just got worse. An enormous unavailable list saw a still promising squad assemble. Zoe VS was now running brilliantly and Mel was still a goer. However, a recent training camp with a rival club saw her boost her weekly mileage from 55 to 90 and she came back a wreck. Mel would finish just one more league race for us. What a shocker after such a wonderful two years: 8 scores, 36 points, taking her quickly to the 16th most prolific Belle of all time in the league, but then *kaboom*. Mel started here, but didn't last long and was in hospital a few days later. Her running days would return, but after a brave effort at the Southern took on a fresh challenge under Nick Anderson [the camp's leader] at Winchester. And now Mel is back with Zoe Doyle at Wycombe. What superb service they gave.

Vale Bowie

After Zoe VS's 8th, the rest did as well as they could but it meant 7th on the day and 100 points off Clapham. We already needed a miracle. My three-line whip didn't work for the next and only four started. What a reversal in fortune, indeed what a mess. Things were better in January, much better – we won. By 70-71 over the now outstanding Clapham squad. My report was pleasing to music buffs as I dropped in nine David Bowie song quotes who had died in the week. There were protein pills and girls floating in a peculiar way... the mice in their million hoards from Ibiza to the Norfolk Broads and poor old Flic probably bore the brunt: "Came on so loaded man, well hung and snow white tan." Mel was described as the mellow-thighed chick who put my spine out of place. Who could fault such lyrics?

I enjoyed the last fixture which had a very fresh look and was a clear sign that "Charlie's Angels" were starting to flourish. It's undeniable that our rebuilding had meant casting the net far and wide for runners, but now it was time to 'go local'. This we did with the thrilling signing of Saron Haileselase, who kept a 2:23 marathoner in Mara Yamauchi at bay, and a squad that went by the moniker of the "Battersea seven". A young Lizzie Goldie-Scot was another to turn the head and blind-side the TMs in 41st. 9th in the league was a bit iffy, but all was due to that horror second match. We were going to be ok.

New look, new excitement

This was confirmed with a terrific start to 2016-17. ZVS was oh so consistent now in her customary 8th, seeing off Saron, with back-up from ZLD, new parkrun pick-up Becky O'Kill and Justine Lynch to see us home. We were just 28 points off the top. This gap grew rather at the next, albeit with another strong squad of double figures; whilst we then unearthed a potential gem at the next in self-confessed "pavement plodder" Sophie Harris who was 10th.

The 2016-17 season kicks off with top 10 Euro cross international Phoebe Law 2477 in line for the win. Two to her right is Megan De Silva, with 1724 another upcoming star in Steph McCal [3rd here]l. Five Belles mean business in ZLD, Zoe VS, Becky Prince [obscured], Saron, Helen White & Lizzie GS. CDM

This was no plodder, but clearly a diamond in the rough who could thrive with a structured training group she was now savouring at Charlie's. Coulsdon for round 4 was incredible. Blanketed in snow, Sophie again led home despite a dreadful fall which led to deep cuts. Sophie the second (Carter) also made a very rare excursion over the country. With Iona Cousland, Bex and Flic closing us in, this was a season to rebuild and take stock. South London were excellent, but we then came through the melee to finish a very understated second, in Charlie's first full season in charge.

Coulsdon left Sophie bloodied but unbowed. Little could we dream of what was to come. CDM [with his wife Fiona as 2784]

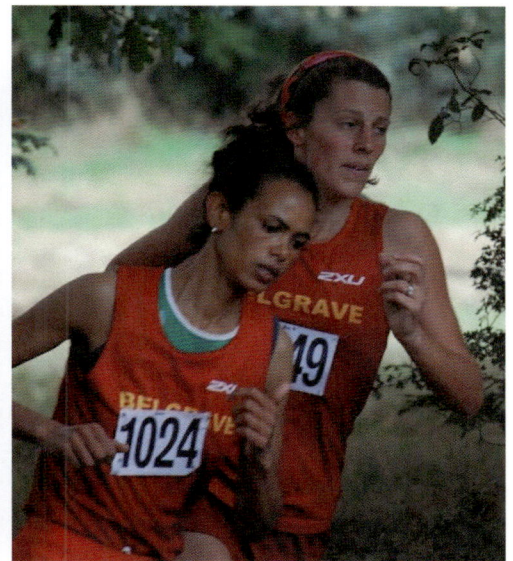

Saron and Zoe; A fine duel between comrades in arms

Amazing feat: Mad about the Harris!

Little could we dream of the thrills that awaited in '17-18. Whilst the team struggled for rhythm, new faces were popping up, and all the while at the front we had the great SGH. And by the front, we mean the very front. Sophie Harris won *all four fixtures* which is the only time this has ever happened for the men or women. Paskar has won four in a row, but over two seasons. It was an incredible feat of top racing, injury and illness avoidance and loyalty to the cause.

Elsewhere, warhorse Saron slogged way and we liked the look of newcomer Mhairi Hall hovering in the early 30s. Elsewhere it was all a tad thin, but we were getting 8 or 9 out and the final damage was 5th in the league, not bad for a squad still under fairly new management and a sea change in the cast.

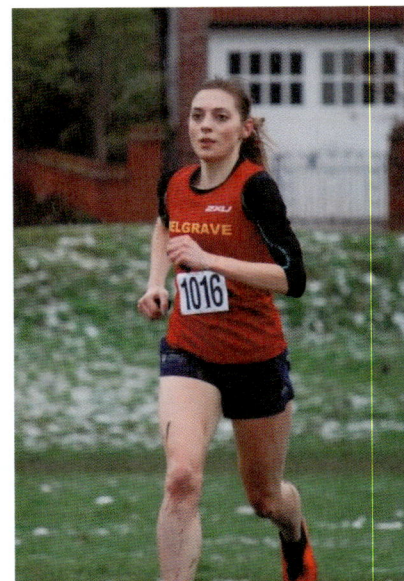

The race to the Grandslam is on! SGH is up against the future world champion in Carla Molinaro [77]... That would be for Land's End to John O'Groats in a time of 12 days flat. The author has been in a four year war with Guinness on that topic as they've waved through a time of 9.1 days for the men by an accomplished chancer who would have only got 14 days – if lucky. But they won't budge – they care nothing for serious sporting achievement anymore – merely stupid records involving faux competition by the masses. It's a great business model but plays absolute havoc with the serious stuff. Elsewhere of note is Clare Elms 164, one of the most prolific racers in the history of the sport and top 6 Olympian Mara Yamauchi [although you wouldn't have known it if you saw the 2008 BBC Beijing coverage].

2018-19

We lost Sophie to Swansea, which let's not sugar-coat, was a disaster, but it's better to have loved and lost... She gave us six Surrey league scores and a maximum 30 points. I wonder how many will equal her 100% winning record in a league season in the next Century. Maybe a couple? We discuss Sophie's loss in more detail in the National 4 stage race of 2018, because to be sure the club can't be signing athletes like this and losing them after a couple of terms.

But we had to crack on. We were going through luminaries like a dose of salts... But we were showing aptitude for replacing them, and on our home patch, Saron finally produced the magesterial run of which we knew she was capable. With company of four into the last 300 of our super fast Wimbledon course, she calmly glided away, and the fragile endurance that she so often struggled with held up a beaut. We then had to go back a tad, but Katie Ellen-French was classy in 19th and old fave Kerimac who we met five long years before, was third home. The Mhairi find continue to develop, and then another sparky kid called Steph Hewitt inside the top 50. Thames however scored 48 points. It was a problem.

Match 2 was pretty grim at Nonsuch although Mhairi was noticeably up to 24th, while Mimi Corden-Lloyd scored for the first time. Things were little improved in Match 3, altho Mhairi rose yet again, and she had company in Alice Reed, who in turn brought along sister Jess. A talented family. Mimi scored again, whilst great things were hoped for from Emma Howsham, but we'd soon lose her to Reading.

116

A large unavailable list saw Georgie Fenn to lead us home in 10th for the final fixture for 6th on the day and 7th overall. Not a great season, but by no means a shocker, and importantly about 10 interesting new names on the books. We looked forward with a quiet optimism.

Epic Chas rebuild

Sophie Cowper of Rotherham had got in touch interested in some second-claim action and we were delight to acquiese. SC was closely followed by another superb signing in Rachel Brown, who had just got our fastest leg up at Sutton Park. She mistimed her kick here to her disappointment, but you know what? We forgave her. Alice Reed had an Ultra looming but heavy legs still meant top 30 whilst Orna McGinley was yet another fresh face. More noted for the track, she was a work in progress. Our day was finished by Camilla Barden and despite being 5th, we were right in the league.

Mesdames Cowper, Brown and Reed remained our key firepower for match two but joined now by the naturally gifted Emily Barrett and Orna closing in, as Alysha Goddard's change of club had yet to come through. This new look squad then bagged a brilliant 2nd at home. We had rehearsed Georgie Fenn thoroughly in training over the course and it all paid off a treat with a magnificent 3rd. Rachel, Emily and Alice were scoring yet again, but then a powerful new runner joined the party in Olivia Papaioannou. Described in dispatches as a 400 metre sprinter, she had a whole new future ahead of her now.

It was a vintage league season with Belles lurking in 3rd behind the mother of all duels some 80 points away between Thames and CC. There will be blood.

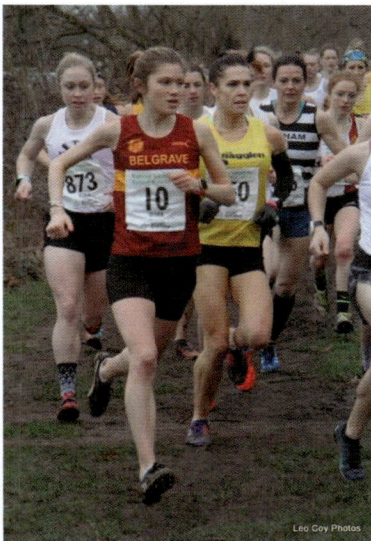

A wonderful 3rd from Georgie on the Common. An even more famous Georgie [Bruinvels] feels the heat, right

Capable of some quite dazzling reps in training, it's no surprise when Emily Barrett scores

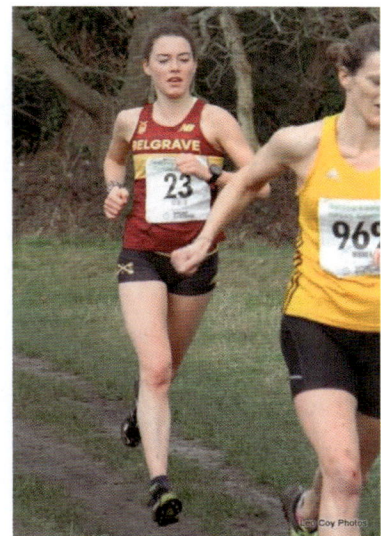

Yet more talent came from Alice Reed, who never seems to have a bad one. Six runs, six scores, 19 points

there was, as Clapham were simply blown away in the final fixture, in fact we all but caught them, falling just 9 points adrift. Thames were sensational and were fully good value for their win. With 11 runners competing, the scorers were now well established, with Georgie still placing top 5, Rachel all but top 10 and then *Paps* (massively on the move), Reed and Hall to see us home. Make no mistake, this was a team on the rise. But then the world stopped.

11 Jan 2020. Whisper it gently, but was Charlie slowly but surely building a remarkable squad? L-R Jess Reed, Paps, Alice Reed, Georgie Fenn, Emily Barrett, Rachel Brown, Camilla Barden, Mimi CL, Jojo Rhodes

Post Covid Mother of all Shellackings

It was clear in Feb of 2020 that the Belles were gearing up to rock the boat in the league. What would 20 months off have done for this band of would-be assassins? Well, it became clear in Covid that one of its phenomena, was that people felt a wee bit frisky and a mini running boom transpired. Attending sessions, when allowed, for those 18 months it became ever so clear that the Belles went from having a handful of 18:20 girls to about 16! Quite incredible. Add in a sub 18 athlete – or 3, with the odd one threatening sub 17 and you surely had one of the most dangerous squads in the country. They rocked up at a stormy Richmond park and as this collage shows, hit the opposition right between the eyes.

Grace Richardson finds a terrific bronze at Richmond. Her season was somewhat becalmed thereafter, and now we've gone and lost her to a Masters at NYU. But she pledges to help out when she can in the coming years

If league chances at the gun stood at about 40% [high, but this was clearly a great squad], after 10 minutes those chances looked more like 94%. What on earth do you do about such an outfit if you're Thames, Clapham or Guildford? Not very much. Over the course the next few months that 94 just kept on rising… to 99 at the end of the second fixture and 100 at the end of the third.

Many thx to SG for this superb collage of a famous day. L-R by row: Adamson, Cowper, Paps, Amend, Hewitt, Vongvorachoti, Corden-Lloyd, Galyer-Barnett, Bray, Goddard, Hards, Vermeulen, Corden-Lloyd, Dewhirst, Goldie-Scott, Bannister

Alix celebrates a great day at the races by putting a traffic sign on her head. Joined in smiles by Mimi, Grace, Lea and Steph

Another Wonderful Turn at Putney Vale

One could but pity the opposition with this claret and gold army marching to the start. The photographer thought back a decade earlier to 2011 at the same venue and recalled the squad about to swallow the bitter pill of relagation. What a brilliant journey it has been since then.

A highlight of this day was the tremendous front-running of Patricia Walker, what a surprise, whilst ever rock steady Rachel Brown led us home. Onto race three and Mitcham and the league was secured in simply resounding fasion, helped no little by the introduction into an already broiling cauldron of Sarah Astin, who took a fine win.

Marching to face the enemy. Even Grace's pony tail is saying: "lemme 'at 'em!"

League title confirmed, after just 75% of the season! Only a severely malfunctioning calculator could persuade the boffins at HQ that the league wasn't put away on Mitcham Common in January, and with a squad like this, it's no surprise. Clockwise from top left: Bethany, Liv, Laurel, Liz, Cat, Mhairi, Ella-May, Flora, Nathalie, Alix, CD, Carmen, Sarah A., Steph, Grace, Sarah D, Lydia & Rachel

Four Mitcham sluggers: Rachel leads Grace, Ella-May's maiden scoring point, with Laurel and Nat keeping watch a little way back

Good things come to those who wait. Jess Saunders roared into the Surrey League points scoring tables with a "triple" at Croydon

And on a low-key season closer [when a hurricane postponed the orginal], we were thrilled to welcome the precocious Maddy Whitman into the squad, aged just 17 and scoring 2nd Belle.

Here's how the scorers landed in 2021-22, for what could be and remain for a long time the greatest Surrey league squad of all time [with due respect to all that Thames and SLH presented down the years].

Grace Richardson	5	4	3		12
Olivia Papaioannou	2	2	2	5	11
Rachel Brown			5	4	9
Sarah Astin			5		5
Lea Adamson	4				4
Maddy Whitman				4	4
Sophie Cowper	3				3
Patricia Walker		3			3
Jess Saunders				3	3
Laura Goodson				2	2
Sam Amend	1				1
Steph Hewitt		1			1
Ella May-Hards			1		1
Mimi Corden-Lloyd				1	1

They have spread the net quite wide, because quite simply, they could afford to, and backing up these fine 14 runners is at least 30 more keeping watch and ready to help if need be. There are 12 backing up in our team image from race three alone.

One of the great pix, which perfectly captures the joy of club athletics. L-R Maddy Whitman, Sarah Dewhirst, Liv Paps, Laura Goodson, CD, Laurel Bray, Jess Saunders [obscuring Jen Beecroft], Laura Shrimpton, Mimi Corden-Lloyd, Steph Hewitt, Cat Hall, Mhairi Hall. SG

All Time Belgrave Surrey League scorers [since October 1979]

First column denotes scores, the 2nd points. 5 points are awarded for the team's top scorer, down to 1 for 5th. See the men's table for more discussion of this system.

138 athletes have scored for the Belles in the Surrey League. 25 names per column.

Name		Score	Points	Name		Score	Points	Name		Score	Points
Tilly Heaton		34	112	Nina Mills		11	25	V Mitchell		3	11
Sarah Murphy		23	103	Morag Andrew		6	24	D Hawkins		4	11
Helen Cole		22	92	Angela Walker		6	23	Chrissie Wellington		2	10
Nikki Haines		16	67	Jacqui Smiter		10	23	Georgie Fenn		2	10
Jacinta Moore		16	65	Rachel Weston		6	22	Pam Davies		2	10
Rosemary Honeychurch		13	63	Mhairi Hall		7	20	J Pearce		3	10
Gabby Collison		15	57	Jenny Webb		6	20	Jen Beecroft		6	10
Tanya Sturton		15	55	Alice Reed		6	19	C.Bruce-Burgess		3	9
Anne Hegvold		17	51	Joanne Warnett		4	19	Christina Pennock		5	9
Catherine Bryson		10	46	Sarah Gailey		5	18	R Elliott		2	9
Juliette Clark		15	46	Olivia Papaioannou		6	17	Karen Fenner		2	8
Zoe Vail Smith		11	43	Jackie Stone		8	15	Wendy Dunsford		2	8
Saron Haileselase		10	42	Wendy Cotterell		3	14	Vicki Clarke		3	7
Fee Maycock		12	40	Maria Sharp		3	14	Kate Dillane		5	7
Zoe Doyle		11	38	Keri Mackenzie		6	14	Sally Underhill		3	7
Mel Wilkins		8	36	Sophie Cowper		3	14	Katie-Ellen French		2	7
Vicki Goodwin		15	33	Felicity Cole		7	13	Annie Briggs		2	7
Samantha Amend		8	32	Georgina Tura		4	13	Kate Houston		2	6
Sophie Harris		6	30	Grace Richardson		3	12	Rieko Trees		2	6
Syreeta Stracey		12	30	Erica Fogg		6	12	Sam Symonds		4	6
Catherine Eastham		16	30	Debbie Hearn		3	11	Emma Howsham		2	6
Jojo Rhodes		14	30	Nelleke Quispel		3	11	Hester Scotton		2	5
Martina Ryan		9	27	Helen Smethurst		7	11	C. Le Poultier		2	5
Tish Jones		5	25	Louise Blizzard		7	11	Rosie Powell		2	5
Rachel Brown		6	25	Tina Jordan		3	11	Iona Cousland		2	5

Name			Name			Name		
Tamsin Growney	1	5	G Husbands	1	3	S.Howard	1	1
Sarah Mulvey	3	5	Stephanie Hewitt	3	3	Amy Linford	1	1
Sarah Astin	1	5	Patricia Walker	1	3	Catriona Knox	1	1
Nici Cahusac	1	4	Jess Saunders	1	3	H.Oriba	1	1
Caroline Shanklyn	1	4	Michelle Dillon	1	2	A. Pike	1	1
Maddy Whitman	1	4	Anoushka Johnson	1	2	Abbie Friday	1	1
Sophie Carter	1	4	S.Couzens	1	2	Madeleine Shott	1	1
Kate Mulvey	1	4	Laura D'Albey	1	2	Gemma Wright	1	1
Christine Bertram	2	4	Justine Lynch	2	2	Camilla Barden	1	1
Vicki Edwards	2	4	Lara Nicod	1	2	K. Charteris	1	1
Rebecca O'Kill	2	4	Lizzie Goldie-Scot	2	2	Carolina Scanlon	1	1
Emily Barrett	2	4	Jess Reed	1	2	S Morrison	1	1
Mimi Corden-Lloyd	3	4	A Coore	1	2	E.Finikin	1	1
Heidi Cayzer	1	3	Susan Pull	1	2	**Total: 138**		
Nikki Neal	1	3	E Bowles	1	2			
Jan Whittington	2	3	Laura Goodson	1	2			
Emily Robbins	1	3	Petra Kasperova	1	1			
J.Oakley	1	3	Ella-May Hards	1	1			
Birhan Dagne	1	3	Sue Porter	1	1			
Sue Clack	2	3	B.Kulidzan	1	1			
Maureen Noel	2	3	H.Saw	1	1			
Orna McGinley	2	3	Rosie Dickinson	1	1			
Linda Sparks	1	3	S.Dyas	1	1			
G Porter	3	3	R.King	1	1			
Rachel Heathcock	1	3	F. Eagle	1	1			

"I used to be the main express... all steam and wheels heading west... but this train don't stop; this train don't stop; this train don't stop here anymore." Coulsdon, December 2013

THE SURREY LEAGUE - MEN

Ahhh, the Surrey league! What can I say? Am I its greatest 'addict' of the last generation or so? Nearly, but not quite. On the all time lists I'm up there somewhere and it's simply because I fell in love with its beauty, charm, ferocity, drama and magic from the end of the last millennium. The league was designed to give athletes a taste for the big time and it certainly succeeds in that quest with dozens of Olympians having passed through its doors – of both genders. It's just a 5 mile cross-country race, but goodness how it sizzles – if you let it into your heart. Belgrave have had a remarkable journey over the 60 years, and nine titles doesn't tell the full story, and admittedly we've struggled for most of the past 50 years, as ten to score is a huge ask, and so often our depth has been found wanting.

Indeed much of my league experience has seen Belgrave toil – rather noticeably – but it hasn't really diluted the pleasure, and the odd relegation battle or three has kept the interest up.

Here's an idea...

The Men's Surrey League was founded on the 3rd May, 1962 at 'The Three Kings', Mitcham, by representatives from Mitcham, Belgrave, Walton, SLH, Surrey AC, Hercules and Herne Hill; although SLH resisted the temptation to compete until 1967.

To some surprise it was Walton who took the spoils in 1962/3 with a 102 point win, Gerry North won the first two races, and Alan Black took the fourth at Addington, with "a power performance that made the rest of the field look like hacks. On a course of heavy snow and occasional patches of frozen plough his effort drew forth superlatives from all sides." 59 years later Alan could still be found supporting his clubmates out on the course, right.

In 1995 Alan Mead [ARM] took over as R&C TM. Alan joined Belgrave in 1958 and by the early 1960's was already editing the Belgravian. He fell in love with the club right from the off, and his performances as athlete, especially in the Southern league were notable and as our Track and Field secretary from the late '70s had really rallied that squad, setting them onto the path to British domination.

Not a purist endurance man, the 4/8 was his metier, Alan nonetheless had the league in his blood, having run it a great many times to build strength for the tartan. Not as a scorer – he didn't do it for that – but he loved the camaraderie and the challenge it presented, knowing how good it was for him. So here he was, stepping up to the plate with a mission that could be described as 'harsh'. For 20 years Aldershot and now Boxhill had raged almost out of control with a league dominance that was hard to envisage breaking. But the thing about Boxhill is that it was more of a project than a 'real' club. Some talented superstars meshing brilliantly with a goal – theirs being Surrey league dominance – and pulling it off. But once two or three of the stars moved on, the house of cards collapsed.

This left an opening, and the league was now up for grabs more than at any time in its history. Thames pounced with fine win in 1995, followed by two somewhat obscure wins from Hounslow, to take nothing from their squads. Thames sharpened their talons and pulled together an astonishingly talented squad that would eventually culminate with one of the most dominant wins ever at the Southern – in the most atrocious conditions – in 2001. Preceding that though were two more league wins in '98 and 99, where they'd regularly get 10 through in 30.

All the while though, the Mead method was to build, oh so slowly, brick by brick. "No easy answers," he headlined an editorial. He needed time. Time that Roman Abramovich would be appalled to give; but the Belgrave committee knew that if someone as organized, diplomatic, personable and passionate as Alan couldn't get us firing, then who?

Elsewhere, help was arriving with some British League superstars who we were trying to turn onto the mud. An outstanding steeplechaser called Lee Hurst started pitching up, as did another great signing Paul Freary, son of the legendary Mike. A new kid called Kevin Nash arrived. And an amazing talent Mark Miles was spotted flying around at the BAL. Gary Staines still had some action in him, having been a real stalwart throughout the last decade. 800 track star Jason Lobo was game, and an under 20 called Quinn looked useful. Messrs Estall, Adams, Alsop, Webb, Foley, Dickinson and Carstairs continued to pump out incisive runs in the engine room. They were joined in the summer of '98 by the author "Billy the kid". And before you knew it, suddenly, a very dangerous squad was in the offing…

Everybody Out!

The message at the start of 1999-2000 was "everybody out for the league - we can win this thing". I had a shocker in that first race but precious few else did. We edged out the Saltires by 35 points to set up the season. Topped and tailed by Staines and Cockerell, we packed a whole lot of goodness in between including the talented – if short-lived – Steve Clarke and Rob McHarg.

A spectacular race followed on Thames' home patch in November as they threw everything at us. But even with Gary getting a stone in his shoe in what turned out to be his last race of a wonderful Belgrave career, we lost by "only" 29 points, with "Gnasher" starting out on an incredible 6 years for us, tracking home Yitbarek Dinku who was 2nd. The euphoria of it all inspired me to the top 30 where I savoured a duel with my pal "Coggie", Paul Coughlan, a friendly and loquacious Kiwi, over to our shores for a couple of years.

In the awfully long run in [the course was 800m longer than today] I was getting mugged by a couple of Thames guys, and Paul just up ahead had two more Saltires on his tail. I could envisage all four of them taking us out and in some hysteria screamed warning – in triplicate – which Paul heeded. He got his guys and I got mine. Great memories. Paul jarred his ankle badly that day, and alas it was never quite the same again, but he made a telling contribution to our affairs during his time here and still follows us with great enthusiasm a generation on.

A bit of a 'mare' followed as Thames ran riot on our home patch before Christmas. They closed in 27, us in 52. Bad news! Our mood was assuaged by a magnificent debut from Mark Miles who duffed up Dave Taylor (4th in the marathon at the '98 Commonwealths) for the win. The loss though was 80 points as we could find only one runner (Rog) between Yitbarek in 7th and Steve Clarke and myself in 32 and 33.

It was a rather depressing day as 75 points to pull back on such a fantastic squad that was only scoring 161 points seemed like a 100-1 shot. A tumultuous decade had ended on a disappointing note.

Impossible to describe euphoria

Ending the 1990s with that minor cliffhanger, we arrived at 5 February 2000 and can do no better than reproduce Alan's magnificent report in full:

Belgrave Harriers top the Surrey C.C. League for the first time in 28 years

1, Belgrave H ....(1, 3, 4, 7, 8, 9, 11, 15, 21, 30) . 109
2, Thames H&H ....(10, 12, 14, 16, 17, 22, 25, 32, 34, 35) . 217
3, Herne Hill H ....(2, 27, 28, 29, 36, 41, 43, 46, 52, 62) . 366
4, South London H ....(5, 19, 20, 37, 39, 47, 49, 51, 55, 58) . 380
5, Ranelagh H ....(13, 18, 23, 31, 40, 45, 48, 50, 61, 66) . 395
6, Aldershot F&D AC ......(24, 26, 33, 38, 42, 44, 53, 54, 57, 74) . 445
7, Borough of Hounslow AC (6, 56, 59, 64, 68, 71, 72, 78, 84.5, 85.5) . 643
8, British Airways ....(60, 63, 65, 67, 69, 70, 73, 75, 76, 77) . 695
9, Met. Police AC were unable to take part due to a fixtures clash

Final League Table 1999-2000

1, Belgrave H	....	800
2, Thames H&H	....	834
3, Herne Hill H	....	1438
4, South London H	....	1559
5, Aldershot, F&D AC	....	1761
6, Ranelagh H	....	1874
7, Borough of Hounslow AC	....	2279
8, Met. Police AC	....	2878
9, British Airways	....	2957

Individual winners

Seniors
D.Taylor (Herne Hill H) .... 6 pts

Juniors
S.Barber (Ranelagh H) 12pts

Veterans
G.Jerwood (Herne Hill H) 11pts

Under 13
E.Rimdap (Belgrave H) 17pts

It's almost too difficult to describe the euphoria that enveloped the Belgrave contingent gathered around the flag on the slopes of Farthing Downs. Not only had we won the race handsomely but we'd come back from a 74 point deficit to carry off the League title in dramatic fashion. The team response to the challenge had been terrific and the sight of so much 'claret and gold' at the head of the field put a spring in the step and brought a tear to the eye of the most hardened Belgrave supporter.

Great win from the Colts

The youngsters set the tone for the afternoon by dominating the youngest of the age groups and carrying off the under-13 title - when did that last happen? Well done Reg Hopkins and Paul and Kim Collier for their enthusiastic organisation. Well done too, Elvis Rimdap, who was awarded the trophy for the best performance in all four races. To see his thrilled expression when he was later awarded the shield was worth the trip to Coulsdon alone.

As the senior men's field assembled it was noted that Dave Taylor of Herne Hill was indeed taking part to give him a 100% turn-out record in the League, and Hounslow's Mike Simpson, fourth-placer from the previous week's "Southern", was also in the line-up. This was to be a classy race.

Our colours were prominent from the instant the race began but one of the sights to remember over a lifetime of athletics came when Captain Roger Alsop, back from Germany just the night before, burst through only a minute or so into the race to lead the field with the whole Belgrave pack falling in behind him in close formation. As the weak February sunshine lit up the downs some eight or nine Belgrave vests crested that initial hill together at the head of the echelon before setting out for the delights of Happy Valley.

When next in view at the 2 miles point it was the home club's Stuart Major making the pace but right behind him was Taylor, and then our own Geremew Wolde and Yitbarek Dinku with Mark Miles tracking all four and looking oh! so comfortable. Three in five ... but this was nothing, for after a very short gap came Paul Freary 6th, Lee Hurst 8th, the bandana'd Charles Herrington 9th and then Kevin Nash and Alaster Stewart inside the dozen. Roger was beginning to feel the effects of German business lunches and that extravagant start, 17th, and then Phil Carstairs closed the team in at 30th. The Thames Team Manager urged on his white vested men, "Come on now. They've got 9 in 17". Tackling the long climb for the second time it was now Geremew making the pace and Mark closely watching everything he did; Taylor was also right behind and there was nothing in it.

The humped back shape of the downs near the finish means that the runners cannot be seen until the very last minute by those waiting at the funnel. Who would it be, Taylor, Miles, even Geremew? Suddenly we knew. As our under-13 team waiting at the final turn leapt up and down and shouted with excitement it was Mark Miles, scything round that final curve with a ferocious finishing burst that Dave Taylor could not answer. Then the Belgrave team streamed home: Geremew 3rd, Yitbarek 4th (what a prospect for the National Junior Champs.), Paul Freary 6th in the Southern but 7th here, Lee holding onto his 8th, Charles 9th (three runs for Belgrave and three team wins), Alaster with his customary strong second lap getting the better of Kevin Nash who was in turn overtaking Thames men at the finish, Roger gritting his teeth and getting home in 21st - and Will Cockerell fighting tooth and nail to become our tenth man yet again. One hundred and ten points to Thames Hare & Hounds' 217. The league was ours by 33 points! Has there ever been such a low team score since the league went to nine teams? Have two clubs ever got below 900 in the same season? The archives will be delved into to answer these questions; but on this day it remained for us to enjoy the curry at Belgrave Hall (thanks to Don Anderson and Val Tanner) and champagne (thanks Gordon Biscoe) to complete a great day. And roll on the "National"!

1, M.Miles (Belgrave) 27:17
2, D.Taylor (HHH) 27:21
3, G.Wolde (Belgrave) 27:38
4, Y.Dinku 27:58; 7, P.Freary 28:13; 8, L.Hurst 28:29; 9, C.Herrington 28:38; 11, A.Stewart 28:51; 15, K.Nash 29:01; 21, R.Alsop 29:31; 31, W.Cockerell 30:11; 34, P.Carstairs 30:23; 53, M.Webb 31:28; 55, B.Barton 31:33; 62, D.Ochse 31:48; 68, E.Lemenager 32:40; 82, A.Luce 33:36; 83, D.Anderson 33:36; 105, J.Mather 35:42; 106, A.Cowmeadow 35:53; 116, R.Bale 37:57; 127 finished.

Under 15 Boys
1, M.Conway (HHH) 16:59
2, P.Graham (Belgrave) .....17:44.
Teams:
1, Ranelagh H 99
2, Herne Hill 100
3, Belgrave 101
Overall:
1, Boro' Hounslow 230.5
2, Herne Hill H 293
3, Ranelagh H 417.5
4, South London H 420.5
5, Belgrave H 538.5
Under 13
1, A.Ulrych 17:27
4, E.Rimdap 21:06; 5, R.Leigh 21:16; 6, J.Kelly 21:20; 7, K.Taylor 21:28; 8, R.Collier 23:08; 9, B.McCarthy 23:42.
Teams:
1, Belgrave H 23
Overall:
1, Belgrave H 129

The site of Roger drifting into the lead of such a stacked field was a true "captain's innings" which he paid for over the next half hour, but he wouldn't change the strategy of his run – it was classic 'leading from the front stuff'.

And if THAT was good…

The following season was a non-event for us, but then we were at it again! A smooth win at Brockwell, a demolition job by Thames on our home patch but then a tremendous win for us at Petersham with an outstanding side. Here's how they rolled in:

1 S Sharp
4 C Moss
5 P Freary
7 A Zawadski
8 L Hurst
18 C Herrington
20 W Cockerell
21 K Hegvold
33 R Alsop
38 J Wolf.

Chas, Knut and Will ran lock step pretty much all way, and the league is nearly secured - despite Charlie parting company with his in motion Kawasaki the day before

It all meant a 549-586 scoreline in the Bels' favour – roll on the decider. If we could come back from 75 points down at Coulsdon in 2000 then surely we could hold onto to 37?

Astonishing climax

But try as he might, Alan found grappling with the team like a bar of soap, as man after man slipped away. What he produced was some dazzling talent, but missing a star - or four. To be sure it wasn't a patch on the 2000 side.

It still appeared as though it would hold as Allen Graffin and Paul Evans is quite the one-two gut-punch. But Thames had parachuted in upcoming Commonwealth steeplechaser Don Naylor from Edinburgh, who went onto win the race in fine style. Allen grabbed second and Paul had a fall but secured the bronze. But then what?!

"Come OOOOOONNNNN!! We're Loooooooosing!"

When strongman Steve Kennefick had to pull out early with a cold, Thames were handed a 40 point gift. Early in the race it was clear that our supporters was on edge, and by half-way they were beside themselves. "Come OOOOOONNNNN!! We're *Loooooooosing*!" They screeched.

Surely some mistake. But concern filled the air like a heavy cloak. Apparently we were a good 10 points adrift. Each runner needed to zap someone. Well it certainly wasn't going to be me, suffering from the ramifications of a hot date-turned-all-night bender. Even my cabbie admonished me at 5am for my lack of sobriety.

Here's Rex Bale's collage of the day to portray some looks of real concern of the lads:

Photos: Rex Bale

But there were heroes too. Recent signing Mike Trees of world triathlon fame, had a blinder in 5th and the rarely sighted Ray Foley, who we never saw in the vest again, took the call and made up at least 10 of the spots on his own, with a marvellous run back in the 40's.

And it meant that amazingly, after four months of hard racing, the league returned to Belgrave by just 6 points! Nothing could quite replicate the euphoria of 2000, but this was still very special.

The team [pictured, in order] was:

2 Allen Graffin; 3 P Evans; 5 M Trees; 9 A Stewart; 17 C Herrington; 20 R Alsop; 23 W Cockerell; 34 J Wolf; 35 K Quinn; 45 R Foley.

Time to reflect…

Yep, this is showing up alright. At an absolutely stacked season opener in 2003, Marty Dent & Sharpy had a superb duel. Marty won. ARM

It was time to take a deep breath and Alan had to consider his priorities and options moving forward. Managing the road and country section is a huge job – especially if you're trying to make it the best in England – as Alan was. And as we well know, throughout these pages, he more than succeeded in that quest.

But something had to give, and the League was it. For the remainder of the noughties, the Bels showed up, and largely kept out of the trouble.

But those next 7 years we could only watch and admire the rise of a remarkable Herne Hill squad constructed by Geoff Jerwood with great skill and dedication.

Thames remained at the top of their game and Belgrave were content to take cover with shellfire all around. We never gave in though and would occasionally turn in a gem, as with our wins at the 04-05 opener at Brockwell and our favourite course at Petersham in Feb of '07, defeating HHH by 37 points and THH by an even 100. The exceptional David Anderson won both those days defeating cross-country specialist Chris Smith in a fine duel. Chris did a few Surrey leagues but was first claim TVH.

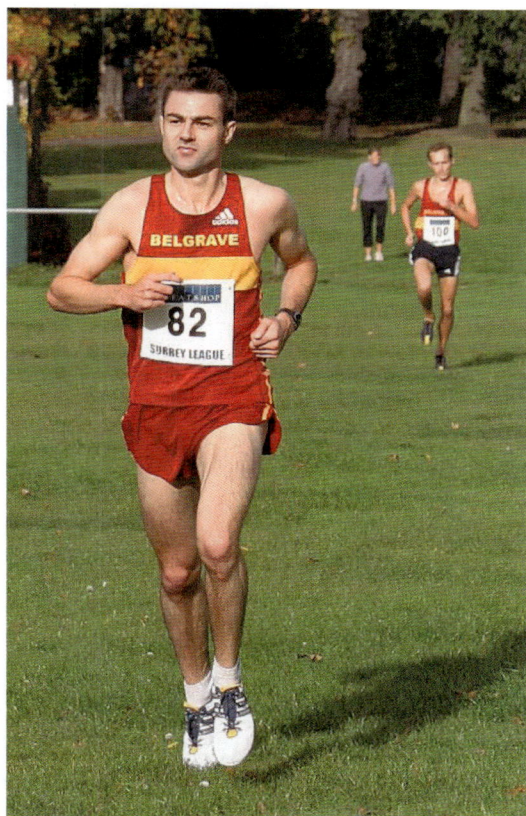

Another season opener [2004], another bridesmaid turn for Stevarino, but at least they're Bels he's falling to. This time to the imperious Danders. Maria looks on forlornly. ARM

10 October 2009. Paskar debuts at the league! He would run it for a decade without missing a race, incredible stuff. Tucked behind PO is John Kimaiyo. Other league luminaries include EE's Will Clark 55, evergreen Jeff Cunningham and the author next along, with league addicts Pete Haarer and James McMullan 411. The Team GB firepower here is incoming from Huw Lobb and Ben Whitby [who would dispose of the Lion]. We spy the thinning thatch of Simon Molden, whilst a remarkable HHH fab four of Keith Newton, Dave Robinson, Alan Barnes and Iain Lockett hunker over on the right. 172 League scores between that little lot, and over 200 when you chuck in Jeff. This was peak Herne Hill time and they would batter the field with 165 points, although Thames placed four in 7 and gasped to a 203. Belgrave were 3rd with an iffy 434. ARM

Chris is one of three Surrey League Podium finishers who tragically lost their lives in recent years. Sam Haughian won at Petersham in 2001 and died in a car accident in South Africa in 2004; and Ed Prickett who placed 2nd at Brockwell in 2002, also died in 2004 in another traffic accident. On 27 October 2020, Chris ventured out for the 15 mile circuit of Meall nan Aighean, Carn Mairg, Meall Garbh and Carn Gorm and died of hypothermia.

Belgrave Harriers remembers all three athletes with great affection and respect.

2010-2019

This decade was notable for two key things – the outstanding performance of Paskar Owor, who missed just a single race and won a dozen of them, to make him the 4th finest Surrey Leaguer in history on the win count, and the astonishing arrival of Kent AC in 2012, who were far, far too good for us and most anyone. To this day there's a little discussion as to Kent's inclusion, but from a personal viewpoint it's brought the standard of the league up hugely and every club had to raise their game an awful lot. There are no more whipping boys in Div 1 and relegation for a club who is going through an iffy spell is a clear and present danger.

One of the finest Surrey League images of all time, brilliantly captured by Leo, our thanks to him. Four terrific runners in Phil, Danny Davis [of Leeds, SLH, AFD and St Mary's], evergreen John Gilbert & the Lion. Richmond, Feb 2014. LC

And also from the above race: The Trondheim Stallion. One of only seven men to have scored in 40+ Surrey Leagues, Knut was placing in the top eight into his 5th decade. Here he is tracked by another loyal slugger in Alex Luce, who has 17 scores of his own. LC

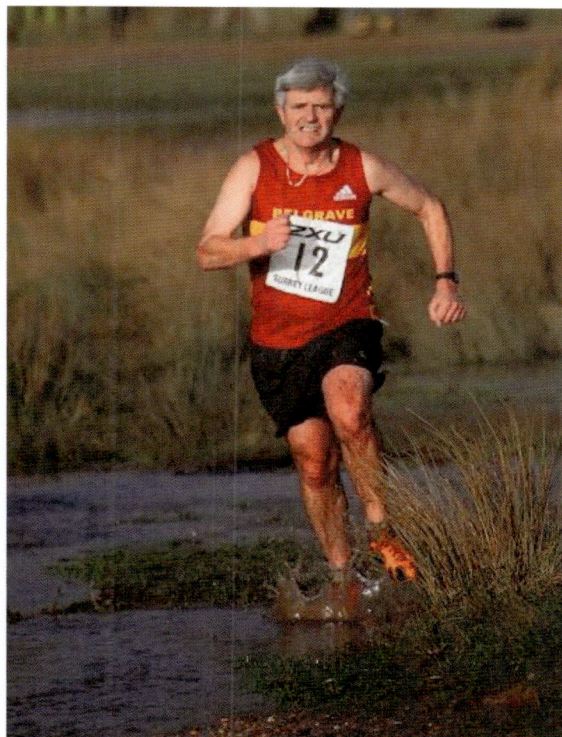

Racing line! 1983 Road and Country skipper 'Donnyboy' Anderson still on the prowl, and remains the club record holder for most Nationals. Throughout his 40-odd years with the club he has been Jack of all Trades [and sometimes Master], and has served a deserved Presidential spell. LC

As uncomplaining a rank and file club man as you'll get, Rob Norville's best distance is arguably the 600m - he would have made quite a few waves with that! But he never shied away from the country and pieced together some important runs down the years and served a spell as Membership sec. LC

The class in this man! We may've only gotten hold of Mike Trees in the perceived autumn of his career, but he still had incredible quality, with a top 5 in the league and very low 24 for a 5 mile relay. And he was very kind to sponsor our 2XU club kit for years. We are always delighted to see Mike and family on UK visits from Japan. LC

I took over the reins from Alan in 2014 and after a fairly smooth opening season (if one overlooks my attracting a grisly five runners to my first race… plus all three Bels R&C TM's who donned the vest, Charlie, Terry and I), we hit trouble the following term. I wasn't too worried as we had an 80-odd point buffer over Clapham in Feb of 2016, but as race day dawned, runner after runner bit the dust. Valentine's Day… a body under a train… nursing a niggle… you name it. Surely we'd still be ok, especially when Ed Auden arrived at 2:59pm and 41 seconds. The counts came in and amazingly we tied with the Chasers over the entire season, but because they got their last man in ahead of us on the last day, they stayed up. It was a brutal reverse, and perhaps we only had ourselves to blame, but I'm pretty pleased with the squad I had on paper at 10am on the Saturday, but losing those 5 men cost around 200 points. And earlier in the season we lost another 60 points when we didn't understand the full rules about athletes being cup-tied.

A relic from the Cold War?! Don't you believe it. Phil Carstairs was still scoring for us deep into the 2010s and won the Cross-country Plate numerous times in the '90s before it officially became a thing. And he was a true Parliament Hill beast. Retirement claimed him a few years ago, altho' in July of 2022 I spied him racing in Battersea. "Soooooo busted," I bellowed. LC

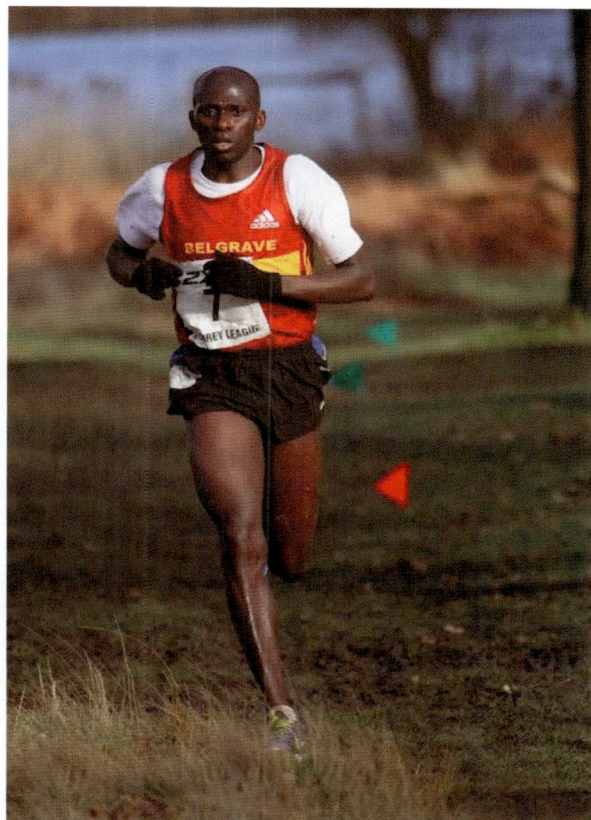

PO canters to the win, having shaken off his fine comrades from the opening image of this salvo. LC

A very nasty moment, yes, but we took our medicine and the lads bounced straight back uncomplainingly in 2017 with a resolute season.

Carl Lawton, perhaps the most prolific Belgravian of all time with some 40 results a year for 40 years, helps out with the results in Nov 2015

A fab four to warm the cockles of any heart, with Bundle, Auden, Williams and AJ ensuring promotion here at Richmond in Jan 2017. And we can't cut out Ollie Garrod, right, one of the most prolific race junkies in the history of the sport, and massive Parkrun world record holder for race wins with over 350. Check out his PO10, but in a nutshell, 810 races since 2008 and he still pings along merrily doing Ultras for Team GB. Makes one weep when you get the old excuse: "can't race… racing again next week." Ollie recently raced four times in one weekend, including the National cross, a Half and two 5ks

The Labours of Hercules

At around this time, the rise of Hercules Wimbledon became impossible to ignore and they all but grabbed the league on a bad day for us in 2018. As for Belgrave, we'd only go down if we turned in the worst performance in our history, and we turned in the third worst, just edging out our friends at Clapham for small revenge on two years earlier.

Oh so slowly though, there were signs that there was a good squad waiting to be built if we could just get the guys to gel. On a broiling season opener in 2018 there was evidence of that gelling

"Hi honey, yes, doing the race now. I'm in the lead pack... Owor's all over the place and not sure what the fuss is about Goolab." Max Nicholls 418 and Anthony Haynes 516 will fade to 7th and 9, but winner Phil Sesemann lurks, centre. 213 is Haward Craske

hotting up. Over 20 around the flag and some damn good runners. Here's the scoring 10:

2 N Goolab
4 P Owor
22 K Touse
36 A Jaksevicius
57 A Cumine
59 A Dumez
62 B Courtney-pinn
69 E Auden
76 R Finlay
79 B Hurley

Arne Dumez tracks the legendary Stuart Major who has a remarkable 89 scores in the league between 1988-2022, and maybe more incoming. 805 is Simon Wurr who himself could become Thames' most prolific ever man were it not for Ben Reynolds being a moving target. 521 is Ian Kenton who is soon to find he's caught the wrong train. SG

Alex Luce has been turning up for the Surrey League since the 1980s, and still goes like a good 'un

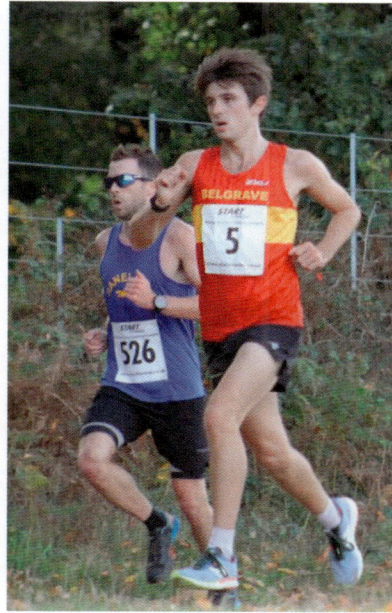

One of the very encouraging new batch who started arriving at the club, Brad Courtney-Pinn, via such paradise hotspots as Truro and the Pontypridd Roadents

This was the following month on the Common in biblical conditions, but our Lithuanian and Greek fighters, Andreas Jaksevicius and Tinos Touse hung in there gallantly. Poor old Nick Goolab saw his assault on the win dip to an unheard of position in the 30s due to horrendous visibility and inadequate spikes.

466 points may sound like a hefty figure but it was good enough for 5th, and showed that the Bels still had some high grade fuel in the tank. Hercules won the league with a very strong squad, with Belgrave finishing the 2010s in 7th, but a long way clear of the drop zone.

The 2020s

Fast forward a year and more progress with Steve and Arne now in charge. This is how the league table looked after a stunning Kent performance:

Men season scores: 2019-20 Div 1

Team scores after 4 matches

Match	KEN	H/W	SLH	THH	HHH	BEL	G&G	C/C	DUL
Match 1	204	297	326	335	451	576	473	743	690
Match 2	197	281	414	418	451	445	547	616	726
Match 3	159	247	474	515	406	431	602	561	700
Match 4	162	270	422	387	395	502	670	581	706
Points	722	1095	1636	1655	1703	1954	2292	2501	2822
Position	1	2	3	4	5	6	7	8	9

Certainly the top two were still somewhat adrift, but 200 points in a league race is not too much, basically 3 good runners. Could Belgrave find those from somewhere? They certainly could, and if Covid 19 hadn't wiped out the next season, we'd have seen that to full effect.

The future then for this wonderful little competition looked good with seven clubs never so strong all at the same time, and from a claret and gold standpoint and post Covid we were ready to rumble.

A cheerful squad show that league athletics at Belgrave is looking healthy at Croydon in Feb 2020. L-R: Will Stockley 14th, Dylan Mitchard 122nd, Nathan Visick 77th, Conall McNally 84th, Steve Gardner 76th, Lawrence Burton 142nd, Arne Dumez 43rd, Matt Edgar 57th, Ben Ireland 126th, Rob Norville 159th, Front: Dave Walsh 128th, Alex Mills 98th, Michael McCarthy 45th, Alex Miller 65th, Paskar Owor 23rd, Alex Janiaud 154th, Will Cockerell 138th

The Boys are Back!

The 2021-22 season was a most enjoybale romp and it was wonderful to have the league back. Steve and Arne put the blinkers on and basically 'declared war' on our circumspect returns over the last decade, and it meant that a hat-trick of Championship races were ignored before Christmas.

It was profligate stuff and given the size of the squad we could probably have afforded to take a look at the South of England XC relay which only needs a quartet to go 5k over the Scrubs, and the two SoTs. But a well run club understands the importance of giving the TMs free reign and trusting their vision. The only flaw in the approach may have been that HW remained so strong that we weren't going to beat them anyway and by halfway they had a 400 point lead on us. Also, one never really knows when a squad is going to "get hot", sometimes things fall into place and amazing things happen. But if you're not there, you'll never know. It also vastly increases the importance of the races you *do* send squads to after Christmas, and we had a run of poor form in the spring despite them being 'ring-fenced' as ones to target.

However, for the league, it all came together: in Race 3 at Mitcham, we WON our first League race since Feb 2007, it was a brilliant return and a great fillip for the new regime.

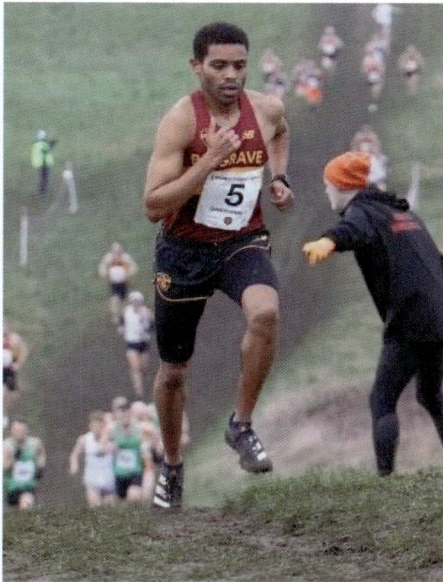

Sammy G is surely one of the top 5 signings of the millennium. A superb runner, but with an unflappable stickability and never say die spirit. SG

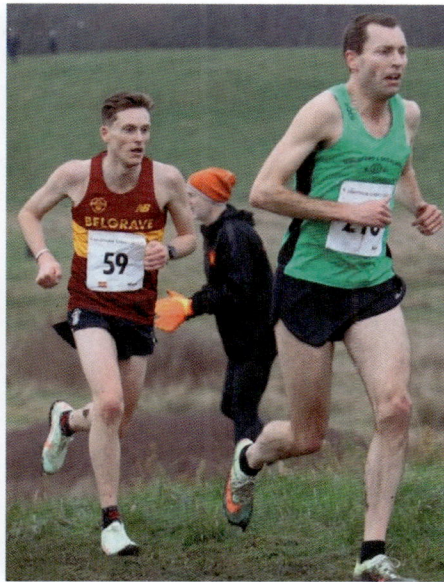

Dylan Evan is a magnificent 2nd claim find, and comfortably won the League title. Here he duels with the great Andy Coley-Maud. SG

Neil Wilson always makes waves when we see him, and here Conall is en route to winning the Cross-country Plate. SG

We then won again in race 4 and could savour boasting the overall league winner in Dylan Evans. In short, for a confirmed *Leagueaholic* like myself I am at ease with Steve and Arne's 'blinkers on' strategy – you have to say it worked. The athletes won't always accept us skipping races, but with a strong foundation and being right up at the sharp end of the league, the rest should fall into place.

Our engine room is spearheaded by the likes of Callum Stewart, Craig Ruddy [remember him?!], Conall McNally, Tommy Taylor, Jonnys Neville & Scott, Angus Lamb and Nick Buckle, and with the plethora of new stars like Sam, Reece Edwards, Josh Trigwell and Dylan, we really are in a position to "rock on" for the coming decade. And the last word goes to my comrade Andy Robinson over at *Reportlab* for revolutionising the league's result's service with his superb website. It really does make all the difference to be able to savour the day's action after 2 hours, rather than 2 days (or 2 weeks, or sometimes 6 weeks, back in the day).

Reece Edwards leads the entire field at Mitcham. It was gung ho stuff and too much gas, but showed crucial intent. SG

"Legga" legs it! The England cricketer Alan Lamb was known as Legga, so if it's good enough for him, it'll do for Angus Lamb, who sprung a real surprise by outkicking Dan Wallis here [albeit sans spikes.] SG

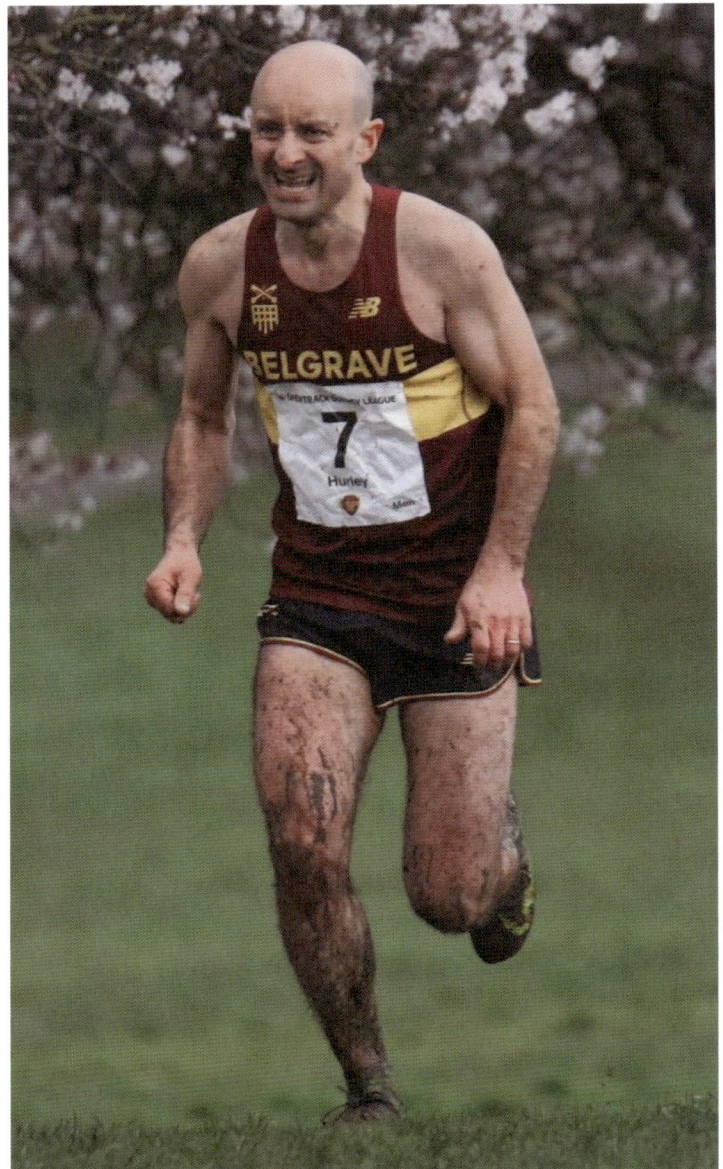

Ben Hurley continues to churn out strong runs for the Bels into his 3rd separate decade of performing with us, and he's well inside our top 100 league scorers of all time. SG

Match	H/W	BEL	G&G	KEN	THH	SLH	HHH	RAN	FUL
Match 1	164	319	444	345	382	465	553	617	806
Match 2	129	369	325	347	576	462	465	643	779
Match 3	233	224	257	344	426	543	521	701	846
Match 4	290	195	384	425	250	467	495	760	829
Points	816	1107	1410	1461	1634	1937	2034	2721	3260
Position	1	2	3	4	5	6	7	8	9

The final 2021-22 table. A superb effort by the Bels and most remarkable perhaps is Guildford seeing off Kent. Just a few years ago such a thing would have been quite unthinkable, but such are the huge swings in fortune in this capricious game

138

Belgrave top 200 scorers in the Surrey League [Founded 1962]

First column denotes scores, the 2nd points. 10 points are awarded for the team's top scorer, down to 1 for 10th. There are more forensic or scientific ways to rank the runners, but after a few scores, the disparity in method is negligible. For instance, Owor's 398 points off 42 scores tallies well with O'Connor's 298 off 50. Or in the battle of the Andersons, Don claims 36 from 17 scores, whilst David gets 38 off just 4. 388 athletes scored for Belgrave in the sixty years of the League between 1962-2022.

The leading scorer over at Herne Hill is Dave Taylor with 354 pts from 42 scores, and for Thames it's Ben Reynolds with 452 pts off 70. The Surrey league record for scoring runs is Stuart Major [SLH] with 89. Stuart's first score was in 1988, and he was still scoring in 2022.

Name			Name			Name			Name		
Will Cockerell	74	480	Frank Ward	23	120	Tony Binda	17	66	Geoff North	8	47
Paskar Owor	42	398	Colin Pearson	25	116	Peter Carton	8	65	Mark Humphrey	15	46
Gerry North	40	369	Bob Richardson	13	113	Nick Goolab	7	65	Bill Kerr	9	44
Pat O'Connor	50	298	Stephen Sharp	11	107	L. Lyons	12	64	C Barber	5	43
John Bicourt	42	276	Adrian Major	21	104	John Gladwin	9	61	Roy Maddams	8	43
Jim Estall	31	255	Bill Weller	15	102	Matt Kinane	9	61	Matt Taylor	6	42
Laurie O'Hara	31	252	Mike Webb	25	97	Tom Ellacott	10	61	Andy North	5	41
John Thresher	31	247	Edward Auden	13	88	Simon Williamson	12	61	Matt Chaston	6	41
Knut Hegvold	40	230	Mark Sinclair	17	86	Ian Duncan	9	61	P. Sanders	7	41
Roger Alsop	40	224	John Abberton	11	85	John Dear	17	60	Gus Upton	5	41
Tony Fairclough	35	206	Malachi Byansi	14	84	Richard Stannard	9	59	Dylan Evans	4	40
Gary Staines	21	195	Leo Coy	24	84	Nick Buckle	9	57	Al Stewart	6	40
Jim Rimmer	33	194	Bruce Barton	18	82	Arne Dumez	9	56	James Fairbourn	9	40
Lionel Mann	34	193	Kassa Tadesse	9	82	P. Richley	7	55	Jonathan Hobbs	5	40
Gerry Adams	29	182	John Stow	12	82	Tim Weeks	15	54	Martin Lake	11	40
Ollie Foote	21	168	Justin Chaston	9	81	Mike Lake	12	53	S Maynard	6	39
Trevor Hart	32	166	Charlie Dickinson	21	79	Chris Steer	10	53	Ben Hurley	9	39
Marcello Bizio	25	142	Simon Holmes	16	79	Warren Lynch	16	52	A. Paton	7	38
Alan Black	25	137	M Hayes	11	78	Pete Willis	9	52	David Anderson	4	38
Andrius Jaksevicius	16	135	Kevin Nash	10	77	Charlie Dabbs	9	52	Owain Lewes	9	38
Dave North	19	134	P. Gilbey	11	73	Dick Piotrowski	7	51	Rob Norville	17	38
Phil Carstairs	34	134	Nick Bundle	11	71	Mel Thorpe	8	51	Alex Luce	17	37
Phil Wicks	14	131	Lee Hurst	8	68	Lander Eguia	8	50	Dave Beaver	8	36
Stuart Paton	18	123	J Wright	7	66	Paul Freary	6	48	Don Anderson	17	36
Mike Trees	20	120	Charlie Walker	12	66	Bob Smith	9	48	Richard Ward	4	36

Name			Name			Name			Name		
Clive Gilby	5	35	Tony Barden	6	26	G Mackie	2	20	Taras Telkovsky	2	16
Callum Stewart	5	35	Kyle Marks	3	26	Mark Miles	2	20	Kieran Gilfedder	3	16
Mike Kazimierski	10	33	Steve Gardner	6	26	Matt Yates	2	20	Craig Ruddy	3	16
Joachim Wolf	8	33	John Kimaiyo	3	25	Will Stockley	2	20	Alex Bodin	2	15
Junior Galley	11	33	Padraic Buckley	3	25	Neil Speaight	3	20	Ray Tubbs	3	15
Matt Welsh	7	33	Kelly Diprose	4	24	Rick Hayman	3	20	Jack Brown	3	15
J Cox	6	32	J Hampshire	5	24	Brian Gorman	8	20	P Whewell	3	15
John Mather	12	32	Patrick McDougall	7	24	Steve Zealey	8	19	G. Tiernan	3	14
Pat Newell	22	31	Konstantinos Touse	3	24	Don McLean	6	19	M Stickles	2	14
Andrew Connick	4	31	Sam Gebreselassie	3	24	A McIntosh	2	18	P Rickley	3	14
Kevin Gadd	5	30	Lee Greatorex	5	23	Geremew Wolde	2	18	S. Hewes	4	14
M Waller	6	30	Stephen Kennefick	4	23	Hassan Raidi	2	18	Mike Shingles	4	14
Rob McHarg	5	30	Charles Herrington	4	22	John Charles	3	18	Peter Hilliar	3	14
James Kelly	3	29	Chris Axe	5	22	Steve Clarke	3	18	Brad Courtney-Pinn	3	14
James Ryle	3	29	Kevin Quinn	5	22	Nick Smallwood	4	18	M Head	6	13
M. Anderson	10	29	Martin Holm	3	22	Adam Zawadski	2	17	M. Nouch	5	13
Marty Dent	3	29	Guy Monnet	4	22	Dave Mason	4	17	Najibe Hliouat	3	13
J Jackson	8	29	Andrew Cumine	4	22	Jason Lobo	2	17	Joe Reilly	2	13
Jason Webb	10	28	D O'Hara	4	21	Ferdie Gilson	2	17	James Browne	4	13
Conall McNally	8	28	Eliot Lyne	5	21	Paul Lowe	3	17	P Hardwick	3	13
Derek Fernee	6	27	Marco Mazzotta	5	21	Reece Edwards	2	17	Josh Trigwell	2	13
B Sawyer	4	27	Zekeriyas Abery	3	21	Matt Hillier	4	16	Peter Sadler	2	12
Tom Dowdall	7	27	Alex Mills	9	21	Rob Harding	5	16	Clayton Scott	2	12
Bill Dance	6	26	J Moore	4	20	Said Chettati	4	16	Lyn Jones	2	12
Paul Coughlan	4	26	Adrian Passey	2	20	Tim Watson	2	16	James Williams	2	11

SURREY COUNTY CHAMPS - MEN

Remarkable sequence, but Gold so hard to mine

Our history at this always entertaining race, the precursor to "the big ones" was magnificent in the first half of the 20th Century, no better displayed than in this pre-war report:

> **1937:** The Surrey County Championship was held at Epsom Downs again this year, on the 2nd January. We were well placed at the start, and after about a mile and a half Hines, of Surrey, was leading, with about nine of ours in the first thirty. At three miles Bert Footer was on Hines' shoulder, having apparently done a bit of "snaky" running when out of the sight of spectators. Penny was next, followed by Carter, Cohen, Ring, and Wood (who won the Surrey Junior Race the week after) in the first twenty places. Our hopes of repeating our win of last year were now very bright; and we next saw the field coming round Tattenham Corner led by Bert Footer. Then came Penny, fifth, Carter sixth, Cohen seventh, Ring thirteenth, and Wood seventeenth. This scoring enabled us to win comfortable from Surrey A.C., thus making our tenth win in the last twelve years.
>
> RESULT:
> 1. Belgrave Harriers   ..   ..   49 points
> 2. Surrey A.C.   ..   ..   98 points
> 3. Herne Hill Harriers   ..   ..   124 points.

Ten wins in 12 years is amazing stuff, and much more was to follow with four wins in the 1940s [half a decade of course], two more in the 50's and two more in the 60's which constitutes a minor wobble, but then amazingly no pay dirt until 1996. What a collapse! That '96 was a great day and a nice surprise as messrs Staines, Foley, Beaver, Alsop, Barton and Chettati brought home a thrilling win by 4 points over the mighty Boxhill. 30 barren years were at an end. A quarter of century later, BB was still a key cog over at *Charlie's Runners*.

By the time I made my debut in the competition in 2000, the club's interest was almost minimal, mainly due to us building on the National not local stage. We had a gutpunch start with Roger and Al in 7th and 8th, but just me and 'Donnyboy' Anderson backing up – what a waste. A sign of life followed in 2001 with Kevin Nash pushing Dave Taylor fairly hard in 2nd, and then a team of engine-roomers nibbled their way to 5th. A sign of life perhaps?

Oh dear no! The next four years were dreadful as we failed to trouble scorers in any of them. It was becoming a minor embarrassment and a shame that we simply couldn't seem to raise the sextet, and were indeed falling some way short. Three good runners in 2005 for instance, but that's your lot.

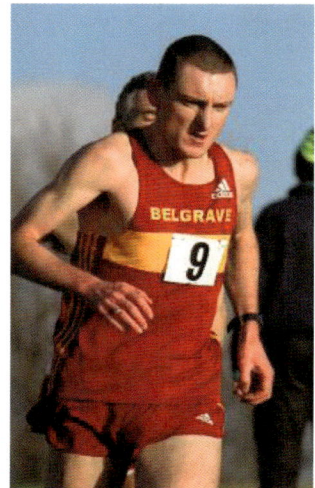

Warren Lynch helped rebuild our aspirations at the County Champs. Warren served us nobly in the engine room for years and was rewarded with a super 2:32 marathon in 2005

A flicker...

Sometimes all you need is the tiniest of spark. Remember the scene in *Cast Away* when Tom Hanks' character is trying to make fire? After endless attempts he sees the smallest puff of smoke... and everything changes. A roaring fire is alight moments later.

The ferociously hard-working John Mcfarlane doled out a harsh lesson in endurance running to Phil in 2006, who toiled somewhat to 5th [but scoring at 2nd]. With myself scoring at 9th, we were in pretty good shape. But our 4th man home was ineligible and 6th had a horror, which meant a modest 7th overall.

In freezing conditions and horizontal rain, Phil wreaked vengeance on all and sundry in 2007. A win by 2:30. Quite astounding. And the team dug so deep.

Jonny Mac out to defend, Phil out for revenge! And boy did he deliver, with a remarkable 2:30 shellacking. Dave Mason is being a wee bit eager in the McEnroe headband, whilst Mal [3] is enjoying his one 'dream' season. Here, he has Jason Simpson and Andy Weir on his tail. Other county luminaries include Nick Hodges 52 and "Rocket Lockett" of HHH, with his compadre Ben Paviour just behind. SW

Mike Trees revelled in the gloop, but alas was not yet Surrey qualified, and Mal continued with his *season mirabilis*. I hated the conditions but went top 20, and with Stanners and Dave Mason running well, we finally had a team to be proud of, but still missing that crucial sixth strong man. It was left to Don to close us in yet again, and instead of 2nd, we had to settle for 5th. But medals were now clearly an option.

I was out covering a story in Addis Ababa in 2008 but we welcomed Oxshott man James Kelly to the squad who backed up another dominant Phil win in 3rd. With Fairbs, Knut and Tim Weeks rock solid we were once again scrabbling for the 6th. He arrived in the form of Richard Merrick, but 87th meant medals lost by just 4 points, and silver by 14. Annoying. Herne Hill were going through their "class apart" phase.

We were clearly improving each year which meant 3rd was looking like our lot for 2009. It was a rock hard course, perfect for fast running and I was much more at home – this was my kinda' cross country. Phil completed his hattrick of wins, yet again by over 2 minutes, in a pretty eye-watering 39:19. JK stalked him from, er, 700 yards back in 2nd. Mike [eligible now] and I had a splendid duel in 14 & 15, while BBC chief sportswriter Tom Fordyce looked good in 41st. One to find. And it was good old Mark Humphrey, talented but unpredictable, who settled the account in 52nd. The bronze was won by a huge distance, whilst up ahead, Thames and Herne Hill had a pretty savage duel. HHH closed in by 20, but Thames elegantly anaesthetised them by 9 points; helped hugely by Stu Major crossing the great divide from SLH. Incredibly they were closed in by James McMullan in 25th, one of the finest runners in the county, but on this day, hungover.

The 2010 race was initially cancelled for the snow, but was reinstated the week before the National, which made it treacherous to hit with full force. But we had a strong team turn out and closed in by 30th. Up front, new road and country star Paskar Owor won a close duel with Nick Torry whilst 'Fairbs' and Landa Eguia had arguably their finest runs in the vest for 14th and 16th. I was a cautious 18th and Malachi and Mike saw us home. Herne Hill were still outstanding with just 87 points but our 116 showed we were an ace shy of winning this.

A very pleasing set of silvers in 2010, with a pretty 'under the radar' squad, clockwise: Mal, Mike, WC, PO, Jim Fairbourn, Landa Eguia & Rob Norville. RX

RESULTS - 2000-2010

2000	-	7 R Alsop; 8 A Stewart; 37 W Cockerell; 76 Don Anderson;
2001	5	2 K Nash; 21 R Alsop; 32 M Byansi; 41 E Lemenager; 43 L Catley; 66 S Zealey
2002	-	20 W Cockerell; 51 M Kazimierski; 99 Don Anderson
2003	-	16 R Alsop; 17 R Ward; 77 W Cockerell [started late]
2004	-	2 K Nash; 22 W Cockerell; 35 W Lynch; 97 Don Anderson
2005	-	17 W Cockerell; 20 K Hegvold; 32 W Lynch;
2006	7	5 P Wicks; 15 W Cockerell; 33 W Lynch; 44 T Weeks
2007	5	1 P Wicks; 15 M Byansi; 19 W Cockerell; 32 R Stannard; 49 D Mason; 149 Don Anderson
2008	4	1 P Wicks; 3 J Kelly; 18 J Fairbourn; 23 K Hegvold; 30 T Weeks; 87 R Merrick
2009	3	1 P Wicks; 2 J Kelly; 14 W Cockerell; 15 M Trees; 41 T Fordyce; 52 M Humphrey
2010	2	1 P Owor; 14 J Fairbourn; 16 L Eguia; 18 W Cockerell; 30 M Byansi; 37 M Trees

A trio of absolute thrillers

A wonderful squad came to race in 2011 and nothing but the win was on our minds. I was in good form, but found only horror… After Wicksy saw off McMullan, James ran to an assured 5th, whilst PO, back from a visit home, could "only" raise 10th some 22 seconds up on the author. One could say it was frustrating he hadn't managed to keep the training up at home, but one can only imagine how many obligations he had. Remarkably, this was my best run in 17 years of doing the Surreys, and this was after being struck down by a knife in the guts in the first half mile. Very bad news indeed. With a team like this, stopping was not an option, but I simply had to get rid of the knife. A family publication such as this doesn't warrant further comment, but suffice it to say that matters were alleviated just enough to get round. I ran with the detached demeanour of a man living a nightmare and just trying to finish. And the result? My best ever Surrey finish. *C'est la vie.*

With Lander and Mike packing well, surely we'd done enough – 77 points is no joke. But Geoff Jerwood was a man on a mission in those days (still is in some ways), and his consistency was astonishing. It was simply a masterpiece in management, as there's no question the team put out was beatable (Busaileh, Henderson, Barnes, Paviour, Taylor and Kettle). But it was just so oaklike, experienced and reliable and knew how to fight for every point. Taylor was just about to turn 47, but still a terrific runner. He remains the only M40er in Surrey league history to win, which he did on his 40th birthday.

They were annoying us now, but all we could do was turn up to Denbies in 2012 and hit them again. For sure after the first lap we were leading, quite handsomely. And deep into lap 2 we were too. But then came the HHH train. Four in a row in the early teens. Remarkable. My dear comrade Kojo Kyereme was a humungous second-claim runner for the Hill in these years, who placed 7th. And then Busaileh, Paviour, Taylor and Barnes packing serious heat in 10-13. Brian Wilder was 21st - only little viewed but in the middle of a magical season which included a 2nd in the league.

Denbies vineyard seen from the top of Boxhill. What a haven for cross-country running and how gracious of the vineyard to have us. The entire course is pretty much here, including the rise and then sharp descent into the finish [top right].

We were very strong as although missing Wicksy had James Kelly in 3rd and then a nifty 2nd claimer of our own in Dan Agustus. Richard Stannard was excellent in 14th but Paskar ran into deep trouble, shutting off all power yet again on his trip home to Nagongera. It was impish and mercurial of him, and again cost us the race, but with a precious gem like that you can't be too cross. I actually caught PO with 500 to go, but he wasn't having that and turned on the charm. Richard Ward had a very brave run. I was concerned about his future when I caught him with two miles to go, but he only leaked two more spots. Gutsy. So the final damage was 74-82, they'd done us again.

A superb portrait of Surrey County cross-country running by Alan - our thanks to him   Too many luminaries to name here, but the most cursory of looks gives up Owor, Kelly, Weir, Slemeck 279, Paviour, McMullan [upside down J], Trees, Ward, Stannard [leading], Kyereme 243, Will Clark 207, Dave Taylor 255, Busaileh 234, Nick Torry 325, WC and Alex Robinson extreme right. ARM

Finally! The gold arrives

After eight years of gritty building, we finally got that dreamteam we craved in 2013. Phil, James and Paskar is one heck of a trio, with their finishing highly unpredictable: PO 1st, James 3rd and a pea green Phil 4th "taking some tough hits for the team in these glutinous conditions". I felt dreadful all race, but it was a day just to grind out a result, whilst Knut and Mike also dug deep. It's pretty scary to think of the experience of that last trio. K & M had both been running since the early 1970s, myself since '81 and

You have to say that's magnificent! Bels win their first County title for 17 years, and by this image, you can see why. ARM

between us we had around 200,000 miles of training under our belts. Chuck in another 100k at least for the top three and this gnarly sextet had close to a third of a million miles in the tank. That's why it's a tough race to win. Hercules and HHH both hit us hard with 105 and 109, but we'd finally done it with 83 – sweet relief!

Three more medals

2014 was another exciting day, and again we hit HHH hard. I had a grim start as the officials at Surrey take great delight in starting races early. It drives me completely mad. I know, I know, we should all be lined up in good time, but the Surrey starter's approach is, "everyone's here, why wait?" *Why wait*?? For about 30 reasons! The person who had a travel nightmare, the last minute dash to the Gents which should be perfectly timed but instead has the athlete chasing the entire field down the way. The last minute tightening of the left shoe… the last minute stride… the wave to the wife and baby, which is affordable because the start's not for another minute, but then BANG! They're off. Yes, I like to cut it fine for start lines, but that is my right. 2pm is 2pm. What's with all the 1:59 and 3 seconds nonsense? Anway, I was just climbing over the waist high partition in 2014 with a good minute to spare and bang, 190 athletes charging off and me straddling the fence. Such an unpleasant way to start, weaving through the masses, and the entire race I'm pretty exhausted having had to do a 5:20 first mile instead of the comfier 5:30. Humph! I notice it happens a fair bit in local track races too. Races sometimes starting 2 minutes early. Just because everyone's there doesn't mean you tear up the rule book.

The ever-strengthening Hercules took the win, whilst we were lacking a little firepower in bronze with me scoring 2nd into my fifth decade. The lion went hungry in 5th place, whilst James Browne had a superb run in 22nd. Newish boys Royston Maddams and Matt Welsh took care of things in the 40s with Knut standing close guard. Nick Bundle was shut out of things on this day, but a year later would win an amazing Southern silver. We had been excited about American Carlos Ryback, a 14:55 man, but he was left shaking his head in disbelief: "Hey I'm from Minnesota. I've never experienced running in anything like this before!"

Cockspur: "Making the party happen since 1884." Well, we're only three years younger than the famous Barbadian rum, and found the conditions decidedly ante-Caribbean in 2014. L-R Browne, PO, WC, Royston and Knut

New regime

2015 was my first year in charge at the Surreys and we did really well to grab a silver, 3 points ahead of the defending champions. Herne Hill were solid as ever, but then we unleashed a fresh, new look of a team. PO had a brilliant win, just one second over Tonbridge's Pearce, whilst new parkrun pick-ups Jaksevicius and Telkovsky were in the top 20. Nick Bundle was up over 40 points on the year before, some improvement that, and with Roy in 29th, we were basically an ace short of a very surprising win. We had to go back to the new gaffer to close in. But it had been a stacked field and was a successful and happy day at the coalface.

There was more of the same in '16, as a team brimming with intent took to the stage. With Phil in great touch for another fine win over Kyereme, we then saw a stunner from AJ from 4th with PO in 5th. It was a magnificent start, but then we had a long wait, some 6 minutes in fact, for more Belgravians, in Roy, Nick Smallwood and myself, packing well, but too far back. It meant 10 points off Herne Hill and 62 off HW, who celebrated another win. It was my 15th and final Counties – what fine entertainment it brought.

2015 was a day when every man fought for every point, which Royston and Nick Bundle demonstrate here

Back to Denbies in 2016 and Phil is all fire and brimstone. AJ can be seen in line for a cracker, and Phil's only challenge would come from Kojo, 165, who now dominates the world stage in Masters running. Number 56 is Luke Caldwell, whose on a Ticket to Ride to a DNF: "I think I'm gonna' be sad, I think it's today, yeah. The [boy] that's driving me mad, is going away...." SW

Gradual pre-Covid decline

I felt very confident that the gang of 2017 would challenge hard for medals, but what colour? We were off to yet another wonderful start with Phil fast becoming one of the most successful runners in the Championship's history [win #6], and the everstrong AJ placed 7th. There was then a small pause before new man James Williams, three months out from winning London Marathon team gold, finished just ahead of Arne Dumez. Yet again Roy ran solidly and we were closed in by a very unfit PO in 44th. Not a

Arne and James Williams fought hard, but we were a little off colour on this day, not the least the Lion in the background

bad run at all from the lads, but Herne Hill yet again were just too strong whilst HW were now on a good gold run.

The instant we met Nick on 7 Nov 2015 with a top 50 in the Surrey league, we knew we had unearthed precious metal. We had to get a lot of rowing out of his system first, but now the climb is well and truly underway to him being one of our most telling Road and Country men of the last 50 years. But we'll know more a decade from now. SG

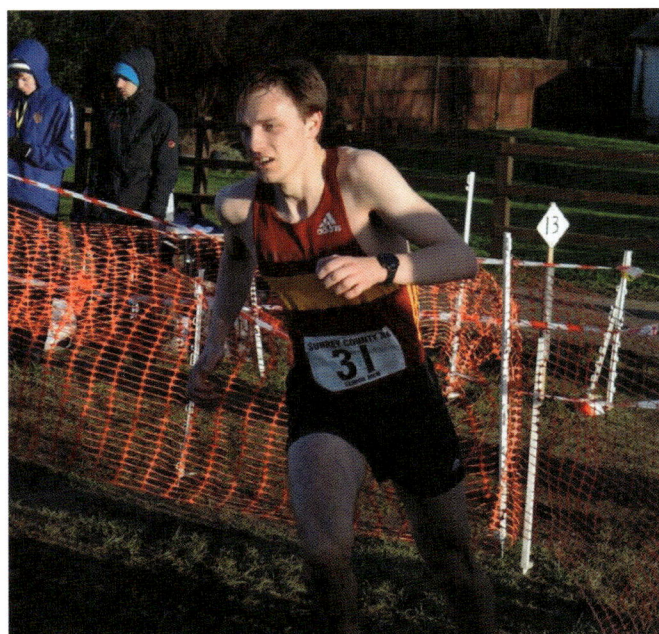

Whither Ross Finlay?! Charming fellow and a loyal trooper but currently MIA. SG

Back to Denbies in 2018 where we were very quiet. Paskar was on form for 5th, whilst Nick Buckle, left, had a stunner in 8th – such a natural talent. But our back up had a bit of a shocker on this day, and although messrs Finlay, Dumez & McDougall did what they could, it was left to an old fave in the form of a visiting Mike Trees to close us home in 99th. A long, epic medal streak was over and we'd come the full circle – back to 7th.

6th wasn't *too bad* in 2019 as we again lacked stars, although AJ was magnificent in 4th. We now had an aging PO on our hands who did well to find 17th and ever reliable Arne ran well for 33rd. Brad Courtney-Pinn and Ross Finlay soon followed, before the always welcome sight of Will Johnson charging along, who is a real fighter. We had a lot of back-up too, with four other runners, so it was not a day to be despondent.

Three VERY different outcomes. DNS, NR, Silver

In the first season of Steve and Arne's reign, the Surrey's were deemed "a race too far" as the squad was focussing on Surrey league mid-pack honour and the upcoming Southerns. It's obviously not the same race without Belgrave and the medal table looked unusual: Hercules, SLH and GG. A change from the norm, and one has to say, good for all the medalists.

Nothing to say about the cancelled 2021 race either, which brought us to a gloriously sunny day at Denbies in 2022, and the Bels were back and here to stay! How strange that we hadn't been sighted for three years – what were the chances? In a dramatic race of great quality, Aldershot were simply unstoppable. Six through in 23 is too good, from a county who straddle the great divide of both Hamshire and Surrey. To be sure it's impressive, but of course it means they can't win both, and placed 4th in Hants behind such outfits as Guernsey [albeit propped up by the great Lee Merrien].

Anyway, we were boasting one of the most exciting line-ups in our history, and it certainly appeared as though the rest of the 2020s would be fertile hunting ground for us at this one. Marathon man Reece

Edwards led the field early before winning a terrific kick finish for 5th; and less than 30 seconds behind was the reassuring figure of Callum Stewart. A small gap followed, but then some wonderful packing. Callum barked to the author that Sam had come out, which I passed on with sadness to the Whatsapp group. Not so! Our brave warrior was just admiring the vines for a moment when Callum had passed, perhaps paying for an over-eager start. He looked in all sorts of bother when he came by early on lap 3,

and I felt that all our next three lads would catch him, but in a display of terrific defiance none could. Our packing was superb with Nick Buckle, and the two Jonnies, Scott and Neville seeing us home inside the top 30.

It was a great performance and equally heartening to see seven more Bels standing guard, including some very useful runners 'on the make'. Any tinge of frustration felt at AFD's brutality was assuaged by the knowledge that they won't be doing that every year and the gaps to the next teams were pretty large. So, we remain at just two triumphs since 1967, but what a journey it's been.

A really super team that was more than a little unlucky to lose. L-R Sammy G, Reece, Jonny S, Jonny N, Nick & Callum. SG

RESULTS - 2011-2022

2011	2	1 P Wicks; 5 J Kelly; 10 P Owor; 12 W Cockerell; 23 L Eguia; 26 M Trees
2012	2	3 J Kelly; 6 D Agustus; 14 R Stannard; 18 P Owor; 19 W Cockerell; 22 R Ward
2013	1	1 P Owor; 3 J Kelly; 4 P Wicks; 19 W Cockerell; 26 K Hegvold; 30 M Trees
2014	3	5 P Owor; 21 W Cockerell; 22 J Browne; 46 R Maddams; 47 M Welsh; 56 K Hegvold
2015	2	1 P Owor; 15 A Jaksevicius; 19 T Telkovsky; 25 N Bundle; 29 R Maddams; 47 W Cockerell
2016	3	1 P Wicks; 4 A Jaksevicius; 5 P Owor; 42 R Maddams; 49 N Smallwood; 52 W Cockerell
2017	3	1 P Wicks; 7 A Jaksevicius; 28 J Williams; 32 A Dumez; 38 R Maddams; 44 P Owor
2018	7	5 P Owor; 8 N Buckle; 55 R Finlay; 62 A Dumez; 70 P McDougall; 99 M Trees
2019	6	4 A Jaksevicius; 17 P Owor; 33 A Dumez; 42 B Courtney-Pinn; 50 R Finlay; 90 W Johnson
2022	2	5 R Edwards; 8 C Stewart; 22 S Gebreselassie; 25 N Buckle; 28 J Scott; 29 J Neville

SURREY COUNTY CHAMPS - WOMEN

A generally pleasing set of returns

The County champs have largely treated the Belles well. Yes, there have been some weighty commercial breaks, but two Championships and five other medals is a good return for a squad whose reach often spills beyond county lines.

A rock solid outfit of Maskrey, Haines, Sturton and Dillane ran to bronze in 2000, a race notable for the participation of Anne Roden in 12th, one of the most pioneering of all British distance runners. One latter highlight was a smooth 2:37 for 12th at Boston eight years earlier as a V45. She would venture back there in April 2000 for run of 2:54 aged 53.

A blank in 2001 was followed by a terrific silver in 2002, with the Eastham reign really starting to motor. It was a diminutive field of just 68 runners, but the Belles could only beat who was before them, and Jules, Erica, Syreeta and Tanya were all through in the top 25%. 36 is an outstanding total, but all credit to SLH for seeing us off by 4.

One of the great races…

A circumspect 13th in 2003 was followed up by the big one! In the midst of their league winning form the Championships were duly claimed as well. No superstars were required for the making of this movie, just rock solid, dedicated, forward placed runners, and in Tilly, Jules, Angela and Erica we had just that.

But would the lack of a major star hurt us? After all the Irrepressibles had runners in 2nd and 5th. They would finish on 37, which was only good enough for 3rd - pretty incredible. In 2nd, Ranelagh reeled of 3, 7, 11, 12. How is that beatable?! Well, technically it wasn't as we tied with them, but by dint of closing in ahead of them, the day was ours. Catherine wrote: "Watching Juliette fight to the line to overtake a Walton athlete made our supporters realise just how much this trophy was wanted."

And it was that kick finish that stole the day – a classic race.

Tilly Heaton, Erica Fogg, Jules Clark and Angela Walker withstood not one, but two kitchen sinks in '04

Frustration followed in '05 with Smurph and Tilly right up there, but no back-up; and it was a direct action replay in 2006. Hmmm, something was getting lost in translation.

The Fab Four

But then all was fixed in 2007 as another superb squad came to race. This time we *did* have a star in former National winner Birhan Dagne in 3rd, behind Susie Bush and Wicksy's future betrothed Emily.

What followed was frankly a bit of a dreamteam in Murphy, Bryson and Heaton. One doesn't quite realise it at the time, but what a collection of jewels that is. All home by 16th, with assured back-up from Sarah Gailey and this time the win was by a comparatively luxurious 14 points. Let it never be forgotten though how tricky it is to assemble a quartet of such classy and hard-working runners.

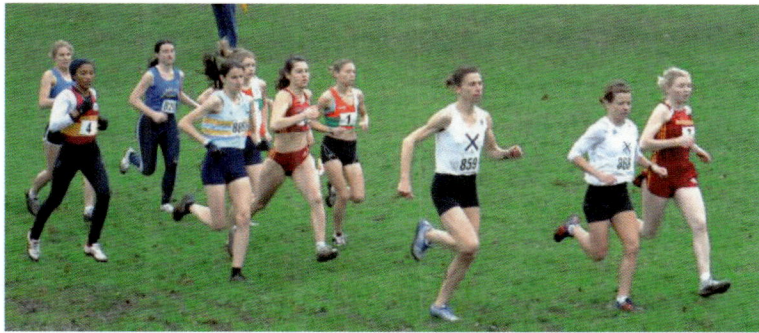

Superb intent from Catherine Bryson. She may end up 10th here, but the message was clear: "if you want to take this race from us, you'll have to do it the hard way." Aussie Naomi Warner duels for the lead and the legendary Rachel Disley is in 3rd. Runner up Susie Bush is #1, with winner Emily Adams [Wicks] on the shoulder of Smurph. Birhan Dagne [4] keeps out of trouble – for now. ARM

RESULTS - 2000-2010

2000	3	8 H Maskrey [Cole]	11 N Haines	25 T Sturton	37 K Dillane
2001	-	10 E Fogg	25 T Sturton		
2002	2	6 J Clark	12 E Fogg	15 S Stracey	16 T Sturton
2003	13	8 M Heaton	13 J Clark	66 J Whittington	72 A Pike
2004	1	6 M Heaton	8 J Clark	10 A Walker	11 E Fogg
2005	-	8 S Murphy	10 M Heaton		
2006	-	13 S Murphy	18 M Heaton		
2007	1	3 B Dagne	9 S Murphy	10 C Bryson	16 M Heaton
2008	-	5 S Murphy	19 K Swanson		
2009	-	4 S Murphy	22 M Heaton	60 C Eastham	
2010	-	4 S Murphy	19 M Heaton		

As if to emphasise this point, we then failed to close in for the next six years as CE's reign as TM gently wound down and I took over the reigns ahead of the 2012 race. Time and time again we'd get Sarah [often in the top 6] and Tilly, but no back-up, although by 2011 all interest in the race seemed to have disappeared, with a no show. League relegation followed the next month. They were pretty desperate times.

I then got a super little four on paper for 2012, but something got lost in translation and Zoe Vail Smith was a no show. "I can't be trusted," she wrote in regretfully, "just take me out for the rest of the season." I calmly replied that she was one of our best runners and I'd be taking her out of nothing!

Goodbye to a Giant

2013 – one runner again, and she was based in Hong Kong now. It was Tilly's last ever race for the Belles, in what was a legendary career, setting attendance records that may still stand 50 years from now. Who will beat her 112 points from 34 league scores? Who indeed. Of the current ranks, Zoe VS and Saron are the nearest chasers on 43 and 42 points, and they are both rarely sighted beasties – for now – but we give up on neither…

As for Tilly, she is back in the UK after many years away and has taken on a fresh challenge at the Chasers with her speedometer down a notch or two. We missed a big trick by not electing her a Life Member when we had the chance, but one never knows when an athlete will suddenly disappear forever. The Far East was seen as merely "a sabbatical or so" away – we had all the time in the world for Life membership pomp and ceremony, did we not?

Finally Back in the Game

We arrived at a very muddy Denbies in 2014, with a fascinating, new look squad of Jojo Rhodes, Debs Noel, Flic Cole, and old hands 'the Vixster' and ZVS. Who would score and how would they fare?

Plenty of squads were up for the challenge, with no fewer than 18 clubs closing in – a superb return. The race had more than doubled in size in recent years. Well, it was a huge scrap from the gun and AFD were quickly seen as untouchable. Thames were then packing mightily, but thereafter it was an eight-way slugfest for the bronze between Dorking, SLH, Ranelagh, HW, Dulwich, HHH, Guildford and ourselves.

Our lines were led by 1,500 child star Jojo who crashed straight into another child track prodegy in the 800 – the author's spouse. It was that 2:06 pace as a 15 year old that saved Dorchie here, although they tied on time.

Just behind, Debs was on sparkling form, but we'd only see her in the vest once more – triathlon being more her thing [plus the small matter of relocating to St. Albans]. A little way back, Flic had another tie with the evergreen Diana Norman, whilst Vicki had one of her finest ever runs in the claret for 38th, in the process showing a clean pair of heels to Zoe. It all meant medals with just 7 points to spare over Guildford's promising youth policy and it was a happy day, with much good humour [plenty of it ribald at the gross conditions], and a fresh feeling of hope in the air.

2015 was another excellent race with JJR again leading the lines. Occasional, but very able, second-claimer Nici Cahusic ran well for 21st and Keri Mackenzie followed just 2 spots back. Ever reliable Flic closed in and we got a hard fought 5th for our trouble.

Medals! Fighting through the gloop, the ladies were good value for their bronze. L-R Zoe VS, Vicki Goodwin, Flic Cole, Debs Noel & Jojo Rhodes

Matters cooled, but ZVS had a notable run for 9th in 2016, whilst Charlie did really well to get no fewer than nine bodies to the line in 2017. We may have been a tad light on quality but it all represented signs of a squad building brick by brick for future cohesion and solidity. Sophie Harris ran to 21st, taking tentative steps to her historic 2017-18 season.

Immaculate packing followed in 2018, but "only" between 30th to 49th. They were well backed up again though, so it was clear that two stars were needed to get back to medal winning ways – 6th here. But then another crash, as Chas drew a total blank in 2019. It can happen like that… 5 become 3, who then take a view, of "is it really worth it with the league next week, and Southerns looming?" Next!

Super run in 2020

And what a next it was. Just the four made the trip to Denbies, but it was clearly a mean, lean fighting machine. Overlooked by one of the classiest striders in our history, President John Gladwin, the Belles put the blinkers on in the chaos all around. First home was Georgie Fenn enjoying a marvellous season, and finding 7th, under a minute from the podium. Emily Barrett is such a talent and though she suffers a lot from niggles and such, when we do get her out it's always 'value added'. This was a good 18th. *Papsrunslaps* was next and with Camilla Barden closing in 38th we knew we'd be up there somewhere, but with AFD out of sight again, there were four clubs vying for two spots. GG packed too much of a

punch for 76; but what of SLH and HHH, such old and classic rivals both? Well they were so busy trying to kill eachother with 104 & 105 that they forgot about us! And we sneaked in with a nifty 91 to surprisingly grab the hardware.

Superb return from the 'Rona'

Post Covid and two years of building saw a thriving and happy tribe return to Denbies. The Belles had blossomed into something quite unseen in their 46 year history. The turnout was nine, but it was the *depth* of the nine that was so notable. None on this day in the top 10, but after a hard fought 13th from Jess Saunders [who was picking up her 4th medal of the season – a lucky charm?]; we then packed a startling six bodies between 24th and 38th, in an astonishing 30-second-choo-choo-train. Pick of the bunch was Lizzie Goldie-Scot, recently engaged to men's star Nick Buckle and perhaps having a little of his magic fairy dust rub off on her. LGS is more noted for standing guard, sweeping up and closing us out, but the subtle flex here was great to see. Nat Beadle as 3rd scorer was another mild surprise, but she does train awfully hard, and the scalp of Ms Goodson was noteworthy. But Laura was in the midst of trying to break the world record of catching Covid the most times in the fewest months.

Mimi Corden-Lloyd and Sarah Dewhirst provided rock solid back-up whilst Fi Maddocks could just be our first President to run a Surrey county champs on a Sunday, at a vineyard in Dorking, for a year ending in two. Sophie Cowper has done some telling runs as a second-claimer – we've been in dialogue with her for years, and it's nice when those conversations pay off. But here was a day to "take one for the team" whilst battling injury.

Reigning Cross-country Plate winner Mimi never stopped fighting for a team medal and ended up just 12 seconds short in 29th

All smiles from Laura, Lizzie, Nat and Jess. Bronze today in a very competitive race

The Belles were right in the heart of an incredible season, this was their sixth podium, and much more was to come.

RESULTS 2011-2022

Year	Pos				
2011	-				
2012	-	26 M Heaton	33 A Hegvold	62 V Goodwin	
2013	-	17 M Heaton	59 V Goodwin		
2014	3	13 J Rhodes	14 D Noel	31 F Cole	38 V Goodwin
2015	5	17 J Rhodes	21 N Cahusac	23 K Mackenzie	36 F Cole
2016	8	9 Z Vail Smith	19 F Cole	45 C Pennock	74 M Bailey
2017	5	21 S Harris	33 I Cousland	35 R O'Kill	40 C Pennock
2018	6	30 I Cousland	32 M Hall	35 F Cole	49 M Bailey
2020	3	7 G Fenn	18 E Barrett	29 O Papaioannou	38 C Barden
2022	3	13 J Saunders	24 L Goldie-Scott	26 N Beadle	27 L Goodson

THE SOUTHERN CROSS - WOMEN

So very, very close to the promised land

What a journey we've enjoyed at this one over the past decade. Although the first decade can be tapped out in a few words… "move along, nothing to see here." It's a strange dearth of activity, but quite simply the race didn't seem to capture Catherine's imagination, nor perhaps that of the runners. There were near misses as the top sluggers Murphy, Bryson and Heaton turned out year after year, but no back up. Strange, but it was what it was.

In my first year at the helm I sniffed a real opportunity to "give it large" at the Southern, still smarting as we were from Surrey league relegation. In new signing Fee Maycock, our woman of the year, and the strength of Sammi Amend, plus evergreen Tilly, we had the makings of a special squad. Hester Barsham-Rolfe gave the nod which meant we'd finish respectably, and with a medal assault underway, could we find one last star? The talent of Nelle Quispel came to the rescue, redemption indeed for not making it to the potential golden team of the Southern cross relay three months before [went to the wrong venue]. But this was more important.

The amazing coup of 2012

But then the night before, Nelle dropped again! We were cursed, and with all respect to Hester, who would finish a strong 128th, it was going to be too profligate for medals. Nelle's problem was not injury or illness, but that she was due for the taping of a TV show at Pinewood Studios as an audience member at 5pm. With her race finishing by 3, I sensed all was not lost, but the only way to skin the cat was a very expensive cab from Brighton. It was deemed affordable and worthwhile, and with a mix of the Belles' XC budget and *BOW* [Bank of Will] we were back in play, with the only proviso from Nelle, that "this better work!"

Could we get some help here please?! For a dozen years where we were plagued by having great runners at "the big ones" but no back-up. In 2009 Catherine Bryson picked her way through to a masterful 8th at Hillingdon. ARM

Superb battling spirit from Sammi, Fee and Tilly. SW

Onto the race and Sam chose this day to have perhaps her finest ever run in the claret and gold – a brilliant 16th and quite impeccably judged, devouring bodies like *Pacman* right to the line. And the rest?! Not so hot… The girls weren't terrible and packed well, but surely had left too much out there, and none were very happy with their runs. But then the results were released and to this day they make me smile:

Pos	Points	Team Name	Placings
1	159	Aldershot Farnham & District AC	(28 33 40 58)
2	203	Serpentine RC	(4 59 68 72)
3	239	Belgrave Harriers	(16 63 78 82)
4	241	St Albans Striders	(37 41 45 118)
5	248	Southampton AC	(1 31 55 161)
6	252	London Heathside	(23 57 85 87)
7	268	Winchester & District AC	(3 29 49 187)

What a logjam! And the perfect example of how every place counts. Sam alone took 5 points in the last 200 yards. It may be a flukey medal, but tell it to the history books. The ladies had done what they could under great pressure – I'd made it clear what was on the line – and now it was straight to a waiting taxi for Nelle, who made her show.

RESULTS 2000-2012 courtesy of A.R. Mead; belgraveharriers.info

Belgrave Harriers – Southern Cross-Country Championships, Female   Senior Women

2000			**Parliament Hill Fields, London**, 29 Jan. — incomplete team; 112 T. Sturton; 359 finished; 47 teams closed in; team winners Shaftesbury Barnet H 39 pts.; individual winner A. Whitcombe (Parkside (Harrow) AC).
2001			**Parliament Hill Fields, London**, 27 Jan. — incomplete team; 55 E. Fogg; 79 T. Sturton; 151 S. Stracey; 327 finished; 34 teams closed in; team winners Shaftesbury Barnet H 63 pts.; individual winner H. Yelling (Borough of Hounslow AC).
2002			**Parliament Hill Fields, London**, 26 Jan. — incomplete team; 45 M. Heaton, 68 T. Sturton; 281 finished; 34 teams closed in; team winners Windsor, Slough & Eton AC 35 pts.; individual winner H. Yelling (Windsor, Slough & Eton AC).
2003			**Bicton Park, nr. Exmouth, Devon**, 25 Jan. — incomplete team; 50 M. Heaton, 97 L. Cooper, 102, A. Walker; 266 finished; 31 teams closed in; team winners Windsor, Slough, Eton & Hounslow AC; individual winner S. Morris (Bedford & County AC).
2004			**Parliament Hill Fields, London**, 24 Jan. — incomplete team; 38 J. Clark, 80 V. Edwards; 297 finished; 38 teams closed in; team winners Highgate H 49 pts.; individual winner L. Damen (Bournemouth AC).
2005	18th	448 pts.	**Parliament Hill Fields, London**, 29 Jan — 24 S. Murphy, 55 M. Heaton, 184 S. Gailey, 185 C. Eastham; 307 finished; 38 teams closed in; team winners Winchester AC; individual winner J. Bleasdale (Hillingdon AC).
2006	13th	344 pts.	**Bicton Park, nr. Exmouth, Devon**, 28 Jan. — 31 S. Murphy; 96 L. Cooper, 102 M. Heaton, 115 C. Eastham; 231 finished; 27 teams closed in; team winners Winchester & Dist. AC 36 pts.; individual winner L. Elliott (Winchester & Dist. AC).
2007			**Holkham Hall, Norfolk**, 27 Jan. — incomplete team; 17 C. Bryson, 25 S. Murphy; 203 finished; team winners Winchester & Dist. AC 68 pts.; individual winner L. Damen (Poole Runners).
2008			**Parliament Hill Fields, London**, 26 Jan. — incomplete team; 23 S. Murphy, 58 M. Heaton, 222 J. Beecroft; at least 10 teams closed in; team winners Aldershot, Farnham & Dist. AC; individual winner R. Townend (Winchester & Dist. AC).
2009			**Hillingdon House Farm, Hillingdon, Middx.**, 24 Jan. — incomplete team; 8 C. Bryson, 89 M. Heaton, 218 J. Beecroft; 311 finished; at least 30 teams closed in; team winners Aldershot, Farnham & Dist. AC 118 pts.; individual winner J. Sparke (Woodford Green w Essex Ladies AC).
2010			**Parliament Hill Fields, London**, 30 Jan. — Belgrave did not take part; 357 finished; 55 teams closed in; team winners Woodford Green w Essex Ladies AC; individual winner J. Sparke (Woodford Green w Essex Ladies AC).
2011			**Parliament Hill Fields, London**, 29 Jan. — incomplete team; 118 M. Heaton; 381 finished; 62 teams closed in; team winners City of Norwich AC 75 pts.; individual winner N. Taschimowitz (Taunton AC).
2012	3rd	239 pts.	**Stanmer Park, Brighton, Sussex**, 28 Jan. — 16 S. Amend, 63 F. Maycock, 78 M. Heaton, 82 N. Quispell, 128 H. Barsham-Rolfe; 335 finished; 49 teams closed in; team winners Aldershot, Farnham & Dist. AC 159 pts.; individual winner C. Mitchell (Southampton AC).

Maddening reversal of fortune

Our great 'luck' bit us on the derriere in 2013 when the SEAA cancelled due to a bit of the white stuff a few days before. I am sure to this day it was vastly premature to pull the plug and an image of the course on the day showed only lush greensward. So frustrating. They rescheduled the race for February and squads everywhere were decimated, including ours.

But those that ran did brilliantly. Hester, no longer with her nose pressed to the glass, roaring to 3rd scorer, and Fee also upped her game, whilst Tish warmed up for the following week's National with a "tough as old boots" 11th. We rounded out the scorers with the affable Petra Kasperova, who went onto become a well known multi-day runner. Petra summed up the "magic" of Parla Hill thus: "It was an incredible experience for me. It was a battle. One had to fight outwardly as well as inwardly."

2014 & '15: a brace of silver thrills

Back again 12 months later and we were plumb in line for great things. We felt only Aldershot could stop us and their first trio duly slammed home a savage 1, 5, 6. What can you do? Well, our ladies refused to give up in the face of such an onslaught and that 4th AFD'er was being shy to show her face, some way behind our fourth. This was still on!

Tish had a marvellous run and was picking off the leaders all race long, before edging into 6th, then 5th, then 4th, then 3rd. Immaculate sharp-shooting stuff, and she may've been a little disappointed not to get the veteran Miranda Heathcote in 2nd, but a master over the mud. Up a little ahead, full credit to the young Jess Andrews for taking the win.

Mel had one of her best runs in the vest for 14th, whilst Sam and ZLD played "no mistake snooker" for 25th and 39th. Zoe came up with one of running's great lines after the race of: "about half way through I thought: this reminds me of giving birth..." Running – don't you just love it?!

Evergreen, just behind, with a very good 53rd, Jojo ensured no mishaps. Now, what of that 4th AFD girl? Oooooh, there was Sarah Rollins in 54th, an unheralded name perhaps, but she'd been around for ages and four years earlier had placed 21st, so no mug at all in her 38th year. All credit to our Hampshire friends, and what a battle.

Zoe fights hard for a place in the top 40, a few steps ahead of former GB 800m junior Dorothea Lee 3111. Zoe would make waves on the world masters stage at the same distance. SSP

Stanmer Heartbreak

In 2015 we were weakened minus Tish; but Zoe, Mel and Sam were back in town, at Brighton's glorious Stanmer park. And this time, in my best Barry Davies voice, "where were the Aldershot? But quite frankly, who cares!" Well, we did, and with Georgie Bruinvels in 2nd we feared more flagellation. But this time the red and green could only find three bodies, oh sweet relief. Could we do it?! It was a remarkably tense race, and although we ourselves could only throw five bodies at the problem, they were all 'scorer worthy' with an epic battle raging for that final medal spot between Jojo and Kerimac.

Poor old Keri; she really is quite 'vision-impaired' without her specs and on a technical course took a really bad tumble on a tight, steep turn. She never gave up though, but it opened the door ajar for JJR to burst through and grab a slim advantage that she'd never relinquish. So, we were closed in 61, and up ahead Zoe turned her 2014 39th into a 30 and Sam her 25 into a 19. This was terrific! With Mel leading Louise Damen early doors before a bit of piper-paying saw her having to give best to this XC legend by 1:39; it was still a superb top 6 finish, with a who's who of Southern athletes in her wake: Taschimowitz, Ansell, Munn and Fullerton.

2011 champion Taschimowitz battles Ansell, Janes, Sanders, Ormerod and Wilkins

Despite a bad fall, Keri never gave up, but Jojo was not to be denied

So, what did it all mean? Well, Herne Hill and TVH were on cracking form and both closed ahead of us, tieing on 133, but we dealt with them on 116. Who else could beat that?! Alas, there was one. The mercurial Winchester, not a club noted for their consistency, but on their day known to conjure up a dazzling performance out of the blue, and this was just such an occasion. After Damen, they packed with a duo of supervets in Lucy Elliott (turning in fine runs since 1983), and another W45 in Kath Bailey; whilst finally our speeders got stopped by the police in copper Kate Towerton, a race junkie who had precisely what it took to snuff us out. Winchester's 5th athlete was 171st, but sadly not a 5-woman race! It was a brilliant smash and grab by them and of course fully deserved.

An hour later and our men also placed 2nd. What a day to manage both squads, but this was *just the moment* my grasp on our Road and Country teams started to weaken and some administerial committee chaos was in store for me, which sadly led to the Belles entering into a brief period of decline.

2016's Tough Day

This was evidenced by 2016 when poor old Mel was still battling chronic injury from a training camp the previous fall, when her diet of 55 miles a week sky-rocketed to 90s. It played hell with her all season and after the first Surrey league of the term [dnf] ended up in an emergency room in big trouble. Mel fought diligently to be fit for her beloved Southern and her heroic 41st, whilst distressing on the back of last year's 6th, was probably one of the bravest runs of her career. Heart-breakingly, it was also her last tour in the claret and gold before as she opted for a fresh challenge at Winchester, where Nick Anderson [the training camp's leader] relieved me of her coaching duties; but we will always fondly remember Mel's stunning shift for the Belles in which she barely missed a race between 14 Sept 2013 to 3 Oct 2015.

We had some difficulty with our back up in 2016, but old faves Cole & Rhodes answered the call before Christina Pennock anchored us home. 16th behind, er, Paddock Wood, was a bit of a jolt, but credit to PW we say.

Training – the daily sacrifice – and its perils

One of Charlie's key skills is the way he rebuilds squads. He reminds me of a spider who makes an attractive looking web, sees it demolished, and with merely a 'nanoshrug', starts weaving again. Women's running squads are very fragile as careers are notably shorter than their male counterparts. There are obvious reasons for this, like starting families, childcare, and post-natal running is laden with multifold extra-challenges while the body adjusts. But women also *appear* to dig deeper in training, and seem willing and able to "beast" themselves more. I am basing this off 25 years of training with both genders and the levels of sacrifice and hard work that women exhibit in sessions compared to men. I was struck with the anxiety my wife would get before sessions when I first got to know her. I have since asked her why, and she replied: "errr, I think you'd be pretty bloody anxious too, if you had to keep up with Lobb and Fitzimmons for an hour!" But they were 14:45 men and she was in 16:15 shape. How about handicapping? How about, you know, letting them go? But no, the flagellation must occur! Got to be tough. It was an honour to run lockstep with Sonia O'Sullivan for a few years in training at the height of her powers. She was in no mood for messin', and I've seen a great many club women train with similar intensity, albeit at a lesser level.

This incendiary approach is of course a risky business though, and it makes women more accident prone, exhibiting a wide-range of deep-rooted injuries which befall men far less. In my eight happy years' managing the Belles, my off-games list used to run to alarming levels of 50%, and the injuries I saw far worse, and sometimes career-ending.

The stats for a Belle's shelf-life compared to a Bel are quite unsettling. In the Surrey league for instance, of the top 40 scorers for both genders, one can expect to get an average of 21 scores from a man, but 8.6 from a woman. There's a quasi-lethal scoring number which many great Belles have hit and don't progress past, and it's around 10. Of recent stars there are the 'ledges' Harris & Jones on 5 & 6, then Amend and Wilkins on 8, and Doyle, Maycock, Haileselase, Vail Smith & Bryson all hovering on 10-12. Only three Belles in 43 years of the Surrey League have got "over the hump" of 16 scores, whereas 35 men have.

Charlie and I have become evermore "switched on" to this problem over the past decade, and try as hard as we can to *reign athletes in*. We then had one, then another, of our best runners leave 'Charlie's Runners' for a rival group that offered more volume, but we could only write that off as 'collateral damage'. Not happy, but sanguine. I have always been of the opinion that if an athlete leaves a session feeling they could have done "a wee bit more," then that's the perfect ingredient right there. Bottle it and sell it! It's those sessions one absolutely batters, and where you're "all in" that are *oh so dangerous*. Yes, you survive one, maybe a dozen. But 15 years' worth? No chance.

The spider gets weaving

CD's rebuild started in no uncertain terms in 2017 with 6th! Back on it indeed with a transitional squad. There was still Sammi of course, and we finally cajoled Sophie Carter onto the mud who was built for it, but hugely sceptical of such a mission. But her run was fine. Christina turned in her final tour for us before leaving for pastures new at London City AC, whilst my parkrun head-hunting unearthed Becky Prince [now the wonderfully named O'Kill] saw us home inside the top 100. This all left us just 1 point adrift of Heathside in 5th – mildly annoying but still a fine day out.

Back to Stanmer for 2018 and the mother of all winter monsoons – dreadful stuff. But we were treated to a wonderful display of front-running fortitude from Sophie Harris in 6th, on her way to stamping down her legendary "4 for 4" record in the Surrey League – a feat never before achieved by either man nor woman. Sammi got a tad stuck in the gloop and was pushed hard by the emerging talent of Mhairi Hall, whilst ever-reliable Lizzie Goldie-Scot closed in for a gnarly 9th team place.

2019 was a mid-sized stutter, although it was now Georgie Fenn's star that was on the rise, and goodness wouldn't she lay waste to that 37th in due course. Mhairi rose to 2nd score, and the excellent, though now sadly departed, Emma Howsham in 3rd. Another 'face for the future' appeared in Mimi Corden-Lloyd. 13th was a touch scrappy, but there was a strong feeling in the air that a fresh new squad was appearing at the club – about the fourth in a decade.

Great squads don't magically appear, they build slowly but surely, and this was a case in point in 2019. Lizzie, Ellen Van der Velden, Mhairi, Emma, Georgie and Mimi showed intent - which would be hammered home 12 months hence

A promise confirmed

This promise was confirmed in 2020 with an immaculate 5th. Georgie was up a cool 20 spots, and we loved the strong, aggressive running of Rachel Brown just outside the big five-oh.

A dozen ticks behind and Liv Paps was starting to make waves; and who to settle the account? We didn't have long to wait. It was Alice Reed in 70th, one part of a very talented sibling duo.

Strong teams like this only prosper with a good subs bench and what quality on there with Emily Barrett, yet another newbie, and Mhairi standing guard a few spots back; not to mention Iona and unthinkably Sammi in 8th Belles spot. Mimi 9th, then another Reed [Jess], followed by one of the girls who set this entire ball rolling way back nine years earlier in Flic. Truly, we'd come the full circle. And with Camilla Barden in the top 26%, our work was done.

Post-Covid Dreamteam

CD built and built during Covid and during the squad's *annus mirabilis* we came to Beckenham Park Place thinking only of bling. And goodness we had the power to back that up. Sarah Astin is a tremendously aggressive and daring runner and it wasn't even medals she was after, it was the win. This ruthless attitute cost her some 30 seconds and perhaps a medal, but the look in her eye indicates: "that's the way I roll…" What a find, and her day will come.

Rachel Brown continued to quietly build on her reputation for churning out high quality, forward placing runs; whilst a little way back we weren't surprised to see "Papsrunlaps" scoring 3rd, but pushed every step of the way by the dynamic Alice Reed – underestimate her at your peril. Sharp eyes will notice no change in that trio from 2020.

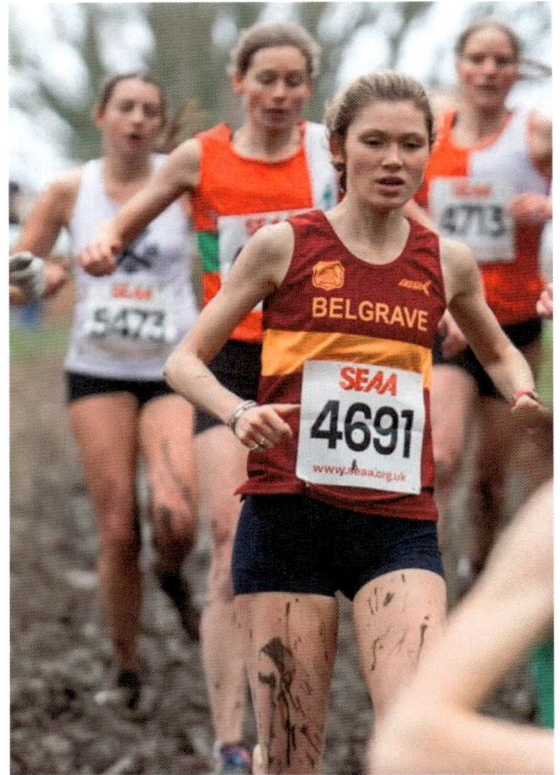

Unpeturbed by one of the South's most experienced beasts, Emily Wicks, placing a bead on the back of her head, Georgie was cold as ice for her 17th in 2020. GG

What followed was by far the most remarkable piece of packing in Belles' history. 60 61 62 76 78 87 89 & 96. Simply brilliant, and one wonders whether the powers that be will ever consider bumping this one up to 5 to score. How many clubs would *really* mind? One can't help feeling that four is a tad on the light side.

A Bel stripping down into racing garb has turned a few heads here. Clockwise: CD, Mhairi, Mimi, Rachel, Alice Keen, Paps, LGS, Steph Hewitt, Laurel Bray, Sarah Dewhirst, Flora Whyte, Alix Vermeulen, Ella-May Hards, SA & Sarah Astin

What the format certainly means is the lesser clubs are brought far more into view, and that's to take nothing away from Heathside and Basingstoke for zapping us. They did so well to grab silver and gold behind Aldershot, but their back-ups were: 41 119 146 240 252 256 & 291, and: 43 101 232 and 239. But a four-to-score race it is, and the scoreboard says it all; and it's not as if Heathside haven't hurt us before. Basingstoke – not so much! CD and friends will never perform so well again for so little return.

RESULTS 2013-2022, courtesy of A.R. Mead; belgraveharriers.info

2013 6th 267 pts. **Parliament Hill Fields, London,** 6 Feb. — 11 T. Jones, 60 F. Maycock; 85 H. Barsham-Rolfe, 111 P. Kasperova, 154 M-R Byrne, 155 A. Heydenrych; 256 finished; 21 teams closed in; team winners Aldershot, Farnham & Dist. AC 11 pts.; individual winner L. Partridge (Aldershot, Farnham & Dist. AC).

2014 2nd 81 pts. **Parliament Hill Fields, London,** 25 Jan. — 3 T. Jones, 14 M. Wilkins, 25 S. Amend, 39 Z. Doyle, 53 J. Rhodes; 66. M.G. Spalton, 158 V. Goodwin, 192 F. Maddocks; 466 finished; team winners Aldershot, Farnham & Dist. AC 66 pts.; individual winner J. Andrews (Aldershot, Farnham & Dist. AC). Belgrave 'B' team placed 19th 469 pts.

2015 2nd 116 pts. **Stanmer Park, Brighton, Sussex,** 24 Jan. — 6 M. Wilkins, 19 S. Amend, 30 Z. Doyle, 61 J. Rhodes, 67 K. MacKenzie; 41 teams closed in; team winners Winchester & Dist. AC) 102 pts.; 352 finished; individual winner L. Damen (Winchester & Dist. AC).

2016 16th 373 pts. **Parliament Hill Fields, London,** 30 Jan. — 41 M. Wilkins, 80 F. Cole, 86 J. Rhodes, 166 C. Pennock, 191 M. Bailey; 501 finished; 53 teams closed in; team winners Aldershot, Farnham & Dist. AC 56 pts.; individual winner N Taschimowitz (Shaftesbury Barnet H).

2017 6th 227 pts. **Parliament Hill Fields, London,** 28 Jan. — 32 S. Harris, 37 S. Amend, 67 S. Carter, 91 C. Pennock, 93 R. Prince, 142 I. Cousland, 196 L. Goldie-Scot, 277 H. White; 574 finished; 63 teams closed in; team winners Aldershot, Farnham & Dist. AC 17 pts.; individual winner E. Hosker Thornhill (Aldershot, Farnham & Dist. AC).

2018 9th 276 pts. **Stanmer Park, Brighton, Sussex,** 27 Jan. — 6 S. Harris, 68 S. Amend, 74 M. Hall, 128 L. Goldie-Scot, 246 G. Farrell; 351 finished; 40 teams closed in; team winners Aldershot, Farnham & Dist. AC 33 pts.; individual winner P. Law (Kingston AC & Polytechnic H).

2019 13th 388 pts. **Parliament Hill Fields, London,** 26 Jan. — 37 G. Fenn, 75 M. Hall, 96 E. Howsham, 180 M. Corden-Lloyd, 211 L. Goldie-Scot, 261 E. van der Velden; 703 finished; 71 teams closed in; team winners Thames Hare & Hounds 86 pts.; individual winner P. Woolven (Wycombe Phoenix H).

2020 5th 193 pts. **Parliament Hill Fields, London,** 25 Jan. — 17 G. Fenn, 51 R. Brown, 55 O. Papaioannou, 70 A Reed, 75 E. Barrett, 78 M. Hall, 131 I. Cousland, 137 S. Amend, 144 M. Corden-Lloyd, 163 J. Reed, 170 F. Cole, 183 C. Barden; 695 finished; 70 teams closed in; team winners Highgate H 66 pts.; individual winner J. Gibbons (Reading AC).

2021 Race not held due to coronavirus pandemic.

2022 4th 114 pts. **Beckenham Place Park, London Borough of Lewisham,** 29 Jan. — 4 S. Astin, 21 R. Brown, 44 O. Papaioannou, 45 A. Reed, 60 S. Amend, 61 F. Whyte, 62, E-M. Hards, 76 L. Goldie-Scot, 78 M. Corden-Lloyd, 87 L. Bray, 89 A. Vermeulen, 96 S. Dewhirst; 366 finished; team winners Aldershot, Farnham & Dist. AC 51 pts.; individual winner J. Gibbons (Reading AC).

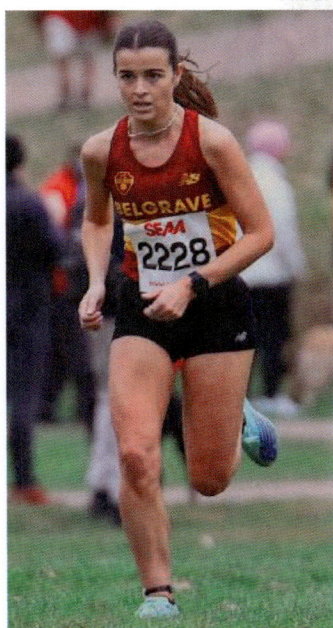

*Sarah Astin prowls to her brave,
never say die 4th in '22. SG*

Most times in the scoring four (including incomplete teams)
7 — M. 'Tilly' Heaton (2002, 2003, 2005, 2006, 2008, 2011, 2012).
5 — Samantha Amend (2012, 2014, 2015, 2017, 2018).
4 — Tania Sturton (1999 as an Under 20, 2000, 2001, 2002 as a Senior)
— Sarah Murphy (2005, 2006, 2007, 2008).
3 — G. 'Gabby' Collison (1986, 1991, 1994).
— Jacinta Moore née Coppinger (1987, 1991, 1994).
— Catherine Eastham (1999, 2005, 2006).
— Melanie Wilkins (2014, 2015, 2016).

THE SOUTHERN CROSS - MEN

We'll start with a bedtime story:

1937   A sad, sad situation

Never have Belgrave been in quite such purple form as the Southern of 1937. But what followed was a travesty as our scribe at the course reports:

THE SOUTHERN 1937:...... at halfway our chances of winning the title from Surrey A.C., not to mention a possible individual winner, appeared very bright and all we could do was to wait until the runners had been out in the country again.

Then followed a long suspense. Suddenly the runners were sighted, but in the wrong direction. The funnel was reversed, but again they disappeared. It was soon evident that the trail had been lost. Meanwhile, an observer from round the course had reported that the 'Bels' had 6 in 12. Then there was a shout and everybody dashed to a barbed wire fence to see the field come straggling uphill over a cabbage field, running from all directions. It was immediately decided to call the race off.

It transpired that the high wind had blown the trail away, but, surely, for a Championship Race, something more definite and not subject to the mercy of the elements as is a paper trail is necessary. Or shall each runner be provided with a map and compass? However, the sad fact remains that the entire field ran about twelve miles over very tough country for nothing; and as for many of the runners the "Southern" is their only 10 miles race, it must have been a very galling reward for their winter's training. No less mortifying was the lot of those clubs who had hoped to have earned a high position in the finishing list. For our own part we feel that Fate has robbed us of what appeared to be a potentially phenomenal win - first two men home, two in the next three positions and the other two scoring men inside the dozen. All of our men had gained ground, including Pat and Jim, who at a short distance from the finish, had increased their lead to 100 yards. Our complete team of twelve would have closed in by the time that the 60th man was home - surely a performance of which even the wildest optimist would never have dreamed.

In the annals of the sport the event will go down as "Race Postponed", but to those who were there (whilst hoping that a similar fate will never befall a race again), I think that it will go down as a moral victory for the Bels.

It was decided some days later to re-run the Senior race on Easter Saturday, at Dartford. In view of the strenuous programme facing our men, some having Service and International engagements in addition to the normal fixture list, and the unsuitability of the date, we decided not to compete. Our feelings were shared by most other clubs and eventually only 32 individuals comprising four teams (as against 33 teams originally entered) competed in the re-run race - a truly farcical state of affairs. It is to be hoped that suitable reference is made in the records as to the conditions size of field etc., of the re-run race, as there can be no credit in a success of this kind, and it is only fair that future generations shall be reminded that no serious "Southern" Senior Championship was decided in 1937.

Since that 'rum old day' we've had great days at this epic event but a last win of 1951 is a rather poor show. Bill Lucas holed the winning putt that day. An interesting example of an iconic Belgravian scoring just one point in their entire club career at the Southern or National cross, but sure making it count. Steve Sharp being the other at the 2004 National.

With no medal since 1971, we entered into the new millennium determined to address our rotten form at by far the longest XC event in the calendar. Not just 15k, but oft over Parliament Hill's unforgiving mud and climbs no less. The event always attracted me, as I'm a glutton for punishment, but rarely did I nail a good run, because I don't have the build or technique for such an affair, but I kept coming back for 18 years because the day has some magic to it, that's for sure.

Some 65 years on from anchoring the Bels home at the Southern, Bill tells Carol Vorderman and Dame Tanni all about it

New Century and a very fine start

We can be quietly proud of what we achieved in the 21st Century after a dreadful preceding 25 years, and it all started with the excellence of 2000. I knew little about what Parliament Hill entailed and only had vague memories of Hampstead Heath from the late 70's and early 80s via my grandparents who lived in Kilburn. I travelled to the venue with a heavy cold, but was determined to give it a go. I was not in the least disappointed by the day, which was enthralling and entailed the typical bad fall, some evidence of which is pictured here.

After 16th in 1999, which was a first team finish for six years, we had a firecracker start in 2000 with Paul Freary briefly leading and settling on 6th, backed up well by Hursty in 15th. 800m specialist Jason Lobo looked good for 25th, while Phil Carstairs always loved Parla Hill and claimed 82nd. After my 103rd we then had rather a wait for stalwart Mike Kazimierski, and were basically an ace off the medals. But a very encouraging day for sure.

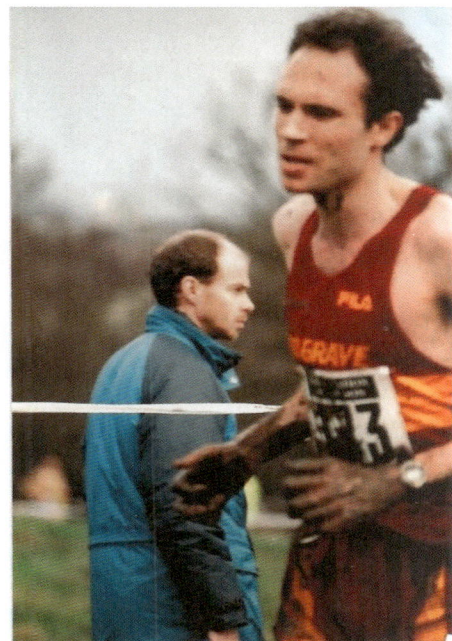

The author gets his hands dirty on Southern debut in 2000

More good fighting spirit entailed in a supreme quagmire in 2001 which I had to skip injured, but the last I'd miss for 14 years. Messrs Lobo and Carstairs were again outstanding. In 2002 I had a good duel with Chas Herrington for first man home, but the superstars had gone MIA, and it was a team of engine roomers who kept us respectable.

The SEAA are fortunate to have such an acqiescing partner in the Heath, but once every three years they have to look elsewhere, and it's here that they come somewhat unstuck. Exmouth's Bicton Park is pleasant but too far to expect so many to travel for. Thus, our 10th was quite pleasing in 2003, and I was sad to be in the form of my life but came down with another cold, missing out on a top 25 chance, and settling for 42nd. Hassan Raidi had one of his rare gems for us in 15th. We should probably have gotten more out of Hassan over the years, but he was mercurial – although would be in the National winning squad the following year.

Some Major Hit and Miss

Maddeningly, three times in Alan's reign we got stuck on five runners, often when looking rather good, and the first of those was '04, before a tremendous looking squad showed up in 2005, although the two big stars then stepped off the heartless course in despair, including dear old Gnasher, with his early retirement starting to creep up on the horizon. We loved what we saw in John Charles and John Clarke though, although both had terribly short-lived Bels careers. We finished a solid eighth.

It's a good start for the Bels in 2005 with Nash, Raidi, Byansi and the author all prominent, but it was a troubled race for the claret and gold. 1162 is the great John Downes who won two years previously and was a true cross-country giant for some 20 years. RO'D

In 2006 I had a wedding in Cumbria but the Southern was in Exmouth. Ooooff, that really is a horror drive and looking back I have to wonder what I was thinking. Especially as we were stuck on just three runners. Straight into the car after the race and six long hours on the road and we arrived just in time for the wedding dinner, slipping into my DJ out of my muddy racing strip at a Service station.

An All-time Wonder Duel

We were blessed that Holkham Hall said yes to the SEAA in 2007 and it was a memorable day. The team was rock solid for 6th with Mal Byansi having that one 'perfect' season for us and Pete Willis and Dave Mason also on cracking form. But it was up front where the magic lay, as Wicksy and Huw Lobb had what many feel to be one of the finest duels in English cross-country in the last 50 years.

It was two contrasting athletes, builds & running styles but for 45 long minutes they simply threw everything at each other. Their dominance over the rest of the field was incredible, with only former National champ Dom Bannister in any way keeping them in check. ARM wrote: *The Belgrave man also appeared to be drifting back a pace or two occasionally but on the other hand, he looked comfortable enough and always closed up immediately. The pair were far ahead now and onlookers gasped at the sheer pace of these two: "How can they possibly run that fast for 15k?"*

162

Finally, in the last mile Phil managed to prise open a slim gap and kept on prising. A marvellous victory for our young lion over a very fine 2:14 marathoner. "A classic race!" exclaimed AW's Martin Duff, as Phil, at just 22, became our 5th winner of the race after Bert Footer in 1933, Tom Carter 1946, Len Herbert 1947 & Gerry North 1967. Great names all.

Double medal assault

To add value to Phil's win, he could "only" find 9th with stitch in 2008 whilst a resurgent Mark Pollard scored a brilliant 7th. But could this wonderful start just mean medals?! Well, with a terrific run from Jonesy in 18th, we were plumb in line. I'd had a lot of time off but held together "ok" for 82nd, and with Richard Stannard tracking my every move we had an agonizing wait for our 6th, so where was James Fairbourn?

Alan powerfully writes: "Skipper Will was on the move now and was leading Richard and James but there was nothing between them as they worked off each other until – disaster – Jim went down like a sack of potatoes, tripping badly on the edge of a path and badly cutting both knees. It was a ghastly moment. Shocked, he was up again, but the crash had taken every ounce of breath out of him and in the next half mile he came out, destined to finish the course in an ambulance."

With that reverse, we had to wait three minutes for our 6th man, in dependable Tim Weeks, and basically, we were an ace shy of Woodford in bronze. But aces don't grow on trees, and we had three anyhow. A fine day though, all round. Oddly enough, Jim's bloody fate mirrored that of Lee Greatorex at the National at the same theatre, two years earlier [in his case, a deep spike gash].

Hillingdon Thrills

Another very strong team came to race at Hillingdon's interesting course in 2009. We had only medals on the mind and the lads fought tooth and nail for every position. None more so of course than Phil, who did his high risk approach of trying to break his man early and then sit on that lead for a great many miles. This time it worked – but would such an approach come back to haunt him? Ben Whitby made major inroads into Phil's advantage over the last lap for the margin to be "only" 5 seconds by the end.

Alan takes us through the travails of our super engine room: "It was always going to be an unpredictable race with the heavy going and waterlogged sections. Some took to it better than others. James Kelly admitted that he just couldn't seem to get his legs going in the mud and Mark Pollard was unable to get near his superb 7th place of 2008 - but Simon Jones, in spite of swearing that he hates cross country, held up well for 28th. As might have been predicted, the ever-present Will Cockerell and Pete Willis filled out the team, although veteran Mike Trees held an impetuous forward position early on before sinking back through the field."

We really felt we'd done enough and Alan said at the finish: "surely a medal, but what colour?" But, alas, we'd not noticed the excellent packing of Winchester, who we speak of elsewhere as a club not often in the reckoning, but extremely dangerous and capable of springing the odd surprise. They duffed us up badly here – in fact everyone – for a superb win, and it was actually Bedford, no less, who we could see in a non-too-distant bronze.

Back to earth with a bump

On a miserable day, our fairly able team in 2010 fell one sandwich short of a picnic. Maddening but there it was. We did have a 6th, but I recall a fairly strong man having a pricey DNS [late arrival].

Club president Hazel Mead hands over the trophy to first Southern man home, James Kelly in 2011

RESULTS 2000-2010 courtesy of ARMead www.belgraveharriers.info

2000	6th	452 pts.	**Parliament Hill Fields, London**, 29 Jan. — 6 P. Freary, 15 L. Hurst, 25 J. Lobo, 82 P. Carstairs, 103 W. Cockerell, 221 M. Kazimierski, 280 D. Ochse, 375, R. Harding, 386 Don Anderson; 966 finished; 82 teams closed in; team winners Blackheath H 212 pts.; individual winner D. Taylor (Blackheath H).
2001	9th	551 pts.	**Parliament Hill Fields, London**, 27 Jan. — 18 P. Freary, 19 J. Lobo, 62 P. Carstairs, 119 M. Byansi, 125 L. Catley, 209 (scoring 208) M. Kazimierski, 252 W. Lynch; 894 finished; 75 teams closed in; team winners Thames Hare & Hounds 130 pts.; individual winner N. Francis (Shaftesbury Barnet H).
2002	14th	1007 pts.	**Parliament Hill Fields, London**, 26 Jan. — 50 W. Cockerell, 58 C. Herrington, 152 M. Byansi, 217 L. Catley, 239 A. Jones, 291 W. Lynch, 499 Don Anderson; team winners Bedford & County AC 99 pts.; individual winner E. DeJonge (Shaftesbury Barnet H).
2003	10th	628 pts.	**Bicton Park, nr. Exmouth, Devon**, 25 Jan. — 15 H. Raidi, 42 W. Cockerell, 70 K. Hegvold, 126 W. Lynch, 170 L. Catley, 209 P. Carstairs, 211 M. Byansi, 524 Don Anderson; scoring – 15, 42, 69, 125, 169, 208; team winners Newham & Essex Beagles 148 pts.; individual winner J. Downes (London Irish AC).
2004			**Parliament Hill Fields, London**, 24 Jan. — incomplete team; 65 W. Cockerell, 134 T. Hadfield, 186 P. Carstairs, 194 W. Lynch, 550 Don Anderson; 800 finished; 65 teams closed in; team winners Newham & Essex Beagles 128 pts.; individual winner H. Lobb (Bedford & County AC).
2005	8th	667 pts.	**Parliament Hill Fields, London**, 29 Jan — 79 W. Cockerell, 85 J. Charles, 106 K. Hegvold, 107 J. Clarke, 130 T. Hadfield, 166 J. Wolf; 208 W. Lynch, 255 A. Porteous, 682 Don Anderson; 830 finished; scoring – 78, 84, 105, 106, 129, 165; 63 teams closed in; team winners Bedford & County AC 99 pts.; individual winner H. Lobb (Bedford & County AC).
2006			**Bicton Park, nr. Exmouth, Devon**, 28 Jan. — incomplete team; 27 T. Watson, 58 W. Cockerell, 129 W. Lynch; 551 finished; 41 teams closed in; team winners Bedford & County AC 165 pts.; individual winner D. Mitchinson (Newham & Essex Beagles).
2007	6th	462 pts.	**Holkham Hall, Norfolk**, 27 Jan. — 1 P. Wicks, 52 M. Byansi, 84 P. Willis, 85 W. Cockerell, 118 J. Kimaiyo, 122 D. Mason, 159 T. Ellacott, 459 S. Baxendale, 507 E. Taylor; 553 finished; 38 teams closed in; team winners Bedford & County AC 68 pts.; individual winner P. Wicks (Belgrave H).
2008	4th	378 pts.	**Parliament Hill Fields, London**, 26 Jan. — 7 M. Pollard, 9 P. Wicks, 18 S. Jones, 82 W. Cockerell, 85 R. Stannard, 177 T. Weeks, 234 M. Whiting, 271 T. Hadfield, 276 W. Lynch, 285 R. Harding, 286 S. Zealey, 466 R. Merrick, 543 R. Poulter, 566 M. Humphrey, 577 L. Rehn, dnf J. Fairbourn; 832 finished; 86 teams closed in; team winners Bedford & County AC 109 pts.; individual winner F. Tickner (Wells City H).
2009	4th	274 pts.	**Hillingdon House Farm, Hillingdon, Middx.**, 24 Jan. — 1 P. Wicks, 28 S. Jones, 40 M. Pollard, 41 James Kelly, 80 W. Cockerell, 84 P. Willis, 99 M. Byansi, 106 J. Fairbourn, 115 M. Trees, 124 L. Eguia, 126 K. Hegvold, 231 M. Humphrey; 672 finished; 52 teams closed in; team winners Winchester & Dist. AC 162 pts.; individual winner P. Wicks (Belgrave H).
2010			**Parliament Hill Fields, London**, 30 Jan. — incomplete team; 25 James Kelly, 46 P. Owor, 89 W. Cockerell, 133 R. Stannard, 428 M. Trees; 806 finished; 81 teams closed in; team winners Bedford & County AC 100 pts.; individual winner N. Hall (Bedford & County AC).

2011 was a near mirror image with our 1, 2, 3 of JK, PO, WC. Jim's magnificent consistency saw a 25th & a 27th while PO oh so dislikes the porridge of Parla Hill, as we got a modest 14th for our struggle; as Lander Eguia did well while Soren Lindner would go much better at the National the following month. Good old Mike Trees closed us in en route to a telling four year run in the scoring six.

"Got Any Ideas?" "Actually, Not..." Phil and Matt's darkest hour

Another teasing quintet showed up to Stanmer Park in 2012. Come on lads, surely one more of you could have got round what is a beautiful and historic course. Especially with Phil and Jim suckin' diesel up at the front. I had one of the best XC runs of my career into my 39th year, but just when it looked as though I'd have a real blinder, I got mugged horribly on the final long descent and lost at least 10 spots. Oh that descent! What can we say, except it was the scene for one of the most upsetting Belgrave losses of all time.

Searching for his 3rd win, Phil had another wonderful run, and in a long, tense assault on glory, with 600 to go, he rounded the corner out of the woods. "Anything?!" bellowed Phil to coach Matt Whiting. One is reminded of Chesley Sullenberger before he ditched Flight 1549 onto the Hudson. "Got Any Ideas?" he asked his co-pilot. "Actually, not..." came the reply. Matt didn't have any ideas either, because from where he was positioned he couldn't see anyone. So "Actually, not," was largely the gist of his reply. But then, in the 6 seconds it took for Phil to scamper off into the distance, the imposing figure of Ben Tickner hurtled round the trees. *Holy shiiiii........* that was not the look of a man who'd settled for 2nd.

Phil Wicks at Stanmer Park. The loneliness of command... the possibility of defeat. SW

The final descent at Stanmer is fairly steep, long and telling. The difference between hunter and hunted could be at least 50 yards and safety not assured. Which was about the case here. Ben simply tore into the unsuspecting Phil, who by the time the final corner was reached with 200 to go was now being severely assaulted, and there was no time for a gear change. He still had to hold on though, for luminaries Pepper, Watts and Heywood were hovering. It was a gut-wrenching defeat, as Phil observed: "I can accept being beaten on any day of the week, but to lose like that is hard to take. I won't forget that for a while."

The car journey home with Matt was very, very quiet, with Matt perhaps being a touch scapegoated, but what could he do? I suppose one option, which he'd probably do now, is to lie and say: "don't relax! He's right behind you!" This could be always defended in court, as say, Tickner was 30 seconds back, Matt could riposte, "as I said, right behind…" another tiny technical impurity was perhaps Matt stood at the wrong angle and was too unsighted. But you know what? Had he have been half-way down that slope, Phil would still surely have been in fatal danger. Such are the glories, the drama, the chaos and the occasional despair of top class racing. Almost unthinkably Phil would not return to the Southern again, although he fully intended to pretty much every time in the next decade, but sickness, injury and a global pandemic cast a deep spell over him; which is all the more frustrating as this race suits men in their 30s more than those in their 20s. One day – maybe 2023!

Namby-pamby officialdom

In fact, Phil was plumb in line to return in 2013, before the SEAA cancelled some five days out due to snowfall. I was really upset; it seemed vastly premature, and indeed on race day all that could be spied on the Heath was greensward. Oh well – '*elf and safety*. The rejig occurred, but the Bramley 10 claimed our star in 49:10. Heh, do the Southern and *then* run 50:30 on the Sunday, Phil, now *that's* marathon training! He'd go on to claim a solid 2:19 at London, leading JK and myself to silver.

Will gets his derriere handed to him, by… Snowie

We had fun at the rerun, with my line drawing a big laugh from Hazel and Alan: "I'm not quite sure about our support today… 'go on Matt… go on Will… go on dog!'" Early on in lap 2 a little white dog took a liking to me and latched on for over a mile, before a policeman finally dove on him. It was an excruciating passage of play. He'd get under my feet, but when I'd try to drop-kick or stamp on the fetid, rancid, runtbeast, he'd scoot away, tossing a delighted look over his shoulder, to say, "try again cockerpillar!"

Elsewhere, we managed to change the flights for Andrew Connick who had an absolute pearl for 15th, while Paskar came to the party in a big way as well. Matt [Taylor] did well to show me the way, whilst Mike [Trees] was excellent and Royston solid. Our 6th was deserved and of course it would have been all that, or better, if on the original date [due to the missing Phil].

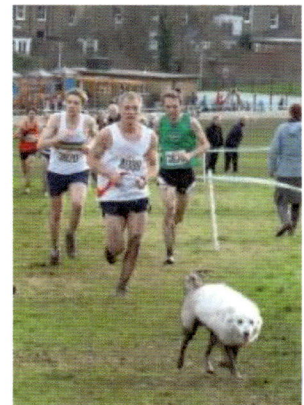

Living his best life. Snowie moves deep into the top 100 - get that man a vest

Which brings us to the end of the Mead era with 2014's iffy return. Paskar was off-colour, Roy found himself as our 2nd man and James Browne, well known around a decade earlier, was solid. I was running out of petrol rather, and we had to dip into the wares of the Trondheim stallion and Tom Corbett to finally settle up in over a thousand points. Whoopsie-daisy. But we finished eight runners and on the whole could be most grateful for Alan's generation of persuasion to afford the race more respect.

It was clipboard time for me after 13 Southerns on the spin, one short of Bert Footer's record streak. And the reason for that, was this was something I had to see! The previous autumn, our Scottish star Craig Ruddy declared an interest in the Southern, to which I replied, "bring it on!" With Stanmer close to Gatwick, it all made sense, and as a huge Brucie bonus, Craig brought along the promising Steven Trainer. Meanwhile, I'd been on the recruit myself. We'd become aware off the running prowess of Alex Miller in the last few years, and the Datchet Dashers were probably a level – or three – beneath him. When ACM started courting none other than Sammi Amend, the situation was right for a poach. Alex was delighted to be asked.

I also became aware of someone giving me more and more trouble at Bushy parkrun. An ungainly but clearly strong Lithuanian fellow. I approached Andrius Jaksevicius and the gist was that pretty much every club in Surrey had approached him, but he was quite happy nursing his parkrun addiction. But those clubs didn't possess my silver tongue, and what followed was one of the great Road and Coutnry signings, as any squad with AJ in it gets a spine and a solid foundation. Now this was looking like a team… with Phil saying yes and another parkrun signing in the talented Taras Telkovsky along for the ride, not to mention the always dependable Nick Bundle, we hit the Friday of the race dreaming *uuuuuuge*. Oh! Did I mention Paskar requested the Surreys off to focus solely on the Southern? [Granted].

There was some heartbreak when Phil came down with a stinker, but such was our depth, the knock was "only" perceived to be around 60 points. Then Taras got sick too, but said he'd give it a go, but on this day had to wave Nick through for the score. In pretty much any other year, the riches of non-scorers Matt Welsh and Roy Maddams would have been gladly plundered.

> ◆
>
> "If you want to win a race you have to go a little berserk."
> —Bill Rodgers
>
> ◆

Onto the race, and when PO targets, he targets BIG. It was nothing less than a podium finish that he desired and he got it with one of the most painful, and proudest, races of his career. Let's pick up the story, via my report, with a packed field still to enter the 3rd and final lap:

 Finally, as the lap progressed, 20 became 12, which became 7 as the last tour was entered. PO dangerously tired now, quite literally losing his mind [he wasn't even sure of the lap count until Mo Aaran put him out of his misery]. But as he came out of the woods, PO reports: "Oh Mr Will, there were girls there, they were *three* Belgrave girls! And they *screeeaamm*! Oh they scream so loud Mr Will. I think, '*NO!* I keep this pace, I do not slow.' "

In the team stakes it was hard to know what was going on, but it was clear Belgrave would be up there somewhere. PO dug deeper, perhaps deeper than he ever has for us before and messrs Pepper and Tickner were stuck to well. Tickner dropped back. PO or Pepper for the win?! But then with the final 600 approaching, Ben T burst through a gap in the middle of them, and the mind returned to Phil's shattering loss here in 2012 when BT came from nowhere to surprise him on the final descent. With 400 to go Tickner led PO by four or five strides as they ran lock step to the final corner. The roars of the crowd were unlike anything I've heard in 17 years of club life. Have we ever seen PO outkicked for us? Once or twice, but he was all in, and three times in that awful last minute he felt the vomit rise to his throat, only to keep it down. Such was his exhaustion it was no longer just Tickner to worry about as Pepper and Alex Bruce-Littlewood started to badly molest our man. But he had just enough left for a fantastic silver in a race some 18 times over his speciality. Hip hip hooray for the Lion – one of the greatest Belgrave XC runs of the last 50 years – and in the conversation for *ever*.

Breath-taking stuff, and now the runners began to cascade down from the mount. Ruds' 21st was fine – we'll take it, while Stephen just keeps getting better. Our Lithuanian dynamo had looked knackered all day, and when Alex caught him, I roared for AJ to stick to him, and for the two to encourage and help each other. Happily that's how it went – superb teamwork and packing. Right, where was our 6th? It was Nick having a blinder, 12 weeks of fatherhood has suited him well. Our work was done but try telling that to Taras who fought to the end as did Matt and Roy.

Bedford and County eh! An incredible sequence of results in this race (around 11 wins from the last 15) and they're National champions of course as well. We're usually over 500 points off them so 'only' 79 is good going. Their team has a fairly new look these days, save for the ageless Darren Deed running in 14th with a bad injury, into his 27th season with the club. But our cushion over our chasers is significant, and there's no doubt the mood in the camp is that we can crack on from here. A big relief to break the 44 year medal duck, but we haven't *won* the race since the reign of King George, and the current monarch is becoming impatient. We'll get there Ma'am!

*[QEII never did witness a Bels win on her watch, but hopefully Charles III will].

1 Bedford & C 150; 2 Belgrave H 229; 3 Highate H 328; 4 Herne Hill H 333; 5 Woodford Gr WEL 425; 6 Serpentine R 453. 55 teams closed in.

It's taken a loooooong time. But we finally medalled at the Southerns again after 34 long years of drought. A team made up of great ability, some feisty recruitment, quite a bit of good fortune, some thinking outside the box, but most important perhaps a thirst to compete over 15 long Kms at a major Championship over a tough course. And you need a good subs bench, which we had. L-R, Miller, Ruddy, AJ, PO, Trainer & Bundle

168

And then relaaaax

The following year was back to norm of big guns dropping like flies and in a minor fit of pique the gaffer discarded his pipe and slippers and came to the ball. It meant I overtook my hero Bert Footer for most scores at the Southern with 15, but my run was not a pretty sight. His dates were 1923-1939 and I expect there would have been more, if not for the war, where he served as a Commando. Mine were 2000-2016. The great news was that the Rudster was back, with barely a discernible run from the year before, and Zek Abery was tidy in 66th. A little behind, a parkrunner I'd been purring over for ages, Paul Lowe, crossed over the bridge from Stragglers, although his first season with us was plagued with minor despair – as he was cup tied for the Surrey League which in turn triggered our relegation horrors. But no such trouble for Paul here. We also had Nick Buckle finding himself somewhat too tall and elegant for Parla Hill, whilst Nick Smallwood kept getting better and better. Alas, the vultures at Cambridge were circling.

Our fighting 10th was improved up to a pretty impressive 8th the next year as our engine room appeared to be really up for the challenge of this brutal race. None more so than the Lithuanian Dynamo, at the peak of his powers and finding a very good 25th. Messrs Buckle and Miller harrassed each other the entire way round: Belgravians like beating athletes from other clubs, but they *love* to beat each other! The fine packing continued with Nick Bundle, a returning Paul, and that all important 6th man came in Arne Dumez.

It's not just the fancy-dan scorers we savour at Belgrave but the great friendships and connections made further down the field. I met and bonded with Eduard Egelie at the savage 2010 Athens Marathon, and he so nearly won a surprise team medal with us at the rescheduled SOT championships that winter, but agonizingly we fell one man short. But EE has kept in touch down the years, and he tested himself against the best at the 2017 Southern

We craved more from Paul Lowe after his big switch from Stragglers but although we got some telling scores it was a case of 'too many daughters, too little time!' He was recently spied in Bushy cantering along though, and who knows, maybe we'll yet see him again.

Alex Miller kicks for the line and has trouble in his rear view courtesy of Bertie Powell, one of the most prolific club servants of all time

A Hard Day's Night as we settled for a well constructed 8th in 2017. Lowe, Bundle, Buckle, Dumez, WC, Miller & Tom O'Beirne

Simply Biblical

Back to Stanmer for 2018 in absolutely horrendous and biblical conditions. Never worse I'm told [I gave it a miss!]. Paskar fought hard and Nick Buckle had one of the best runs of his career to push him all the way. Miller and Bundle were back which made it all quite déjà vu on 2015 and their runs were strong. We then enjoyed the sight of two unlikely but valuable lads closing us home in Ross Finlay, and remarkably Patrick McDougall, into his 50s and placing in close to the top third of the field. And that was our lot! So to be this short on manpower but still find 9th was a terrific effort.

A small stumble, but then more progress

2019 saw us continuing to shore up our defences, as Andrius, Paskar and 'Nick Buck' were yet again to the fore, with the welcome sight of Steve Gardner as our 4th man. Patrick and Alex Mills saw us home, with James Morris on loyal sentry duty, lest accidents occur and come the National he would indeed be required. This weaker year was corrected 12 months later with Covid encroaching. Callum Stewart gave us a nice surprise by nicking the lion who had now scored in this one eight times. James Nutt had a superb run in 79th, whilst Arne was way up on his best. Scoring honours completed by two promising new men in Andrew Cumine and Matt Edgar, with Alex Miller to the surprise of some edged out, but goodness would he correct that at the National; whilst four more men lay in wait, the most notable being a certain C McNally – having a horror here, but also in line for a National correction. The new Dumez-Gardner regime was off to an encouraging start [11th].

This is like the Blackadder scene at Hadrian's Wall where the Romans' skirts got shorter... and shorter.... but you have to hand it to Patrick, he has the legs to pull it off. Elsewhere AJ, Alex, James, PO, Steve and Nick savour a tough old day when all but 7 of the lads stayed away. 17th in 2019

A Covid Declaration of Intent

We arrived at Beckenham's truly bizarre, appallingly marked course in 2022 bristling with intent. Spikes were swiftly dispensed with as this was more of a road race, on rock hard pathways, and a grisly 4 laps. Yes, the South struggled to find a venue, but with the tens of thousands of pounds they grab for the race, the least they can do is get enough marshals and mark out a clear route to the finish. It was vague conjecture where finishing athletes were supposed to go, or the racing-line required, especially in the early races where there was some chaos and medal positions compromised.

But onto the race and we had a spell-binding squad to savour. Could they medal? Reece Edwards ran superbly all day and hovered at the back of a lead group of nearly 20 for some half an hour before going to work and starting to pick off the enemy. His clock finally stopped when just seven fidgety souls remained. The next day, maybe with the endomorphins still buzzing, Reece reeled off a 50K run, which duly broke him, and we never saw him again for the season. Running: play with fire, and you will get burned.

A quartet to warm the cockles. In the background is Tommy Taylor, so often keeping close watch on our scorers and ready to pounce, but this was about 12k too long for him really. And then Conall, Jonny and Nick severely accost Saltire skipper Richard Ollington. SG

Callum confirmed his low-68 marathoning form for a position well inside the top 50, with some humurgous packing displayed by the 'smiling assassin mountain goat' that is

Jonny Neville, the head-rolling Conall who all but collapsed on the long finishing straight (although he'll say, just another day at the races); Nick Buckle yet again, to enter our leaderboard of most SEAA scores with 5, and co-TM Arne. And what about that back-up! No fewer than eight of the little terrors, with Tom Lole's run the cream of the crop. But seriously, well played to the management, it presses our club record of 16 starters in 2008 hard. 5th was a wee bit of a harsh return for such a good day, maybe 4th was more like it, but for that you perhaps need one more star, and for medals, two more.

The most important thing though is all were agreed: the Southern will remain as a key target for the club going forward – and quite right too.

Callum Stewart is one of our most able and loyal men, who is starting a notable career in the claret and gold. A fine 44th was his reward here. SG

Into the gloaming, a hard-working squad savours a long, tough race. Back row l-r: Reece Edwards, Arne Dumez, Tom Lole, Toby Fletcher, Callum Stewart, Ewan Somerville, Nathan Visick, Matt Edgar, Nick Buckle, Jonny Neville, Conall McNally. Front row l-r: Frank & Ben Hurley, Valentin Rigori.

2011 14th 739 pts. **Parliament Hill Fields, London**, 29 Jan. — 27 James Kelly, 80 P. Owor, 102 W. Cockerell, 153 L. Eguia, 164 S. Lindner, 213 M. Trees, 386 R. Norville, 423 P. Carstairs, 427 D. Mason, 479 W. Ireson, 591 A. Lang; 885 finished; 93 teams closed in; team winners Bedford & County AC 129 pts.; individual winner N. Hall (Bedford & County AC).

2012 **Stanmer Park, Brighton, Sussex**, 28 Jan. — incomplete team; 2 P. Wicks, 16 James Kelly, 70 W. Cockerell, 258 M. Trees, 275 L. Eguia; 745 finished; 79 teams closed in; team winners Highgate H 157 pts.; individual winner B. Tickner (Wells City H).

2013 6th 424 pts. **Parliament Hill Fields, London**, 6 Feb. — 15 A. Connick, 29 P. Owor, 63 M. Taylor, 72 W. Cockerell, 99 M. Trees, 146 R. Maddams, 215 J. Needham, 290 T. Hadfield; 541 finished; 31 teams closed in; team winners Bedford & County AC 57 pts.; individual winner F. Tickner (Wells City H).

2014 19th 1112 pts. **Parliament Hill Fields, London**, 25 Jan. — 60 P. Owor, 126 R. Maddams, 145 J. Browne, 152 W. Cockerell, 235 K. Hegvold, 394 T. Corbett, 525 F. Logan, 529 T. Hadfield; 986 finished; 110 teams closed in; team winners Shaftesbury Barnet H; individual winner R. Goodman (Shaftesbury Barnet H).

2015 2nd 224 pts. **Stanmer Park, Brighton, Sussex**, 24 Jan. — 2 P. Owor, 20 C. Ruddy, 24 S. Trainer, 51 A. Miller, 54 A. Jaksevicius, 73 N. Bundle, 86 T. Telkovsky, 125 M. Welsh, 131 R. Maddams, 330 L. Pikett, 567 A. Carpentier; 854 finished; 55 teams closed in; team winners Bedford & County AC 144 pts.; individual winner B. Tickner (Brighton Phoenix AC).

2016 10th 737 pts. **Parliament Hill Fields, London**, 30 Jan. — 28 C. Ruddy, 66 Z. Abery, 82 P. Lowe, 133 N. Buckle, 154 N. Smallwood, 274 W. Cockerell, 287 T. O'Beirne, 440 J. Goymor, 731 R. Norville; 1026 finished; 70 teams closed in; team winners Highgate H 162 pts.; individual winner J. Hay (Aldershot, Farnham & Dist. AC).

2017 8th 580 pts. **Parliament Hill Fields, London**, 28 Jan. — 25 A. Jaksevicius, 80 N. Buckle, 82 A. Miller, 101 N. Bundle, 122 P. Lowe, 170 A. Dumez, 270 T. O'Beirne, 388 A. Mills, 830 E. Egelie; 1068 finished; 69 teams closed in; team winners Highgate H 121 pts.; individual winner A. Maud (Highgate H).

2018 9th 767 pts **Stanmer Park, Brighton, Sussex**, 27 Jan. — 54 P. Owor, 56 N. Buckle, 99 A, Miller, 105 N. Bundle, 179 R. Finlay, 274 P. McDougall; 740 finished; 55 teams closed in; team winners Bedford & County AC; individual winner J. Gilbert (Kent AC).

2019 17th 1090 pts. **Parliament Hill Fields, London**, 26 Jan. — 32 A. Jaksevicius, 48 P. Owor, 115 N. Buckle, 188 S. Gardner, 353 P. McDougall, 354 A. Mills, 707 J. Morris; 1154 finished; 77 teams closed in; team winners Aldershot, Farnham & Dist. AC 105 pts.; individual winner H. Pearce (Tonbridge AC).

2020 11th 543 pts. **Parliament Hill Fields, London**, 25 Jan. — 48 C. Stewart, 53 P. Owor, 79 J. Nutt, 90 A. Dumez, 123 A. Cumine, 150 M. Edgar, 240 A. Miller, 303 C. McNally, 346 B. Hurley, 353 N. Visick, 839 J. Morris; 1173 finished; 81 teams closed in; team winners Aldershot, Farnham & Dist. AC 97 pts.; individual winner A. Hickey (Southend on Sea AC).

2021 Race not held due to coronavirus pandemic.

2022 5th 474 pts. **Beckenham Place Park, London Borough of Lewisham**, 29 Jan. — 8 R. Edwards, 44 C. Stewart, 98 J. Neville, 100 C. McNally, 110 N. Buckle, 114 A. Dumez, 145 T. Lole, 153 T. Fletcher, 159 T. Taylor, 169 E. Somerville, 172 M. Edgar, 179 N. Wilson, 209 B. Hurley, 286 B. Vigori; 685 finished; 46 teams closed in; team winners Southampton AC 131 pts.; individual winner A. Coley-Maud (Guildford & Godalming AC).

*N Wilson in 2022 should read N Visick, and B Vigori V Rigori

A list for the sluggers! Nick Buckle starts to climb, Paskar has eight, which is good going for an 800 star, and Don Anderson has a range of 21 years. We are still in close touch with Lionel and Leo, and that's good Steeplechase prep for John Bicourt, weaving his Southerns around his two Olympics of '72 and '76.

With another double Olympian in Paskar also giving the Southern a lot of attention, it's a great reminder of how crucial club athletics is to toughen up and advance athletes. John Thresher was a classic miler, and we were very sad to lose Tony Fairclough in 2022.

Most times in the scoring six (including incomplete teams)
- 15 — Will Cockerell (2000, 2002-2014, 2016).
- 14 — H.E. 'Bert' Footer (1923-1928, 1930-1936, 1939).
- 13 — Charlie W. Walker (1952-1964).
- 11 — Pat O'Connor (1969, 1972-1980, 1982).
- 10 — C.T. 'Tom' Carter (1933-1939, 1946, 1948-1949, spanning the missing war years).
- 9 — Jack W. Brown (1950-1953, 1955-1957, 1961, 1963).
  — Gerry A. North (1963-1971).
  — Lionel Mann (1969-1971, 1973-1975, 1977-1979).
  — Don Anderson (1983-1984, 1988-1989, 1991, 1993, 1997-1998, 2004).
- 8 — A. 'Tony' Fairclough (1965-1969, 1971-1972) .
  — Leo Coy (1975, 1977-1978, 1980, 1982, 1984-1985, 1986).
  — Arthur W. Penny (1929, 1931, 1933-1934, 1936-1939).
  — Paskar Owor (2010-2011, 2013-2015, 2018-2020).
- 7 — Arthur Allum (1929-1935).
  — Eric Gebbett (1956-1962).
- 6 — John Thresher (1964, 1966-1969, 1971).
  — Laurie O'Hara (1963, 1965-1967, 1973-1974).
  — John Bicourt (1970-1973, 1975-1976).
  — Mike Lake (1985, 1987-1988, 1990-1991, 1993).
  — Mike Webb (1991-1995, 1999).
  — Phil Carstairs (1998-2001, 2003-2004).
- 5 — J.E. 'Jack' Flower (1930-1934).
  — E.S. 'Ted' Stimpson (1939, 1948-1951).
  — Len W. Herbert (1946-1949, 1951).
  — Mike Hayes (1984-1987, 1989).
  — Nick Buckle (2016-2019, 2022).

THE NATIONAL - MEN

Ah, National Sweet National. It is truly one of the greatest footraces in the world and I personally have found none better. The atmosphere, aura, surroundings and brutal nature of the challenge make this the ultimate bucket-lister. Not only have I not missed the race for 23 years, I have never come close to giving it a pass. I am more likely to swerve the latest Bond at the cinema, or Kate Bush in concert… and I do love a bit of Kate.

There are many reasons why I think the National is one of the greatest races in the world, but here are four:

1) It is, quite simply, berserk. But in a hypnotic, breath-taking manner that leaves you stunned, gasping for air, and saying: 'you've got to be kidding me'. The challenge is one of "no let up" and indeed more than any race I've ever done, you're under *constant pressure*. And by constant I mean, if you have a bad mile and you can lose 80 spots – or 180. Brutal.

2) The start. Some 2,000 runners, all sprinting like maniacs for that first turn. Very fit 1,500 meter runners versus very fit marathoners… a sea of colour, chaos and carefree joie de vivre.

3) The courses. Wonderful stuff! The cynical ECCA could easily give us more variety for the Southern edition though, refusing to move us away from the dreaded Parla' Hill. Don't get me wrong, it's a terrific sporting theatre, but there are loads of other places they can take it. But the City of London are very generous and it's a huge money spinner to take it there. However, the *obsession* with such a massive profit line means the runners are deprived some iconic glimpses of elsewhere in Southern England, which the ECCA seem to have no idea is a glorious part of the world, to stick us in the urban jungle of North London, since the wonderful race at Stowe over a generation ago.

But that grumble aside, a fine time is had by all, and this Century we've all loved three fabulous and contrasting courses in Leeds, plus Wollaton Park [albeit thrice], Alton Towers, Bristol, Durham, Sunderland, Birmingham and Leicestershire.

4) The excitement of the team race. More than any other this is about 'taking one for the team'. Runners have horror runs all the time at the National, but many times they stay the course, simply for the club, knowing a drop out could cost, say, 500 points. Battling for every spot, and indeed getting into the scoring 6 can make one forget about one's own misery. I found 18 scores at the National, and no fewer than six were in the anchor role. It's always a good feeling the 'stop the team's clock'. I recall the mild despair in the horrendous race of 2011 of standing at the finish watching our 5th man come home in the low 230s with a fine team spot incoming, and waiting for our strong 6th man, due any minute. Make that 7 minutes! Yuk, instead of top 10, we were 19th. But that's the National.

2000-2003 some origami, a surge, and a worrying dip

So with all that said, how have the Bels fared this Century? And the answer is, by all accounts, pretty darn well, and when one compares to 25 years before, very fine indeed.

My first National was on the tough Newark course in Nottingham in '99. There was much running through ploughed fields and I was stunned by the speed and severity of the start. But I was fit, and it remains one of the best races of my career. For the entire 45 minutes I had one thought on my mind: "there's not enough time… there's not enough time…" It's the best possible thought one can have in a race because it means the runner is solely focussed on catching as many as possible and is not fatiguing. For about 97% of my races, and indeed the National, the thought is, "oh, please let me finish." Our TM Arne Dumez said exactly this at his debut in 2017. After 3k he had one thought on his mind: "I may not finish this…" It is a mindset that afflicts so many runners.

We should've been 9th that day, but we suffered a deeply negative turn of fortune when Najibe Hliouat was flung out of the race for "number mutilation". We'd put enormous effort into rousing a fine squad, and everyone fought so hard, but we had to pay six places for that. Basically, Najibe had folded over the sponsor's name – a silly, but innocent mistake. Quite the punishment though – how about a 20 point penalty? It did though trigger one of Alan's great lines: "We did try to explain to him what happened, but Najibe's English does not stretch to the nuances of origami."

Lots of leaderboarding

It did though perhaps make ARM all the more determined to pay back the race at the glorious environs of Stowe School in 2000. David Niven did not tell a lie when describing the idyllic surrounds in which he used to romp with Piccadilly courtesans.

The squad assembled was by any mark, a "ripper", and when I walked into the 1030 team meeting, Alan threw a projectile at me. But what was in this curious package? I unwrapped it to find an Asics raintop in dark blue and claret, emblazoned with Belgrave in bright gold lettering. I was enormously flattered, as was not close to the A team, maybe slated to score at 10th. "Really?" I asked. "Sure, you're part of the squad," Alan replied. It made me feel part of something quite special, surrounded as I was by members of Team GB and indeed a big City marathon winner leading our lines.

What would happen on this exciting day? In retrospect perhaps having the big team tub-thumper some 4.5 hours out from the race was too early, because it wound us all up something awful! After a slightly interminable boxing analogy from Rob McHarg, Alan started the lethal guessing game of finishing spots. The problem was that anything he said would be shot back by the runner with interest. "75th?" he'd say to one… "50th!" came the reply. 60th? To another… "45!" Suddenly everyone was a better runner than they appeared. And I'm sure if Alan had said to me "200th?" that I'd have been appalled. Of course, I was 209.

So we got to the course and now had some three hours to kill. It's too much with all that nervous energy and maybe we then went into the race a tad flat, with a mixture of also being too wound up… a bad mix, which meant that everyone went out too fast and then bonked! And that was the least of our problems. Dear old Paul Evans, of 2:08 marathon fame who so brilliantly won the Chicago Marathon three years before, broke down en route to the race and had to be rescued by Bill Laws and John Jeffery. He arrived somewhat fuming, and declared: "Alan, I'm not being cocky, but when we reach that first turn, I'll be in the lead…" Ugh. A recipe for disaster with everyone going out at 4:20 miling. Paul was as good as his word but dropped out soon after with a tweaked hammie. Would he have finished without the car fail? We'll never know.

Paul keeps his promise to Alan. Our other Paul somewhat eagerly tucks in behind, and Kev Nash is about to pay 200 spots for that little stunt on the left. Godiva's Tromans 831 eyes up the first of three National wins. KM

My slated 10th scoring spot became 7th as the remarkably talented Kev Nash had a shocker, but goodness, how prescient Alan was to write: "his time will come." In truth though, top 6 was what we wanted, and we got it.

Better execution

The squads of 2001 and 2002 were a little weaker, but our racing was sharper and more "*à point*". Durham was particularly good with an 8th, with no sub par runs. It was a glorious course, and day – albeit immediately followed by a spectacular snowstorm. How lucky we were. And at Bristol, in horrendous conditions with many ending up in first aid with hypothermia, a solid 9th. I was still drunk during the race after an all-night bender, and injured. But I managed to find an electrifying finishing burst only for a marshal to block my path to the gantry: "another lap to go old son," he chided. Big trouble…

We got Allen Graffin out for two Nationals, and this was 2nd, having to give best to Sam Haughian. We'd get him out again two years later for something even more special in the team stakes…

2003 was destabilising as a subpar team pitched up for London. One could be forgiven for worrying that perhaps our National dreams were already over. Because if 28th was all we could manage in our home city, then heaven help us for Leeds a year on. It was left to me to narrowly edge out Rog for the Parker Bowl.

"An Historic Day for Belgrave"

We are still in good touch with Pat Footer who's the daughter of the founding father of Belgrave cross-country Bert. This tremendously tough runner and equally human became determined to make our Harriers a "going concern". Year after year he'd show up at the National with little or no support, but he built us up, brick by brick. What a pioneer.

His progress can neatly be tracked here:

1925			**Hereford Racecourse**, 14 Mar. — running as an individual and finishing in an unknown position beyond 30 H.E. Footer; 245 runners; 19 teams closed in; team winners Birchfield H 78 pts.; individual winner L-Cpl W.M. Cotterell (Royal Corps of Signals AC).
1926			**Stacey Hill Harm, nr. Wolverton**, 13 Mar. — running as individuals 42 H.E. Footer, 136 J.G. Flatt; 321 runners; 18 teams closed in; team winners Birchfield H 43 pts.; individual winner J.E. Webster (Birchfield H).
1927			**Crewe Hall Park, Crewe**, 12 Mar. — running as an individual 56 H.E. Footer; 429 runners; 32 teams closed in; team winners Hallamshire H 36 pts.; individual winner E. Harper (Hallamshire H).
1928	17th	711 pts.	**Leamington**, 10 Mar. — 63 (86) W.G. Webb, 79 (105) H.E. Footer, 95 (121) A.D. Pyer, 141 W.L. Bayliss, 149 A.E. Smith, 184 A.G. Jones, 250 F.G. Ford; 375 runners; 34 teams started, 27 closed in; team winners Birchfield H 49 pts.; individual winner J.E. Webster (Birchfield H).
1929			**Lord Burnham's Estate, Beaconsfield, South Bucks.**, 9 Mar. — incomplete team; 73 (87) W.G. Webb, 104 (120) A.W. Penny, 106 (122) W.L. Bayliss, 178 (197) F.G. Ford, dnf A.E. Smith, A. Robertshaw, W.S. Mitchell, H.E. Footer; 247 runners; 29 teams started, 20 closed in; team winners Birchfield H 91½ pts.; individual winner E. Harper (Hallamshire H).
1930	6th	320 pts.	**Graves Park, Sheffield**, 8 Mar. — 17 (20) H.E. Footer, 36 (42) S.H. Warboys, 47 A. Allum, 65 W.G. Webb, 74 F.R. Webb, 81 E.A. Duffett, 133 W.A. Rice; 334 runners; 23 teams closed in; team winners Birchfield H 94 pts.; individual winner W.B. Howard (Kettering Town H).
1931	9th	329 pts.	**Wickstead Park, Kettering**, 14 Mar. — 4 (5) A. Allum, 36 (48) S.H. Warboys, 46 (61) A.W. Penny, 67 (86) H.E. Footer, 83 (105) W.G. Webb, 93 (115) J.E. Flower, 113 (140) E.A. Duffett, 165 (194) C.T. Carter; 348 runners; 35 teams started, 30 closed in; team winners Birchfield H 104 pts.; individual winner J.H. Potts (Saltwell H).
1932	10th	433 pts.	**Stacey Hill Harm, nr. Wolverton**, 12 Mar. — 21 (34) J.E. Flower, 22 (35) H.E. Footer, 87 (109) S.H. Warboys, 91 (114) C.T. Carter, 97 (120) E.A. Duffett, 115 (139) W.G. Webb, 151 (180) F.R. Webb, dnf A. Allum, A. Robertshaw: 289 runners; 29 teams closed in; team winners Birchfield H 66 pts.; individual winner J.A. Burns (Elswick H).
1933	3rd	233 pts.	**Alderley Edge, Alderley Park, Cheshire**, 11 Mar. — 4 (4) A.W. Penny, 5 (5) H.E. Footer, 34 A. Allum, 48 C. Mains, 62 J.E. Flower, 80 A.R. Shaw, 94 C.W. Tame, 126 F.R. Webb, dnf C.T. Carter; 344 runners; 37 teams started, 32 closed in; team winners Birchfield H 80 pts.; individual winner T. Evenson (Salford H). [1]
1934	3rd	113 pts.	**Himley Park, nr. Dudley**, 10 Mar. — 4 (5) A.W. Penny, 9 (13) H.E. Footer, 16 (22) A.E. Taylor, 20 (27) A. Allum, 28 (38) J.E. Flower, 36 (48) H.W. Shields, 62 F.A. Walker, 91 W.A. Rice, 95 C.T. Carter; 297 runners; 35 teams started, 26 closed in; team winners Birchfield H 88 pts.; individual winner S. Dodd (Wirral AC).
1935	1st	97 pts.	**Hall Barn, Beaconsfield**, 9 Mar. — 11 (16) H.E. Footer, 14 (21) D. Patience, 15 (22) J. Ginty, 18 (25) A.E. Taylor, 19 (26) C.T. Carter, 20 (27) H.W. Shields, 37 (46) A.R. Shaw, 42 A. Allum, 57 J.E. Flower; 295 started, 248 finished; 30 teams started, 28 closed in; team winners Belgrave H 97 pts.; individual winner F. Close (Reading AC).

Source belgraveharriers.info, research by ARM

The table tells us all we need to know about what it takes to succeed. In a nutshell 10 years of *hard yakka*. Belgrave then became one of England's great cross-country squads, winning the National three more times, with Bert scoring in two of those [three in total], and Tom Carter in all four! On either side of the war to boot. WWII surely cost Belgrave much hardware, but to utter such a thing is crass. Losing some 12-14 years of the 20th Century to global conflicts was the same for everyone, and fairly little is said about it in sports literature, because what is there meaningful to be said? Perhaps our own Bill Lucas put it best: "Hitler cost me two Olympics, so I went and bombed him."

We arrived at Temple Newsam and got a bit of a shock when we instpected the course on the Friday night. That hill was a shocker! But in reality, despite the 12 minutes of hard climbing in the race, this was a course that suited us much better than Leeds in their own backyard. It was largely mudfree and very straightforward, fast running. I recall coming into the last mile and glancing up: everyone was up on their toes and starting to kick, not a great sight…

We had five stars and then four strong men to back us up in Hassan, myself, Rog and Simon Marwood. Who would fill that precious last berth? It was Hassan – a mercurial but extremely gifted runner who ended up a remarkable 48th. Actually, the 6th spot went to a pea-green Sharpy, who was running on memory in lap three and even that was not a pretty sight. I shadowed him well in 99th, and felt very much a part of things as a great squad is only as good as its subs bench, and it's when you don't have that 'custodian' that things quickly fall apart. Messrs Graffin and Barden were immaculate up top and with Paul and Kev having the races of their lives, we destroyed Leeds in what was the perfect day.

It had taken Alan a year less than Bert Footer to build a non-existent National squad into the best in the land. Some more copy on this race may be found in the introduction.

Two fine years but no luck

For everything that went right in 2004 it went wrong in '05 and '06. Not drastically, but Spen dropped out at Birmingham which was hugely costly for medals, altho I was able to stop the bleeding in 111th. Up ahead, early in the race, Richard Partridge shouted to ARM: "Milesey's going to medal, do you want to bet on it?!" Not wishing to trade against his own man, Alan declined, but Mark, after a bad tumble at the start, ran the perfect race to take the bronze. Wonderful! In some 15 years with us, that was the only National we could persuade Mark to do, but hey, it could've been none…

Indeed, at the time of writing we never got Nick Goolab out for the National, and he won it twice as a junior… however, in one dreadful moment, Nick did pop up asking to do it, but I'd not gambled on him in the race entry. In a draconian directive, the ECCA asked for entries seven weeks in advance which in this technological age is nothing but an outrage. The hapless TMs simply *can't* enter everyone and even by doing a fair amount of gambling hand over some £20,000 to the ECCA in excess runners who have no intention of setting foot on the course. To be sure, the system disgusts me and there is no excuse for it except the organizers hoodwinking the clubs into entering around twice as many runners as they need to. It goes without saying that when I begged them to allow Goolab to run a week out, I was given very short shrift. One of these days goodwill to the clubs will prevail, the sharking will cease, and a more sensible entry system will take hold.

**Postscript.* *A few weeks after writing these strong words, the National reduced to a four week entry. What a relief for thousands of TM's up and down the land. Now to get them to reduce to a sensible and pragmatic 2.5 weeks.*

2006 was 'solid as a rock', and we enjoyed the sight of a young Wicksy leading us home a few pips up on Dave Anderson. We now boasted returns of 1 6 6 7 8 9 for the century [not in that order], but nice grouping.

Do you want to bet on him? Err, yes please. Mark Miles ran the near perfect race

A wee splutter

Herrington Country Park in Sunderland is a nice venue but honestly, what a silly place to have the National. It is way too far off the beaten path. I decided to fly, which is a saga in itself, and after the race in 2007 (where we were a circumspect 17th), I could not get out of the carpark for love nor money… so I abandoned my ride and found myself cruising the backstreets of Sunderland, with a Newcastle plane to catch. I have had many 'filthy' commutes to the National down the years, but this was the most jarring. The drive to Alton Towers is a shocker too. Expecially as they make you drive the scenic route around Alton which adds on some 25 minutes to an already harsh 3:45 ride. In future, and this is a lesson to us all, when a race official flings up a sign saying: "Runners take diversion" it is legal to ignore it! We are still allowed to take drives around quaint English towns, the last time I checked.

ECCA sell us short

The Alton Towers course was terribly short in 2008 which is a really bad show from the organizers, especially given the above rant and their huge profits. All that money taken, all that draconian attitude, and they couldn't be bothered to give us the 12k, but more like 10. Phil had an incredible duel up at the front with Tom Humphries, who was white-hot that year. But we had no back up, in fact I was next in followed by a worthy engine room.

Back to Parliament Hill for 2009 and more chaos as our top Aussie Russ Dessaix-Chin, had a spike come through his undersole, with a hoped for top 25, early doors. Nothing is more uncomfortable, so both shoes had to go… on a very muddy course. Russ's 186 was pretty impressive all things considered, and Alan's summation that 13th "was not bad for an iffy day" was about right. Wicksy placed a brilliant 4th.

RESULTS 2000-2010 *courtesy of ARMead www.belgraveharriers.info*

2000	6th	390 pts.	**Stowe Park, Stowe, Bucks**, 26 Feb. — 32 L. Hurst, 36 J. Lobo, 47 P. Freary, 74 A. Stewart, 77 C. Herrington, 136 R. McHarg, 209 W. Cockerell, 245 K. Nash, 258 P. Carstairs, 385 D. Ochse, 428 R. Harding, 770 Don Anderson, dnf P. Evans; scoring – 30, 34, 45, 72, 75, 134, 206, 242, 255; 1419 finished; 122 teams closed in; 4th from 51 teams at 9 to score, 1093 pts.; team winners Tipton H 138 pts.; individual winner G. Tromans (Coventry Godiva H).
2001	8th	628 pts.	**Maiden Castle, Durham**, 24 Feb. — 49 L. Hurst, 56 A. Stewart, 64 P. Freary, 147 R. McHarg, 161 R. Alsop, 165 W. Cockerell, 194 N. Hliouat, 201 M. Byansi, 279 P. Carstairs, 832 Don Anderson; scoring – 47, 54, 62, 145, 158, 162, 191, 274; 1228 finished; 108 teams closed in; 9th from 37 teams at 9 to score 1916 pts.; team winners Bingley H&AC 162 pts.; individual winner M. Openshaw (Birchfield H). [5]
2002	9th	693 pts.	**Ashton Court Estate, Bristol**, 23 Feb. — 2 Allen Graffin, 46 A. Stewart, 69 C. Herrington, 155 L. Hurst, 201 J. Wolf, 220 W. Cockerell, 286 James Browne, 336 M. Byansi, 392 A. Jones; 1220 finished; 95 teams closed in; 10th from 42 teams at 9 to score 1707 pts.; team winners Bingley H&AC 184 pts.; individual winner S. Haughian (Windsor, Slough, Eton & Hounslow AC).
2003	28th	1905 pts.	**Parliament Hill Fields, London**, 22 Feb. — 92 W. Cockerell, 106 R. Alsop, 167 K. Hegvold, 319 S. Zealey, 334 P. Carstairs, 887 Don Anderson; 1258 finished; 101 teams closed in; team winners Leeds City AC 181 pts.; individual winner M. Smith (Tipton H).
2004	1st	160 pts.	**Temple Newsam Park, Leeds**, 21 Feb. — 5 S. Barden, 6 Allen Graffin, 16 P. Freary, 22 K. Nash, 48 H. Raidi, 73 S. Sharp, 99 W. Cockerell, 159 S. Marwood, 211 R. Alsop, 255 T. Hadfield, 257 J. Wolf, 291 W. Lynch, 957 Don Anderson; scoring – 4, 5, 14, 20, 46, 71, 97, 155, 208; 1399 finished; 117 teams closed in; 2nd from 50 teams at 9 to score, 620 pts.; team winners Belgrave H; individual winner G. Tromans (Coventry Godiva H).
2005	6th	362 pts.	**Cofton Park, Birmingham**, 19 Feb. — 3 M. Miles, 32 K. Nash, 53 David Anderson, 66 T. Watson, 97 H. Raidi, 111 W. Cockerell, 175 J. Clarke, 182 J. Charles, 229 T. Hadfield, 450 P. Carstairs, 990 Don Anderson, dnf S. Barden; 1316 finished; 102 teams closed in; 5th from 39 teams at 9 to score, 948 pts.; team winners Salford H&AC 188 pts.; individual winner G. Tromans (Coventry Godiva H).
2006	7th	437 pts.	**Parliament Hill Fields, London**, 25 Feb. — 41 P. Wicks, 44 David Anderson, 60 T. Watson, 70 D. Gauson, 92 P. Freary, 134 W. Cockerell, 166 P. Willis, 180 T. Ellacott, 192 T. Hadfield, 223 M. Byansi, 278 W. Lynch, 934 Don Anderson, 978 H. Corbett, 1083 S. Baxendale, dnf L. Greatorex; 1288 finished; 100 teams closed in; 4th from 45 teams at 9 to score, 976 pts.; team winners Leeds City AC 234 pts.; individual winner P. Riley (Leigh H).
2007	17th	1178 pts.	**Herrington Country Park, Sunderland**, 10 Mar. — 71 S. Jones, 92 M. Byansi, 194 W. Cockerell, 244 J. Kimaiyo, 250 D. Mason, 331 M. Whiting, dnf B. Poore, P. Willis; scoring – 71, 92, 193, 243, 249, 330; 916 finished; 72 teams closed in; team winners Leeds City AC 162 pts.; individual winner F. Tickner (Wells City H).
2008	19th	1228 pts.	**Alton Towers, Staffordshire**, 23 Feb. — 2 P. Wicks, 191 W. Cockerell, 223 K. Hegvold, 237 M. Byansi, 257 J. Fairbourn, 318 T. Weeks, 392 D. Mason, 462 M. Whiting, 498 S. Zealey; 1244 finished; 99 teams closed in; 12th from 40 teams at 9 to score, 2580 pts.; team winners Leeds City AC 183 pts.; individual winner T. Humphries (Cannock & Stafford AC).
2009	13th	938 pts.	**Parliament Hill Fields, London**, 21 Feb. — 4 P. Wicks, 72 James Kelly, 151 W. Cockerell, 186 R. Dessaix-Chin, 201 M. Byansi, 324 P. Willis, 331 K. Hegvold, 342 L. Eguia, 438 T. Fordyce, 564 M. Humphrey, 754 A. Luce, 831 T. Hadfield, 1356 Don Anderson; 1455 finished; 112 teams closed in; 11th from 46 teams at 9 to score, 2049 pts.; team winners Newham & Essex Beagles 214 pts.; individual winner F. Tickner (Wells City H).
2010	7th	567 pts.	**Roundhay Park, Leeds**, 27 Feb. — 16 D. Mulhare, 41 James Kelly, 89 P. Owor, 103 M. Pollard, 153 J. Fairbourn, 165 W. Cockerell, 232 M. Byansi, 290 L. Eguia, 1008 R. Harding, 1254 Don Anderson, dnf M. Trees; 1428 finished; 107 teams closed in; 10th from 45 teams at 9 to score, 2097 pts.; team winners Aldershot, Farnham & District AC 182 pts.; individual winner A. Vernon (Aldershot, Farnham & District AC).

Amazing effort under the radar

2010 was one of our best ever efforts with a team that was very much "under the radar" grabbed 7th. Hill 60 at Roundhay is incredible, and I loved the course, perhaps my personal favourite of the circuit. Dan Mulhare and James Kelly were terrific, Paskar was a bit wan and 'Polly' was in a world a pain, and said for the entire way, "I'm dropping out", which he did – at the finish line – such a good boy. And with the talented but short-lived James Fairbourn nicking me, we had sprung a real surprise.

Our struggles started in earnest at a return to Alton Towers where conditions were so bad the course was slashed by 2k again. It didn't affect the times though, which came up the same! Phil yet again was a wonder in 7th, and James Kelly immaculate too in conditions polar opposite to his perceived strength, but then again JK's strength was his strength. We enjoyed Soren Lindner's brief time in Bels colours and with Fairbs and I swapping spots on last year, we just had one more to find. But as described above, poor old Malachi got completely swamped and his mooted 275 became 725, nasty!

2012-2020   Flattering to Deceive

Not a vintage nine year spell this, as the Bels "hung in there" with flashes of brilliance, but an overall decline in value. 2012 and '13 were punctuated by outstanding runs from James Kelly, particularly in the snowy hell that was Sunderland: "I must have died a 1,000 deaths in the last K…", and then Paskar had an epic assault on the leaderboard in 2014 at a glorious Wollaton before settling at 18th. My first year as TM saw us find a sound 15th with some very fine packing, but thereafter it was was a grim slugfest, with venues such as Donington Castle and a return to Wollaton really catching us cold.

Worse was to follow at Parliament Hill, before we hit rock bottom with a an eye-watering 3,765 points at Harewood House. What a magnificent course that was, although I was in no fit state to enjoy it; but at least our club record for most ever points scored at the National was unmolested, which is surely safe for all time: 1991's 5,232 points. But you know what? I see those lads as pioneers, they came, they saw and they got stuck in, and you can't say fairer than than, particularly as we closed in a miserable four times between 1989-1998.

Phil heads to yet another Parker Bowl in 2015, awarded to the first Bel home. SW

The new Dumez-Gardner regime arrested the decline with 36th at a Wollaton course that was fairly benign in 2014, then got much worse in '17 and by 2020 was simply a flooded swamp.

Our thanks to Steve Gardner for these wonderful images of swampy Wollaton in 2020. The one of Conall is surely one of the greatest Belgrave images of all time, and Ben Hurley's is pretty good too! Ben is tracked by Team GB Ultra runner Matt Lynas. SG

The TM puts his money where his mouth his. Great running from Arne. 381 in 2017 has become 397, so real consistency. SG

He's a swamp beast! Unlike Arne, Dave Walsh is better suited to the muck and it's clear from this picture why he scored and ran so well. SG

And for inexplicable reasons the ECCA designed the course into four ever increasing circles which is miserable for all involved: bewildering for spectators and soul-destroying for the runners, not to mention coming out well over distance at 13k. Maddening and capricious stuff indeed. Particular kudos should go to Michael McCarthy for leading us home in 259th and winning the Parker Bowl – straight out of left field but all credit to the lad.

Back with a mini post-Covid revival

We were plumb in line for the top dozen post-Covid as the gaffers entered a barnstorming 39 souls. Sensational stuff, albeit only starting 23. The 23rd was I, who was reduced to a survival shuffle a quarter through. I'd done fairly well to make the start after a winter of gyp, but not nearly enough conditioning. A little way up, give or take 1,500 spots Phil roared nobly to his 7th Parker Bowl for first Bel home. It's a marvellous record of achievement and certainly when Gerry got his 10th in 1977 folks thought: no-one is *ever* getting close to that! Well, Wicksy is 70% up the mountain, and that's over a 16 year period [to Gerry's 14], so he could have got even closer... still could. It was a glorious sunny day, but the course was still gnarly and very sticky. We used to do 2 very large laps around there but now it's a tortuous 2/3rds of a lap before two slightly less large ones than normal. As ever the head fry around that is annoying. I got to the end of lap one and the thought of two much bigger ones filled me with horror.

After Phil, Henry Hart ran very well for 127th. HH has been a racing junkie since he was bashing out 10k in 38 as a 15 year old, which is wicked stuff. And thereafter the running journey has just kept on going... low 2:50 marathons as a U20... which all built to a 2:29 to win Dorney Lake in 2021. Six clubs he's seen in his short life, but we hope we can stop he club count here and now. What a fasinating mongrel of a runner, with a remarkable sub 15 at parkrun and a huge ultramarathon in the following weeks [for which he'd pay a dear price at MK].

Next up was the smiling assassin. How remarkable that Jonny Neville was our 3rd scorer. He is as unflashy and humble a runner as you'll get but as the saying goes: "Beware... of the runner who turns up with his stuff in a brown paper bag." And JN is a bit like that: he leaves it all out there, trains hard, races harder, and crucially is a mountain goat. Hill reps with him on the Common make one feel like the boy from Kentucky who stubbed his toe running to meet his sweetheart: too big to cry, but far too badly hurt to laugh.

Then some super packing with Scott, McNally and Lamb bridging the 300 divide in close order. Tough uncompromising souls and we thank them for their service. And they had to get a move on with the likes of Nutt, Edgar, Fletcher and good old Mike McCarthy standing guard. The value of his Parker Bowl from 2020 just went up a notch or ten.

As for the rest, troopers all, a classic Harriers day, and their names may be admired below. Surely our presence at the National is on solid ground for the coming years, whatever swamps we face. I love the race more than ever, and really look forward to us going top dozen again soon. Just need another star or two, or of course some of the above can do a subtle flex. Warm congrats to the TMs for such a cracking turn-out.

2011 19th 1334 pts. **Alton Towers, Staffordshire**, 19 Feb. — 7 P. Wicks, 54 James Kelly, 144 S. Lindner, 169 W. Cockerell, 236 J. Fairbourn, 724 M. Byansi, 729 R. Harding, 847 A. Lang, 1098 Don Anderson, dnf David Anderson; 1302 finished; 95 teams closed in; 16th from 34 teams at 9 to score, 4008 pts.; team winners Leeds City AC 188 pts.; individual winner S. Vernon (Stockport H&AC).

2012 25th 1709 pts. **Parliament Hill Fields, London**, 25 Feb. — 42 James Kelly, 169 W. Cockerell, 284 M. Holm, 338 K. Gadd, 356 M. Byansi, 520 L. Eguia, 537 T. Weeks, 599 K. Hegvold, 899 T. Hadfield, 1553 Don Anderson; 1689 finished; 125 teams closed in; 23rd from 62 teams at 9 to score, 3744 pts.; team winners Leeds City AC 219 pts.; individual winner K. Gerrard (Newham & Essex Beagles).

2013 **Herrington Country Park, Sunderland**, 23 Feb. — incomplete team; 25 James Kelly, 204 W. Cockerell, 1034 Don Anderson; 1085 finished; 80 teams closed in; team winners Morpeth H 153 pts.; individual winner K. Gerrard (Newham & Essex Beagles).

2014 21st 1349 pts. **Wollaton Park, Nottingham**, 22 Feb. — 18 P. Owor, 155 K. Marks, 243 W. Cockerell, 257 M. Trees, 298 R. Maddams, 378 D. Morton, 477 F. Logan, 671 R. Norville, 693 M. Young, 1387 Don Anderson; 1657 finished; 127 teams closed in; 17th from 56 teams at 9 to score, 3190 pts.; team winners Bedford & County AC 265 pts.; individual winner S. Vernon (Stockport H&AC).

2015 15th 1073 pts. **Parliament Hill Fields, London**, 21 Feb. — 38 P. Wicks, 72 T. Telkovsky, 173 A. Miller, 192 R. Maddams, 255 N. Bundle, 343 L. Pikett, 361 N. Smallwood, 433 W. Cockerell, 503 P. McDougall; 2007 finished; 145 teams closed in; 13th from 74 teams at 9 to score, 2370 pts.; team winners Notts AC 213 pts.; individual winner C. Hulson (Sale H).

2016 25th 1829 pts. **Donington Park, Derbyshire**, 27 Feb. — 92 P. Owor, 185 Z. Abery, 232 N. Bundle, 370 N. Smallwood, 463 W. Cockerell, 487 T. O'Beirne; 1730 finished; 123 teams closed in; team winners Morpeth H 130 pts.; individual winner J. Hay (Aldershot, Farnham & Dist. AC).

2017 27th 1703 pts. **Wollaton Park, Nottingham**, 25 Feb. — 29 P. Wicks, 52 A. Jaksevicius, 272 J. Williams, 306 P. Owor, 381 A. Dumez, 663 W. Cockerell; 1763 finished; 131 teams closed in; team winners Tonbridge AC 289 pts.; individual winner B. Connor (Derby & County AC).

2018 39th 2441 pts. **Parliament Hill Fields, London**, 24 Feb. — 72 N. Buckle, 122 P. Owor, 421 A. Dumez, 544 W. Cockerell, 610 A. Mills, 672 P. McDougall, 1141 T. Oldman, 1473 W. Johnson, 2161 Don Anderson; 2328 finished; 162 teams closed in; 37th from 90 teams at 9 to score, 7216 pts.; team winners Tonbridge AC 131 pts.; individual winner A. Hickey (Southend H&AC).

2019 52nd 3765 pts. **Harewood House Estate, Leeds**, 23 Feb. — 88 P. Owor, 147 A. Jaksevicius, 216 N. Buckle, 910 W. Cockerell, 1129 S. Jones, 1275 J. Morris; 2008 finished; 146 teams closed in; team winners Leeds City AC 110 pts.; individual winner M. Mahamed (Southampton AC).

2020 36th 2609 pts. **Wollaton Park, Nottingham**, 22 Feb. — 259 M. McCarthy, 377 A. Miller, 397 A. Dumez, 470 C. McNally, 549 B. Hurley, 557 D. Walsh, 652 B. Ireland, 705 W. Cockerell, 1020 R. Norville, 1476 T. O' Neill; 1716 finished; 115 teams closed in; 25th from 59 teams at 9 to score, 4986 pts.; team winners Tonbridge AC 246 pts.; individual winner C. Johnson (Gateshead H).

2021 No race due to coronavirus pandemic.

2022 19th 1409 pts. **Parliament Hill Fields, London**, 26 Feb. — 68 P. Wicks, 127 H. Hart, 290 J. Neville, 295 J. Scott, 313 C. McNally, 316 A. Lamb, 333 J. Nutt, 398 M. Edgar, 403 M. McCarthy, 409 T. Fletcher, 459 J. van der Brande, 497 B. Hurley, 501 T. Lole, 616 A. Elsadig, 619 J. Williams, 628 D. Walsh, 655 V. Rigori, 712 R. Kelly, 892 M. Horn, 1037 L. Burton, 1112 P. McDougall, 1363 S. Hodges, 1547 W. Cockerell; 2087 finished; 132 teams closed in; team winners Southampton AC 209; individual winner M. Mahamed (Southampton AC).

Most times first Belgravian home, (and since 1951 the recipient of the The '**Harry Parker Memorial Trophy**')
10 — Gerry A. North (1963, 1964, 1965, 1966, 1968, 1969, 1970, 1971, 1974, 1977).
 7 — Phil Wicks (2006, 2008, 2009, 2011, 2015, 2017, 2022).
 5 — H.E. 'Bert' Footer (1925, 1926, 1927, 1930, 1935).
 4 — J.W. 'Jack' Brown (1951, 1953, 1956, 1957).
   — John Bicourt (1973, 1975, 1978, 1982).
   — Mike Webb (1991, 1994, 1995, 1997).
 3 — Vernon Blowfield (1948, 1949, 1952).
   — Ian Duncan (1979, 1980, 1981).
   — Ollie Foote (1985, 1989, 1992).
   — Lee Hurst (1998, 2000, 2001).
   — Paskar Owor (2014, 2016, 2019).
 2 — Bill Webb (1928, 1929).
   — Arthur W. Penny (1933, 1934).
   — Len Herbert (1946, 1947).
   — Pat Newell (1958, 1959).
   — James Kelly (2012, 2013).

Most times in the scoring six (including incomplete teams)
18 — Will Cockerell (1999, 2001-2003, 2005-2014, 2016-2019).
13 — H.E. 'Bert' Footer (1925-1928, 1930-1937, 1939) [7].
12 — Gerry A. North (1963-1971, 1973-1974, 1977).
11 — Charlie Walker (1952-1962).
10 — Pat O'Connor (1969, 1974-1982).
   — Don Anderson (1983, 1986-1987, 1991, 1994-1995, 1997-1998, 2003, 2013).
 8 — Tom Carter (1932, 1935-1939, 1946, 1948, spanning the missing war years).
   — Mike Webb (1991-1992, 1994-1999[8]).
 7 — Arthur W. Penny (1929, 1931, 1933-1934, 1936, 1938-1939).
   — Eric Gebbett (1956-1962).
   — Lionel Mann (1970-1971, 1973-1974, 1977-1979).
   — Martin Lake (1984-1985, 1987-1989, 1992-1993).
   — Phil Wicks (2006, 2008-2009, 2011, 2015, 2017, 2022).
 6 — J.W. 'Jack' Brown (1950-1953, 1956-1957).
   — Eddie A. Short (1952-1954, 1956, 1960-1961); plus, Junior scorer (1948-1949) and Youth scorer (1946).
   — Tony Fairclough (1965-1967, 1969, 1971-1972); plus, Junior scorer (1962-1964) and Youth scorer (1961).
   — John Bicourt (1970, 1973-1975, 1978, 1982); plus, Junior scorer (1965-1966) and Youth scorer (1963-1964).
   — Paskar Owor (2010, 2014, 2016-2019).
 5 — W.G. 'Bill' Webb (1928-1932).
   — Arthur Allum (1930-1931, 1933-1934, 1936).
   — Clive Shippen (1958-1962).
   — John Thresher (1964-1965, 1967-1968, 1971); plus, Junior scorer (1959-1961) and Youth scorer (1958).
   — Leo Coy (1975, 1977, 1980-1981, 1984).
   — Roger Alsop (1990-1991, 1999, 2001, 2003).
   — Malachi Byansi (2007-2009, 2011-2012).
   — James Kelly (2009-2013).

Most consecutive completed runs
23 — Will Cockerell (1999-2022).
12 — A. 'Tony' Fairclough (1961 as a Youth, 1962-1964 as a Junior, 1965-1972 as a Senior).
   — Pat O'Connor (1971-1982).

The founding father of Belgrave at the National. Bert Footer [seen here winning the Southern in 1933]. Many thanks to AR Mead for the image

THE NATIONAL - WOMEN

The Glacial climb

What a journey this has been. From tortuous beginnings where for some reason we simply couldn't get going at all, the Belles have boxed above their weight and carded some remarkable returns, including a magical spell of form between 2013-15.

Tania Sturton travelled up to Durham in '01, but she was unaccompanied, whilst slogging again to Bristol in '02 at perhaps the UK's most inaccessible course. She started 5 minutes after the field and dropped out when the clarity of her mission hit home. Otherwise a dazzling run from Anne Hegvold lit a small fire in the darkness.

Birhan takes the Title

A masterful run came from our Ethiopian star Birhan Dagne in 2004. Out more for a training recce, and no lover of the mud, she scented an opportunity and brilliantly pounced. For our original report on Birhan's achievement, consult the Introduction.

2005 was a thrill and shows just what can be done when a quorum is assembled. 12th! Where did that come from? Well, it came from three of the great club servants in Belles' history in Smurph, Tilly and Lou; with Liz Horrobin in "one-trick pony" mode to see us home. Some frown on one-trick ponies, but they perform a critical role in all amateur sports clubs the world over, and in this case took a team that was not to trouble the scorers to one that was top dozen in the land. We'll take it!

More good solid fare in 2006 [15th] whilst 2007 was oh so frustrating. How can we ship up doyennes in Sarah and Catherine Bryson to Sunderland with no back-up?! It must have been terribly frustrating for those two (having crackers in 37th and 41st). "What we have here… is a failure to communicate…" as the line in *Cool Hand Luke* goes.

Just the stalwarts of CE and Jen Beecroft at a benign day at Alton Towers in 2008, whilst a flicker of activity in 2009 in London, but Jen would happily admit she shouldn't be performing anchor duties, but we were most grateful that she did. Two more aces followed in the next two years, but they both fought alone. Shades of Bert Footer for the men in the 1920s.

After claiming World Junior Team Silver in Durham at the 1995 World Cross, Birhan claimed asylum in Britain due to assault by a soldier back home. The UK government refused her but she won on appeal. She became a Life member of Belgrave in 2022.

2012 A race to target

I took over the XC reigns from Catherine and although the 'Blasted Heath' was a little frustrating in 2012 [16th], my report's headline summed up the day: "Assault on top 10 a no, but not a never". We were led home by Belle of the Year in Fee Maycock, and it was good to know that from Surrey league relegation in 2011, we were now back in 'the Premiership' of Cross-country clubs.

Apocalypse Now!, But Wonderful With It

2013 was surely the most brutal XC day I've had in my 24 years with the club – and there have been a few. It ticked all the boxes of the early rise, the logistics, the journey, the weather and the course, and all for one of the world's most intense races; a day doesn't get more "full-on". And we do this for fun?

About 10 of us met at St. Pancras at 7am for the long slog to Sunderland, and by York the weather closed in and snow was in the air. Heavy snow. It had lifted by the time we reached Herrington Country Park, but under an inch of the white stuff, there was a dark and boggy morass. Ghastly. And it was, oh so cold. In the build up Sammi had a problem with frozen blocks for feet and she wondered about how to compete. "Well… I haven't come all this way not to f***ing start," she opined. Fair point, well made. Tish was perhaps as ripped as I'd seen her, gym rat that she is, and no-one feels the cold more. But I never heard a peep of dissent all day, she just got on with it – imperiously! Our wonderful image shows an athlete making a move and turning heads. Behind, everyone fought so hard. It was Lou's

Birth of a ledg. The road to World Championships Marathon qualification started here, with one of the bravest runs of Tish's career

first cross-country race for a while and she was in a real jam all day. Sam never gave up but for much of the race had to admire a stormer from Jojo Rhodes, and Fee was gnarly as ever to see us home, with Hester standing guard just 44 spots back.

The look of surprised delight when Jojo scanned the results was a treat: "Will! 6th!" Now we could relax on the long ride home knowing we'd given our best, whilst also absorbing the convoluted performance of Hester's "wet wipes bath", before a party she was headed straight to. A surreal end to a surreal day.

Oh So Close to the promised land

Ahhh, high level sport doesn't give up her wares easily and we had strengthened big time in the year that followed with the signings of Mel Wilkins and Zoe Doyle. It was a "Dream Team" that we could proffer Wollaton Park, but there was no way I was going in without Sam, who alas was a no. We entered into negotiations to massage that no to a better place, and it was actually easy. Sam sacrificed the other race in her diary, her personal requests were far from outlandish, and she could see the big picture of National medals beckoning. I felt I'd been most diplomatic, but as is often the case, getting the athlete on board is the easy bit, but the coach is often the far bigger problem, and I got it in the neck soon after in a rather torrid online blog. But the battle between a TM and a coach is as old as sport itself, especially for such an individualistic sport as athletics. What does the coach care about the team stuff? But the most important thing is that Sam was fine.

The fab four were ready to rock but then disaster: Zoe Doyle was to be in Tenerife with the family for half-term. She came up with the remarkable suggestion that she semi-ruin the holiday, leave James [husband] there with two of the children, and fly back early with toddler daughter on lap. It was an amazing gesture but a great insight into what goes on behind the scenes to raise these fine sides: "Just happen," they don't.

Williiiiiiiiiiiiiiiiiiiiiii! ➤ Inbox ☆

Z **zoe doyle** 29/01/2014
to me ∨ ↩ ⋮

Hi Will,

I am on the phone to travel agents. Going to change the flight. Just checking you definitely need/want me to!!!!!

Thanx

Zoe

The perfect example of the selfless sacrifices athletes make for their beloved club. What a wonderful gesture from Zoe – and for that matter hubster James

Race day dawned and big trouble as Mel appeared with a cold. She dug in as best she could and leaked maybe only 30 spots for her trouble [67th]. Tish had problems with nerves and nausea (strictly kept from the gaffer on the day), but actually it may've helped as she started super conservatively and was perhaps 16th after the first lap. Then the after-burners were lit, and she romped to a magnificent 7th.

With Sam in cracking form [41st], it was interesting to see what the Tenerife stunt was worth. I thought it'd only be around 30-40 points, but it was 99 [Zoe's 47th vs Jojo's 146th].

Such a tense day! We all fought so hard to win those medals, but it wasn't to be. Tish keeps the leaders in sight, before settling for 7th

As the dust settled, my phone rang with Sammi on the end: "Do you know where we've come?..." she asked, as only a mother could talk to a child.

"Tell me…" I braced.

"4th!" It seems amazing now how bad that sounded, considering what a wonderful result it was, but at the time we were pretty gutted. Who reckoned on Rotherham?! Not us, but a very fine performance on the day from them with a rock solid squad, and a reappraisal of the results indicates it's touch and go of whether Mel's cold cost us a medal. My feeling is that we'd still have been a handful of points short as Rotherham were 35 up. Up ahead, the great Charnwood were in sight and AFD at Galactic level.

RESULTS 2000-2014, courtesy of A.R.Mead www.belgraveharriers.info

Year	Pos	Pts	Details
2000			**Stowe Park, Stowe, Bucks**, 26 Feb. — Belgrave did not take part; 398 finished; 44 teams closed in; team winners Shaftesbury Barnet AC 56 pts.; individual winner T. Kryzwicki (Charnwood AC).
2001			**Maiden Castle, Durham**, 24 Feb. — incomplete team; 113 T. Sturton; 336 finished; 37 teams closed in; team winners Sale H Manchester 61 pts.; individual winner E. Yelling (Bedford & County AC).
2002			**Ashton Court Estate, Bristol**, 23 Feb. — incomplete team; 32 A. Hegvold; 384 finished; 38 teams closed in; team winners Shaftesbury Barnet H 67 pts.; individual winner E. Yelling (Bedford & County AC).
2003	31st	801 pts.	**Parliament Hill Fields, London**, 22 Feb. — 86 A. Walker, 153 J. Whittington, 256 A. Pike, 310 C. Eastham; 398 finished; 43 teams closed in; team winners Chester-Le-Street & District AC 48 pts.; individual winner H. Yelling (Windsor, Slough, Eton & Hounslow AC).
2004			**Temple Newsam Park, Leeds**, 21 Feb. — incomplete team; 1 B. Dagne; 454 finished; 54 teams closed in; team winners Bristol AC 100 pts.; individual winner B. Dagne (Belgrave H).
2005	12th	448 pts.	**Cofton Park, Birmingham**, 19 Feb. — 39 S. Murphy, 67 M. Heaton, 134 L. Cooper, 208 L. Horrobin; 451 finished; 50 teams closed in; team winners Bristol & West AC 55 pts.; individual winner H. Yelling (Windsor, Slough, Eton & Hounslow AC).
2006	15th	427 pts.	**Parliament Hill Fields, London**, 25 Feb. — 47 S. Murphy, 88 M. Heaton, 116 H. Smethurst, 180 C. Eastham, 211 L. Cooper, 260 S. Gailey; 444 finished; 47 teams closed in; team winners Charnwood AC 68 pts.; individual winner E. Hall (Herts Phoenix AC).
2007			**Herrington Country Park, Sunderland**, 10 Mar. — incomplete team; 37 C. Bryson, 41 S. Murphy; 297 finished; 28 teams closed in; team winners Winchester & District AC 41 pts.; individual winner E. Yelling (Bedford & County AC).
2008			**Alton Towers, Staffordshire**, 23 Feb. — incomplete team; 333 C. Eastham, 354 J. Beecroft; 495 finished; 61 teams closed in; team winners Winchester & District AC 96 pts.; individual winner E. Yelling (Bedford & County AC).
2009	21st	660 pts.	**Parliament Hill Fields, London**, 21 Feb. — 41 S. Murphy, 121 M. Heaton, 143 A. Hegvold, 355 J. Beecroft; 546 finished; 63 teams closed in; team winners Charnwood AC 49 pts.; individual winner H. Dean (Hallamshire H Sheffield).
2010			**Roundhay Park, Leeds**, 27 Feb. — incomplete team; 46 S. Murphy; 505 finished; 61 teams closed in; team winners Charnwood AC 73 pts.; individual winner S. Twell (Aldershot Farnham & District AC).
2011			**Alton Towers, Staffordshire**, 19 Feb. — incomplete team; 93 S. Amend; 552 finished; 67 teams closed in; team winners Charnwood AC 45 pts.; individual winner L. Damen (Winchester & District AC).
2012	16th	591 pts.	**Parliament Hill Fields, London**, 25 Feb. — 118 F. Maycock, 129 M.G. Spalton, 157 M. Heaton, 187 A. Hegvold, 302 H. Barsham-Rolfe, 340 E. Orlando, 365 R. Trees née Takayasu, 388 M. Noel; 650 finished; 73 teams closed in; team winners Hallamshire H 156 pts.; individual winner G. Steel (Charnwood AC).
2013	6th	289 pts.	**Herrington Country Park, Sunderland**, 23 Feb. — 17 T. Jones, 79 S. Amend, 92 J. Rhodes, 101 F. Maycock, 145 H. Barsham-Rolfe, 201 L. d'Albey, 234 L. Blizzard née Cooper; 427 finished; 46 teams closed in; team winners Aldershot, Farnham & District AC 42 pts.; individual winner L. Damen (Winchester & District AC).
2014	4th	162 pts.	**Wollaton Park, Nottingham**, 22 Feb. — 7 T. Jones, 41 S. Amend, 47 Z. Doyle, 67 M. Wilkins, 146 J. Rhodes, 262 A. Heydenrych, 459 H. Brown; 708 finished; 83 teams closed in; team winners Aldershot, Farnham & District AC 21 pts.; individual winner G. Steel (Charnwood AC).

Another near miss

More terrific squad action followed in 2015 but we were without Tish, with a resurgent Jojo taking her place in an otherwise unchanged line-up. We were treated to the entertaining sight of Mel leading the entire field up Parla Hill's cruel start. It's a poisoned chalice of course and our comrade Andy Lea-Gerrard of Herne Hill celebrated his 50th birthday by leading the National up the hill in 2003, before settling for a 1226/1258 finish. The chances that the leader will win the race is pretty tiny, as generally people prefer a nice tow up there, which Mel benevolently gave them.

Mel buys herself a one-way ticket to hell, by leading the National by some distance, after the famous starting climb. Maybe her body wouldn't notice

Pacing the first mile of a tough cross-country like this is so critical and having led the great Louise Damen out at the Southern the previous month we mused as to whether Mel might take a chill pill and not up the ante. It meant she was in a sea of lactic for the rest of the race and was so tired that on occasion her legs buckled, but a final position of 17th was still excellent and got us off to a great start. We actually shipped 130 points on the previous year though with ZLD circumspect [about 1 in 12 races does she have a damp squib], and we didn't like getting nicked by Herne Hill by 16 points, while that bronze was again claimed by Rotherham, what a double from them.

2016-2020 a steady rebuild

Still, we could hold our heads high by a hat-trick of top 6 National finishes, which felt pretty special at the time, and in the intervening years only grew in value. A purple patch of form indeed for a race that only requires 4 scorers, so the volatility is high.

With Charlie taking on the Belles to leave me to focus on the men, were massively up against it for the next two years but all credit to the runners who insisted that we close in, before a return to form of sorts at Parla Hill in 2018 for 18th, which included a frisky top 30 from Sophie Harris.

Georgie Fenn then led the team home twice, with a stubborn team 20th at glorious Harewood House, followed by a super 11th in 2020 just before Covid shut down our beloved sport. The packing was superb in conditions so foul they beggared belief, but GF [up from 98 to 41], Liv, Alice and Mhairi seemed to revel in the mayhem.

It's conga time as Liv leads her rivals on a merry dance through the gloop. AR

A mixture of concentration, amusement, but most of all enjoyment for Mhairi, who had a stormer. This is why we do it... SG

With great back up from Mimi [Mhairi thawing], left, who nobly won the cross-country plate; Paps, Alice and Georgie savour 11th in the land

Glorious "Hobbsesque Failure"…

In the long, hot summer of 1925 the world's finest cricketer Jack Hobbs got into a bit of a pickle. He couldn't find his 126th first-class Century to break WG Grace's world record. After four consecutive 100s and with one more to find, time after time he'd threaten to reach the landmark, only for headline wags to write: "Hobbs Fails Again…"

This was the paradox that faced the Belles after an almighty National assault with a squad sent straight from the angels. And yet, and yet… only 5th… with a team like that? What do we have to do? It was certainly superior to the 2015 squad which also got 5th – I revere them like children, but this was a step up in class. And our staggering depth meant it also deserved better than 2014's famous team that got 4th.

To the race and Lea Adamson burst out of the traps like a startled greyhound, and was our second scorer for a good while. Lea could just be our most naturally gifted runner and her smooth, incredibly long stride is something to behold. [To be uber pedantic it could just be an over-stride]. Anyway! It was all too good to last and nausea set in for the drunken sailor. [A metaphor, no achohol was consumed during the construction of this run]. But she'll be back.

Up ahead Sarah continued her superb Southern form with 13th and it was left to old fave Rachel to yet again turn in one of those clinical and reliable runs for us in 54th. Blister horrors awaited at a triathlon to put her out for the remainder of the season, but we got the best of her here. Under glorious skies, *Papsrunslaps* timed her progress to top fitness of her season to perfection, just 13 spots back; now who to see us home? It was only Grace! What stunning quality to close in a National squad. She was 3rd in the first Surrey league, but had her trials and tribulations since, but never stopped fighting.

Our work was done, with Ella-May seperating herself from a huge pack of Belles – we had 5 in 25 in the early to mid 100s, quite incredible. Now for that nervous wait for medal news. It was Heathside who won the bronze – shades of

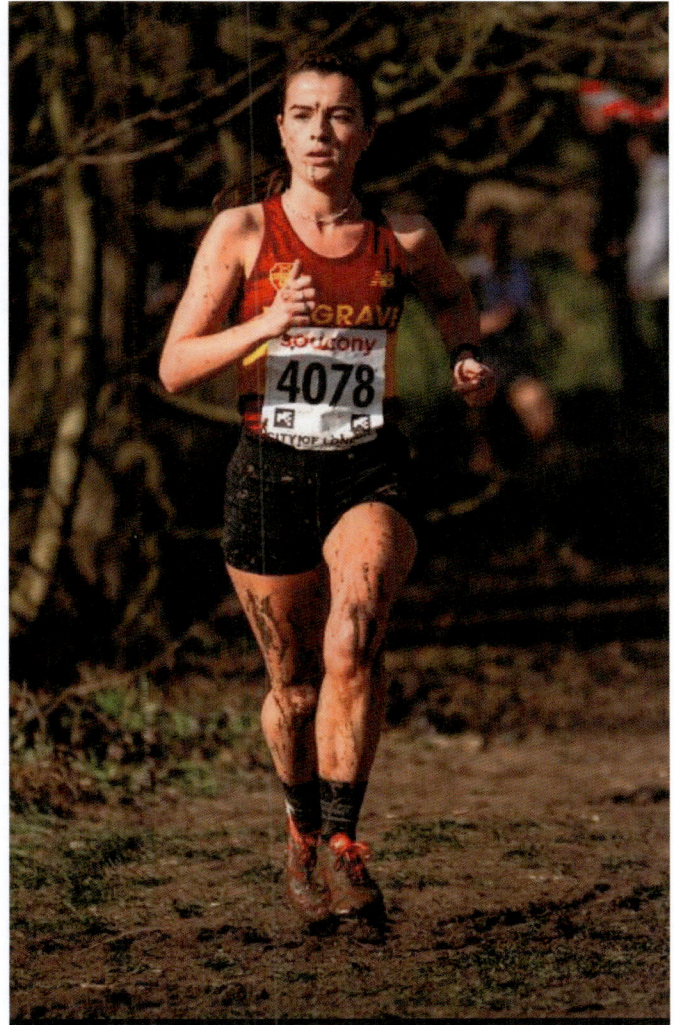

Another superb run came from Sarah, albeit having a minor malfunction with her mascara. Or it could be mud. Leonard Martin

Rotherham 2014 – unexpected but most deserved. And Tonbridge showed it's not all about the men. Kudos indeed.

Oh! And a coda to that Hobbs story? He *did* break the world record and then pulverised it, lengthening it from 127 hundreds to 197, a figure that still stands today. The Belles should take that analogy and run with it.

The classiest runner ever to close in a Belles team?! Grace was 3rd in the league four months earlier, and since then battled to maintain form, but she never gave up, and kept her spot in a cracking side

Chas looks content enough, but the cogs are already whirring: "what do I have to do?!" Clockwise from top left: Grace, Mimi, Liv, Rachel, Alix, Lea, Nat, SA, CD, Sarah D, Ella-May & Flora. Full names in results

RESULTS 2015-2022, courtesy of A.R.Mead www.belgraveharriers.info

2015	5th	292 pts.	**Parliament Hill Fields, London**, 21 Feb. — 17 M. Wilkins, 69 S. Amend, 82 J. Rhodes, 124 Z. Doyle, 147 Z. Smith, 168 F. Cole, 174 G. Farrell, 310 R. Trees née Takayasu, 496 A. Heydenrych; 865 finished; 93 teams closed in; team winners Aldershot, Farnham & District AC 38 pts.; individual winner L. Partridge (Aldershot, Farnham & District AC).
2016	30th	837 pts.	**Donington Park, Derbyshire**, 27 Feb. — 56 S. Amend, 213 C. Pennock, 263 L. Goldie-Scot, 305 M. Bailey; 739 finished; 84 teams closed in; team winners Aldershot, Farnham & District AC 47 pts.; individual winner L. Partridge (Aldershot, Farnham & District AC).
2017	37th	1060 pts.	**Wollaton Park, Nottingham**, 25 Feb. — 185 S. Underhill, 272 L. Goldie-Scot, 274 F. Maddocks, 329 M. Bailey; 728 finished; 93 teams closed in; team winners Aldershot Farnham & District AC 22 pts.; individual winner J. Judd (Chelmsford AC).
2018	18th	559 pts.	**Parliament Hill Fields, London**, 24 Feb. — 29 S. Harris, 56 G. Fenn, 189 J. Reed, 285 J. Rhodes, 309 L. Goldie-Scot, 327 F. Cole, 659 S. Underhill; 1113 finished; 112 teams closed in; team winners Sale H Manchester 76 pts.; individual winner P. Law (Kingston AC & Polytechnic H).
2019	20th	727 pts.	**Harewood House Estate, Leeds**, 23 Feb. — 98 G. Fenn, 125 R.A. Brown, 199 M. Hall, 305 M. Corden-Lloyd, 337 L. Goldie-Scot; 1034 finished; 114 teams closed in; team winners Leeds City AC 47 pts.; individual winner E. Hosker Thornhill (Aldershot Farnham & District AC).
2020	11th	348 pts.	**Wollaton Park, Nottingham**, 22 Feb. — 41 G. Fenn, 84 O. Papaioannou, 109 A. Reed, 114 M. Hall, 264 M. Corden-Lloyd; 920 finished, 94 teams closed in; team winners Aldershot, Farnham & District AC 48 pts.; individual winner A. Moller (Aldershot, Farnham & District AC).
2021			Race not held due to coronavirus pandemic.
2022	5th	203 pts.	**Parliament Hill Fields, London**, 26 Feb. — 13 S. Astin, 54 R. Brown, 67 O. Papaioannou, 69 G. Richardson, 93 E-M. Hards, 123 S. Amend, 126 F. Whyte, 127 L. Adamson, 144 N. Beadle, 148 A. Vermeulen, 182 S. Dewhirst, 209 M. Corden-Lloyd; 1010 finished; 104 teams closed in; team winners Leeds City AC 54 pts.; individual winner J. Gibbon (Reading AC).

Most runs

6	— Samantha Amend.
5	— Sarah Murphy.
4	— Catherine Eastham
	— M. 'Tilly' Heaton
	— J. 'Jojo' Rhodes
	— Lizzie Goldie-Scot.
3	— Pam Davies (plus at least 9 other runs as a member of Selsonia Ladies AC).
	— Georgie Fenn.
	— Mimi Corden-Lloyd.

SOUTHERN 6 STAGE ROAD RELAY - WOMEN

Four Sacks of Silver

Four silvers at this one is very good going for the ladies, especially when one considers their returns at the autumn's 4 stage. The extra depth and distance required have suited them.

Catherine was a good, tenacious relay manager, who wrestled with its complexities, admitted when things could have been done differently, and then tweaked her approach the following year, sometimes to a completely contrasting degree. The oldest conundrum for a relay team is whether to back-load, front-load or plunk for something in the middle. Catherine ensured that the Belles turned up to MK for seven straight years before a couple of fallow years, when I stepped in to have a crack.

After 2000's blob, we came a glorious last in 2001 - by 3:25! Whew, it's may seem a somewhat iffy return to the naked eye, but I love the spirit and the never say die of this squad, who in turn can say that out of some 600 clubs in the South, only 20 could fell the Belles. Also, the only way was up and took all the pressure off 2002, and in Tanya Sturton and Juliette Clark we clearly had the makings of a 'midfield'.

A Meteoric Rise

Fast forward a year and boom! That last had become 4th. "Meteoric", wrote CE, and just shows what can be done when the initial declaration of intent is made. The only slight critique of the day was too much front-loading which somewhat fed our more inexperienced girls to the wolves; but I honestly don't think Catherine believed that Juliette Clark would bring us back in a 41 second lead on two! But all the same, to have star Maria Sharp on one and then Jules was too top heavy and meant Jayne Lawrence and Syreeta Stracey [who started out with us as a 12 year old sprinter and long jumper] were attacked quite severely.

Tanya Sturton held firm in bronze though on 4 and the excellent Julie Mitchell actually gained a spot on anchor. I think Juliette on two and Maz on four were their places in hindsight. When one has only two "stars", one must point blank ensure that they're *always* chasing, and never being chased, every step of the way. It made for a very lonesome run for Jules as she took out Dulwich early in her run; but still, what a wonderful performance.

Syreeta was a loyal Belle for years

In 2003 Catherine rejigged her approach and kept Maz for last. That's too isolated the other way, as the gaps are too large! But it was fine restraint from the gaffer and two spots were gained from the Sharpster as 9th became 7th. The race was becoming a little more popular and competitve, and we had to bide our time in 2004 with 7th again. But the ladies were only 53 seconds off the medals after 2 hours and 6 minutes of racing. Two notable names came to race in Helen Smethurst and Tilly Heaton – a club juggernaut in the making – and here ripping 11th into 8th on four.

2005 - Lift-Off!

A key flaw in our strategy on this momentous day came when CE writes:

"Hoping for a fast, competitive race, Birhan Dagne elected to take the first leg."

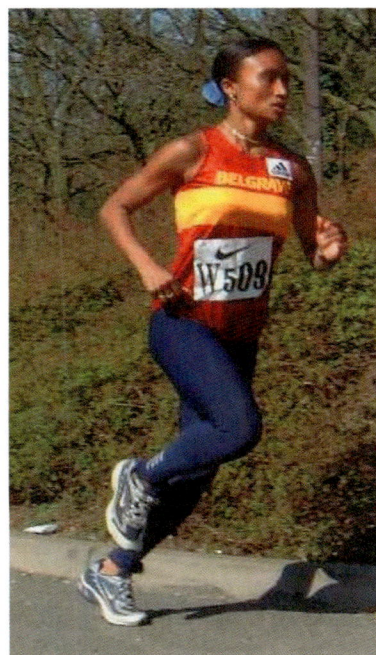

No! Runners don't "elect" to take 1, they are given it by management. The moment you start letting runners elect themselves for first, there will be blood, because most would want it. Birhan was the previous year's National cross champion, and to wipe out our superstar, with SLH's Eleanor Baker merrily drafting just behind, was too benevolent of us. Jules then did what she does best and clung on well, dropping to 2nd, although her time won't have pleased her. Christine Bertram shone briefly for the Belles around this time, and found a way past SLH before having to give best to Wells. It was a wonderful race though, as Wells were seen as unlikely winners. Helen Smethurst was always a reassuring sight in the vest and clinically reeled them in. We were back in the lead! But only by 7 seconds, with Highgate and SBH queueing up.

Tilly Heaton was in the eye of the hurricane, and no mistake. Both our hunters had aces but Tilly refused to give up and ended up just 27 seconds down on silver, and 50 on gold, to give the talented Vicky Clarke a shout of something. She ran a rock steady race, reeling in Highgate's big lead, who rather disappeared, and had a great duel with Shaftesbury. The margin at the end was just 18 seconds and one can't help but wonder what would have happened if we'd given Birhan more to do. 18:48 is an ok time from Birhan, but she was better than that. To leave her till last is too late, fine, but how about leg 5 for such a strong team? That's where you need your strength in these tense and critical moments.

Catherine herself wrote: "Yes, lessons will be learned from the race and there were lots of what ifs and maybes, which could have seen us win Gold."

2006-09 A steady decline leading to two DNS's

The 2006 vintage had some very nice talent on paper but had in no way matured. The future "Catherine the Great" Bryson, being a case in point, only holding Smurph's solid 10th on 2. But the ladies ran fairly strong all day, and Tilly once again claimed three spots to zoom from 10th to 7th on 4. Catherine B then put in a great year's running and we let fly with her in 2007 with again a strong squad that missed a star or two. 7th after 5 was good after a riotous run from Jules [+5], but then the TM then found herself being looked at lasciviously… Not really part of the plan, but Catherine [Eastham] only dropped 4.

2010 - Quiet start, but it's another launchpad

After two fallow years, it really was a beg, steal and borrow to field a side post the CE era, in my management debut at the race, but we managed it with a rarely sighted Anne Hegvold of 2001-02 relay fame, race-walker Maureen Noel, engine-roomer Jen Beecroft, Vicki Goodwin kicking us off, and then a new signing who agreed to race straight after the Reading half. Very generous of Ms Samantha Amend, and little did we know of the force of nature we were unleashing onto the world! The ladies scrapped oh so hard, and it perhaps wasn't such a bad day for Tilly for go off course by some 2 minutes. It meant that Sam went off in a lowly 16th on anchor and came back in 11th. A new star was born.

Fast forward to 2011 and medals were "*Forever Gentle On My Mind*". The squad had rebuilt itself favourably and we had the exciting prospect of a charming Czech *au pair* that Sammi noticed finishing races high on leaderboards. I pounced and although Lenka was amenable to my pleas, she was an *au pair* for a reason: to look after sproglets at weekends; so it was really her employers I needed to sweet talk for occasional foray on to the race course.

Sarah Gailey was a talented runner who we only got out very rarely due to injury and Triathlons, but when we did she invariably made it count. 7th on one set up Flic Cole, another recent signing to hold steady, before Zoe Vail broke open the door with a rise of two and Lenka to rip us into the medals. What excitement and the race was a pot-boiler.

Sam's bonkers day

SA's day was simply savage: Before heading out into the tension of a bronze medal run on 5, she'd had 4.5 hours of driving and the Kingston 16m Breakfast run in 1:37. Pretty harsh! She fell straight into trouble with a stitch and Norwich's Jane Clark went by. But finally Sam's exhausted frame hove into view and we set off another promising new signing in Mary Grace Spalton to hold us steady with the medals a little over a minute away by the end. All in then it was a happy, exciting day and only whetted the appetite for more.

We wanted a good, solid start in 2011 and Sarah Gailey delivered. LC

7th was a fine start, now Flic had to hooooold it, before we wheeled out the heavy mob. LC

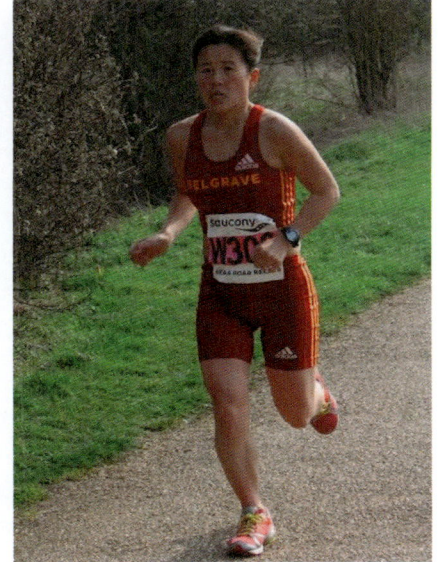

Such was our strength that we had the luxury of Rieko Trees on the subs bench for this one. LC

RESULTS 2001-2011

Milton Keynes, Open University:													
Year	Team	Name (team pos.)	Time										
2001	21	T Sturton (17)	21:40	J Smiter (22)	29:13	J Clark (21)	19:56	J Emery (22)	27:48	C Eastham (22)	26:20	D Hearn (21)	24:02
2002	4	M Sharp (2)	19:19	J Clark (1)	19:33	J Lawrence (3)	21:41	T Sturton (3)	21:12	S Stracey (5)	21:51	J Mitchell (4)	19:46
2003	7	J Clark (14)	21:01	R Powell (11)	20:38	T Sturton (10)	21:46	L Cooper (8)	21:32	H Alsop (9)	21:50	M Sharp (7)	19:45
2004	7	J Clark (6)	20:10	H Alsop (12)	21:47	H Smethurst (12)	21:20	R Powell (11)	21:27	M Heaton (8)	21:31	L Cooper (7)	20:39
2005	2	B Dagne (1)	18:48	J Clark (2)	20:56	C Bertram (2)	21:40	H Smethurst (1)	20:42	M Heaton (3)	20:16	V Clarke (2)	20:11
2006	8	S Murphy (10)	20:26	C Bryson (10)	21:31	H Smethurst (10)	20:53	M Heaton (7)	21:18	C Shanklyn (8)	22:10	V Clarke (8)	20:43
2007	11	C Bryson (7)	19:19	H Smethurst (9)	20:36	R Powell (11)	21:35	S Gailey (12)	21:18	J Clark (7)		C Eastham (11)	23:12
2010	11	V Goodwin (19)	22:44	M Noel (18)	24:03	A Hegvold (15)	21:11	J Beecroft (16)	26:55	M Heaton (16)	24:20	S Amend (11)	20:44
2011	4	S Gailey (7)	20:01	F Cole (7)	20:55	Z Vail (5)	20:44	L Vseteckova (3)	19:29	S Amend (4)	20:50	MG Spalton (4)	21:16

Fresh Theatre of Dreams

The 2012 race was frustrating at the new Stantonbury venue, as we lost a few stars in the build up. A great warrior returned in Birhan, but a shadow of her former self, whilst the likes of Anne, the Vixster and Rieko held us steady. Up front, woman of the year Fee Maycock found 12th, which is where we finished with little deviation. Nelle had a good run on 2.

Agonizing Medal Miss in '13

We also cover 2013 in the National report as the Southern race was cancelled and then piggy-backed onto that. The girls fought hard but it was an odd day as the early runners struggled to make an impression. By the time that a tremendous run from Tish on four, and a good run from Sam occurred, it was left to Fee to anchor us home in 5th which counted as 4th with the removal of the AFD B's, just 12 seconds behind Bedford. Surely we had another 12 ticks in us, but it was just one of those days where the machine spluttered before finally catching light. Afer Jojo's opener of 10th [remember, this was the National, so less Southern clubs], Rose was unable to make headway, and then Lou found a solitary spot, but with a time 1:28 down on the previous year. So all told, one of those off-colour days that crop up once in a while.

Back on form – Kinda'! But it's still silver

A year of yet more building followed and we knew we were plumb in line for good things come 2014. A team crackling with talent commenced with a seemingly cautious 15th by Jojo, but a closer look showed that the race was ever-growing in depth and they were all lined up ahead... Nelle reached for her drill for some root canal on seven souls, running within 2 seconds of Jojo. We now expected Mel to really make hay after a terrific first season with us which included 16th at the Southern cross. But not so! In the first of the day's two reverses, Mel came in a minute down on prediction. Goodness would she correct that, a year hence. But it was still a spot gained and although there was some genuine concern at 7th at the half, Tish laid waste to the field, ripping us into 2nd with the day's 4th fastest with a run that she enjoyed thoroughly. AFD were on another planet and meanwhile a fine run from ZLD extended our lead over bronze to some 3 minutes.

But in an incredible twist, great drama awaited. I'd been after Sophie Carter for literally years, feeling that her strong reliable running would suit us so nicely. After SC pondered my invitation for a year or so, she concurred to make the switch from Woodstock, but in the same breath informed she was pregnant. Another year or so passed and we had our runner. As it went (oh the best laid plans!), Soph was a nigh on write-off for XC in her time as a Belgravian as she simply couldn't get her head around it, a very solid Southern aside. But on the roads we did get some very fine action, including a National gold in the Vets.

Here, Soph admitted to a suspect ankle, after a National medal winning team run in the Reading Half, but was nearly 2 minutes up on what a reserve in the Bs could offer, so what would the niggle cost her? She tested it out and declared herself good to go. However, the run quickly became a nightmare and behind her the excellent Rebecca Murray of Bedford was going 3:20 faster! Mercifully, the finish line engulfed Soph with 10 seconds to spare, but we had learned a good lesson: to grill athletes with niggles even more closely. But there has to be trust as well.

Some fashionable eye-wear here as the women savour silver. L-R, Zoe, Mel, Sophie, Nelle, Tish & Jojo

More silver service

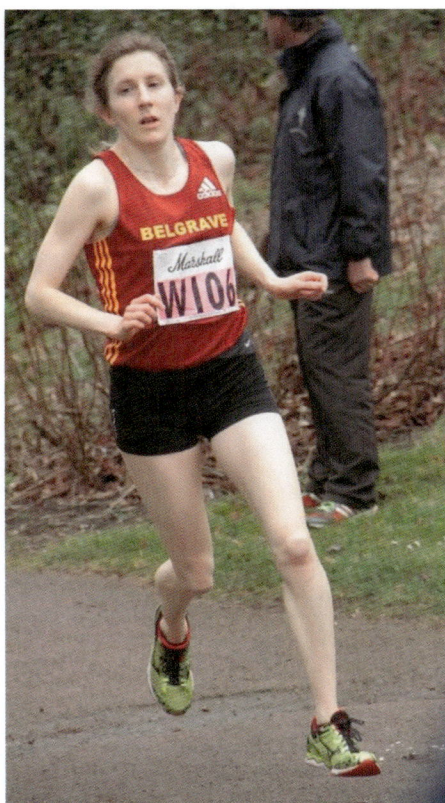

A hattrick of openers from La Metronome, JJR! LC

Anyway! It was a bullet dodged and still a very fine day out, with plenty to cheer. The squad had lost Tish a year later, but remained rock steady. The question was who should have been the 6th athlete into the squad? All my calculations had both Fee and Rose in 18:30 shape. Who to choose? I quizzed the runners and Rose very gallantly said Fee should take the spot due to her superiority in their head to heads, as in the 26 seconds to Fee at Sutton Park. Wrong call! We switched them a month later for Sutton Park, but wrong again! The solution to the problem perhaps being that Sutton Park favours the strength runners and MK is better for the speedsters. But the error was "only" 14 seconds, and Rose had eight more runners to chase, where Fee was up in the top 15, and surrounded by talent who weren't giving her much of a slipstream, as in GB International Jo Wilkinson, pictured.

Fee fully warranted her inclusion in the side, despite dodging a coin flip due to Rose's benevolence. Team GB marathoner Jo Wilkinson hunts her prey. LC

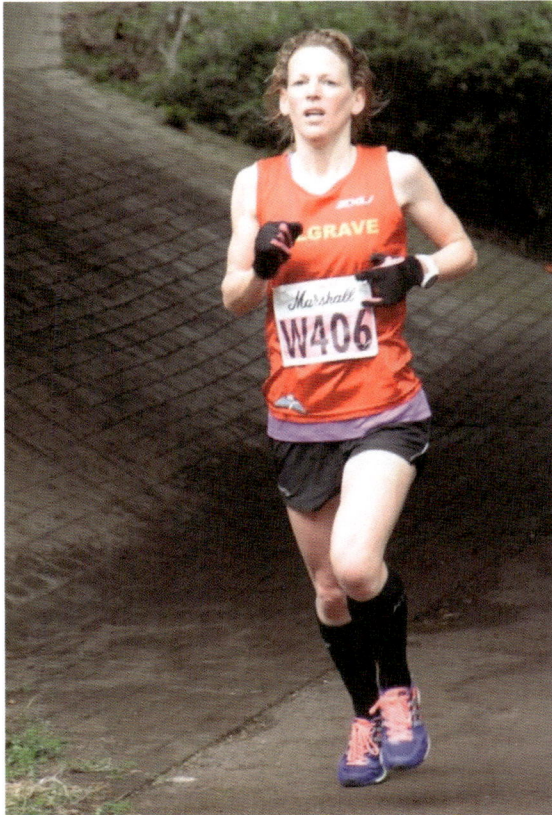

Just like the previous year, our metronome Jojo took 15th, and with Fee finding a one spot rise, it was left to Zoe D to bring us right up into the reckoning to 7th and this time Sophie was right on the money with an 18:33. We were now 4th and what could Sammi do? In a brilliant run just 3 seconds off SC, 4th became 2nd. Such clinical running. It meant a fair bit of pressure for Mel, and she didn't disappoint; probably leaving 20 seconds out there through insurance but still our quickest and a cushion of over 1:30 over Cambridge. It was notable that the race had 45 teams start and that our B's claimed 20th, which was a very fine effort. The future looked bright.

That's more like it! After 2014's horror run, Sophie showed us how it's done. LC

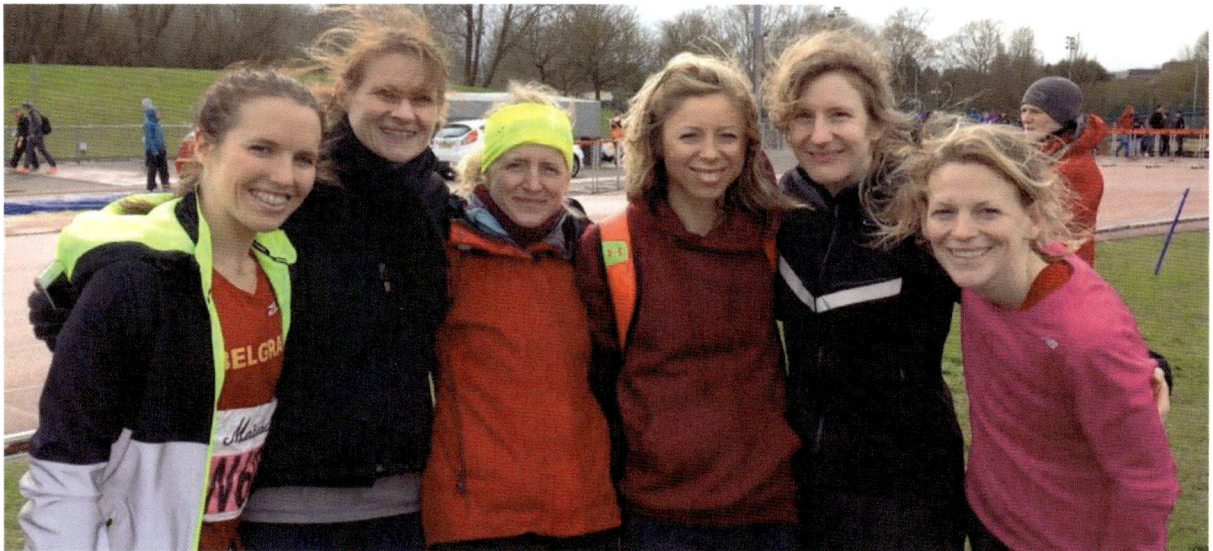

A somewhat scruffier bunch than 12 months earlier, and just the two switches as Fee and Sam come in for Tish and Nelle; and one might say an injury-free Sophie for a crocked one

Transitional period

The South went on the road – to Gravesend cyclopark - and the squad underwent some severe biomechanical adjustments including my stepping down to focus on the struggling men. Chas had the matter bravely in hand though and fielded a new look squad. Keri Mackenzie will always be one of the most talented runners in the club, but goodness does she pay for that skill with fragility. But when she's smokin', opposition beware! Non more so than at the opener in 2016 when she set us up in 9th. Rocking stuff and now it was the historic first ever long Southern leg as the National's remit from 2015 was followed. Flic came back with profuse apols in 18th, but no need, if not her, then who? Heh, well Saron perhaps, but she preferred short and three spots were claimed, whilst ZVS cemented her cracking season with one of her best runs for a rise of four and 7th best on the stage – her first Southern 6 stage since that thriller five long years earlier – when Flic was also involved.

Rose was in good form on 5 to take us up another pip to 10th and it was left to Jojo to enjoy an absolute cracker to go 59 secs quicker than RO'B and cement that spot, by seeing off Ipswich but having to give best to a peach from Brighton's Emma Dixon. It was clear that not having that 2nd strong longey really hurt us here, but the day was an aberration: for the last 20 years it is clear that Belles like to go long, we just lost about eight potential candidates on the day!

After a strong 6th at the Southern cross, the engine-room were raided in a very big way in 2017, but all credit to Lizzie, Becky O'Kill, Saron [again swerving the long, but remember, she is a purist 800 runner], Sammi, and then two welcome engine-roomers in Helen White and Megs Bailey. Their attritional runs made for a very attritional day!: 19th, 18th, 17th, 16th, 16th, 17th. I don't think I've ever seen such little movement in a squad that said, "we may not be at our best today, but NONE SHALL PASS!" Ok, just the one for luck.

2019s wabble of wowdy webels

…As Pontius Pilate in *Life of Brian* might say, when gazing upon his hyped-up flock. After snow and ice cancelled 2018, Charlie summoned no fewer than 16 back to Stantonbury in 2019 – that's wonderful stuff. It was a talented team too, although had one disaster as after talented new find Alice Reed kicked us off in 13th, poor old Sammi was hit by a frigtehening dizzy spell during her run, and had to give a few spots back. About 1 in 20 does she give us a sub par run, maybe 2013 at Sunderland was her last?! Rachel Brown though was clearly another name for the future and she had more to chase than expect and enjoyed picking off three very much, to hand over to Olympic marathoner Jane Vongvorachoti to claim three more.

The club's marquee name was now Georgie Fenn [the day's 11th quickest] and suddenly we were 7th which in turn became 6th with Mhairi's slightly traumatic run on a gammy knee. However, mild amusement was in store as up ahead Colchester's athlete in 4th took in a 2nd tour of the property – not something menched in Chas's report, but completely maddening for them. There is a fork a mile from the finish and if an athlete/marshal are not vigilant, disaster can occur. Hey, we'll take it.

Not so very far behind another huge story was the B's – 15th! Say what?! Yes, Fi Maddocks, Jess Reed, Steph Hewitt, Mimi Corden-Lloyd set us up nicely for 24th, upon which Kerimac and the alas-soon-to-depart Emma Howsham took careful aim and fired.

Post-Covid dreamteam!

A week out and with his *season mirabilis* largely tucked under his belt, I noted to Charlie the bind he must be in trying to fit 10 into 6! "Already done it," he shot back. And when reeling off the names, I saw he was probably right, but what chance one of those diamonds left on the cutting room floor coming to nip him and prove him wrong? Huge. Truly, it was an embarrassment of riches. Then he lost one – the dynamo Rachel Brown – after a superb season, savagely slashing her foot open with an horrendous blister, the likes of which I'm not sure I've seen [no way you're getting a picture]. It was from a triathlon and I guess wet feet and no socks can be a bad mix. Now Charlie's trouble really started. It was at least four into one! He went with Jess Saunders, as he needed a 'slugger' for the long stage, who in turn had had a rock solid season.

To the start and it was pretty profligate with Grace Richardson off on one. You may have picked up that I get very squeamish about front-loading, but in this case, Grace had experienced an up and down season, and really needed to get the confidence back. A leg one straight race, with some 2 hours to correct any problems, would do that. A no frills 9th was her reward – she's better than that and it will come for sure, but this was the tonic she required. It all gave Jess a perfect platform with runners in close proximity. A sharp time was missing this day – maybe too many miles in the legs and not enough of that speed that we all gasped at when she was a 'Charlie's Runner' the year before.

And behind Jess the imposing talent of Patricia Walker in the B's beat her by 25 seconds! It's not that Charlie was blind to PW's skill, we saw it in abundance at Wimbledon in November, where she actually duffed up Jess by almost a minute, but we hadn't got her out since due to injury, so CD went with what he knew. But Patricia is pure class, and not for the first time in these pages [with others], left her dart at the A team too late. Next up was Steph Hewitt who we're always delighted to see in the squads as she's such a fighter. But all through the season her great pace was undone by endurance issues and niggles, and here she came under fearsome attack by Alix Vermuelen in the B's who was simply getting better and better in training, and the remarkable newbie Anna Price. I witnessed Anna do a fairly obscure charitiy 10k in London weeks earlier [placing 2nd] and she can destroy people in handicap reps in training, but she's so new to the sport! As we say, what breathtaking riches we have at our disposal and both Alix and Anna saw off Steph, who in turn "got the job done" by turning 11th into 8th.

Another who was down to run on this day before having to bow out was Emily Kerr – with us for nearly a year, but yet to get a vest on her. But we will, and when we do, watch out! And yet another firestorm raging in the Bs was child prodigy Maddie Whitman kicking them off in 16th only 35 seconds behind Grace. Chuck in a bit of Flora Whyte and the always sparky Alice Reed and it's no surprise that team finished 8th. Incredible really.

And let's pay tribute to the C's while we're at it, who were a very solid 19th/33. Goodson, Goldie-Scot, M Hall & Hards all have great potential and with the President next up, followed by the reliable Cat Hall gaining a pip at the death, that's not such a bad A team from years gone by.

With all those breathtaking selectoral conundrums whamboozling the stopwatch boffins, a superb race was raging. Surely we would medal, but 8th at the half was surprising. Time to send for SA – our second SA – not Sammi Amend but Sarah Astin. A momentous run follow which was so strong and secure, and is off the back of over 17 years at the running coalface where she's served six clubs under five coaches, all over the world, from Manx to Virginia. Anyway, this sub 16 runner not only picked off four like a sniper but she set up Paps with the mother of all lobs to smash away.

Liv too had had a mix season, and the obligatory Covid woes, but she was 'back on it' now for sure and loved the challenge before her. Lewes' outstanding outfit were finally dealt with and it was a rare victory for us over the great Aldershot. We don't fell them very often, but when we do it's a great feeling, and to be sure they never stopped firing. Over to debutante Naomi Lenane who's crossed over from Epsom. It was a fairly high pressure run, knowing the "Shots" were back there somewhere, but she returned a solid, no frills run, and the selectors had got it right with her – by just 3 seconds! Up ahead, we can but pay tribute to Cambridge. To be sure, Aldershot aside, that's one of the greatest relay squads of all time. They beat us by 3:50! Far too good, but can they now keep such a remarkable team together? We shall see. [They imploded at the National with the DNF].

All in all, the day was like a dream for the Belles and surely they can go on and enjoy great riches over the coming decade. But then just a fortnight later the warning shot came to NEVER relax. Total capitulation – no National – where they'd surely have medalled in what was very weak race. Amazing stuff and a jarring end to an otherwise gem of a season.

Southern 6/12 stage results 2022					
Leg	Bel A	LEG TIME	POS	TOTAL TIME	POS
1	G Richardson	00:17:44	9	00:17:44	9
2	J Saunders	00:32:18	14	00:50:02	11
3	S Hewitt	00:18:10	5	01:08:12	8
4	S Astin	00:29:05	1	01:37:17	4
5	O Papaioannou	00:17:32	2	01:54:49	2
6	N Lenane	00:17:55	4	02:12:44	2
Leg	Bel B	LEG TIME	POS	TOTAL TIME	POS
1	M Whitman	00:18:19	16	00:18:19	16
2	P Walker	00:31:53	11	00:50:12	12
3	A Vermeulen	00:18:05	4	01:08:17	9
4	F Whyte	00:34:14	18	01:42:31	11
5	A Price	00:17:58	3	02:00:29	9
6	A Reed	00:18:42	8	02:19:11	8
Leg	Bel C	LEG TIME	POS	TOTAL TIME	POS
1	L Goodson	00:18:48	22	00:18:48	22
2	L Goldie-Scot	00:34:15	23	00:53:03	23
3	M Hall	00:19:21	16	01:12:24	21
4	E Hards	00:34:57	23	01:47:21	20
5	F Maddocks	00:19:50	16	02:07:11	20
6	C Hall	00:22:00	22	02:29:11	19

Summation of a remarkable day's play

A really outstanding team, selectoral headaches aside. Naomi, Liv, Jess, Grace, Sarah & Steph savour their late, late show

RESULTS 2012-2022

Stantonbury, Milton Keynes

Year	Team	Name (team pos.)	Time										
2012	12	F Maycock (12)	18:48	N Quispel (11)	19:11	B Dagne (13)	20:16	A Hegvold (12)	20:04	V Goodwin (11)	20:36	R Trees (12)	21:36

Sutton Park (in conjunction with the National)

| 2013 | 4 | J Rhodes (10) | 18:28 | R O'Brien (10) | 18:56 | L Blizzard (9) | 19:03 | T Jones (5) | 16:51 | S Amend (5) | 17:44 | F Maycock (4) | 18:30 |

Stantonbury, Milton Keynes

| 2014 | 2 | J Rhodes (15) | 18:39 | N Quispel (8) | 18:41 | M Wilkins (7) | 19:08 | T Jones (2) | 16:52 | Z Doyle (2) | 18:31 | S Carter (2) | 20:30 |
| 2015 | 2 | J Rhodes (15) | 18:51 | F Maycock (14) | 19:50 | Z Doyle (7) | 19:10 | S Carter (4) | 18:33 | S Amend (2) | 18:36 | M Wilkins (2) | 18:12 |

Gravesend Cyclopark

| 2016 | 10 | K Mackenzie (9) | 15:53 | F Cole (18) | 25:26 | S Haileselasie (15) | 16:12 | Z Vail Smith (11) | 23:41 | R O'Brien (10) | 17:16 | J Rhodes (10) | 16:17 |
| 2017 | 17 | L Goldie-Scot (19) | 17:11 | R O'Kill (18) | 25:39 | S Haileselasie (17) | 16:53 | S Amend (16) | 24:17 | H White (16) | 17:56 | M Bailey (17) | 18:30 |

Stantonbury, Milton Keynes

| 2019 | 6 | A Reed (13) | 19:11 | S Amend (16) | 29:40 | R Brown (11) | 19:08 | J Vongvorachoti (8) | 28:26 | G Fenn (7) | 18:26 | M Hall (6) | 20:49 |

Stantonbury, Milton Keynes [adjusted course]

| 2022 | 2 | G Richardson (9) | 17:44 | J Saunders (11) | 32:18 | S Hewitt (8) | 18:10 | S Astin (4) | 29:05 | O Papaioannou (2) | 17:32 | N Lenane (2) | 17:55 |

SOUTHERN 12 STAGE ROAD RELAY - MEN

2022's squads. Standing l-r: Will Cockerell, Euan Campbell, Sam Gebreselassie, Ewan Somerville, Nick Buckle, Valentin Rigori, Jonny Neville, Conall McNally, Nick Goolab, Rob Kelly, Henry Hart, Lizzie Goldie-Scot, Maddie Whitman, Sarah Astin, Charlie Dickinson. Kneeling l-r: Hillory Wallis, Steve Gardner, Dan Wallis, Scott Mills, Brad Courtney-Pinn, Grace Richardson, Steph Hewitt, Liv Papaioannou, Alix Vermeulen, Ella-May Hards, Fiona Whyte, Mhairi Hall.

22 Years of absorbing struggle

"I love this day…" Thus spake one of the team's most loyal supporters Bill Laws in around 2007. He was referring to the Southern 12, a race steeped in Bels folklore, and completely reinvented in the

This sharply dressed group is of the last Belgrave team to win the London-Brighton (Southern edition), in October 1963. L-R: Pat Newell, Bill Kerr, Geoff North, Ron Linstead, Bill Lucas DFC (President), Tony Fairclough, Barry Sawyer, Charlie Dabbs, John Thresher, Gerry North, Laurie O'Hara & Alan Black. Chas Walker was 'absent without leave'.

Over 52 years later, Pat, Bill [Lucas], Tony, Charlie & Alan were pictured together again at Belgrave Hall for a gathering to mark Bill's 80 years as a Belgravian.

*see page 214 for an image of five of these souls in 2016

21st Century by MKAC, Mick Bromilow and the alluringly memorable Open University course. Spectating was good – once you figured it out, which could take years – the wind was often ferocious, and the longs slogs around the lakes pretty savage.

There were some fairly strong concerns for a while whether the community could justify a Southern 12 anymore, and the SEAAs limp marketing of the day didn't help, and in around 2010 I wrote a paper suggesting we ring-fence the National 12 stage, but perhaps reduce the Southern to 10 legs. Surely it would boost participation by around a dozen clubs and take the edge off the day's length. But competitions do evolve and slowly but surely the race has rebuilt its competitive hue, and is now a six or seven-way slugfest which is superb, and hopefully safe in the calendar for the coming generation and beyond.

Two mini thrillers

We medalled at the Southern 12 stage for a dozen years in a row – a remarkable achievement. In 1999, outside the remit of these pages, a dazzling but mercurial team grabbed silver, in a day most notable for Mark Miles smashing out the day's fastest, and Hassan Raidi getting lost and even being seen to walk. He got a few years on the naughty step for that. ARM raised a splendid dozen for the 2000 race, eyeing up perhaps one better. And then they started to fall – like ninepins – as is so often the way. At 7pm on the Saturday night he called on the 6th reserve who'd placed 235/253 the previous year, and had done an enormous Frank Horwill sesh that morning. But I was delighted to get the call!

EASTALL, J	0:25:44	22	22	
NASH, K	0:16:15	1	3	+19
STEWART, Alaster	0:25:11	8	4	-1
CARSTAIRS, P	0:18:15	18	6	-2
ALSOP, R	0:24:51	7	6	
CLARKE, S	0:17:34	5	3	+3
FREARY, P	0:24:21	3	3	
HUTCHINSON, A	0:16:55	1	1	+2
HURST, Lee	0:24:26	1	1	
QUINN, K	0:18:14	9	2	-1
COCKERELL, W	0:26:13	11	3	-1
GILBEY, C	0:17:47	9	3	

*shld read Estall

I was handed the graveyard shift of leg 11, a thankless task to many, but the marathoners lap it up. I arrived at the flag during leg 6 and announced: "ok you can stop panicking, here I am…" John Jeffery whirled on me: "it's you who better start panicking - we're about to go into the lead!" Whuh?! This was a big surprise as we were in such damage limitation mode, but the boys had done well. After messrs Estall, Nash, Stewart, Carstairs, Alsop & Clarke had fought for a podium spot, a riotous Paul Freary closed right in on the leaders, setting up Canadian International Alex Hutchinson to rip us into the lead. Lee Hurst was no mug at all to keep us in the lead, but now it was the turn of young Kevin Quinn on leg 10, who 20 years later would be one of the most respected club men in the UK, but was still very much a work in progress and had to let Shaftesbury go.

My SBH opponent was Nick Francis, a 23 minute man, while I'd run 29 the previous year. So a bit of a mismatch and Shaftesbury were now dead certs, but could we find a silver? I was soon caught by the redoubtable Karl Corpes of AFD, but I loved the thrill of getting into his slipstream and we ran lockstep the rest of the way. It was left to Clive Gilbey to hopefully repeat his fine kick for silver the previous year. Vince Garner was a tough cookie though, and there was no way he was going to allow that, but it was still a pleasing bronze.

The following year was more of the same, Windsor in red hot form and SBH strong again we never had gold or silver in mind, but the battle for medals with Bedford was terrific and on anchor I ran in terror with the thought: "if the Bedford man catches me, I'll have to let him go, I have no fight left…"

I shall hand over to this nice little historical vignette from Alan which shows that our dutiful website reportage stretches back well over 20 years. One has to dig seriously deep into the WayBackMachine archives for this! Look at some of those interesting names and clubs at the sharp end, and an insight into how the landscape has changed today, and let's face it, a pleasingly improved depth:

Stage 12. So it was down to Our Will. He'd held on last year to keep us in bronze – could he do it again? He went out with a 27 second advantage over Bedford and shortly, as supporters who had been out on the course returned to the finish area they brought back tales that his lead was conflictingly down to 20 seconds or up to 30 seconds. The wait on that final corner before the slope up to the finish seemed interminable; but suddenly there he was, still in 3rd having taken another 42 seconds out of our rivals. Bronze again!

1, WSE&H 4:12:00; 2, Shaftesbury Barnet 4:13:26; 3, Belgrave 'A' 4:16:21; 4, Bedford & County 4:17:30; 5, Thames Hare & Hounds 4:22:37; 6, Aldershot F&D 4:22:42; 7, Brighton & Hove 4:25:32; 8, Phoenix AC 4:26:27; 9, Cornwall AC 4:33:11; 10, Exeter H 4:32:56; … 31, Belgrave 'B' 4:46:42 (2nd 'B' team to WSE&H – 28th).
Fastest: D.Brien (Shaftesbury B) 16:46; W.Cockerell 17:49 (4, =36); D.Anderson 20:42 (31, =243).

299 men completed the 7.978 kms long stage and 293 the 5.506 kms short stage. 54 teams started and 44 finished.

Fastest long stages: S.Haughian (WSE&H) 23:43; N.Francis (Shaftesbury Barnet) 23:56; J.Fitzsimmons (Shaftesbury Barnet) 24:04.

Fastest short stages: K.Cullen (Chelmsford) 15:49; G.Amos (City of Norwich) 16:09; D.Brian (Shaftesbury Barnet) 16:40.

2002-2006 Sheer dominance

What can we say? We never took the race for granted, but for whatever reasons there was a fair amount of weakness elsewhere, and there were still some fine racing, but this was Belgrave at its best. 2002 was a dreamteam that I was unable to find a way into post injury, but the quality was astonishing with the likes of Evans, Anderson and Sharp running riot, we won by nearly 6 minutes.

1	107	R Alsop	25:03	11
2	207	N Hliouat	17:15	4
3	307	K Nash	25:16	3
4	407	R Hayman	17:31	2
5	507	R McHarg	25:43	3
6	607	K Quinn	18:07	4
7	707	R Ward	25:13	4
8	807	S Clarke	17:25	4
9	907	P Freary	24:34	4
10	1007	F Bernard-Gaudin	17:41	4
11	1107	A Stewart	24:44	3
12	1207	W Cockerell	17:49	3

1	109	K Nash	24:42	5
2	209	S Sharp	16:33	2
3	309	P Freary	24:49	1
4	409	K Quinn	17:31	1
5	509	C Herrington	25:48	1
6	609	David Anderson	16:28	1
7	709	L Hurst	24:46	1
8	809	R Ward	17:15	1
9	909	P Evans	23:47	1
10	1009	J Wolf	17:34	1
11	1109	A Stewart	24:41	1
12	1209	R Alsop	17:24	1

2001 [top] & 2002

1		**Belgrave Harriers 'A'**	**4:07:23**	
1	111	R Alsop	24:50	7
2	211	R Ward	16:25	1
3	311	P Freary	24:34	2
4	411	David Anderson	15:51	1
5	511	K Nash	24:18	1
6	611	J Blackledge	16:46	1
7	711	W Cockerell	25:03	1
8	811	C Herrington	17:20	1
9	911	M Dent	23:49	1
10	1011	S Kennefick	17:42	1
11	1111	A Stewart	24:45	1
12	1211	S Sharp	16:00	1

Looking fresh from logging by far our fastest Long Stage, Paul Evans savours SEAA12 Gold again, a cool dozen years since his last

The 2003 boys ran almost without fault

2003 another resounding 'dreamteam', with 'Danders' tying Keith Cullen for the course record of 15:51. Only Mo Farah would have something to say about that in 2010, but not by much. We also saw blinders from Marty Dent, SS, Wardy and YJB [Young Jonny Blackledge.]

A classic Bedford duel

2004 was a wonderful race as Bedford threw everything at us. The lead went back and forth for hours and during leg 7 simple maths said: 'we were cruising for a bruising'. We were behind, and leg 11 was Cockerell vs Lobb who'd just holidayed together in the Tenerife mountains [not as romantic as it sounds, I got the huge double bed, and Huw slept in a cot at my feet]. Huw was the Southern cross champion and one of the fittest men in the land for sure. So if we were 2nd after 7, we were going to have to find a minute over Bedford before then... Maybe we were 25% for the win?

Enter Wardy! He always loved a scrap and took out Neil Miller by 26 seconds, and so we led by 17 seconds going into the final third. Paul Freary then took 45 seconds out of Steve Herring and there was the minute we needed. We worried for Simon Marwood a tad but he was more than equal to the task, and now Huw had a 1:38 problem. Of course I didn't know it to be this much and it was a very long slog, with Huw, his tiny frame in black *raybans* looking like an angry bug, and later admitted to be "flying", eating into my lead with every step. Pat Mead gave it to me straight with a mile to go: "He's closing, but you're fine..." It's well chosen words like that which make all the difference to a lonely, leading relay runner. 66 seconds was the dent in my chassis, and we still had Blackledge up our sleeve; a superb runner who laid waste to the Bedford man by another 50. All was well, and as Alan said in his report: "hats off to them. Yes, we were missing a few, but so were they!"

1		Belgrave Harriers 'A'		
1	109	M Trees	24:12	4
2	209	R Alsop	17:16	3
3	309	C Herrington	25:19	4
4	409	S Sharp	16:22	1
5	509	H Raidi	24:43	2
6	609	J Beech	17:39	2
7	709	K Nash	24:40	2
8	809	R Ward	16:38	1
9	909	P Freary	24:43	1
10	1009	S Marwood	17:17	1
11	1109	W Cockerell	25:23	1
12	1209	J Blackledge	16:41	1

2004

2005 was great fun for all until around leg 8 when we finally broke free. I had a wee shocker on 1 [16th], and with Woodford front-loading massively, Thames in the form of their lives, and Bedford and Newham both strong we were second after 7 after Mark Warmby's brilliant run, who won a cruel duel with a hot little kid called Wicks. Amazingly, Thames had savoured the lead at the half.

1		Belgrave Harriers 'A'	4:13:09	
1	108	W Cockerell	25:38	16
2	208	C Moss	16:30	3
3	308	H Raidi	25:29	2
4	408	J Charles	17:45	4
5	508	T Watson	25:01	4
6	608	T Ellacott	17:27	2
7	708	P Wicks	24:21	2
8	808	S Sharp	16:21	1
9	908	David Anderson	24:34	1
10	1008	C Herrington	17:34	1
11	1108	K Nash	24:47	1
12	1208	K Hegvold	17:42	1

2005

What could messrs Sharp, Anderson, Herrington, Nash and the Trondheim Stallion Knut Hegvold do about these yapping Beagles? A lot! A very juicy quintet with only Gnasher losing his head to head duel. Knut was at his best when training with the likes of Joachim Cruz before JC's 1984 Olympic win over a generation earlier, but he still fired off the stage's 3rd fastest to comfortably see us home.

2006 was a bit of a non-event and there had to be real concerns about the viability of the race with such little competition, for yet another cracking team. But nigh on 7 minutes is far too much to win by.

1	7	Belgrave Harriers 'A'	4:12:38	
1	107	Andrew Swearman	26:08	20
2	207	Will Cockerell	17:23	11
3	307	Simon Jones	24:54	6
4	407	Peter Willis	17:44	3
5	507	Hassan Raidi	24:48	1
6	607	Stephen Sharp	16:28	1
7	707	Tim Watson	24:52	1
8	807	Jonathan Blackledge	16:33	1
9	907	Philip Wicks	24:04	1
10	1007	Tom Ellacott	18:00	1
11	1107	David Anderson	24:08	1
12	1207	Richard Ward	17:36	1

2006

2007 - One of the great races

For several reasons the team was a tad all over the place the next year, and Alan was intent on giving runners what they wanted. It's all very well to strongarm the best runners into the long stages, but if they're really not up for it, bad feeling can occur and niggles can flare up.

It meant that our team was *phenomenal* going short, but the longeys looked about as unusual as it gets: Byansi, Willis, Wicks, Ellacott, Buckley & Cockerell. An almost unthinkable line-up, and yet we still felt we had a chance.

Mal ran great for 9th, Shugri Omar killed it to move us into 2nd, the wind floored poor old Pete, so back to 10th and then Sp8y ripped out a 16:14 to go back to 3rd. We were up and down the leaderboard like demented squirrels. SBH were a long way up, but enter Wicksy with a phenomenal 23:20 (on a slightly shorter course). We were now 55 ticks adrift, which became a mere 10 after a stunner from Jon. Tom Ellacott on 7 was in the slime, up against SBH stalwart James Trapmore. But Tom gave up "only" 1:08 and Sharpy promptly took nearly a minute back. What a race!

Padraic Buckley had to give up 25, but a terrific run from a slightly unfit Wardy versus the man SBH were trying to hide, gave me a lead of 29 seconds on 11 over another training partner Orlando Edwards, who'd taken 3:30 out of me at the National cross. We had a splendid duel, and the crowd around the course screamed themselves hoarse. Brilliant stuff, and why we all love the club scene. "Come on Willie, let's go faster," urged OE when he caught me at half-way. Not what I wanted to hear. But I clung grimly on and there were only 2 seconds in it, handing over to the talented but very young Alex Bodin. He ran well but Shaftesbury's Renfree was too good and we had to settle for a 30 second loss after a startling day's racing.

2		8 Belgrave Harriers 'A'	4:14:13	
1	108	Malachi Byansi	24:53	9
2	208	Shugri Omar	16:43	2
3	308	Peter Willis	27:05	10
4	408	Neil Speaight	16:14	3
5	508	Phil Wicks	23:20	2
6	608	Jonathan Blackledge	16:19	2
7	708	Tom Ellacott	26:17	2
8	808	Stephen Sharp	16:13	2
9	908	Padraic Buckley	25:53	2
10	1008	Richard Ward	17:22	1
11	1108	Will Cockerell	26:12	2
12	1208	Alex Bodin	17:42	2

Duffing up AFD in their back yard

2008 was another classic, this time up at Rushmoor Arena. We awoke to a blanket of snow, and the heart sank. But then a joyous text from Alan: the race was ON! We were around a minute behind a flying Aldershot after 5, and Alan was getting one or two quizzical looks from our lads [and supporters]. Were we going to win this? But the likes of Steve Davies and Nick Goolab singed the overnight snow off the roads with scorching runs. Also worthy mention must go to Neil Speaight's terrific silver on leg one. However, with just two stages to go, there were only 11 seconds in it. We'll hand you over to Alan for the denouement, and results:

"Jonesy" was taking on Elliott Robinson, a redoubtable performer, but our man has raised his game exponentially in the last two years and he wasn't about to let his reputation slip. Looking smooth and pacey as he toured the first circuit in 13:06 Simon enquired of a Belgrave supporter in his lilting Welsh accent, "Have I dropped him yet?" Well, you don't exactly "drop" a man who's running a top-15 time but we were back into a 45 second lead and with another master blaster to come in the shape of Blackledge, J., we were looking for the fat lady to make her entrance. Much was the delight of Simon when it was later confirmed that he'd run a second faster than "Sp8y".

Jonathan took off as if the opposition were right on his shoulder – in fact he had a rather uncomfortable middle section where he realized that he'd overdone it a bit – but he recovered and stopped the Belgrave team time on 4:00:01 and was third best short-stager of the day. A minute and 24 seconds later AFD crossed the line and the bare results made it appear fairly comfortable. It wasn't!

1 Belgrave H 4:00:01; 2 Aldershot F&D AC 4:01:25; 3 Woodford Green wEL 4:04:23; 4 Newham & Essex Beagles 4:06:48; 5 Thames H&H 4:14:40; 6 Harrow AC 4:14:06; ... 26 Belgrave H 'B' 4:37:10; ... 48 teams started; 37 teams finished.

A – N Speaight (team position 2, ranking on stage 2) 26:14; N Goolab U20 (1, 3) 13:03; P Freary M40 (3, 9) 27:56; S Moralee (2, 2) 13:06; W Cockerell (2, 9) 27:53; S Davies (2, 1) 12:34; J Kelly 26:47 (2, 2) 26:47; S Sharp (1, 1) 12:37; M Pollard (1, 4) 26:58; K Hegvold M45 (1, 5) 14:01; S Jones (1, 2) 26:13; J Blackledge (1, 1) 12:39.

The 2009 squad was outrageous, and primed to do serious damage at the National (which they duly would). We severely backloaded and yet were still in the lead by leg 5. It wasn't actually a bad effort by Aldershot to keep us within 4 minutes. The highlight was Phil's stunning 23:08, but did a relay team ever pack a greater final third punch than: Wicks, Speaight, Dessaix-Chin & Mulhare? If so, let's hear about it.

1		9 Belgrave Harriers 'A'	4:09:53	
1	109	Stephen Sharp	24:45	3
2	209	James Fairbourn	18:07	5
3	309	William Cockerell	25:43	5
4	409	Michael Trees	17:28	4
5	509	Simon Jones	24:13	1
6	609	Nicholas Goolab	17:01	1
7	709	James Kelly	25:13	1
8	809	Mark Pollard	16:48	1
9	909	Philip Wicks	23:08	1
10	1009	Neil Speaight	17:05	1
11	1109	Russell Dessaix-Chin	23:55	1
12	1209	Daniel Mulhare	16:27	1

Bidding farewell to Mo

2010 was notable for it being Mo Farah's last ever club race, with global domination incoming. An honour to share a race course with him for exactly a decade and all in all we handled him ok, maybe a score draw versus Mo-led teams? But Newham were phenomenal on this day, the nigh on perfect team, with the late Bob Smith at the peak of his powers. Our team was strong, although having Wicks and Goolab on short was a tad profligate, but Phil was on the comeback trail and it meant he had the confidence to really let rip. But there was nothing we were ever going to be able to do against a team like that, a cool 5:39 up the road.

2		6 Belgrave Harriers 'A'	4:12:43	
1	106	Stephen Sharp	24:35	5
2	206	James Fairbourn	17:51	4
3	306	Paskar Owor	24:48	3
4	406	Richard Stannard	17:18	2
5	506	William Cockerell	26:15	2
6	606	Lander Eguia	18:02	3
7	706	Mark Pollard	25:22	3
8	806	David Anderson	16:54	3
9	906	James Kelly	24:58	3
10	1006	Philip Wicks	16:06	2
11	1106	Daniel Mulhare	24:05	2
12	1206	Nicholas Goolab	16:29	2

Very merry chaos in 2011!

The squad was all over the shop in 2011 and for the first half of the race we floundered, half asleep. 17th after 4… crumbs, unthinkable stuff. It appeared we'd come maybe 8th and it'd all be a slightly embarrassing damp squib. But not a bit of it! We finally came to life via Jon Blackledge on 8, who only gained a spot, but cast a deep spell over those up the way who he couldn't see. Finally, the teams were running out of men – at the same time! Great stuff and there was a crackling atmosphere for those next three legs. James Kelly set off loving the challenge set before him – let's face it a close and exciting race is often as fun as an easy win, and 7th had become 5th. Sp8y wasn't especially fit but he ran like a man possessed and suddenly, almost unbelievably, were into the medals.

Slight problem: we had men approaching their 5th and 6th decades to see us home. Woodford flew past me on the graveyard shift, but had gone too soon, and I re-arrested Mark Burgess and ended up handing a 17 second gift to Knut on anchor in 3rd. But the Trondheim Stallion was turning 50 in five months and this was an ask too far, especially as he was up against the impeccable Matt Shone (of 1:46 800 fame).

5		6 Belgrave Harriers 'A'	4:21:21		
1	106	Michael Trees	27:27	28	27:27
2	206	Hassan Raidi	18:30	23	0:45:57
3	306	Nicholas Goolab	24:01	16	1:09:58
4	406	Malachi Byansi	18:41	17	1:28:39
5	506	Paskar Owor	24:55	10	1:53:34
6	606	Stephen Sharp	16:44	7	2:10:18
7	706	Richard Ward	25:58	8	2:36:16
8	806	Jonathan Blackledge	16:40	7	2:52:56
9	906	James Kelly	25:05	5	3:18:01
10	1006	Neil Speaight	17:45	3	3:35:46
11	1106	William Cockerell	26:14	3	4:02:00
12	1206	Knut Hegvold	19:21	5	4:21:21

And 83 seconds behind, Knut had a 14:08 man on his tail in Nick Altmann, which just isn't cricket. Knut held on as long as he could to 4th, but finally the inevitable happened and 5th was our lot. But we were happy – it had been a long and fascinating day.

New venue, new look team

The decline accelerated somewhat in 2012 at Stantonbury, but we could hold our heads high in 9th. We had to resort to some seriously unlikely lads toward the end, but thanks to the likes of Stuart Kollmorgen for standing in. Lovely chap. 5th after 8 was still good fighting spirit though, before hanging on grimly. 2013 was cancelled due to snow and ice and we withdrew from National's double-header due to reasons described in that chapter. Alan's final Southern 12 stage for a quite spell-binding reign, was a cautious 10th, but just as in 2012, we never stopped fighting, and were able to throw plenty of welcome new faces at the problem like Doug Morton, Rob Norville, Sam Shore and "Frase the Laze" Logan. Even Knut was back in play (and ran very well).

9	6 Belgrave Harriers 'A'	4:12:57	
1	106 Andrew Connick	25:15	21
2	206 Steve Davies	14:52	3
3	306 William Cockerell	25:23	8
4	406 Richard Ward	15:54	8
5	506 James Fairbourn	27:01	12
6	606 Stephen Sharp	15:11	9
7	706 Paskar Owor	23:35	4
8	806 Neil Speaight	16:27	5
9	906 Malachi Byansi	27:46	8
10	1006 Stuart Kollmorgen	17:51	8
11	1106 Lander Eguia	26:34	9
12	1206 Mike Trees	17:08	9

2012

10	05	Belgrave Harriers 'A'	4:20:14	
1		105 Paskar Owor	23:19	2
2		205 Samuel Shore	17:29	8
3		305 Craig Ruddy	24:06	3
4		405 Richard Ward	17:07	6
5		505 William Cockerell	25:52	4
6		605 Doug Morton	17:13	6
7		705 Michael Trees	26:39	8
8		805 Knut Hegvold	17:36	9
9		905 Roy Maddams	26:13	8
10		1005 Robert Norville	17:56	9
11		1105 Peter Willis	29:09	10
12		1205 Fraser Logan	17:35	10

2014

WVLC presides over the devil's number, 666

In my first TM season, I had an absolute peach of a team a fortnight out in 2015, and as around 6th reserve, I shut off all power in my training. Bad idea! 2nd reserve the night before saw me head to a 40th birthday party grimly foreseeing my getting

completely *whammed* and then two more dropping out overnight, which is of course what happened. Mark Pollard had a torrid run on opener in 24th and it was all I could do in the haze of hangover, little sleep (or running), to hold that. My oppo hadn't even started shaving. It meant for a long, fairly glorious fightback though, and perhaps we held PO back too long on 11 who ran superbly.

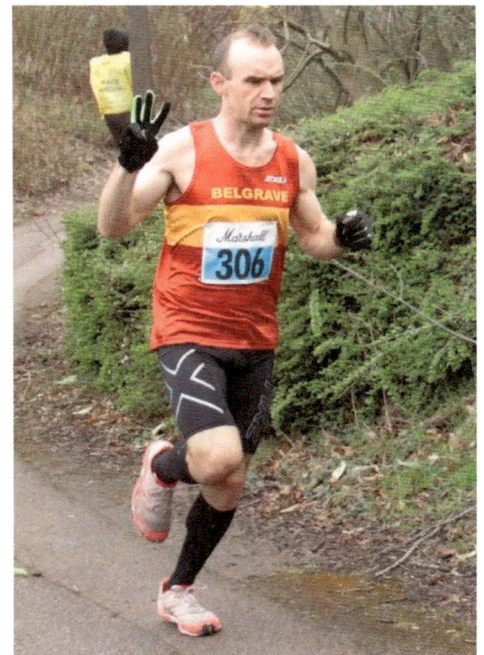

The fightback is on! Miller signals a hattrick and is not done yet. LC

The oh so gifted Ed Auden enjoyed cantering through 25% of the field. He became a calm and diplomatic club captain in the years that followed. LC

Alex Miller really enjoyed the challenge on 3 and grabbed 4 spots, another five fell to Ed Auden and six more to the Rudster. The fightback was well and truly on. The team's second half-dozen ran well to turn 9th into 6th and in the end we were "only" 1:22 off the medals. Goodness, we lost about 5 minutes in the days leading up… But such is the capricious nature of relay running.

He goes way back. A decade since his debut at the SEAA 6 in 2005. Kris Gauson can always claim to have once looked at his Garmin during a National 12 Stage and seen 4:34 miling. LC

6 06	Belgrave Harriers 'A'		4:10:16	
1	106	Mark Pollard	26:27	24
2	206	Will Cockerell	17:30	24
3	306	Alex Miller	25:36	20
4	406	Ed Auden	16:12	15
5	506	Craig Ruddy	24:09	9
6	606	Stephen Sharp	16:40	9
7	706	Gus Upton	25:24	9
8	806	Nick Bundle	16:17	8
9	906	Kris Gauson	25:11	8
10	1006	Andrius Jaksevicius	16:38	9
11	1106	Paskar Owor	23:46	6
12	1206	Taras Telkovsky	16:26	6

2015

More of the same

I was feeling even cockier in 2016, but several dropped and then the important Matt Taylor bowed to a cold late on Saturday night. We put in Tom Chandy who looks like a runner, but wasn't ready for this, and dropped 15 on two. Some might say, "well, leave him for last", but he had gone fairly well in training, and if you mean to medal, like we did, you put out an order that means it. There's a great saying in golf and backgammon: "play it like you love it." And front-loading is only done by TMs who don't love their line-ups. Why else would you give the easy legs to the good runners and the hard legs to the weaker ones?

So it all meant another huge rescue job, as we languished in 13th at the half. But still we had Phil and Nick Goolab to come… could we get close to the medals? The race had clearly smartened up in quality and depth. Kris Gauson couldn't make an impression on 7, but did set up Gus well on 8, who looked superb. What a talent that man has, but oh so fragile. Phil ran well on 9 but the shortness of the course didn't help our cause, and we were simply too far back. Roy held on, and then Mr Goolab ripped out a beauty but we were still 2:37 off the hardware, for Nick Smallwood to hold us steady. Quite simply we were missing two strong men on this day.

6	Belgrave Harriers			'*A*' 3:24:45		
1	Zekeriyas Abery	(6)	19:55	2 Tom Chandy	(21)	15:40
3	Edward Auden	(17)	20:35	4 Will Cockerell	(18)	14:16
5	Paskar Owor	(15)	19:53	6 Nick Buckle	(13)	13:57
7	Kris Gauson	(13)	20:31	8 Gus Upton	(11)	13:36
9	Phil Wicks	(9)	19:05	10 Royston Maddams	(9)	14:04
11	Nick Goolab	(6)	18:55	12 Nick Smallwood	(6)	14:18

2017 was something of an action replay with late replacements being raided. AJ on one was solid, whilst messrs Bundle and Buckle kept us steady before we slipped in Alex Mills who had to give back 11. 25th after 4, and it was going to be a *looooong* way back. That journey started with the first of our triple whammy as PO grabbed a 13 spots and the race was suddenly exciting again. Gus ran well again and we were 10th at the 'turn'. This was going to be a fascinating second half. I wasn't messing around with Goolab this time and flung him in on 7 for maximum impact. His run was superb and it was a pity he ran out of road after tying with Maud for the day's fastest, and we were up to 6th. We now had to hide another runner in Ted Oldman who toiled rather [-3] before Ed Auden kept 9th. We weren't giving up though, and altho' Matt Welsh begged for more contact of an early stage he was too good for that, and applied himself well to gain a spot. Right! Poor old Phil was 3 minutes off the medals – it was too much to ask, but he never gave up and landed within two seconds of Nickyboy's time.

Only a spot claimed for all that effort, the field had concertinaed. On an absorbing last leg, Alex Miller went off right on the shoulder of 6th (who he promptly dealt with) and chased the excellent Hartley of Kent, but not to be. After all that drama, a final leaderboard of Tonbridge, Serpentine, Highgate, AFD, Kent, Belgrave, Bedford, Herne Hill & Woodford wasn't a bad reflection. And all credit to the Serpies – they sometimes produce blinders like that.

1	A Jaksevicius	13	20:24	2	N Bundle	12	14:01
3	N Buckle	13	21:17	4	A Mills	24	15:18
5	P Owor	11	20:25	6	G Upton	10	13:51
7	N Goolab	6	19:07	7	T Oldman	9	15:35
9	E Auden	9	20:47	10	M Welsh	8	14:01
11	P Wicks	7	19:09	12	A Miller	6	13:54

The astonishing race of 2019

After more weather chaos in 2018 causing an abandonment, we returned to Stantonbury for my last SEAA 12 as TM, and you guessed it, I was pretty darn confident of medals. It was an immaculate team, with almost no weakness, but crucially missing Phil on long. It was an hugely competitive race, surely the deepest field in its history. I know some of those races in the 1970s and 80s were "hot", but this was no joke, as evidenced by any of the top 7 having a realistic medal shout. Rounding them out were 'team of the moment' Hercules, who were pretty peeved to only find 7th with an outfit like that. And in 6th were Tonbridge who won the 2018 National 12 stage by some margin. Wow… Very long gone were the days of say, 2006, where we were wondering if the calendar could justify the fixture in its current format. To my happy surprise, I think it's now secure for at least the next generation, which is terrific news.

A poorly lit but atmospheric pic of an excited squad at Euston: Ben MacCronan, WC, Andy Fyfe, Steve Gardner, Brad Courtney-Pinn, Arne Dumez, Tinos Touse, PO & Nick Buckle

To the race, and Andy Fyfe was stunned by how fast he was travelling but how many were up ahead. But we didn't worry about his position, all we cared about was his time, which were clearly 'pukka'. Tinos Touse also ran his socks off, but another shaking his head in mild dismay. Only one spot gained. That must be the fanciest ever brace of runners to only find 19th. We now turned to a bit of Aussie magic to kick-start us for real. I wanted to give Ben MacCronan as much action as possible, but didn't really expect him to be chasing so many. But after AF and KT's hard work it was the mother of all playground's to which Ben was flung, and he loved every minute. Runner after runner fell to his calm, elegant stride and our total was all but halved.

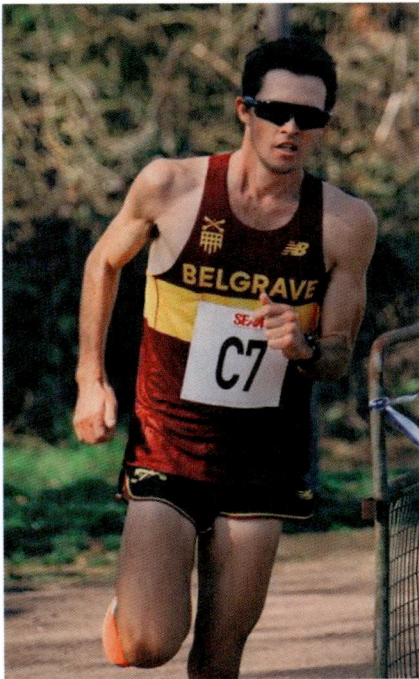

The draught was being felt by the rest up ahead too, and it was left to Steve Gardner to have the best run of his Bels career, so far, to 'take a hattrick'. Up to 6th then, and after consolidation from PO and a solid run from Arne to only leak one, we wheeled out Goolab. What followed was pure mayhem as he creamed an absolutely sensational run. It was the day's fastest by about 40 seconds and we were now up into 3rd.

There had been a wee bit of front-loading going on though, and as it went the winners, Aldershot, were chilling back in 6th. But they had a really incredible fab five to come, whilst we were "only" solid. Brad Courtney-Pinn enjoyed himelf to only let Kent squeeze by, whilst poor old Nick Buckle had a quite savage task on his hands with the likes of Jonny Hay and Chris Greenwood flying past. It was simply one of the angriest stage 9's I'd ever seen.

A cracker from Craka. Yes, the front-loading is generous, but we wanted to give our mileage junkie Ben MacCronan on tired legs every chance of an ok run, and with so little experience of British relay running, some bodies around him

We'd have dearly loved Phil on it, but he was nowhere near ready, and did very well to keep us in 5th on 10, as did AJ and Alex Miller on their tours. Well done to both. Especially Andrius who turned up to the venue a day early in error, and then pounded out a tempo 23 miler in Richmond Park in anger. Upon his return from that run, I was on bended knee pleading with him to reconsider his withdrawal, which he benevolently did. It was such a silly, trite miscommunication. Paskar put out on email to the team: "see you Saturday guys!" I immediately corrected him with "Sunday, Paskar, Sunday…" But the damage was done. Andrius saw my correction, but thought I was joking. What can you do?

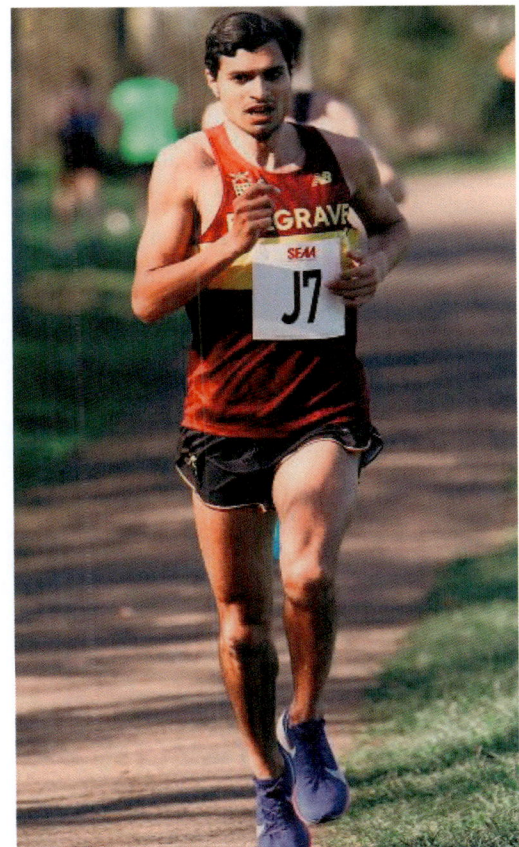

Was this Goolab run the finest Long Stage at the SEAA 12 this Millennium? We believe so… a little superior to Phil Wicks' epic run in 2009

5		**Belgrave Harriers**	**4:01:48**	
1	A07	Andrew Fyfe	24:34	20
2	B07	Konstantinos Touse	16:15	19
3	C07	Ben MacCronan	23:46	10
4	D07	Steve Gardner	15:57	6
5	G07	Paskar Owor	24:20	6
6	H07	Arne Dumez	16:24	7
7	J07	Nick Goolab	22:19	3
8	K07	Bradley Courtney-Pinn	16:01	4
9	M07	Nick Buckle	25:08	5
10	P07	Phil Wicks	15:33	5
11	S07	Andrius Jaksevicius	25:06	5
12	T07	Alex Miller	16:25	5

Totally Bizarre Post-Covid Return

After three long lurgified years we were back in play, although Covid was still playing havoc, depriving us of as many as three, including Wicksy – sometimes I think he's jynxed when it comes to SEAA events. That's 29/34 SEAA Championship races he's had to let go since that gruesome loss to Tickner in 2012 – yes, 8 of those are the lesser SEAA cross-relay [and we've skipped a couple], but the one year he could do it? You guessed it, the South rejected him as a tardy entry, after computer malfunction their end. Of course he's become a family man in that time, with added responsibilities at work, but it's a classic insight into just how tough Team management is when you're getting a 15% strike-rate off your biggest gun. [With respect to Nick Goolab who's not such an XC man]. And *to be clear*, this is a gun who with the exception of Paskar and the author [both rather curious cases] is by far and away the most prolific road and country Belgravian of the millennium with 62 Championship scores.

Typically, Phil *could* do the cancelled SEAA 6 of last September (run without Championship credentials), but the loss of Phil is always a gaping two+ minute hole in any team, and hopefully that will remain the case for a few more years! Such a ledg. Elsewhere, Steve and Arne took quite a few other hits as well but they generally affected the Bs. I couldn't find a way into them, but then almost overnight became their 5th best man.

We began with Callum Stewart who was given the gift of leg 1, which is too benevolent for a 68 half marathoner. 68-minute men are "past masters" at long, lonely, isolation running, and therefore must take their medicine at the relays, and given no easy ride! But Steve and Arne do like to start well… It meant that Arne had a much trickier task before him on 3 [I'd prefer that cat on one - or Hart or Fox], and then a major blunder came when Henry Hart severely underestimated the toll that a 58k ultra run took a fortnight earlier. When he set off I thought, "ummm, that looks circumspect" not knowing he had legs were filled with led. The run concluded, in our reporter's words: "leaving poor Henry cowering in the tent reconsidering every life decision that led to this point. Lessons learned all round!"

An almighty trio

We than hit the race our triple crown of Sam, Dan Wallis and Nick G. But the gaps were enormous. Still, Sam was marvellous as ever, while poor Dan saw only chaos. Still not quite *au fait* with the subtleties of being 'ready for the off' in a relay, he got fed duff info and remarkably none of us were on the ball enough to help him with the sight of Sam entering the stadium. What a stupid snafu. We had all been talking about it, but when Dan said: "someone told me I'm off at 2:40" I believed him. Sam appeared at 2:36. About 7 seconds were lost, and some major obstacles to deal with as Dan started in the finishing not starting strait! Pandemonium… and then he tried to run a 4:30 mile to make up, and he was still fighting the after effects of Giardiasis picked up in Kenya and a concussion incident from the gym. Oh! And then he took a wrong turn. Not by a lot… we were saving that up.

Nick Goolab then ripped out an outstanding time to advance us 3 spots and it was over to the flying Conall to show how much he's come along this season. The one drawback with this oh-so-tough athlete is that in digging so deep he does become a wee bit dullally. We were concerned at the SEAA

Cross that he was going to collapse on the final straight as he had the 'Grobelaar spaghetti legs', and here the poor soul turned right instead of left at a junction, and headed off across motorways and through fields before finally righting himself.

The course isn't 'perfectly' marked, but the runners simply must be willing to take 4% responsibility. We can't ask the course markers to take 100%. It's too much to ask people to stand in a spot for four hours that only 1 out of 400 are going to get wrong, when two very clear signs will do. Anyway, Conall had no complaints, it was simply his moment of madness, but what a shame for it to occur when he's "all in". But of course that's probably why it happened. James Fox smoothly repaired some of the damage, a warm welcome to him, and Nick Buckle as ever did what he does best: rock steady, no nonsense running – and darn quick too, by far our fastest short of the day.

Foxy stuff from James on 11. SG

Southern 6/12 stage results 2022

Leg	Name	Leg time	Pos	Total time	Pos
1	C Stewart	00:27:22	17	00:27:22	17
2	E Campbell	00:16:17	24	00:43:39	18
3	A Dumez	00:28:42	28	01:12:21	22
4	E Somerville	00:16:18	13	01:28:39	19
5	H Hart	00:29:38	29	01:58:17	23
6	J Neville	00:16:16	14	02:14:33	20
7	S Gebreselassie	00:26:37	4	02:41:10	18
8	D Wallis	00:16:29	15	02:57:39	16
9	N Goolab	00:25:49	2	03:23:28	13
10	C McNally	00:17:49	25	03:41:17	15
11	J Fox	00:28:02	9	04:09:19	13
12	N Buckle	00:15:38	4	04:24:57	13

All in all a pretty mad race. I was tearing my hair out after that sequence of 6, 6, 6, 5 on my watch - it felt like I simply couldn't catch a break. Turns out, matters could have been a fair bit worse. What odds of us not cracking the top dozen here at the start? Maybe 250-1? Simply a crazy day – but this is sport and there will always be problems.

For an image of the squad, see start of chapter

THE NATIONAL 12 STAGE - MEN

A journey just beyond the imagination

A fine piece of Belgrave road relay history with many of the Bels' most notable road runners from the past gathered to mark Bill Lucas' 80 years as a Belgravian in February, 2016. L-R, George Flanagan, John Stow, Leo Coy, Tony Binda, Bob Taylor, WEL [club debut 1937], Lionel Mann, Tony Fairclough, Alan Black, Bill Laws, Ken Miller, Charlie Dabbs, Pat Newell & Charlie Dickinson. This image hangs in Belgrave Hall with a detailed caption about each runner

"Many clubs never cease to wonder how Belgrave maintain their high standard in this race. Over a period of many years our record is second to none and this year proved to be no exception."

Although these words were written about our fortunes at his one over 60 years ago, they could've come from 2011 not 1961... and yet, and yet...

What a barnstorming, bonkers, brilliant and brutal race the 12 stage is. To say it was an "easy ride" for us at any stage this millennium would be far from the truth. Basically, 20% dreamboat, 80% nightmarish in its depravity.

But would we do it all over?! Oh, of course. After all, only the mediocre are always at their best.

Coming into the new Century, it would be true to say that Alan was a tad discombobulated on how to tackle this slippery eel. The previous year of '99 he noted our drop-out rate was so alarming that we had to start pulling spectators into the team, in order to keep going. We finally ran out of humanoids on leg 10.

2000 wasn't much better... But look at the title of that report! The gaffer was refusing to lie down. This was simply another puzzle to be solved: "One day we'll hit the jackpot."

National 12-stage - one day we'll crack it!

AAA 12-STAGE ROAD RELAY, SUTTON PARK, 29 APR 2000

Against all odds the Bels. finished a team in the AAA 12-Stage Road Relay at Sutton Park, Sutton Coldfield for the first time since 1994 - but what a struggle. It was only the tenth time that we have managed to get to the finish line in this event since the race left the Brighton Road after 1966.

We all love to call to mind the names of athletes not available on the day who "could win it" for us and this year we could name a further dozen who weren't even entered in the first place because we knew they would be elsewhere. Somehow the combination of the track & field season starting around the same time and the lure of warm weather training combines to decimate our running squad at the end of April. On "black" Thursday before this race no less than five men pulled out and in the last 24 hours even the reserves started to crack. All credit to those who ran, though, and gave the Club their highest placing since 1990. One day we'll hit the jackpot.

Nerves were stretched to breaking point as race time neared and the majority of the team, in two cars, were still driving across Buckinghamshire, looking for the M1, having left a horrendous traffic jam back on the M40. 'Phone calls to Paul Freary, already on the race course, got the team registered and fortunately the start time was put back 15 minutes as at least ten other teams had not yet shown up. With the first two runners declared we'd sort the rest out when we got there but the previously agreed running order was thrown out of the window.

Not only did Paul stand in as admin. man, he then proceeded to run a cracking 26:39 to place the team 7th after one stage with a time which puts his name right up in lights near the top of our all-time list just ahead of Gerry North and only behind Evans, Tadesse, Darren Mead, Geoff North and Halliday. Young Richard Hayman held up well under pressure but the crash was going to come and an unfit Jim Estall bore the brunt of it having volunteered to step out of the car and into number three slot while the rest of the team was sorted out. Thereafter, a crew made up of the running injured and the less than fit

>>

51

The Belgravian, May 2000

For a team in a minor shambles, this was actually good stuff, and more than "respectable", but it shows what high hopes the manager had of getting these guys into the top 10 and beyond.

Fast forward a year and Alan released a team sheet that had a phenomenal, cosmic power all of its own. A liberal sprinkling of Internationals and some outstanding club men. It must surely have been a hot favourite to return the beautiful trophy to Belgrave hands for the first time since 1951, after a break of exactly 50 years.

A day of drama – and tears

At the London Marathon that year our superstar Paul Evans came out at Tower Bridge. One of the reasons he gave was to save himself for the Belgrave 12 stage team, "and it's a good one." But the problem Paul had refused to clear and that was a 2 minute hole in a ship slated to win by 3 minutes… so, still a minute to spare!

My 60th at London got me the reserve spot, so up I ventured to the hallowed macadam of Sutton Park for the first time. What drama I witnessed.

We kicked off with real strength in the form of Kasse Tadesse, former World Junior Half marathon champion. Maybe KT could find us a top 3 position. 35th! Blimey, what a disaster, and not a great look to have him stopping to vomit at the side of the road 2k from home. But that long stage is a "giant-slayer" for sure. Were we goners? I wondered aloud. "It's a 4 hour race, Will, long way to go," Donnyboy Anderson reassured, and how right he was.

A violent game of 'Space Invaders' ensued with 18-year-old Richard Ward zapping everything in sight before he ran out of road proclaiming he'd enjoyed his tour so much he'd make the race a priority for the next 20 years. We got him for 14! Not bad…

took on long legs when they wanted short ones, late stages when they wanted early, to nurse the Belgrave team back into the top twenty. Best of the runs were probably Roger Alsop's dip under 15 minutes and Don Anderson's last leg effort to run some 15 seconds faster than last year to keep our position respectable.

1, Salford H 4:08:04; 2, Tipton H 4:10:32; 3, London Irish 4:11:39; 17, Belgrave H 4:28:57; 59 teams started, 56 finished.

1	P.Freary	(7)	26:39
2	R.Hayman	(10)	15:25
3	J.Estall	(28)	29:33
4	S.Clarke	(22)	15:10
5	P.Coughlan	(27)	29:51
6	R.Alsop	(22)	14:59
7	R.McHarg	(20)	28:41
8	K.Quinn	(17)	15:41
9	A.Stewart	(15)	29:23
10	B.Barton	(15)	16:04
11	P.Carstairs	(16)	30:11
12	D.Anderson	(17)	17:20

215

Into the top 20 now, and Paul Freary had good fun halving that. A spot nibbled for Rick Hayman as we started to wheel out the heavies. Triple Olympian Justin Chaston could "only" find 2 spots for his trouble, but up ahead the field had dramatically concertinaed. Gnasher made it to 4th and now what could Milesy do? *Whammooo*!! He came home in the lead, quite incredible, what a fightback.

Was our win now assured? Not quite… we had one superstar to come, one ace and three strong men. Maybe 75% wins from here? Roger hit his run as intended and International Spencer Barden pushed our lead up to around a minute. Weakest link Rob McHarg ran fine with a 15:14 but now it was *only* 15 seconds to protect for Al Stewart over Tipton's Stirk – a really classic 'club man' – who had the big advantage of chasing Al. But however hard Nigel tried he could barely dent the gap and after 20 minutes Al went into beast mode. The suffering etched on his face was memorable to see and by the end 20 more seconds were added onto the tab, to give Lee Hurst a 35 second gift.

Another like-for-like match up vs Danny Gibbons [3&5k pbs: LH 8:22 & 14:34; DG 8:24 & 14:31]. Ten'll-get-you-one for a Belgrave win now… We briefly describe this stunning denouement in the preface, but suffice it to say that Lee's mission was a torrid one, full of that inimitable sickening tension that only a big relay run can bring. There was maniacal Tipton support out on the course, whereas most of the Belgrave claret and gold had drifted back to the finish to see our colours burst through the winning tape. We heard signs that the lead was coming down, but never expected the runners to be nearly together at the final turn for the cruel minute's climb to the finish. Gibbons muscled his way past, but Lee refused to yield and edged ahead again approaching the final 100… but he had gone too soon and Gibbons had yet another gear, the rarely utilized gear 7… And Lee was defeated, by a run sent straight from the angels. Danny would never log another athletic performance on *Power of Ten*. What a note to bow out of athletics on – the ultimate "mic drop".

2	Belgrave Harriers		4:10:33
	K Tadesse	(35)	28:06
	R Ward	(20)	14:40
	P Freary	(10)	26:38
	R Hayman	(9)	15:17
	J Chaston	(7)	26:22
	K Nash	(4)	14:42
	M Miles	(1)	25:45
	R Alsop	(1)	15:06
	S Barden	(1)	26:20
	R McHare	(1)	15:14
	A Stewart	(1)	27:11
	L Hurst	(2)	15:12

There was real shock in our tent and a grown man or two cried. It had been a long, emotional day. But when the dust settled, we were the second best in the land and it was clear where we could find not just the missing 6 seconds, but *minutes*! This was a team with a long way to go, and six months later we'd win the 6 stage at the same venue in an equally thrilling race.

2002 Dreamteam

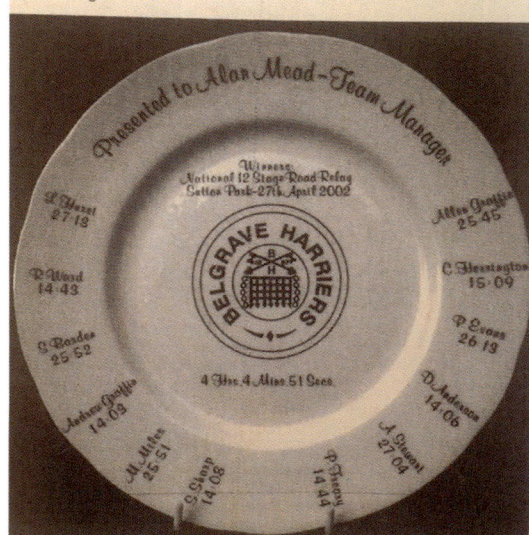

The superb commemorative plate later presented by Mavis and Eric Hall to the Team Manager.

The slight frustration with this race is that when it goes well, it seems to go perfectly and when things are off, everything seems to go wrong. Ie. our days are either a 10/10 or a 3! Some more 8's would have been nice, but that's the thing about 12 stage running: getting the team together is a logistical nightmare, and at least three of the runners will have a problem on the day, by law of averages. No such problems in 2002 though. A perfect day it may have been, but an exciting race it was not!

It's a sensational team, packed with stars and old favourites. The Graffin twins were rarely sighted by us, but when we were fortunate enough to get one of them

out, a team would be semi-transformed, and get them both – watch out!
The PA announced before Leg 9 that Belgrave were
"struggling so much for runners they were having to resort to
some guy called Paul Evans". A bit of Brummie humour for
you… But wheeling Paul to the start was preceded by pure
panic: during leg 8 the TM observed him strolling along with
an ice-cream without a care in the world and clearly not in
racing garb. Alan asked Paul in no uncertain terms what he
was doing and Paul replied that since it was only Stage 6 that
he had plenty of time. When disabused of this notion, ice-
cream was scattered, and the mad search for racing flats and
vest ensued. That's the thing with Big City Marathon
winners: you're in safe hands.

With Birchfield in silver 6:26 behind, one wondered just how
much we could dominate in the years to come… but it didn't
quite work out like that. This is sport,
and anything can happen.

1	**Belgrave Harriers**		**4:04.51**
	L Hurst	(17)	27:13
	R Ward	(9)	14:43
	S Barden	(1)	25:52
	A Graffin	(1)	14:03
	M Miles	(1)	25:51
	S Sharp	(1)	14:08
	A Graffin	(1)	25:45
	C Herrington	(1)	15:09
	P Evans	(1)	26:13
	D Anderson	(1)	14:06
	A Stewart	(1)	27:04
	P Freary	(1)	14:44

Suave defence

I narrowly found a way into the 2003
team post-"*marathon diabolique*" and it was
another peach of a side. Minus the
Graffins perhaps, and Paul was now
raging against the dying of the light, but
still a riotous ensemble.

Indeed, perhaps the only alarm bell of
the entire day was awaiting perhaps 40
seconds longer than we anticipated for
my leg to begin as Paul turned in his last
Bels performance. We may not have
gotten him out much down the 14 years,
but he
cast a
huge

*Two great stalwarts in "Gnasher", Kev Nash, and Sharp. Kevin shone like
a beacon for us over road and country for some 7 seasons, before
suddenly retiring, body and mind exhausted. The steeplechase can do
that to a man… SS still had another decade or so at the 'Sharp end' to
go. MS*

spell over our affairs in that time, and when I first started reading
about great runners in around 1996 when I started running
seriously in Boston, Paul's was one of the first names that really
struck me [well before I was a Belgravian].
And then, seven years later, I was 'taking a pass' from him, in
football parlance, in the lead in a National relay. Such are the
mysteries and magic of club running.

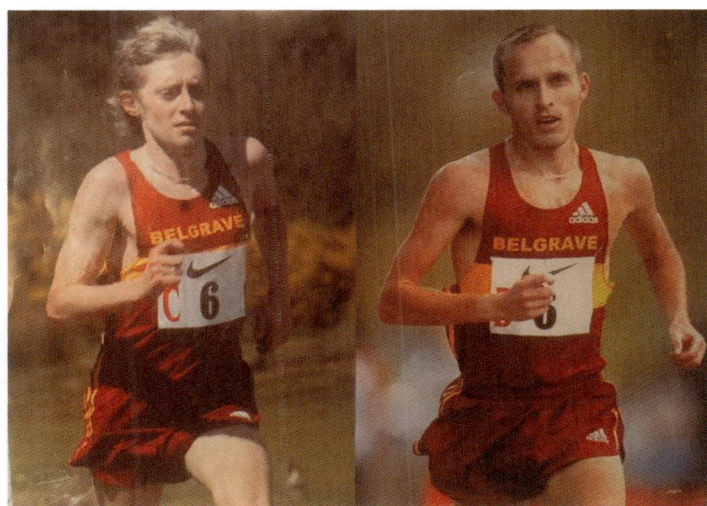

*Al Stewart was a vaguely terrifying relay
oppo for all and sundry, and it's
documented elsewhere how he
convinced one poor soul that retirement
was the only option, after a savage duel.
The amazing battle with Nigel Stirk in
2001, also lives long in the memory, and
here he found his best ever long stage
under nearly zero pressure and just the
bike for company. MS*

So just the lead bike for company then – an experience I'd repeat 10 years later on the same stage. It's a curious experience of fear, panic and glory. The lead bike is probably worth nearly 1% to the leader. All will play the game of trying to catch the bike. Not really possible, because "Father Christmas" as we knew him due to his majestic white beard, could just look into his mirror and rev it, but it's a great target to shoot for. I wonder if the races would be closer without it? Perhaps, but there's no denying the National leader gets a great tow. Better get into the lead then!

With young Jon Blackledge probably 'man of the match' here, our winning margin had come down to 2:07 though, so no room to relax for 2004.

1	Belgrave Harriers		4:08.55
	P Freary	(10)	26:47
	S Sharp	(2)	14:11
	K Nash	(2)	27:00
	D Anderson	(1)	14:17
	A Graffin	(1)	26:44
	J Blackledge	(1)	14:40
	M Dent	(1)	26:19
	R Ward	(1)	14:48
	P Evans	(1)	27:39
	W Cockerell	(1)	15:05
	A Stewart	(1)	26:53
	A Zawadski	(1)	14:32

The winning National 12 Stage team of 2003. Clockwise from top left: **Jon Blackledge, Al Stewart, Kevin Nash, Adam Zawadski, Marty Dent, Paul Freary, Paul Evans, David Anderson, Stephen Sharp, Richard Ward, Alan Mead (Team manager), Will Cockerell & Allen Graffin**. The team defeated silver medalists Tipton Harriers by 2:07, with Birchfield in bronze.

A dreadfully sad day

We arrived to the course in 2004 to find it in a state of shock. The young, charismatic, superstar Sam Haughian, one of the finest young runners Britain had ever produced, had died in a car crash in South Africa. It was a terrible blow. He had been a quasi-training pal at Kingston [usually in a different group of course], and the Bels had fought – and lost – plenty of splendid duels with him, over road and country. His free-flowing style was quite simply poetry in motion. His coach Alan Storey stood shell-shocked at the start… "I just can't believe it," he said, through watery eyes. Many from our squad had known Sam well, but not as well as poor Chris Thompson of AFD who'd been out with the camp in South Africa. How could Chris be expected to run now? Well he would – for Sam.

A pretty special trophy haul for the season; but Alan's pre-race pep talk was cautionary: "I've got a funny feeling about today..." L-R Tim Watson, Roger Alsop, SS, WC, RW, Spen, Paul, Charlie Herrington, Gnasher, Jon Blackledge, ARM

I'd had a good London and ripped out a pearl of a last 2.2k (7:40ish) one of the best 25 in the race to indicate I was 'good to go'. But Alan worried dearly about what Sutton Park does to marathon legs – or vice versa – and I missed the cut by the finest of margins. I took it well but it triggered one of Alan's great lines: "after Will had good naturedly questioned my parentage, we had our team…" But Sutton Park's long stage takes no prisoners and after a modest 30th from Adam Leane on 1, it was followed by a horror from Tim Watson on 3. But I can't really complain – Tim's a better athlete than me, he just got the dreaded "jelly legs" at the half-way turn, and wondered if he'd even finish. More Space Invaders from Wardy took us to 18th after four. We had serious quality to come, but this was going to be a slog.

Despite a couple of other chinks in our armour we edged up to 2nd, before Spencer Barden was thrown into the fray on 11. His opponent was the bereft Thommo. What a dramatic denouement. Never was more emotion seen on a relay run, as a red-eyed Chris, totally drained, just chanted to himself throughout: "Come on Sam, get me up this hill, get me through this." How do you chase a man you cannot see? Spen never saw his quarry and despite a fine run from Jon we ended up over a minute shy of our Hampshire friends. What a race, and all credit to them for catching us short.

2 Belgrave Harriers		4:11:47
A Leane	(30)	28:17
C Herrington	(25)	15:08
T Watson	(22)	28:43
R Ward	(18)	14:26
P Freary	(9)	26:54
S Sharp	(6)	14:14
M Miles	(3)	25:48
S Marwood	(2)	15:02
K Nash	(3)	27:12
R Alsop	(3)	15:15
S Barden	(2)	26:15
J Blackledge	(2)	14:33

A crown reclaimed, followed by three bonkers years

I was team skipper between 2004-08 and at my little tub-thumper at breakfast I mused to the gang whether any team in the world could handle us on this day. We knew Birchfield were throwing no fewer than three Kenyans at us, but *Danders* was nonplussed: "Forget the Kenyans; just leave them to me, Spen and Milesy!" How right he was. Kiharah, Taragon and Yacqub ran 78:18, whilst Anderson, Miles and Barden ran 78:29. Thank you, and good night.

1	Belgrave Harriers		4:08:36
W Cockerell	(23)	27:59	
R Ward	(22)	15:19	
E McRae	(14)	27:06	
T Watson	(6)	14:35	
P Wicks	(1)	26:51	
J Blackledge	(1)	14:38	
D Anerson	(1)	26:34	
K Nash	(1)	14:40	
M Miles	(1)	25:50	
S Sharp	(1)	14:24	
S Barden	(1)	26:05	
C Moss	(1)	14:35	

*Anderson [sic]

1:46 man Chris Moss cruised round in style

Our domination in this one, and the real secret to a great 12 stage team, was in our short stagers. It is of course where teams hide their weaker runners, whilst the Bels just kept throwing 14:30 boys at the problem. Savage.

St. George's Day I believe, or else the Bels have picked up a few admirers. Clockwise TL: Moss, Miles, Sharp, Ward, Anderson, Barden, Blackledge, Wicks, McRae, Watson, Nash, Cockerell

220

Nightmares are made of this

2006's team was also very strong, and I couldn't find a favoured long stage, but Alan gifted me the excitement of 2. I went for a nice warm-up and returned to the tent, having tweaked my training to handle a much shorter, faster race. Wardy greeted me with a hammer blow: "We've lost one…" Whuh?! And it was a big one too in Paul Freary, who was stood by the tent looking fit as a flea. Chaos followed, as Alan having argued desperately with the officials for 20 minutes was told: "if you run him, we will disqualify you." On this occasion, having the world's most organized TM counted against us. With two teams we were allowed to enter a whopping 72 names. And Alan, fearful of leaving someone on the cutting room floor, entered 72 names. Tragically though, Paul slipped through the cracks. Maybe if Alan had been a tad less thorough and only entered, say, 40, he would've noticed the flub.

It was a horrible thing to happen, and purely human error. Bizarrely Wardy wasn't in the programme either. The officials said: "sorry our mistake." Alan said: "you see? We all make mistakes", but they were unmoved.

Our trouble was only just starting. We had about 7 minutes to completely rejig our running order, find a new Leg 1, and raid the *baby Bees*. A recently breakfasted Tim Watson kindly stepped into open the batting, and I moved up to long, very worried I hadn't done the work. Pete Willis was nicked from the B's and we were back in play. We never stopped fighting all day, and it would have been a wonderful race with Paul in the team. But I believe a terrific Newham squad would have still nicked us. Mo Farah was "hot and ready" at the start of leg 9 and let out a huge cheer of "Oh Yes!" when he saw his man in 2nd hove into view at the end of leg 8. No prizes for guessing what happened next.

3 Belgrave Harriers A & B		
T. Watson	(12)	27:03
R Ward	(7)	14:56
S. Jones	(5)	27:09
P Willis	(8)	15:34
W. Cockerell	(9)	27:52
D. Gauson	(7)	14:49
S. Sharp	(7)	26:45
C. Moss	(6)	14:27
P. Wicks	(5)	26:35
K. Gauson	(4)	15:15
D. Anderson	(4)	27:24
J. Blackledge	(3)	14:20

As late as leg 11 and we still had a breath of hope, but Dave's calf twanged early, when we needed him to have the race of his life for a 25:50. Instead it was 27:24, which is remarkably courageous on 1.5 pins. Jon Blackledge ripped us into the medals on anchor with a superb 14:20, pushing Leeds into 4th, whilst all credit to Sale who were 30 secs ahead in 2nd & 1:30 off NEB.

More fumbling in the field

A minor deja-vu occurred in 2007 when we lost another ace on the morning, as Mark Miles awoke with a looming cold, and so he wished to save himself for London, where he would have helped us to Gold – if only he'd worn his club vest! I was on the train to spectate as reserve, when my phone pinged with the news: "Leg 6"… the previous night's spicy 8-miler looking a tad ill-advised. But I had worked hard on it, in glorious weather, weaving throught the crowds of Hammersmith pub-goers spilling out along the river, in something of a blue funk at not being in the team. A reserve's job is a thankless one.

Young Jonny Blackledge, or an illegal, underage imposter. The lens of Steve Wicks saves the day

We then had Alan accused very publicly in front of the officials of blatant cheating by a rival TM; of running an underage, ineligible athlete at the Southern 12. ARM was incredulous, but it was further explained that the athlete claiming to be Leg 6, Jon Blackledge, was not him. The proposition was doubly absurd as who on earth would ever sub-out such a creature? Anyway, fortunately our online report of the race carried the above image of Jon, where for once his youthful look and ethereal beauty had counted against him.

If that wasn't enough, more madness occurred on 5, when Sharpy's guts failed him. A dreadful feeling on a training run, but a nightmare in the National 12 stage. Modesty was preserved, but nearly a minute lost. "I tell ya' if it wasn't a relay, I'd've come out," he gasped after.

Leeds were perfect on this day, and after a brutal duel between two old warhorses Mark Hudspith and Paul Freary on 11, we had to let Morpeth go, but looked to have the bronze sorted. Wardy cantered off, but by the half was grimacing… [I know, Rich always grimaces, but this was notably clenched…] and a minute behind, Newham's Mark Warmby was going like the clappers. Rich still had this, but he couldn't relax. Final score: MW 14:31; RW 15:41. Ouch. But Rich had it under control (he'll tell you), and yet more Sutton Park bling was ours with just 11 ticks to spare. Phew!

3 Belgrave Harriers

Malachi Byansi	(28)	27:51
P Buckley	(20)	15:23
Neil Speaight	(14)	27:20
Shugri Omar	(4)	14:54
Stephen Sharp	(11)	27:17
Will Cockerell	(12)	15:34
Phil Wicks	(8)	26:40
J Blackledge	(6)	14:37
Simon Jones	(4)	27:06
Mark Pollard	(3)	14:36
Paul Freary	(3)	27:44
Richard Ward	(3)	15:41

The 2007 bronze medallists. Some luminaries here and no fewer than eight club presidents. Back row, l-r: Gerry North, Gordon Biscoe, Bill Laws, Brian Pritchard, Tom Osment, Maureen Pritchard, Zara Chidoub, Mark Pollard, Jon, Janet & Mike Blackledge, Neil Speaight, ARM, Padraic Buckley, Paul Freary, Eric Hall, Pete Willis, Hazel Mead. Front row: Mavis Hall, Charlie Jones, Richard Ward, Simon Jones, Mal Byansi, Will Cockerell, Pat Mead & Phil Wicks.

Sp8y Magic

The following year, 2008, was the only time Alan and I fell out in 16 years of him managing me. It came down to fitting four of Cockerell, Freary, Stewart and Ward into three. It's not an easy choice, but Al hadn't raced for us for years, Rich was off his A game, and I'd nabbed Paul at the Southern. I thought I was safe. But the days went by and I started to get really worried. Finally the call came:

"Will, everyone wants you in the team... but they're not sure you should be..." It was a crusher, but there are so many close calls.

I had the idea of drawing lots as it really was so close, and it is rather personal to the discarded athlete, especially one who has done all the season's races. Paul wrote back though: "no thanks, I'd rather be picked on merit." With my victory at the Southern, I was in then, yes?! Haha, Paul is quality, and remember, he'd had an awful misfortune of his own, two years earlier.

To the race, and Sharpy kicked off with a brilliant 3rd, whilst Wardy came back apologizing in 11th. For sure he is better chasing than being chased. And after that a long, difficult day in which we struggled to make an impact. Paul and Al were solid, and if not obvious choices over me, can't be deemed blunders. The day's great drama though was left to Neil Speaight who set off over a minute back from Andy Robinson of NEB on anchor. AR turned in a sound 15:30, whilst Neil found a quite stunning 14:09 to nick us a narrow bronze for the 3rd year in a row. The medal streak continued.

```
3  Belgrave Harriers

   Stephen Sharp     (3)  26:26
   Richard Ward     (11)  15:38
   Paul Freary      (11)  28:00
   Nick Goolab      (10)  14:37
   A Stewart        (11)  28:06
   Shaun Moralee     (8)  14:56
   James Kelly       (9)  27:31
   J Blackledge      (5)  14:18
   Mark Pollard      (5)  27:24
   Stephen Davies    (5)  14:18
   Simon Jones       (4)  26:35
   Neil Speaight     (3)  14:09
```

Dream Team – Part Three

Alan announced the phenomenal 2009 team nearly a fortnight out with me in my somewhat over-familiar reserve spot. But given the way runners tend to fall, I was fairly sure I'd sneak in somehow. Not to be! Everyone held rock solid for another huge win. The frustration is how little went our way in the three years preceding, or the three after. So the marks out of 10 for those seven years are roughly 5 5 5 10 5 5 5. What about a few 8s or 9s?! But that's not the way the 12 Stage rolls.

```
1  Belgrave Harriers          'A'  4:04:43

   James Kelly      (18)  27:15
   Steve Davies     (11)  14:41
   Mark Miles        (1)  25:49
   Stephen Sharp     (1)  14:58
   Simon Jones       (1)  26:27
   Nick Goolab       (1)  14:45
   R Dessaix-Chin    (1)  26:21
   Mark Pollard      (1)  14:45
   Phil Wicks        (1)  25:13
   Neil Speaight     (1)  14:33
   Martin Dent       (1)  25:42
   Daniel Mulhare    (1)  14:14
```

The day was most notable [a riotous Miles aside], for Phil's stunning run. The fastest SP long stage for some 30 years and comfortably quicker than what Mo Farah managed in '06. And the team itself pipped that gem from 2002 by 8 seconds.

2009s untouchable body of men. Clockwise top L [names in results]: MP SJ JK NS NG MD RDC DM PW SS MM SD. ARM

Death by Eyjafjallajökull

When the volcanic ash descended and turned air traffic control into a nightmare, we doubled down on our Sharp/Goolab sagas. The little treasures had booked the wrong dates for their warm weather training and there was no way we'd be going into SP without them, so at some grim expense we changed their flights, only for Eyjafjallajökull to strike, leaving them stranded! What a huge nuisance and some 3:30 added to our bill. With luck not running our way elsewhere either, our damage limitation topped out at 8th.

2011 - What FUN!

More of the same in 2011 with runner after runner hitting trouble, but goodness we had fun with it. After a somewhat circumspect Goolab left the course in a huff after leg on one, we front-loaded the living daylights out of the race to creep to 4th after 2 courtesy of a Davies blinder, and then PO ripped us to the top with a cracking run, and Speaight, Mulhare, Anderson and Kelly preserved that lead for a lovely little 2 hours at the top. But our problems ran oh so deep. We had more trouble with Sharpy as sick as a dog and being cared to by nurse Maria in the tent. Malachi set off in the lead on 8 and afterward uttered this brilliant line: "it was the greatest feeling of my running career... and also one of the worst!" Our lads had run their socks off but try as they might, the field hovered like vultures for the kill – six of them. Poor old Mal dropped to 7th.

Wardy then gamely took on a long stage [he did a half-marathon in 70, seven years earlier, don't you know?], whilst Mike, myself and Steve kept us in the top 10. It was a wild ride.

And a stunning chase in '12

I then came down with a nasty cold in 2012, which was a terrible feeling to let the side down and we drafted in Martin Holm at a very late hour for cover. It was a really tremendous chase, as went went from 50th to 6th. Epic stuff, and everyone enjoyed themselves. It was a farewell to Jon Blackledge, one of the finest relay runners in our history, and I don't think my trouble actually cost us a spot, and certainly not a medal.

2013

We won't say much about the actual racing of 2013, because our result has been withdrawn from the history books. Those who were there will recall a heart-stopping Belgrave win with myself, JK and Sp8y all having monster duels on legs 10-12 for a 10-second or so win, but some months later Alberto Lozano de Pedro tested positive for EPO in Spain. The moment we heard about this we contacted the organizers to withdraw us from the race. You won't find a straighter arrow than James Kelly who had befriended the Lozano brothers as training partners in Madrid. Our inclusion of one here was within the rules, but we caught some flak for it, from one rival TM in particular. I reminded him that he in turn had medalled with a top South African international of late. "Yes, but he was dating one of our girls," came the reply... I think if we were going to say Internationals were only kosher if they were having a romance with members of women's teams, things would become

8	Belgrave Harriers		
William Cockerel	(34)	28:08
Hassan Raidi	(31)	15:29
David Anderson	(21)	27:36
Richard Ward	(21)	16:12
James Kelly	(21)	28:14
Simon Jones	(20)	15:24
Paskar Owor	(16)	27:28
Mark Miles	(14)	14:37
Daniel Mulhare	(9)	26:14
Mark Pollard	(9)	15:18
Philip Wicks	(8)	26:54
Neil Speaight	(8)	15:09

10	Belgrave Harriers		
Nicholas Goolab	(15)	27:06
Steve Davies	(4)	14:23
Paskar Owor	(1)	26:34
Neil Speaight	(1)	15:09
Daniel Mulhare	(1)	26:42
David Anderson	(1)	15:12
James Kelly	(1)	27:33
Malachi Byansi	(7)	16:25
Richard Ward	(9)	28:44
Michael Trees	(10)	16:03
William Cockerel	(10)	28:35
Stephen Sharp	(10)	15:15

6	Belgrave Harriers		
Martin Holm	(50)	29:22
Stephen Sharp	(34)	14:43
Andrew Connick	(32)	28:18
Nicholas Goolab	(22)	14:47
James Kelly	(20)	27:23
J Blackledge	(20)	16:04
R Dessaix-Chin	(16)	27:21
Neil Speaight	(13)	15:29
Michael Mulhare	(10)	26:55
Richard Ward	(9)	15:30
Paskar Owor	(7)	26:42
Stephen Davies	(6)	14:27

unthinkably convoluted. The rules of residency for foreigners have since been amended, and of course we stick to them closely.

Anyway, it was of course a sad and jarring incident, but on the whole, the community were of the opinion that "accident's happen," and appreciated how quick we were to hold up our hands to an innocent error. Terrible things happen to great sports clubs, and this was a hefty bump in the road. It cost us the Southern win too which was run in concert [congrats to Bedford for the Southern – and of course Leeds for the National); and also the previous winter's XC relay in Mansfield. Doh! Three Championships gone in the blink of an eye, but we wouldn't have won any without Lozano anyway.

Gaffer's farewell

I have been enormously fortunate with sickness and injury in my 24 seasons with the Bels, but just as in 2012, I fell sick the night before, slated for leg 1 again, this time with a vomiting issue. Can one run with such a thing? Up to a point. Third gear is fine, but anymore and all hell breaks loose. Alan didn't want to upset the lads in their order preps, and I thought maybe my trouble would only cost a minute or so, but it was more like three. The whole thing was a harrowing and very embarrassing experience, but, well, I came, I saw, I beat Wolverhampton. The team was creaking at the seams in a big way anyhow [more reason for ARM to stick to his guns], and maybe my trouble only cost us a pip. 19th it was, with Alan writing: "us earning the right to win."

19	Belgrave Harriers		
William Cockerel	(61)	30:14
Richard Ward	(58)	14:33
James Kelly	(50)	26:07
Stephen Sharp	(46)	13:56
Paskar Owor	(33)	25:26
Nick Bundle	(32)	14:15
Craig Ruddy	(23)	25:19
Royston Maddams	(22)	14:07
Mark Pollard	(22)	27:19
Fraser Logan	(23)	14:50
Stephen Trainer	(20)	26:32
Michael Trees	(19)	14:15

**Note the course was tweaked here for around a 2 minute reduction of both loops.

2015-2019 -- Hanging tough

My years as TM were up and down. Two excellent performances for 10th and 8th and twice we didn't start. It really is such a fiddly fish to fry, but it was great fun seeing Dan Mulhare - and Sharpy in a nostalgic run – taking us briefly into the medals in 2015, whilst Gus Upton and Paskar were exceptional too.

10	Belgrave Harriers		
Kristopher Gauso	(22)	28:21
A Jaksevicius	(20)	16:28
Paskar Owor	(6)	27:25
Gus Upton	(4)	16:10
Craig Ruddy	(4)	27:42
Nick Bundle	(5)	16:31
Daniel Mulhare	(3)	27:32
Stephen Sharp	(3)	16:42
Taras Telkovsky	(6)	29:16
Mark Pollard	(6)	16:31
Alexander Miller	(8)	29:52
William Cockerel	(10)	17:27

Into the bling! Somewhat against expectations, Dan Mulhare ripped us into the medals in 2015, which SS then held. Four engine-roomers then battled to staunch the flow. LC

More sellotape! More!

After a blob in '16, the 2017 team was one of the bravest Bels squads ever. The squad existed only just beyond the imagination, but Bill Laws and Chas urged me to "hang in there." The lads were patched up with stickytape for sure: Andrius was six days off a marathon, JK just off the 'red eye', Phil had a calf ready to explode at any moment, and on and on it went. We were treated to the great sight of Dan Wallis debuting for us, in what was an extremely competitive race.

A brilliant club debut from Dan Wallis [to tie with Wicksy], hauled us into 7th on a fairly brutal Leg 11 with many big guns out to play

A squad that ran to survive... Problems ran right through the team, so 8th was a fine return in 2017. Clockwise TL: Alan Black, Simon Haileselase, CD, Nick Bundle, Ed Auden, Matt Welsh, Arne Dumez, Dan Wallis, James Kelly, author, PO, Bill Laws

8 Belgrave Harriers

Paskar Owor	(12)	26:57
Matthew Welsh	(21)	16:45
A Jaksevicius	(18)	28:00
Gus Upton	(18)	16:21
James Kelly	(20)	28:38
Arne Dumez	(19)	17:09
Philip Wicks	(16)	26:25
Alexander Miller	(16)	16:48
Craig Ruddy	(12)	27:25
Edward Auden	(11)	16:21
Daniel Wallis	(7)	26:25
Nick Bundle	(8)	16:43

Some unlikely but welcome phizogs

In 2018 we were rebuilding as I'd gone down in flames at committee and handed over the reigns to a care-taking Matt Welsh, where the team placed a merry 25th. With Mr Wallis again to the fore, some unlikelier lads in Scott Mills and Will Johnson kept us going, while Steve Gardner turned some heads early doors. Messrs Fyfe and Welsh tied on a tangy 28:35. We were gutted to lose Andy the following year, an outstanding talent with a 3:53, 8:13 and 14:16 range. We're still in touch and wish him nothing but the best.

In their to-and-fro battle of the silver foxes, Patrick took out Will by just 2 secs

25 Belgrave Harriers

Paskar Owor	(9)	26:42
Steve Gardner	(18)	17:05
Matthew Welsh	(23)	28:35
Gus Upton	(23)	16:48
Nick Bundle	(25)	29:01
William Cockerel	(30)	17:59
Daniel Wallis	(21)	26:35
Patrick Mcdougal	(23)	17:57
Andrew Fyfe	(22)	28:35
Scott Mills	(23)	19:05
Ed Auden	(24)	29:36
William Johnson	(25)	18:27

No amount of engine roomers was going to make a trip to the great race worthwhile in 2019 though, and little did we dream it'd then be lost to the world for three years.

2022 Back with a fun-filled, low-key romp

Goodness what hits we took with Covid still hovering in the air. I reckon I was 45th reserve for this one, but still I got the nod on the Friday evening. The atmosphere amongst the lads though was still cracking. Yes, we had the top 12 in mind a month earlier (or top 8?), but for now it was, 'be happy to be there, and blood some new lads' into the exceptionally competitive world of club distance running.

Any team with Nickyboy [+15 from 18th to 3rd, with the day's quickest] is worth the trip to the midlands alone [that's an ARM line referring to another doyen – Mark Miles – in 1999, when we didn't even finish]; and we loved the sass and elan of the likes of Sam up front with an imperious run. Speedster

A future TM in waiting. Steve Gardner ran well after long-term injury

Tommy [with a hacking cough] somehow tied with Jonny and got within 5 ticks of Conall, sluggers all. Arne had a major uptick on his MK run, and his scorecard decline is way harsh, whilst pick of the shorties was Ewan's run, who also got "buried alive" on the scoresheet.

26 Belgrave Harriers

S Gebreselassie	(6)	26:18
Ewan Somerville	(18)	16:30
Nick Goolab	(3)	25:23
Rob Kelly	(7)	16:56
Arne Dumez	(15)	28:40
Ross Christie	(18)	17:21
Conall Mcnally	(20)	29:04
Steve Gardner	(20)	16:58
Jonny Neville	(22)	29:09
Valentin Rigori	(22)	18:19
Tommy Taylor	(23)	29:09
William Cockerel	(26)	18:49

This field is *tough*. I would have loved to 'hang on in there' with a peaceful end to the festivities, but three illustrious clubs in Tipton, Liverpool and Herne Hill were vultures all. One thing I think we're all agreed on though: it was an intriguing day, we fought like tigers, and a return to top 10 land at the glorious National is certainly within our remit. But perhaps don't go down to the 57th best runner in the club next time.

New man Ross Christie showed plenty of promise albeit carrying the air of a man on the run from the law. LC

THE NATIONAL 6 STAGE - WOMEN

Some super returns

Our ladies have had a really fine go at the big season show-stopper and have averaged 12.3 in their 13 finishes. It's a tough old race – much tougher than the autumn event as those two extra bodies are so hard to find. The more required, the more the depth of a club is examined, and it is depth where the true mark of quality in a club lies.

Also, since 2015 the women have had to find two long stagers. I am responsible for that! I campaigned with the ERRA for a year as I thought it was old-fashioned and disingenuous to not entrust a couple of girls with the longer distance. I also did it for selfish reasons as I had so many endurance junkies under my command, in particular Tish Jones, who I didn't feel was given sufficient "bang for her buck" during her brave run in 2014. The same went for one of her key opponents in Leeds' Susan Partridge.

Storey Time

When I excitedly blabbered to legendary coach Alan Storey in 2015 that the women going long was my idea, he snarled back, "*yooouuuuu twat*!" It's a typical AS response, and I am very fond of him, curmudgeon that he is… We go way back and his imprint on British endurance stretches over 50 years and AW were running features on him as early as 1982. But his somewhat capricious personality means he's been out of the limelight for a good many years now, although continues to do great work "on the lowdown."

My first run-in with him was most jarring. In 2000 I didn't really understand how the Championship race at the London Marathon worked so entered the main field instead. When illuminated, I called the marathon office and got Alan, explaining my problem. I was in line for 2:30ish, I didn't comprehend that a different form was required, so could he kindly switch me over? He pointblank refused. I tried buttering him up and told him a little about myself, and 40 minutes later we were firm friends as we had an exhaustive chat about the history of the marathon. Finally, I said, "Well Alan, I must let you go, this has been delightful, so if you could kindly flip me across…"

"Sorry, unable," came the reply.

I wrote him a long, sob story of a letter. No reply… so I called a month later to see if he'd gotten it. "Yes, thank you, but I can't switch you." I asked why, and he said, if he had to switch every 2:30 marathoner that entered the main instead of the championship, it could get very tiresome… I asked how many made this mistake each year. He replied I was the only one so far, but he was not for turning. I was really upset and couldn't believe how harsh he'd been.

A month later the phone went at work: "Hi, this is the marathon office. Did you know that given your best time and predicted time, you could be in the Championship race and not the Main race? You get to start right at the front, you get your own tented village and enough toilets to run a small town…" Yes, I replied dejected, "but the office won't let me switch".

"Oh! I can do that for you," said the voice… "I just have to take the tick out of this box… and put it in this box… done!" I hung up the phone, dumbfounded.

Alan Storey puts the author and Sonia O'Sullivan through their paces. Saltire Andy Weir is in the background. RO'D

Two years later I joined Alan's legendary training group in Kingston and we became good pals in a very *Storeyesque* way. Certainly, I never got a reply to an email or text from him and his reason for the texts is that his inbox was full and he could no longer receive texts. "Oh! You can delete old ones Alan, to make room!"

"But I don't *want* to delete any texts! I like them just the way they are!"

Beneath that prickly veneer though is of course a superb session-setter and brilliant coach; and his speech to Sonia O'Sullivan before her Olympic silver in 2000 was hauntingly word perfect. He doesn't mince his words, as with the time I ran a 5:02 opening mile with Liz Yelling at the Bristol Half. "Too *f***ing* quick, Liz!" he bellowed from the crowd, in fury at his charge.

So, what of the women going long, then? And was Storey correct to chide me so sharply? No. On the whole it has clearly been a great success. I've scoped the women at the long stage at SP ever since and quite frankly I see little or no difference in their form on the long or short stage. They cope with either absolutely fine. And for Belgrave there's no question that the extra distance has been a boon to us. For the five years before the switch we averaged 14.2 and for the 5 after 9.75.

I do get the occasional utterance of: "I wish you hadn't done that, Will," from our gang, and I know it's dumped Chas into a quagmire or two over the years, when he's found himself short of at least one 'longey'; but on the whole it's been well in our favour, it's the same for everyone, and look at all the controversy with the women going longer in Cross-country! Which, perhaps perversely, I don't agree with: 8k of XC is a more than ample test of endurance; and the days would be so much longer for the already freezing and aging officials, and only 50% of women run than men, at lesser speeds due to their gender and a smaller talent pool, so the Southern and National would take some ladies in excess of 2 hours 15 mins. It's quite simply not palatable.

"Brilliantly bonkers!" Is how I described the great Emelia Gorecka in this historic image which captures the first ever long stage for women at the road relays. "I love bonkers!" she replied. EG treated the challenge like a fox let loose in a chicken hutch, which she came to regret about 10 minutes later, but for sure she set the tone – and the ladies have never looked back

Magnificent Start

But let's start at the top in 2002 and it really is the top, because with "beginner's luck" our first foray to this one saw a superb 5th.

TM Catherine Eastham loved to hit her opponents "right between the eyes", which with weak teams is the traditional way to go. Here however, Birhan would have been much better used elsewhere as giving your superstar the easiest leg means that

5	Belgrave Harriers		1:45.39
	B Dagne	(1)	16:19
	T Sturton	(10)	18:54
	E Fogg	(11)	18:24
	M Sharp	(6)	17:07
	J Clark	(4)	17:17
	A Hegvold	(5)	17:38

weaker runners have much harder legs, and poor old Tania here was placed in the proverbial tumble drier which must have been pretty rough. But thereafter things settled down and it was a terrific effort from all the team to reach such lofty heights and improving from an impeccable 7th at the previous Autumn's 4 stage. Perhaps a simple switch of Maria and Birhan would have been the order to go with here... but maybe Maria didn't fancy it. Or maybe Juliette. The key thing though with a super team like this is to get your runners in the right position and ensure that people are always chasing, and not being chased.

More fine fare followed in 2003 and this time Maz *did* open the batting to fine effect [9th] and the team settled on 11th before a blob in '04 and reasonable 21st in '05, altho Catherine didn't like having to step out of her tracksuit for both those years and wished to be excused for 'player-manager' duties. Well, she had to deepen her roster then... This she managed for a gnarly 17th next term with a notable charge from Tilly at the death; and then back up to 10th in 2007. A fine effort indeed, but more naughtiness with Birhan up top... By this time Catherine Bryson was in her halcyon years, a tremendous "contact" runner and was a better candidate, or else the redoubtable Vicky Clarke.

The Belles then disappeared from this for three years as CE slowly wound down her years at the helm. I took over the road-side of things in the autumn of '09, but by the spring it was still a group desperately light on numbers. Smurph and Sammi were not to be denied though, and I had to scrape them off the course kicking and screaming in a smooth 15th after two, but alas no back-up.

The Big Rebuild

A very hard fought 24th followed, well done, troopers all – sometimes you have to rebuild the hard way; and we lit the touchpaper again with 11th in 2012. It was a seamless progression of a run as we went 26-24-21-15-13-11. Oh, now that's lovely! Every runner deserves a call-out here from Sarah's tidy start, to the rarely sighted but evergreen Mary Grace Spalton, to a nostalgic farewell run from Birhan, to Sammi right at the top of her game, and the same could be said for the "Maycock Massive" at the end of a brilliant first season, and culminating with what I believe to be the best run of Lou's Belgrave career.

I think the team was even stronger in 2013, but the result slipped a tad to 13th. I don't know what it was but while everyone was perfect in 2012, here it took us an awful long while to "hit our straps". But finally they did with Tish roaring from 27th to 14th on four. Sammi then claimed another place before Fee held the ship the steady. Too steady as it turned out as this doubled up as the Southern, and the result there was a bit of a heartbreaker as medals were just out of reach, but see that chapter for its report.

An even stronger team arrived in 2014, with an up and coming Mel Wilkins shoring us up, although she'll be the first to admit that the cruel Sutton Park hills crucified her at this one and had to bow to Jojo Rhodes, with Nelle Quispel just a second further back. I held Tish back until leg 5, and her smash and grab was an even more riotous 18th to 9th, which we preserved. But still I didn't think the Jones girl was being given a broad enough canvas on which to display her art.

Year	Team	Name (team pos.)	Time										
2003	11	M Sharp [9]	17:01	L Cooper [17]	19:49	H Alsop [17]	19:19	A Walker [14]	19:26	H Smethurst [11]	19:09	J Clark [11]	19:28
2004	-	R Powell [29]	18:54	J Clark [21]	17:44	H Alsop [19]	19:12	L Cooper [20]	19:21	C Eastham [21]	21:41		
2005	21	S Murphy [36]	18:35	B Dagne [15]	16:44	M Heaton [14]	17:59	H Smethurst [13]	18:51	L Cooper [15]	19:50	C Eastham [21]	21:13
2006	17	J Clark [28]	18:03	H Smethurst [28]	19:28	C Bryson [24]	18:27	V Edwards [24]	19:57	L Cooper [22]	19:09	M Heaton [17]	18:55
2007	10	B Dagne [3]	16:23	V Clarke [3]	17:47	S Gailey [9]	19:04	M Heaton [10]	18:18	J Clark [10]	18:27	C Bryson [10]	17:16
2010	-	S Murphy [18]	17:43	S Amend [15]	17:55								
2011	24	L Vseteckova [16]	17:30	A Linford [29]	20:04	L Blizzard [27]	18:55	V Goodwin [25]	19:45	M Heaton [22]	19:38	R Trees [25]	22:29
2012	11	S Murphy [26]	18:04	MG Spalton [24]	18:44	B Dagne [21]	19:15	S Amend [15]	17:18	F Maycock [13]	18:29	L Blizzard [11]	17:35
2013	13	J Rhodes [29]	18:28	R O'Brien [30]	18:56	L Blizzard [27]	19:03	T Jones [14]	16:51	S Amend [13]	17:44	F Maycock [13]	18:30
2014	9	Z Doyle [24]	15:48	S Murphy [26]	16:34	J Rhodes [21]	16:14	M Wilkins [18]	16:18	T Jones [9]	14:39	N Quispel [9]	16:19
2015	8	S Amend [12]	32:54	S Carter [9]	33:10	M Wilkins [7]	17:58	Z Doyle [7]	19:33	J Rhodes [8]	19:08	R O'Brien [8]	19:57
2016	8	S Carter [18]	32:05	S Haileselase [12]	19:02	Z Doyle [16]	20:25	S Amend [12]	31:59	Z Vail Smith [9]	18:26	J Rhodes [8]	19:30
2017	15	S Amend [18]	32:40	S Underhill [18]	20:03	S Haileselase [17]	20:09	J Rhodes [18]	35:41	L Goldie-Scot [17]	20:27	Z Doyle [15]	18:47
2018	-	S Amend [25]	33:25	S Haileselase [17]	17:55	G Fenn [13]	18:49	M Hall [16]	35:04	L Goldie-Scot [15]	21:07		
2019	8	T Jones [5]	29:05	A Reed [7]	19:53	K Mackenzie [8]	20:06	G Fenn [9]	32:10	J Reed [8]	20:25	R Brown [8]	19:26

2014 course shortened for the year, and the short-stage thereafter runs around a minute longer

She was in 2015 though, with the Long stages in! But Tish was now injured… oh the best laid plans. But look at us go, as a weaker team on paper bumped up their game. The organizers bizarrely made the two long legs go Stage one and two, which is *so* not the way to go and it triggered huge gaps; but Sammi and Soph made hay and we found ourselves in the lofty heights of 9th, which Mel, ZLD [Zoe Doyle], JJR and RO'B improved by a spot. Poor old Rose had a very isolated run on anchor, and could be forgiven for a time a tad beneath her as she never saw a soul all day. But little did she know is that up ahead Bedford had completely imploded, and instead of running 18 mins as expected, their athlete found a 22. Had Rose known of this, the 7 seconds between us and one of our dearest foes could have been dealt with, but we all learnt of the *snafu* too late.

A pioneering run, as Sam Amend becomes the first Belle to ever do a long stage in British relay running history. No-one better for the job of course! LC

Chas to the Fore

The Dickinson era began in 2016 and he held us steady as a rock. Soph and Sam were again entrusted to the long grind and both responded wonderfully, with times just 6 ticks apart. It was yet another 'mini dreamteam', and with Saron chasing brilliantly, a slightly off-colour Zoe Doyle leaked a few, but it was a 16-12-9-8 finish, with the highlight being Zoe Vail Smith's wonderful run on 5 to move us from 12th to 9th.

Only minor disruption followed in 2017 for 15th, and it was a huge ask to throw a long leg at Jojo, but there was the kink in our ruse! Everyone's got a plan until they get punched in the mouth. But looking at the others, Jojo was the athlete for the occasion with Saron unfit and ZLD becoming more of an 800 metre runner by the day.

2018 – disaster! A tremendous team lost Sophie Harris on the day – during the race in fact - to nausea the night before, and our promised top 8 became a dnf. After expert runs from Saron and Georgie Fenn, Mhairi Hall bravely stepped in for a torrid go at the long, to keep us in the race and to give SGH more time, but it wasn't to be. Years later Sophie wrote to club to apologize for not overriding the directive of her coach and "having a crack".

2019 and the ship was superbly righted. It was a big surprise and hugely welcome to slot Tish back into the team. I think her on 4 and Georgie Fenn on 1 would have been a better look as Tish was in 2:31 marathon shape and leg 4 is so isolated. But it may well be that as it was her first relay for years, and she had light mileage after years of injury trouble, that Tish was very low on confidence and desperate for a normal race. The gaffer Charlie explains: "a difficult one when you have one elite athlete and the rest good club level as in this case. I was once never forgiven for putting an elite last, and you yourself once led off with a lesser light who was not only extremely nervous but got swamped and ran a disappointing time. Sometimes we get it right!"

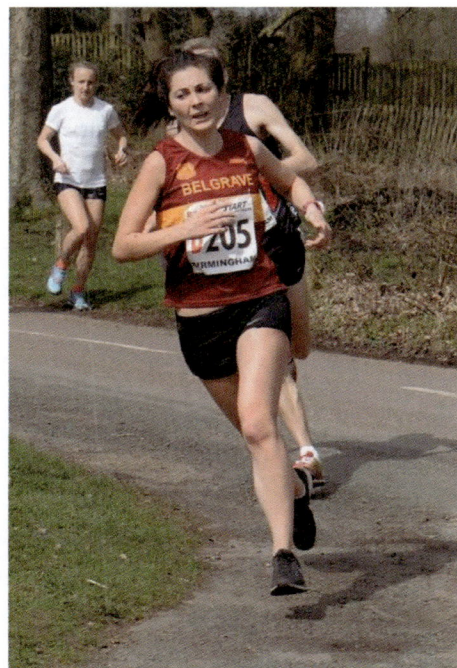

Mhairi bravely steps up to long in 2018 to 'keep the kettle boiling'

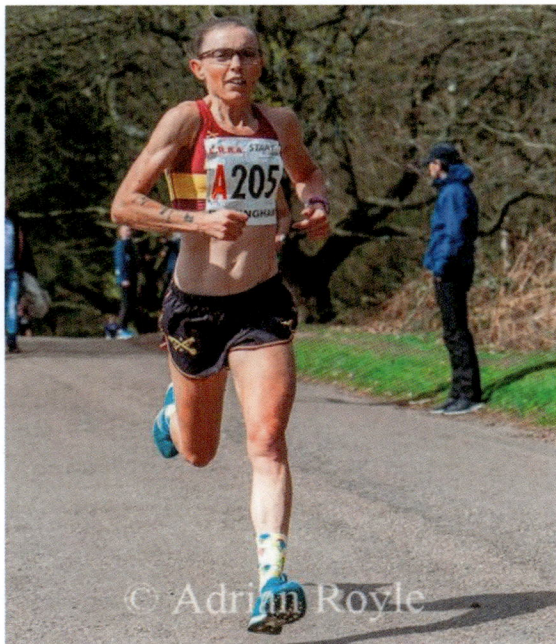

It was wonderful to welcome Tish back into the side, after some 5 years away. World Championship marathon qualification incoming! AR

It meant some serious front-loading, but the evergreen and hugely talented Reed sisters held steady in the turbulence all around, Georgie leaked just a single spot on long, and Kerimac and Rachel B held things very steady. A fine effort indeed and yet another top 8, which of course is an important position, as it signifies a "quarter-final" spot were it a tournament.

We then had a post-Covid *season mirabilis* in 2021-22, but the trouble with flying too close to the sun, as Icarus will tell you, is that your wings melt. The Belles crashed into the sea, bless them, for a DNS, but nothing can take away from the preceding eight months of that term, and their Sutton Park adventures will return.

LONDON MARATHON - WOMEN

Incredible success rate

The Belles have been magnificent at the marathon – it has probably been their best event, with 3 National titles, four bronzes and a silver – superb stuff.

We started as we meant to go on with Helen Maskrey (2:56), Rachel Weston (2:57) & Nikki Haines 2:58 packing very snugly to be the only club to find all runners sub 3 for bronze.

In 2002, more bronze as an electrifying run from Juliette Clark in 26th (2:52), was well backed up by Tilly Heaton (3:05) and Lou Cooper (3:06).

And two years later, a fantastic Gold! With Tilly improving by a couple of minutes and Lou going thru' the roof with a 2:54, and was left to Birhan Dagne to rip out a superb 2:34 in 11th, and give us the win by "only" 6 minutes. Quite a fragile margin over Bristol considering the quality of our team.

We appeared to be in an on-off cycle now (although 2005 was still an excellent showing in 4th), with medals returning in '06. I was busy at the team hotel in the days before promoting my book on great marathon races, which included inscribing one to Deena Kastor, which read: "To Deena, 2:19:37 here we come…" The next day at the post-race party DK accosted me on the dancefloor to say:

"I beat your prediction by 1 second, but next time, could you write something a little faster?"

Nikki Neal had a fabulous run in 2:54 and questions were raised as to whether she broke the Channel Islands record, whilst Lou reported: "It was all going to plan early on. I think I realised that my 6:40-something miles were creeping closer to 7-somethings, and then I was trying desperately hard to get there [3 hours], but think I hit the wall with a mile to go – nightmare!!" She'd miss the barrier by 55 secs. But Lou taps more into the magic of the marathon:

"It's been a range of emotions since finishing, sometimes pleased, but more often than not, reflecting over and over again on what I could have done better to get me under 3 hours. Having done my first London marathon aged 18, and run everyone since (number 13 yesterday!), I think I was smiling because I just love the race so much!!! Couldn't believe how much support for Belgrave there was on route, and want to thank everyone who gave me a shout!!"

To this day 16 long years later, Lou may be found prowling the course with a streak of some 25 [now in Warrington colours]…

Sandwiched in between Nikki and Lou was Vicki Clarke with 2:57. Birhan Dagne was off colour in 2:49, but didn't wear the vest anyhow… Probably cost us the gold - the men would suffer similar fate the following year.

More medals arrived in 2009 with Tilly, Smurph and Lou to the fore, with slower efforts of 3:08, 3:11 & 3:26. It's a tad surprising that this triggered an entry onto our honours boards, but a spot check with Smurph indicates that although she doesn't recall a medal, she *does* recall a cheque, which team medals come with. Memories can work like that, especially in a largely amateur pasttime.

Stunning passage of play

Sarah would go on to a 3:03 the following year but not enough back-up, before an excellent outfit showed up in 2011. Sammi and I had travelled to Amsterdam for their marathon in October 2010 where she found an excellent 2:42 (whilst I endured the mild horror of a 2:30:01), and was looking to go better here and perhaps even worry the 2:40 barrier. But it wasn't quite her day, stopping the clock at 2:44, whilst Tilly and Lou both found a 3:06. It meant a dramatic duel in the perhaps unlikely form of Cornwall, but a good insight into how broad this competition is. They saw off every last bit of England, save for its toenail! All credit to the Kernow ladies who ran 8:52 to our 8:57, with Stockport 3rd in 9:06. Some range in locales.

As ladies TM by now I was particularly 'switched on' to the riches to be mined from the race as we had several fine endurance junkies. It was also around this time I started the unusual and onerous pracice of going through the marathon results looking for sub 3:20 marathoners who were unattached. It's only around a 3% strike rate of those one writes to compared to those who becomes Belgravians, but such was the fragile state of the squad around this time, it was a necessary business. And from out of it all we unearthed the gem in Fee Maycock, who would perhaps be the missing link for gold in 2012.

At day's end, after the ladies had performed superbly with Sammi scoring another 2:44, Fee 2:55 and Lou 2:58, but I was disappointed to find out we'd been edged out by Serpies. Too good… I texted the gang with the bad news who by now were arriving home in the evening. "Bugger!" came the reply from Fee. For reasons unknown, I clicked on one of the Serpies' results to see the image of one of our vanquishers and to my bemusement found not the red and yellow humanoid I was expecting, but some sort of ninja, bedecked head to toe in black! A club uniform it was not, and I instantly reported the happy news that the Serpies had fallen foul on London's strict sartorial rules and we had done it. I guess our friends may have been a victim of their own success in that for the last 20 years Serpentine really nailed Google's search engine listings for London running clubs and saw their membership rocket from a few hundred to over 2,000 in under a decade. But in this case a trainsient member, possibly an overseas athlete, hadn't bothered with the vest.

The three musketeers were back in 2013 – could they repeat the dose? Oh yes – did you ever doubt them?! They were the perfect mix of strength, experience and unflappability. [As a slight aside, I once described a top American backgammon player as unflappable, to which he commented on the piece: "does that make me a bird?" But he loved the term and claimed it

Defending their National title! Our ever unflappable trio of Sammi, Lou and Fee

as his moniker. To this day, some 15 years later, he is known in tournaments around the world as UBK. Unflappable Bob Koka.]

Incredibly the ladies ran identical time to 2012 – 8:52! [Sam gained a minute, Lou lost one, and Fee saw no deviation in fortune.] It was a terrific little trio and fully deserved to defend their title.

Thereafter, Sam was lured away from London's streets by the frying pan of Barcelona in 2014 which was as hot as it sounds, and then the cooler climes of Manchester and Edinburgh in the following years, with other forays to such delights as Frankfurt, Chester, Valencia, Isle of Man, Seville, Goodwood and Dorney Lake. A remarkably varied menagerie indeed, but all the while gearing herself to go longer, much longer! An exceptional GB career in ultras is enveloping her, including the British 100m record (14:10) and we hope and trust our Club President has plenty more gas in the tank yet.

No Sam in our ranks has seen the marathoning Belles cool off in recent years, but with the squad growing so large, their team exploits may be ready to return. Individually, we loved the thrill of seeing Tish Jones run to a 2:33 in 2017 and then a remarkable 2:31 flat in 2018 which secured her World Championship qualification with not a moment to spare. [See cover image]. She did not manage to start in Doha, but then returned to a Covidized London in 2020 to find a gutsy 2:36 when half-fit.

LONDON MARATHON - MEN

Near misses, close calls and one great day

The men too have fought at the marathon, and bronze, silver and gold is nothing less than they deserved. I hit London hard for some 15 years and ran the full gamut of emotions the glorious distance doles out. Good runs, bad runs, dnfs, shockers and about half a dozen 'run of the millers'.

I was very fit for 2003 but went out far too quickly. Such a dreadful blunder, as you only get one or two shots a year at the marathon. Out in 69 back in 79. Such a waste and probably the worst day of my career. I was much more circumspect the next year in lashing rain, and went well under 8 mins for the last 2.2k, which was around 25th[th] best in the whole race. "How are the legs"? Asked Alan, with the 12 stage coming up. Fine! I replied. I had shown respect and restraint and finish on fire. But it wasn't enough and I was shut out of a strong team. However, two went into the long stage slightly 'iffy' on the distance and got eaten alive. How would I have done? We'll never know. One of those devilishly tough selectoral decisions, and of course it is provocative to run a marathon before a big relay selection.

Medals came for Belgrave with me on a mid-career marathon sabbatical in 2005. The key was a fit and firing Kassa Tadesse – the former World Junior Half-marathon champion – running lock step the whole way round with one of my training partners Huw Lobb. Huw noted how it was the perfect run for the both of them as they had identical stride length and literally ran as a clinical tandem together to the line. A few weeks later the medals arrived in the post and I appalled Kassa by mailing him his. He called on the phone: "thank you for sending me a medal – but what do I do with a medal?! There is money, no?" Yes, there was, and it duly followed. About £250, split three ways. But don't give up the day job, KT.

Warren Lynch had a superb run in 80th and a 2:32. A marathon purist, he'd be the first to admit he wasn't up to 'too' much elsewhere for us, albeit scoring in a useful dozen championship races for us over a decade, but goodness, didn't WL make the most of his ability – stringing every last shred of equity out of himself. I recall him also helping us to National medals at the half-marathon the following year. With the little sighted Craig McMillan firing off a 2:37 [also in '05] that put us into the best three in the land – a satisfying raid on the swag.

Oh Dear Mark, No!

The rules for wearing the club vest are extremely strict at London and in the last dozen years some really stupid other rules have come in, like insisting a runner runs in the Championship race, and not the elite. This is berserk, as it punishes a club for getting an athlete to the quality of the elite start line. To my horror, since Hugh Brasher took over, London have also separated the main and elite fields, even though they begin together. It is a disgusting move which flies in the face of 125 years of Big City Marathon history. The message is clear, elitist, crass and hideously knuckle-headed. It is: "did you get an appearance fee, or flights, or hotel? No? Then you WON'T be able to compete with the elites." And yet we're all doing the same race. So we now have the ghastly situation of the elites blowing up and having shockers, and the leaders from the main field taking them out, but none of it counting in the results. An elite can run 3 hours and still be given 17th at London when he was actually 2,000th! And a championship racer gets zero credit for mixing it with the big boys. There is no excuse or reasoning for this except for corporate greed and a complete blindness to the grassroots of the sport. I used to love shooting for the top 40 at London, but nowadays such a goal is about 12th, but then you have to tell people: "that's with all the good runners taken out," and they sigh and lose interest.

Anyway, I was given a 36th in 2007, which *did* include the whole field before the hideous split. It was a very hot day and myself and Malachi had blinders. Mal got 32nd! I caught him at about 19 miles after he'd had my number all season, and I looked across. He was sweating furiously and clearly rather put out that after 8 months of beating me, I was surely going to get the best of him. But no! To my amazement, Mal put his head down and charged. I never really saw him again. It takes superb fitness and belief to come back from the dead like that in the marathon and dear old Mal showed it. Thames' Andy Weir who split us that put it best, saying to me later: "Mal will never run that well again…" he was right, but what a day to do it – his perfect day.

Up ahead we had none other than Mark Miles, suckin' some serious diesel. The heat hit him baly, but 2:19 was still no joke. Had we done enough for the gold? – Oh yes, comfortably – with one flaw: no club vest for Mark! It was a major clunker all round and no single person gets the blame. 11 years earlier, Alan had been all over this issue for Paul Evans and cleared it with the organizers to run in his sponsor's vest. Much to'ing and fro'ing occurred – Paul got the green light and we got the gold.

Mal's perfect day, but it'd still end in minor despair. Also pictured the evergreen Andy Weir, so often the executor of a marathon masterclass

For some reason, all of Alan, myself and Mark dropped the ball here. Mark due to uncertainty of the rules (and probable ignorance as to how strong we were), Alan probably due to worrying about such matters as the riotous 12 stage the week before, which crucially Mark missed due to a sniffle. Perhaps a conversation would have been had there… I think it would. And then there was me – desperate for a medal and knowing the rules and that Mark was running. Silly Billy. To add insult to injury Mark said he would have been delighted to wear the vest, if so directed. It was all a great shame, but a decade later the curmedgeonly rule would work in our favour.

Farewell medal for the 'Pillar

After exactly 20 years at the marathoning coalface, and into my 40th year, I did get my London marathon club championship medal – a precious silver in 2013. I didn't have a very good run, but was gnarly, whilst up ahead, James Kelly ran to a superb 2:21, whilst Phil toiled to 2:19. Toil is a strange word for such a good time, but Phil was a 62 minute half-marathoner, so I only use it out of great respect and esteem. Anyway, what an honour to back those two up, and we were looked down on but just the one team in the land, who I can't quite recollect!

Huge Slice of Luck, a three way tie, and it's GOLD!

In 2017 we brought an interesting little trio to attack the Capital's streets. Catherine Bryson got in touch and kindly asked me to take a look at and advise her fiance James Williams. This was clearly a seriously talented guy, who knew how to dig deep. We embarked on a very pleasant year together with the aim of a sub 2:30. His 2:30:05, whilst a delight to his coach was extremely frustrating for James. I had to gently explain that getting within 6 seconds of a marathon goal is about a 10 to 1 shot – probably 20. Maybe I did it twice in 20 years.

Craig cruises to his bizarrely satisfying time. Our thanks to KM

James then embarked on an Ultra career which included an assault on the World record for John O'Groat's to Land's End. After 10 minutes of researching his target I could see he was chasing a phantom and thus began my four year war with Guinness to take it down. It's just a couple of idiots having a laugh. But despite the clear impossibility of what the guy is claiming (who was a barely serviceable Ultrarunner), Guinness just stonewall everything I throw at them. Ugh, one day redemption shall be mine! But pity poor old James having to do such a brutal event at 10% quicker than is meant. Like an 800 metre runner being told they have to run 1:30 instead of 1:40! Yes, it's that stupid. They were scraping James off the side of the road early on day 5, and will be doing so for others who chase it over the next 100 years, but Guinness simply don't care and refuse to listen to reason. And this from a body that owes its entire existence to distance running via Bannister and the McWhirter twins. Tragic.

For the record the correct FKT [fastest known time] is Dan Lawson's 9d21h, and positively not the fake 9d2h.

Back to the race! The poor old Belles should have gotten bronze but the capricious rule book stung them badly. And we should have gotten bronze too, with both Notts and Aldershot fielding outstanding teams, but they were wiped out by the blazer brigade, the bureaucrats and the dissemblers. All such nonsense. They were clearly by far the best two marathoning clubs in the country – give them the bloody kudos.

But with all that nonsense going on, James found himself crowned as National marathon team champion, backing up Craig Ruddy's bizarrely satisfying time of 22222 [insert colons where appropriate], and the amazing Andrius running 2:23, just a fortnight after a 2:24 at Manchester. Incredible stuff. Good back up came from Mark Pollard 2:32, Kris Gauson 2:34 and Paul Lowe 2:37.

The result after removal of the big guns was an epic thriller as Serpies ran 221, 227 and 227, and Kent an equally scary 222, 226 and 227.

That mean ALL three clubs came to the same time on minutes! Simply amazing. But when the seconds came into the equation, we'd scraped home.

» Ruddy, Craig (GBR)	Belgrave...	1642	18-39	01:10:02	02:22:22
» Jaksevicius, Andrius (GBR)	Belgrave...	1786	18-39	01:10:06	02:23:24
» Williams, James (GBR)	Belgrave...	1249	18-39	01:14:03	02:30:05
» Pollard, Mark (GBR)	Belgrave...	1764	18-39	01:16:11	02:32:51
» Gauson, Kristopher (GBR)	Belgrave...	1650	18-39	01:16:11	02:34:44
» Lowe, Paul (GBR)	Belgrave...	1763	18-39	01:14:55	02:37:48

It was all hugely satisfying and one in the eye for the unseen pedants who for over 100 years have taken such satisfaction from complicating our gloriously simple sport. I wrote about this a lot in my first book about the terrible controversies that the rules' officials brought to the 1908 Olympics. As one American said: "as far as strengthening diplomatic ties, it has been a disaster."

109 years on and there's some of the same old trouble – but for once, we'll take it!

In 2018, Dan Wallis ran a superb race at the hottest London in history and placed 15th overall with a 2:19. It was a race the athlete most enjoyed and he absolutely confirms he'd prefer to execute a perfectly judged race in torrid conditions than a less well done race in perfect conditions. Ie, would he wish for 2:17 and 26th, or 2:19 and 15th. He'll take the latter every time – understanding that racing is, well, about racing. Times are secondary.

Dan laudably won the Championship race and along with Matthew Cox [2:25] and Andrius Jaksevicius [2:33] came away with a well deserved bronze.

Dan Wallis wins the 2018 Championship London Marathon with a simply immaculate run in the heat

MISCELLANEA - MEN

The range and scope of Belgrave Road and Country doesn't stop with the 14 Championships in this book. Far from it! Up and down the land we compete, either individually or as a team. But to go into detail about such affairs would be too broad in scope. 50 years ago there were twice as many races in the calendar and an awful lot of road relays. Ever growing traffic issues put paid to most of them, and one supposes we should be glad for the five big ones that remain.

There are also National 5k, 10k and half-marathon Championships, but by and large they're dreadfully marketed, and one needs a firm grasp of geography and historic governing bodies to really follow what's going on. There's the ERRA now, which used to be the AAA, and there's UKA, and British athletics. One supposes now that the big 10k to go for is the Vitality 10,000 in May each year, which attracts a stellar field and deemed the UKA Champs and is the 'one to win'. Three lads running sub 30 is required for that, and the Belles have attacked it strongly too.

Here's a tangy little venture. The catchily monikered 'European Club Champions Half Marathon Championships'. And a fine reason to get the triple London champion Antonio Pinto [2] into the book, who was a tad podgy, and the author got within 3 minutes of him on the broiling streets of Lisbon in Oct 2002. Al Stewart, Roger Alsop, Chas Herrington & Knut Hegvold also in shot, with Lee Hurst, who had a troubled race, still out there somewhere... Belgrave placed 9th out of the 13 nations. We came, we saw, we beat San Marino

We have benefitted in our propaganda from this marvellous photo from of Nicky-boy in 2019 slicing and dicing it with the one... the only... four years earlier I went with a long walk with Nick after the same race when he'd had a painful time [30:46], and he mused about retirement. I gently observed that it was his first race for yonks and getting duffed up by Andy Vernon was no disgrace. So this day was all the sweeter, even if Sir Mo did take care of our man!

One of the finest Belgrave images of all time. Our warm thanks to JHM photography

And here's Nick outleaning Andy Butchart at the 2016 Vitality mile in 4:00:

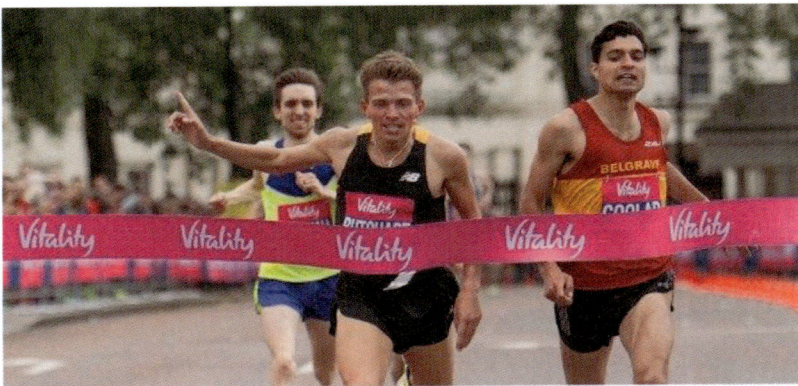

When it was the AAA 10k, we had a splendid win in 2003 after a silver the previous year. I ventured to the unlikely environs of Bradford and Bourton-on-the-Water for those races, and they were thrilling days. In 2003 I recall nicking a couple of guys yards before the finish which made our win by 2 points all the more satisfying.

Here's ARM's atmospheric report – a battlefield indeed. As can be seen there was confusion as to whether it was a 3 or 4 to score race. 'Twas 3, which we felt spelt doom for us, but not so!

And so to the finish. As expected, the Kenyan trio had the race stitched up although Taragon was in danger of being caught as the group of leading male Brits had split asunder in their efforts to win the individual AAA Championship. City of Stoke's Rob Whalley prevailed but Dave Anderson finished strongly, overtaking Hepples in the last metres to win AAA 'silver'. He might have gone better still but for a very nasty blister. Amazingly, Hassan had also maintained his high placing, a minute or so faster than expected, and Will was another to overtake men in the final stretch to reduce our score by what proved to be a very valuable couple of points. Charles, running in Buckinghamshire colours, was close behind Will - and at that stage we believed that with four to score we had won by a mile. An ecstatic Warren Lynch carved no less than 1:40 from his previous best!

The village green was like a battlefield as runners fought tooth and nail down the straight and then collapsed on the grass to recover; and now the women were finishing. Our eight runners had set out determined to run their best 10kms and no less than four came back having achieved personal records. The the announcer shouted: "Here comes a Belgrave athlete, and here's another Belgrave athlete, and here's yet another Belgrave athlete..."

Men

1 J.Kibet (Kenya) 28:42; 2 W.Koga (Kenya) 29:24; 3 W.Taragon (Kenya) 29:39; 4 R.Whalley (City of Stoke) 29:44; 5 David Anderson 29:48; 12 H.Raidi 30:29; 36 W.Cockerell 31:32; 42 C.Herrington 31:58; 84 W.Lynch 33:11; 140 S.Zealey 36:20; 157 G.Reid M40 37:16; J.Browne dnf; 384 finished.

Teams: 1 Belgrave H (1, 8, 30) 39; 2 Bedford & Cnty (6, 10, 25) 41; 3 Newham & Essex Beagles (12, 18, 36) 66.
...

Some "Other" races as they appear on our Honour's board are as such:

Men:

AAA 5km
Winners: 2006.
Placed: 2005.

AAA 10km
Winners: 2003, 2011
Placed: 2002, 2004, 2005, 2006, 2007, 2008, 2013
(UKA).

AAA Half-Marathon
Winners: 2002, 2004, 2007.
Placed: 2003, 2005, 2006.

AAA Marathon
Winners: 1996, 2017.
Placed: 2005, 2013, 2018.

South of England AA 10k
Placed: 2007

And then plenty of Surrey County 5, 10k & 10 mile gongs.

The Half-marathon Championships were imperious stuff. The 2002 race was an amazing team, pictured right, and at Ackworth in 2004 we had seven in 24. David Anderson ran a beauty of a 65 on a tricky course, and our top three of David, Hassan Raidi and Paul Freary were 3rd, 6th and 7th. Pretty remarkable for a National Championships. We did not get Hassan out much over the years and he was very inconsistent, but he does have the "mic drop' claim of winning the National team gold for Cross-country, 10k and Half-marathon.

The great Paul Evans was a nice foundation to build a cracking National half team around in 2002. Chas Herrington, Kassa and Al Stewart kept him company. ARM

We did well to pick up silver at Wilmslow in 2003 [Cockerell, Stewart & Freary; running 66, 66 & 67]; Hastings '05 [McRae, Raidi & Cockerell] and 3rd at a Silverstone wind tunnel in '06, where myself, Tom Hadfield, Joachim Wolf and Warren Lynch placed 9th, 11th, 13 & 15th – some tight packing there.

And in 2007 Phil Wicks won the English and UK individual and team prizes at Bristol. Four gold medals – pictured, left. Not a bad haul for 64:43 of work.

Sammy G breaks the magic 30, and doesn't he know it! With imperious splits of 15:04 and 14:54 Sam Gebreselasie ran 29:58 at the Vitality 10k and led the Bels to a top 10 UK placing, backed up nicely by Steve Gardner and Henry Hart who bridged the 33 minute divide. [Craig Ruddy]

MISCELLANEA - WOMEN

AAA 10km

Winners: 2006, 2013

Placed: 2014

AAA 10 miles

Placed: 2013

AAA Half Marathon

Winners: 2013, 2014

Placed: 2002

The most startling win here was the 2006 gold, detail of which may be enjoyed here:

Birhan Dagne found herself in trouble, suffering from the return of a knee problem, but with it being a one lap course there was no point in pulling out. She slowed but kept going forward, completing the race two minutes slower than in 2005. What a good job she did, for with 'Jules' Clark and Tilly Heaton finishing not too far behind, the team were amazed to find that they had snaffled silver medals - and were a mere seven seconds behind the winners, Arena 80. But there was more drama to come as two days later it became clear that the results showed an ineligible runner among Arena 80's squad and the Belles were upgraded to GOLD!

Men. 1 P Riley (Leigh) 29:02; 2 K Cullen (Highgate) 29:24; 3 J Mayes (Kent) 29:40; 11 S Sharp 30:09; 29 R Ward 31:51; 40, K O'Connell 33:27; 840 finished.

Teams: 1 Wells City 1:31:14; 2 Belgrave 1:35:27; 3 Newham &EB 1:36:34.

Women. 1 H Yelling 32:31; 2 N Harvey (South L) 33:53; 3 J Wright (Shaftesbury B) 33:57; 10 B Dagne 35:47; 19 J Clark 2nd-W40 37:57; 31 M Heaton 38:58; 88 C Eastham 44:49; 534 finished.

Teams: 1 Belgrave 1:52:42; 2 Brighton &H 2:03:18.

2013 saw Tish run to a superb 33:10 at Leeds, with fine back up from Lou and Fee in 36 and 37 for the gold.

And those half-marathon wins around the same time were immaculate with Sammi Amend and Sophie Carter also very much to the fore. I have dark memories of 2014 though, when my charge Tish placed 2nd in the National trial at Reading ahead of the World Championships for that event, and the selectors picked an incomplete team of two runners, and took 3rd instead of Tish! I know, don't ask. Completely maddening. GB athletics took more managers than athletes to Copenhagen and our written appeal was rejected because there, "wasn't an appeals process in place for this race."

At the Worlds four weeks later, Aly Dixon [who Tish handsomely beat at a very windy Reading] ran to a superb 70:38. If Tish had run [she smashed the course record at Paddock Wood on the same day], we would have placed 5th in the world. What can you do in a sport run by dissemblers?

London XC Champs

Then there are the London XC Champs, a race that Belgrave have traditionally overlooked as we veer more to being a Surrey club. There used to be complex qualifying criteria for the race as well, which were a turn-off, but now it is largely seen by us as "a race too far…"

Having said that, *Charlie's Angels* have begun to attack it with some glee and no little skill and 2021's venture was a case in point, as Rachel, Paps, Jess and Sam [right] closed in 24 to see off TVH by just 5 points for the gold. Nice work ladies.

Reigers

I am very fond of the Reigate Priory Relay, and we go way back to the '90s, when I turned up after an all-night bender, ran a good leg, and after 10 minutes rest Alan asked if I'd care to anchor the Bs. 'Beats a warm-down,' I thought. The following year we beat Herne Hill in a thrilling race, with the 'auld enemy Dave Taylor cooking up a hurricane on anchor, but on this occasion we were far enough ahead "not to feel the draught."

The men have been fleeting since then [due in part to a clash with Mansfield]; but it's always a fun if low-key day out on that stone-cold bonkers course. Well, that's harsh, 75% of it is serious and sober, but goodness the two climbs are "full on" and the descent is savage and way above my pay grade. For 20 years my strategy has been the same, whether it be the League or relay: "you can risk life and limb going hell for leather, but *I'm* going to sacrifice 10 seconds here and get down safely." I don't know how there aren't more serious injuries and I they've tweaked the course right at the top to make it less hairy.

A classic Reigate day out. This from 2019. Clockwise TL: James Morris, Phil Wicks, Mhairi Hall, Steph Hewitt, Emma Howsham, Paskar Owor, Keri Mackenzie, Mhairi McDonald, Saron Haileselassie, CD, Jurgita Levertaviciute, Sam Amend, Alex Miller, Simon H.

The race is as quintessentially English and obscure as it gets and it'd be disingenuous to get too excited about the Belles' astonishing sequence there. Sometimes there's competition, and sometimes not. But year after year Charlie has used it as a really nice piece of team building which is of course vital, as is the experience of tough racing in a mixed race with the men.

And before our reappearance, Catherine likewise found success there. Check this out as defending champions in 2004 with a whopping four teams:

Teams: 1 Belgrave H 'A' 47.21; 2 South London H 48.29; 3 Medway & Maidstone AC; 6 Belgrave 'B' 50.44; 11 Belgrave 'C' 53.31; 21 Belgrave 'D' 57.52.
A – S.Murphy (3) 16:03; C.Bryson (2) 15:22; J.Clark (1) 15:56.
B – M.Heaton (6) 16:22; H.Smethurst (7) 17:04; L.Cooper (6) 17:18.
C – C.Bertram (14) 17:31; S.Galley (15) 19:04; S.Murphy (11) 16:06.
D – C.Eastham (31) 20:00; A.England (26) 19:14; D.Hearne (21) 18:38.
Fastest: 1 E.Baker (South London H) 14.59; =2 C.Bryson Belgrave 15.22 and A.Simkova (Medway &M) 15.22.

For the record, this is a neat summation from CD:

Belles record at the Priory from 2014

The women have had a remarkable run of success in this event since returning to the race in 2014:

2014; 1st, 51;12, Rose, Catherine, Keri.

2015; 1st, 51:43, Lizzie, Jojo, Zoe S.

2016; 1st, 48:19, Sam, Beccy, Zoe S.

2017; 2nd, 49:26, Saron, Katie, Sam.

2018; 1st, 47:55, Keri, Sam, Saron (15:03, 14th fastest of the day including all the men).

2019; 2nd, 52:49, Georgie, Camilla, Mhairi.

2021; 1st, 48:51, Liv, Sam, Lea, and 3rd, Natalie, Patricia, Jurgita.

And 2021s winning squad:

l-r: Olivia Papaioannou, Jurgita Levertaviciute, Patricia Walker, Charlie Dickinson, Sam Amend, Lea Adamson, Natalie Beadle.

THE VETS

I'm not sure why, but ever since the great Laurie O'Hara was ripping up the record books in the 1970s, Belgrave have been slightly blind to Veterans' athletics. Not that we haven't had some right superstars down the years and some splendid moments to savour, both individually and teamwise. The women's TM was European Masters champion once, don't you know… But an actual dedicated Vets' section run by at least one or two souls has been surplus to the committee's requirements. In short, it has been left to the athletes to sort ourselves out, but without a cohesive leader, the section will always splutter and misfire. We lost the imposing presence of Roger Alsop to Herne Hill due to not having a Vets section [perhaps he could have built one for us, instead of going to a ready made one elsewhere?]; and I wrote a detailed memo to committee about how we could structure our Veteran's athletics, but I never heard back. My belief of the committee's stance, and I have to say I agree with it in part, is that if we started to look too closely at the Vets, that we could take our eye off the Seniors, and that for sure would be a bad thing.

I myself largely ignored Vets' athletics throughout my 40s due to living in denial. And as for the diabolical M & W 35 divisions: scrap them today! Total and utter garbage. Whoever came up with such a moronic premise should be strung up. What next M/W30?! If history has told us anything it's that endurance athletes deep into their 30s are some of the very best in the world. Olympic golds for Constantina Dita and Carlos Lopes to name two, not to mention Chris Thompson and Mo Farah, but of course there are countless others.

So this isn't really a gripe from me against the committee, but perhaps if Belgrave created a men and women's Vet's division, then we would start travelling more to Championship events. There is a Whatsapp group for the 1998-2014 relay juggernauts and some of them seem to think that even with their Zimmer frames they can still move at pace. I'll believe it when I see it.

In 2016 the M40's had good fun at Sutton Park and it was great to see Sharpy and Paul back in the saddle. We didn't have a stormer, but it was an encouraging foray, and we grabbed 4th.

We were a bit creaky on this day, but still found 4th. L-R: Miller, Freary, WC, SS, PO, Bundle

I write in detail in the Management chapter about the bewildering peccadilloes of constructing 2015 women's National 4 stage Vet's team, and perhaps a part of that confusion was due to it being "only" a Vets' race, and hence me running into such a brick wall. But it was a terrific performance, with Sophie Carter winning the opening stage and the ladies running it home in various degrees of a leader's terror. Here's that team celebrating:

The following year they came to defend and so, so nearly pulled it off. See result below.

I agree with you - this quartet doesn't look in the least Vet-like but blame on the horrors of misguided officialdom. But Sophie Carter, Lou Blizzard, Kate Rennie and Zoe Doyle celebrate their National road relay title in 2015

Almost defending! What a remarkable finish this was from Zoe, Sam, Lou & Sophie, see result

Another pioneering escapade was the women winning National bronze at the BMAF XC relay champs at Long Eaton in 2016 with a team of Zoe Doyle, Sophie Carter and Fi Maddocks. Good fun and quite tense stuff.

(nn) is team position after the appropriate stage.

1   Salford Harriers & Ac W35   'A'   1:14:00

Julie Cook	(11)	19:09
Tessa Robinson	(3)	17:35
Hayley Kuter	(3)	18:15
Beverley Simons	(1)	19:01

2   Telford Ac W35   1:14:02

Claire Martin	(1)	17:05
Michelle Clarke	(1)	18:21
Lucie Taitharris	(1)	19:04
Rachel Coupe	(2)	19:32

3   Belgrave Harriers W35   1:14:07

Sophie Carter	(2)	17:47
Louise Blizzard	(4)	19:33
Samantha Amend	(2)	17:34
Zoe Doyle	(3)	19:13

4   Heanor Running Club W35   1:14:14

Looking around, none of us are getting any younger, and there are some very nippy silver foxes on the prowl. It's pretty clear there are fun times to be had in the coming decade, but people need that little nudge, and I think it will come from either a real pioneer, or committee's guidance. It wouldn't take too much organizing, but I think my role in its affairs ended with the straight bat played by the club to my memo. One doesn't like to push these things if the club doesn't want it.

A conversation for another day.

The astonishing denouement of the 2016 National Vet's 4 Stage

THIS IS OUR YOUTH

And they do this for fun?! A gaggle of 11 Bels in various states of euphoric, exercise-induced endomorphia contemplate life. Mickey Bradley Sanna's look, top right, says it all. TO'N

As with the Vets, wrestling the youths to great things is like trying to have a reasonable discussion with a cut snake. A squad leader needs nerves of steel, the temperament of a monk, the patience of Job and the stickability of Sticky the stick insect stuck on a sticky bun.

Youth athletics is the trenches of coaching and management. For sure it's not for the faint-hearted and an approach anything other than calm temerity and insouciant charm will end in tears.

One is reminded of Jack Woltz in *The Godfather*. "For five years we had her under training… singing lessons… dancing lessons… acting lessons… I was gonna' make her a big star! And then what happens… Johnny Fontaine with his olive oil voice and guinea charm. And she runs off… she runs off just to make me look ridiculous…!" Ok, this could apply to a senior or two down the years as well, but you catch my drift.

Poor old Woltz. All that effort, and what's the return? A $600,000 horse's head in the bed. Fortunately, Terry O'Neill is dealing with slightly lower stakes, but most Olympians start off life as a junior, and we've had some shining beacons in our time, who remind us why we have a junior section. The inspiring and haunting stories of nurturing a young Phillips Idowu would assuage the most cynical, and there are multifold others. Here's John Bicourt, right, creaming to 4th at the Southern Junior in 1963. Some 59 years and two Olympics later, John could still be found cheering us on at the Surrey league.

The likes of George Flanagan, John Stow, Tony Binda, Tony Fairclough, Alan Mead & Alan Black are also all the proof one needs that some careful nurturing as a youth can lead to a lifetime's involvement in the sport, and great success in senior athletics.

But that bridge crossing over to the seniors is similar to the one in *The Temple of Doom*: Why is the bridge to trepidous and the water filled with crocs? Oh a hundred reasons… too much too soon, studies, injury, illness, boredom, relationships, booze, parties, temptation and the need to dedicate oneself to a career. For every Eilish McColgan, Mo Farah, Charlotte Purdue, Chris Thompson, Paula Radcliffe & Scott Overall, there are 50 that didn't make it over the grand divide, let alone make it big.

When you look at it like that, why bother? For two reasons: the joy of athletics for a youth is still very real, great fun to watch and can certainly be life-changing; and if they don't keep it up, is that really the end of the world? Of course not. But for the few halcyon years that kid was an athlete, the memories, happiness, and discipline it instilled will be ingrained forever. And for the 5% that crack on as seniors – well that's marvellous too.

Terry observes: *"Well, for me it's about giving something back to the sport that's given us so much, usually from super Coaches (like Frank Horwill) who expected nothing in return other than that we tried hard & did our best, for ourselves & for our club/club mates."*

Would you put your trust and faith in someone who chooses to do this on a Saturday afternoon? Well, Belgrave has, and at least Terry leads by example. SG

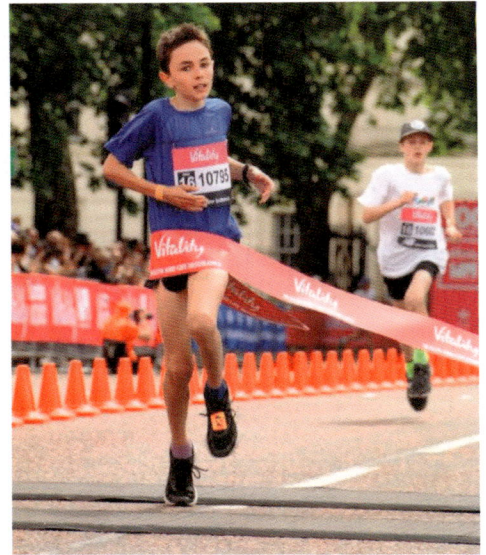

The search for the next Roger Bannister is ON! Hey, you gotta' dream. Here Seb Cockerell contemplates life with the great man at the Westminster mile. Five years later, Seb would win his race at the same event, right, followed closely home by our own Lucas Ebert

Enough preamble – where are we?

So with all that background, one gets more insight into what Terry's been merrily wrestling with this past eight years or so: A menagerie of talent, some Mary Poppins impersonation of running an unofficial creche [he has the same cut-glass cheekbones], some terrific runners and much happiness and laughter. When he's not wishing to fondly strangle a little treasure for some impish jape, he is there, rain or shine knowing he's right at the start of something. But what is that something?!

Oh look how sweet they were! Lucas Ebert 8 and Max Simpson 18 are about to have an absolute stormer at Effingham in 2019. Seb 5 would just lose to Ollie 6 a short way back whilst Mickey 4 would have to bow out on this day. Faisal Abubakar looks forward to the U15/17s.

To riff on a little Morgan Freeman, being at the start of a promising junior career is akin to being: "so excited I can barely sit still or keep a thought in my head. I think it's the excitement only a free man can feel…

"A free man at start a long journey whose conclusion is uncertain. I hope I can make it across the border… I hope I can see my friend and shake his hand…"

The border here of course refers to the grand, gaping divide between the Juniors and the Seniors.

Our youths cover a bewildering array of sections – around 10 [5 per gender]. The U13s, 15s, 17s, 20s and then there's the really little ones who aren't even allowed to compete in the U13s. Indeed just getting someone 'U13 legal' is a journey in itself.

Cast of Characters

What news then of how they've done? In short there has been much success and many fine results. The full breadth and scope of that story is outside the remit of these pages, but we would be remiss not to name check London Youth Games winner Blaine Robinson, a superb athlete and hopefully not lost to the sport forever, but currently MIA.

And we have a wonderful triumph to report in Maddy Whitman who after many years in the youths made the bold step up to the senior Surrey league in Feb 2022 and placed a majestic 9th on a very muddy 5 miles course at Lloyd Park. We knew she was good, but didn't dare hope for such audacity early doors. Yes, the field was depleted at the rearranged fixture, but it was still one of the great Belgrave runs of the last 10 years.

A classic example of the great divide is Nick Goolab, who won the Junior National in both 2009 [here], and 2010. But the long delay to see him there in senior colours at that race continues. We'll wait

A grainy image, but a critical one. Maddy Whitman makes her debut for the seniors in the League in Feb 2022, and promptly scores second, aged just 17

My sprogs flatter to deceive and Seb has hit trouble in responding to the chimp on his shoulder in races that says: "stop running, right now." So being a good, obedient kid, he does. Trouble is that Dnf'ing can become addictive. He'll grow out of it, and for passion and 'runners' build' he gets high marks. All we can do is wait for the acorn to grow and build on a 9:55 3k from the summer of '22.

Imogen has always had blinding speed, which she gets from her mother who travelled the world competing against Russians twice her size back in the '90s. But much as we'd like Immy to run more, she also has loads of football, BMX, hockey & cricket clamouring for her. So much sport, so little time. But she had a full season in 2021-22 and there was some good stuff, culminating in an 11th in the Surrey league, after an 'oh so painful' National.

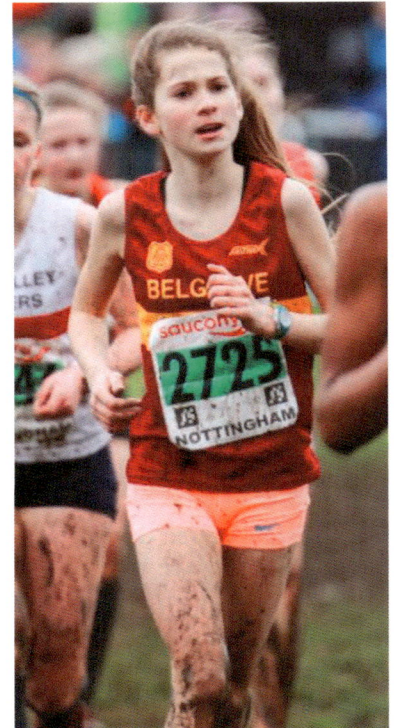

Three gung-ho Belles tackle the brutal National of 2020. Lucy Jodrell, left, had a good battle with Lina Colas, right, whilst Palmer Newson exclaims to Terry in her best Graham Taylor voice: "Do I Not Like This!"

However, in concert with Honor Barclay, Daisy Larkin and Evelyn Marley, the "fab four" reeled off a top 20 position in the land at the Parliament Hill National, which was a super effort, and with the clubs so tightly packed it's very easy to see top 10 bang on the horizon. The Surrey League was 5th, and all our squads often land a top 10 team spot in a race there, but consistency is tough.

A really classy squad could be brewing for the U13 & U15 Belles, here at the league opener in 2021. L-R Isabel Shamlian, Fiona Ebert, Honor Barclay, Yoda, Daisy Larkin & Imogen Cockerell

Honor is clearly is special talent, as is Daisy, who trains so hard and whose easy demeanour belies an inner steel and ferocious grit on the race course. Another determined soul is Daisy's little brother Alfie – all fire and brimstone and destined to set the world alight should he so choose! Evelyn is a mildly thrilling find, and we have some back up there too in the likes of Isabel Shamlian and Fiona Ebert.

Boys in the Hood

Over in the lads, we have a future superstar in the making in Jediael Yared. Such a humble, kind and friendly lad who loves to get stuck in and mix it with the seniors on the track [as in a 4:23 1500]. To be sure, if he wants it, he could have a marvellous career in athletics. Minor details like navigation to races, punctuality and correct footwear will come with maturity, but for now we're often just delighted he makes it at all! TO'N recalls:

Honor Barclay - a special talent

"Jediael arrived at a SLAN meeting too late for his 800m so he ran in the 300m & blithely turned in a 39.9."

Alexis Delaney has terrific leg speed and going 2:10 in 2022 as a U15B shows that he will only get better. Now to find some endurance! The same might be said for the elegant Rohan Singh.

Oscar Kinirons has a maddening birthday of 31 August which it would be harsh to blame him for, but cuts him loose from the year below, but all that will resolve itself in the next XC season when the lads come up to the U17s. For now, Oscar holds a candle to JY for natural ability,

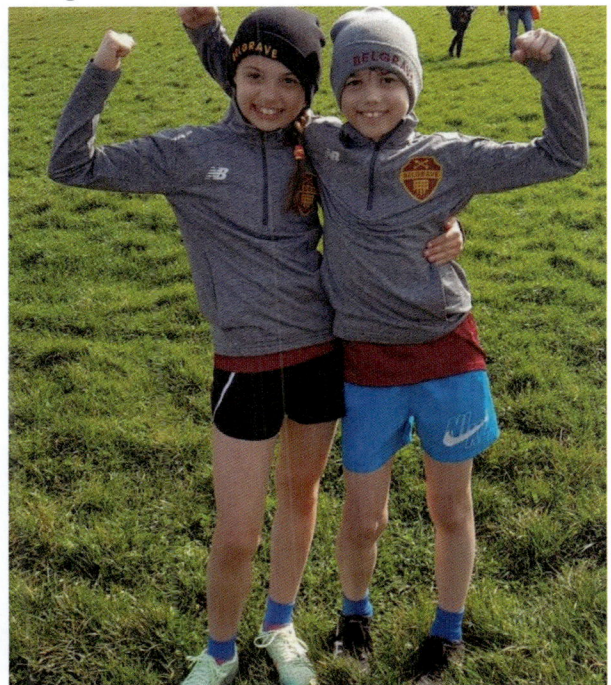

The Larkin siblings, Daisy & Alfie. Wonderfully spirited and out there rain or shine. Daisy is one of the top 120 1,500 runners in the land now, and that figure will only improve. Alfie places top 10 in the U11 Epsom League

and boasts a top 3 at the London schools to his name and bronze at the 2022 County champs with 4:21.

Do not underestimate this young man! The author has in Saturday morning sessions and was left shaking his head in disbelief. Harry Jodrell is seriously talented and we all hope he sticks with it.

All of these will start training full-time with the seniors soon, hopefully to be joined by perhaps the most loyal attendee of the last six years in Ollie Cunningham. A real talent with a classic style, Ollie was responsible for inspiring Seb to "up his game" in the early days, and get dragged along in Ollie's wake. I sometimes saw them as 'the twins' due to their similar look and ability and one can but hope that Ollie has much more running in him yet and that he defeats the ongoing spectre of injury. He is also a brilliant swimmer.

Going back a bit, we loved what we saw in the Juxon twins, now embroiled in the cruel and unusual punishment of Eton College for their sins. We always love to see Monty and Jago though, and hopefully they'll keep up their connection to the Bels. Monty found a stunning 14th at the 2019 National.

And then of course there is the Jodrell dynasty. TO'N writes: "Harry Jodrell has seen elder siblings Eddie & Lucy move through the Juniors, with Eddie now a good Senior & Lucy not far behind, with all three family members huge Belgrave fans. Harry is a gritty U13 who is a big favourite with his team mates, takes his running seriously, has just moved up to Group 1 & loves competing against his older colleagues. He continues to improve & has a charming personality - it's hard not to laugh when he asks a cheeky question."

Three ever-improving guns. Alexis Delaney is an 800 specialist and already down to 2:10; Seb is well into the 9's for the 3k, whilst the outstanding Jediael Yared mixes well with the adults in the 1500.

We can't name check everyone sadly as we've had well over a 100 pass through the ranks in recent years and leaving someone off the roll call could cause offence. But suffice it to say that you're all contributing to the Belgrave legacy and mentions a plenty await you in dispatches if you stick with it and enjoy your athletics.

Imogen Cockerell, left, places the gentle "graze of death" upon Julia McDonnell's hip at the denouement to the Mitcham Surrey League of January 2022, whilst Poppy Guest [402] is also in line for unwanted attention. These fields are deliciously bunched. Meanwhile, ever game Noah Gomes-Coley puts in a shift in the engine room. And the sky's the limit for Evelyn Marley, who not only sounds like a movie icon in Evelyn Mulwray, but has Faye Dunaway's daring spirit from Chinatown, as evidenced by improving from 46th to 20th between two Surrey Leagues. She was also a key cog in us going top 20 at the National.

Clockwise, TL: Rohan Singh, Khuran Gurveer, Ismail Sissoko, Seb Cockerell, Alexander Wilson, Alexis Delaney, Ollie Cunningham, Jediael Yared, Oscar Kinirons, Timmi Annon, Victoria Gomez Villamizar, Maddy Whitman, Elena Delaney, Daisy Larkin, Harry Jodrell, Alfie Larkin

ACKNOWLEDGEMENTS

My profound thanks to all the Belgravians who have made this last quarter of a century such a pleasure. At the top of the list of course is the Mead dynasty, Alan, Pat and Hazel, whose support and incredible sacrifice and hard work inspired one to compete for, and succeed with, the club.

There are many other luminaries as well, and my comrade Charlie Dickinson has been a great support, particularly when things became rather frosty for me in my management years. We all miss the irreplaceable Bill Laws so much and his encouragement to me was enormous for 20 years. Alan Black, Leo Coy and Lionel Mann continue to offer great solace and friendship through good times and bad. As do the likes of Phil Wicks, Nick Goolab, Paskar Owor, Sammi Amend, James Kelly, Hester Scotton, Terry O'Neill, Zoe Vail, David Anderson, Tilly Heaton, Stephen Sharp, Jon Blackledge, Neil Speaight, Sarah Murphy, Tish Jones, Chas Herrington, Paul Freary, Richard Ward, Mark Miles, Laura Goodson, Ben Hurley, Alex Luce & Bruce Barton.

Steve Gardner's photography is magnificent, thank you so much, and to all the other generous snappers in these pages.

And thank you to Jojo Rhodes for her well chosen words on a Saturday run from the Hall, which acted as the catalyst for this book. I couldn't quite see the angle, as I didn't wish to clash too much with Alan's history site, but by just going with Road and Country of the 21st Century, as Jojo advised, made the cross-over fairly minimal, and as Alan himself notes: he was too close to some of these stories to comfortably write them himself.

Finally, thanks to Steve Green and Donald Hale for all their help and encouragement in the publishing process.

INDEX

Printed in Great Britain
by Amazon

10276658R00156